ART OF WAR

NICCOLÒ MACHIAVELLI

ART OF WAR

Translated, Edited, and with a Commentary by
CHRISTOPHER LYNCH

The University of Chicago Press
Chicago and London

The University of Chicago Press, Chicago 60637
The University of Chicago Press, Ltd., London
© 2003 by The University of Chicago
All rights reserved. Published 2003
Paperback edition 2005
Printed in the United States of America
12 11 10 09 08 07 06 05   3 4 5

ISBN: 0-226-50040-3 (cloth)
ISBN: 0-226-50046-2 (paperback)

Library of Congress Cataloging-in-Publication Data

Machiavelli, Niccolò, 1469–1527.
    [Arte della guerra. English]
    Art of war / Niccolò Machiavelli ; translated, edited, and with a commentary by
Christopher Lynch.
        p. cm.
    Includes bibliographical references and index.
    ISBN 0-226-50040-3 (cloth : alk. paper)
    1. Military art and science—Early works to 1800. 2. War—Early works to 1800.
I. Title.

    U101.M1613 2003
    355.02—dc21

                                                                        2002045578

*To Catherine O'Loughlin Lynch
and to our children,
Emily, Henry, and Grace*

CONTENTS

———⌣⌣⌣———

ABBREVIATIONS

AW   *Art of War*
D   *Discourses on the First Ten Books of Titus Livy*
FH   *Florentine Histories*
P   *The Prince*

TRANSLATOR'S PREFACE
AND ACKNOWLEDGMENTS

The purpose of this book is to provide English-speaking readers the opportunity to understand the only major prose work Machiavelli published during his lifetime—the *Art of War*. The book's centerpiece is a translation of the *Art of War* that seeks to be as faithful as possible to the original. The translation is the first to incorporate the many significant discoveries included in the recent critical edition of the Italian, edited by Jean-Jacques Marchand, Denis Fachard, and Giorgio Masi. The new Italian edition reconstitutes the text as it was first published in Florence in 1521 as *Libro della arte della guerra di Niccolò Machiavegli cittadino et segretario fiorentino*. For details regarding this Italian edition and an explanation of the principles that guided the translation, please consult the note on the translation. My introduction and footnotes to the text (as well as the interpretive essay at the back of the book) are merely tools for helping contemporary readers overcome some of the obstacles that lie between them and Machiavelli's intention and teaching in the *Art of War*. If these tools become impediments in turn, I encourage readers to leave them aside and proceed straight to the *Art of War* itself.

The introduction orients readers to the general character of the *Art of War* and provides basic information about that work's historical context, sources, influence, contemporary relevance, and treatment in the scholarly literature. It is meant to be of use to anyone unfamiliar with the *Art of War* in particular or with Machiavelli's works more generally. In the interpretive essay, I put forward my own understanding of the *Art of War* in light of its military, political, and philosophical or literary aspects.

Many individuals and institutions made possible and improved this book. The translation is much better for the suggestions of Wayne Ambler, Harvey Mansfield, Anne McDonald, Christopher Nadon, Davide Papotti, and Nathan Tarcov. Valuable criticisms of various drafts of the introduction and interpretive essay were made by Stephen Gregory, Edmund Jacobitti, Mark Lutz, Harvey Mansfield, Jonathan Marks, David McNeill, Nathan Tarcov, Paul Ulrich, and Paul Yingling. The entire manuscript was much improved by Steven Lenzner's corrections, criticisms, and advice. Svetozar Minkov (assisted by Gabriel Pihas, Lydia Mulvaney, and Jason Laine) prepared the word glossary and did an outstanding job tracking down difficult-to-find sources; Paul Eiting prepared the name index. Their work was funded by the John M. Olin Center for Inquiry into the Theory and Practice of Democracy at the University of Chicago. David Bemelmans copyedited the whole with great care. Emily Lynch and Aaron Krager helped with proofreading. Any remaining errors and infelicities are my responsibility.

My interest in Machiavelli and in political philosophy more generally was initially sparked by the charm and intelligence of Henry Higuera at St. John's College. He later introduced me to Allan Bloom who oversaw my first years of graduate study at the University of Chicago. Unlike any other, Mr. Bloom's voice knew how "to descend into the netherworld of every soul." At Chicago I was fortunate to have the chance to learn from many talented teachers, including Hillel Fradkin, David Grene, Walter Kaegi, Leon Kass, Ralph Lerner, Clifford Orwin, and, especially, Nathan Tarcov, whose encouragement, guidance, and example have been indispensable. Assistance for graduate studies related to this project was provided by the Olin, Earhart, and Bradley foundations. My greatest debts are to my first teachers, Leland Lynch and Mary Martin.

Support for an important phase of writing and revision was provided by a Bradley Foundation postdoctoral fellowship at Boston College's department of political science. Students in my classes on Machiavelli at Boston College and Carthage College have taught me far more than they likely imagine. Insightful criticisms offered by the referees of the University of Chicago Press led to significant improvements in the manuscript. John Tryneski's wise stewardship of the entire process was invaluable. The dedication expresses my most heartfelt thanks.

INTRODUCTION

The importance of war in Niccolò Machiavelli's life and writings can hardly be overstated. His long career of government service was dominated by his fateful efforts to found a strong military force, one controlled by the republican government in Florence and drawn from its Tuscan dominions. The goal of this enterprise was to free his native land from a debilitating dependence on mercenary and foreign forces. These martial actions were more than matched by the writings that came to outshine them, Machiavelli's *The Prince* and *Discourses on Livy*. He declares in the former that "a prince should have no other object, nor any other thought, nor take anything else as his art but that of war and its orders and discipline; for that is the only art which is of concern to one who commands" (*P* 14). This categorical advice complements what can be called Machiavelli's truest truth, proclaimed in the *Discourses on Livy*: "[I]t is more true than any other truth that if where there are men there are no soldiers, it arises through a defect of the prince and not through any other defect, either of the site or of nature" (*D* I 21). The decisive fact about human beings is that at any time and in any place they can be made into soldiers; the most urgent or important task of politics is to make them so and to use them well. No excuse is to be accepted for failing to shape human nature according to the most fundamental necessity, that of war. Machiavelli's words and deeds alike thus direct our attention to his *Art of War*, the only major prose work he published during his life.

As Machiavelli's most sustained and detailed treatment of war, the *Art of War* offers a revealing angle from which to approach his thought as a whole. Indeed, through the *Art of War* one is witness to:

- the birth of modern military thought
- a "revolution in military affairs" at least as radical as our own
- Machiavelli's critical assessment of the results of his own efforts as Florentine Secretary to give his native city "arms of its own"

- a synthesis of the "Western" and "non-Western" ways of war
- a host of brilliant battlefield stratagems and ruses
- an extended reflection on the enduring elements of civil–military relations
- an appeal to, and simultaneous attack on, the humanism of his day
- the announcement of the author's long-term project for the political and spiritual transformation of the West

In addition to providing such a useful vantage point, the *Art of War* is an entrée in another sense as well. Because Machiavelli chose to publish it during his life, in Florence in 1521, the work affords the opportunity to see him as he wished to present himself to his contemporaries, namely, as Florence's preeminent civilian expert on military affairs. By the time of the posthumous publication of *The Prince* and *Discourses on Livy*, Machiavelli was already well known for his military writings as well as for his military projects as Secretary of the Second Chancery of Florence. Over the course of his fourteen-year tenure as secretary, Machiavelli bore the longest sustained responsibility for military matters of any government official. He was immersed in virtually all areas of military affairs: he personally observed and reported to his government on the size, composition, weaponry, morale, and logistical capabilities of the most effective militaries of his day; he created Florence's first native fighting force in over one hundred years, writing the law on its composition, handpicking its troops, and vetting its potential "captains" (as Machiavelli called military leaders); and he planned or observed significant sieges and skirmishes. His proclamation in the preface to the *Art of War* that he is inexperienced in war because he was not a soldier must therefore be taken with more than a grain of salt, much like his humble disclaimers in the dedicatory letters to *The Prince* and *Discourses on Livy*. Machiavelli had intimate familiarity with the warfare of his day as practiced by numerous types of warriors.

It was the greatest type of warrior, in Machiavelli's estimation, that was demanded by the Florence and Italy of his day. Lacking adequate forces of their own, they required a captain who knew not only how to command an army, but also how to make one from scratch. Most of the *Art of War* is devoted to cultivating this double virtue that deserves a twofold glory and praise (*AW* VII 199–206; cf. *D* III 13.4 [in citations to *Discourses on Livy*, the number after the period refers to the paragraph number in the Mansfield–Tarcov translation]). Regarding the creation of a new military, the work lays out the fundamentals of military organization and their attendant political conundrums: the topics of how soldiers ought to be conscripted, armed, ordered, trained, and encamped are entwined with such political questions as which citizens or subjects should be chosen and whether and how their military and civilian educations and occupations might conflict. Regarding how to command a military already in existence, the work constitutes a veritable armory of precepts, prescriptions, and examples concerning such topics as how to motivate one's own soldiers and demoralize one's enemy's, avoid ambushes, terminate a war, invest a recalcitrant city, and gain the tactical and strategic advantage in countless circumstances. Throughout the work Machiavelli draws on the exploits of great ancient commanders like Caesar and Alexander, and those of such moderns as Cesare Borgia and Francesco Sforza, well known to readers of his other major works. But the brightest stars of the *Art of War* are founder-captains such as Alexander's father, Philip of Macedon, the legendary Roman king Tullus Hostilius, and Cyrus the Great of Persia—all men who first created great armies then led them with brilliance.

It is clear, then, that Machiavelli constructs neither his army nor his stratagems out of thin air. He relies on what he has seen in his own lifetime, but also on what he has read regarding the military art of the ancients, especially that of the ancient Romans. His stated purpose is, in fact, retrogressive: to draw the contemporary military back toward "ancient modes" and give it "some form of past virtue" (*AW* pr. 10; cf. I 112). He draws repeatedly on two ancient Roman military authors in particular, Vegetius and Frontinus, often following the order in which each treats his various topics. Considerable use is also made of the Greek writer Polybius, whose history of the Roman republic contains one of the most valuable extant records of Roman military practices. Machiavelli makes such frequent reference to these authors that many interpreters have gone so far as to conclude that the *Art of War* is a mere compilation of ancient sources.[1] If that were so, however, one would expect the author to follow the practice (common even then) of naming his chief sources at some point, much as Machiavelli did in the very title of his *Discourses on Livy*, at least ostensibly a commentary on a part of Livy's history of Rome. But the names of the authors he draws on most in the *Art of War* are not so much as mentioned, while those he does name (Thucydides, Josephus, and Livy) are touched on only lightly. Furthermore, examples taken from all these ancient texts are frequently altered by Machiavelli, often in minor ways that are difficult to detect, but sometimes in striking ways accompanied by exhortations to compare the text with its presumed ancient source (e.g., *AW* VI 18–29, VII 215). Occasionally, examples presented as histor-

---

1. See, e.g., Sidney Anglo, *Machiavelli: A Dissection* (New York: Harcourt, Brace and World, 1969), 157; Walter Goffart, "The Date and Purpose of Vegetius' 'De re militari'" in *Traditio* 33 (1997): 92–93; for a nearly exhaustive collation of passages from the *Art of War* and their corresponding ancient sources, see L. Arthur Burd, "Le fonti letterarie di Machiavelli nell'*Arte della guerra*," *Atti della Reale Academia dei Lincei*, 5th ser., *Cl. di scienze morali, storiche e filologiche* 4 (1896): 187–261.

ical would appear to be sheer invention on Machiavelli's part (e.g., *AW* VII 192–93). What is more, he states explicitly toward the end of the work that he uses only those aspects of the ancient sources that serve his particular purposes given his particular circumstances (*AW* VII 181–82). For similar reasons, some interpreters of his other works have suggested that Machiavelli uses the ancients to provide cover for purposes of his own that entail radical innovations rather than retrogressive reform.[2] It is thus something of a puzzle whether the *Art of War* is a mere compendium of ancient texts, a rough-and-ready updating of those texts, a grab bag for practical contemporary reform, or a radical innovation camouflaged as a pious tribute to antiquity. This puzzle can be clarified—if not solved—by recurring to what is commonly called the "context" of the work.

No book by Machiavelli is more charged with its political and intellectual context than the *Art of War*. Because it was published during his lifetime, it reflects the constraints of his times more than his other major prose works. Indeed, Machiavelli draws our attention to the most crucial of these constraints by making the work a dialogue that takes place in a location bearing particular intellectual, political, and military significance: the Rucellai family gardens in Florence, known as the Orti Oricellari.[3] These gardens were located near the margins of Florence proper, just within Florence's outermost defensive walls, by the gate leading to the town of Prato. At this nearby town in 1512, the army founded by Machiavelli himself while serving as Florentine secretary suffered the disastrous defeat that led to the fall of the republican regime and the end of Machiavelli's political career. Thus the very location in which Machiavelli sets his chief discussion of the military art calls to mind a major military failure directly associated with his name, a failure that bore the gravest of political results. Machiavelli wrote, just as the characters in his dialogue speak, in the shadow of that failure.[4]

2. See, e.g., Leo Strauss *Thoughts on Machiavelli* (Chicago: University of Chicago Press, 1958), 85–86; "Niccolò Machiavelli," in Leo Strauss, *Studies in Platonic Political Philosophy* (Chicago: University of Chicago Press, 1983), 211–14, 217, 223; Harvey C. Mansfield and Nathan Tarcov, introduction to *Discourses on Livy* (Chicago: University of Chicago Press, 1996), xix–xxvii.

3. Regarding the setting, see especially Felix Gilbert, "Bernardo Rucellai and the Orti Oricerllari: A Study of the Origin of Modern Political Thought," *History: Choice and Commitment* (Cambridge: Harvard University Press, 1977), 215–46; cf. Harvey C. Mansfield, *Machiavelli's Virtue* (Chicago: University of Chicago Press, 1996), 194–96; Hannah Pitkin, *Fortune Is a Woman* (Chicago: University of Chicago Press, 1984), 68.

4. For a reliable account in English of Machiavelli and Prato, see C. C. Bayley, *War and Society in Renaissance Florence: The* De Militia *of Leonardo Bruni* (Toronto: University of Toronto Press, 1961), 276–84. Bayley makes clear that the failure at Prato cannot be used to impugn Machiavelli's military judgment: the limitations imposed on the enterprise by Florence's financial and political circumstances could have been overcome only with considerable time and authority,

Perhaps more significantly, the Orti Oricellari were a major center of humanism, a school of thought that reveled in the rediscovery of ancient writings and strove to bring them to bear on the modern—that is, the Christian—world. The gardens themselves had been cultivated at considerable expense and effort by the wealthy and politically influential Florentine Bernardo Rucellai. His wealth and influence derived in some measure from his many connections to the Medici, the family that had been the *de facto* rulers of Florence for much of the fifteenth century and that would rule again well after Bernardo's death. A true humanist, Bernardo longed to bring the ancient world to life, a goal he pursued in part by filling his gardens with imported plants representing all the species mentioned in classical literature,[5] as well as with the busts of famous rulers and writers.[6] A close disciple of Marsilio Ficino (1433–99), the famous translator of Plato and founder of a humanist academy under the patronage of Lorenzo de' Medici (1449–92), Bernardo sought to provide a place for serious discussion and study. The discussion staged in the pages of the *Art of War* literally begins with Bernardo's grandson, Cosimo Rucellai, explaining to a puzzled guest that the unfamiliar trees in whose shade they sat had been famous among "the ancients" (*AW* I 14). From this initial mention of the ancients, Cosimo and his guest launch into a friendly but pointed argument about whether, how, and in which activities the ancients ought to be imitated, as well as which ancients should be chosen as models. Machiavelli thereby dramatizes the question regarding the imitation of antiquity. While the *Art of War* clearly reflects the humanistic use of ancient sources, the manner and meaning of that use is itself at issue in the work.

The gardens provided a venue not only for theoretical discussions, however. They became the intellectual seat of aristocratic conspiracy during Florence's republican years (1498–1512) and then of republican conspiracy when Bernardo's grandson, Cosimo, presided over new gatherings in the years following the return of the Medici in 1512. It was in this latter period that Machiavelli, now forced (and freed) from government service by the Medici's return, frequented the Orti Oricellari. The humanism that was nurtured there prized not only ancient literature and political philosophy, but also ancient military and political actions, access to which could be had only through ancient historical and military texts.

In the early pages of the *Art of War,* Machiavelli narrates the discussion that takes place in these gardens, but names neither the date of the discussion nor

---

neither of which Machiavelli possessed. He concludes that "Machiavelli, the superlative bureaucrat, wrought on this unpromising material with all the effect that administrative intelligence and boundless energy could achieve" (ibid., 283); cf. *AW* I 148–70, VII 241.

5. This is the only feature of the gardens explicitly alluded to in the work (*AW* I 13–15).

6. Gilbert, *History,* 229.

that of its narration. It can be inferred, however, that the discussion occurs in late August or early September of 1516, whereas the year of Machiavelli's narration of the discussion is 1519.[7] Although the conversation can be presumed to be fictitious, the active participants are all historical figures. The chief participant is Fabrizio Colonna, a prominent mercenary captain who, we are told, was just then passing through Florence after fighting honorably in Lombardy for the "Catholic King," Ferdinand of Spain (*AW* I 9). It is not mentioned that Fabrizio, like other successful mercenary captains, had been employed by many of the major powers contending in Italy since the 1494 invasion of Italy by Charles VIII of France. Thus Fabrizio cut the ambiguous figure of most condottieri: at once the honorable warrior and the faithless mercenary.[8] But the dialogue itself puts Fabrizio's loyalties into question in another way. His young host asks whether his allegiance is to his king, whom he serves both as peacetime counselor and wartime captain, or to the art of war as a means to his own ends (*AW* I 94–110). Fabrizio's emphatic—if ultimately unconvincing—answer is that his loyalties lie with his king, peace, and politics rather than with his own profit and war.

The allegiances of the others depicted as taking part in the discussion are also in doubt, but in their cases the doubt is due to events following the work's publication. In 1522, the year after the publication of the *Art of War,* these other participants were all exiled for principal roles in a major conspiracy to oust the effective ruler of Florence, Cardinal Giulio de' Medici. They, like Cosimo, were young friends of Machiavelli and were as much "on fire for great and magnificent things" as was Cosimo (*AW* I 3, 11). The conspiracy they helped instigate was led by the Soderini, the family of Piero Soderini, head of the republican government Machiavelli had served.[9] The ambitions of his young friends would seem

---

7. For Fabrizio Colonna was then returning to Rome after the Treaty of Noyon ended the wars in Lombardy on August 16, 1516; also Fabrizio is said in the dialogue to be in Florence to visit "the Duke," presumably referring to Lorenzo de' Medici, who was named duke of Urbino by his uncle, Pope Leo X, on August 18, 1516. The narration is presented as occurring just after Cosimo Rucellai's death in 1519.

8. See Michael Mallet, *Mercernaries and Their Masters: Warfare in Renaissance Italy* (Totowa, N.J.: Rowman and Littlefield, 1974), 57–58; Frédérique Verrier, "Machiavelli e Fabrizio Colonna nell'*Arte della guerra:* il polemologo spoddiato," in *Niccolò Machiavelli: politico, storico, letterato: atti del Convegno di Losanna. 27–30 settembre 1995,* ed. Jean-Jacques Marchand (Rome: Salerno, 1996), 175–85.

9. For the suggestion that Machiavelli instigated the plot, see Maurizio Viroli, *Niccolò's Smile: A Biography of Machiavelli,* trans. Antony Shugaar (New York: Farrar, Straus and Giroux, 2000), 210. For a summary account of the conspiracy in English, including reliable bibliographic information on more exhaustive accounts, see J. N. Stephens, *The Fall of the Florentine Republic* (Oxford: Oxford University Press, 1983), 117–21. Machiavelli devotes the longest chapters of his most

to have led them to seek to overthrow a princely government in republican garb in order to install a more truly republican form of government.

The source of Fabrizio's divided loyalties, his dual role as warrior and peacetime counselor, can be said to be *the* problem addressed by the *Art of War:* the relation between the military and civilian ways of life (*AW* pr. 1). Are these two essentially at odds? Is military discipline the schoolhouse of the citizen's patriotism? Or should civilian life be used to temper the harshness of military life? Related questions are raised by the divided loyalties of Fabrizio's young questioners: Should civilian life be spirited and republican, or can it be lived just as well in a principality? Taken together, these questions lead into the thick of scholarly debates about Machiavelli's thought as a whole. For those scholars who follow in the wake of Hans Baron's approach (such as J. G. A. Pocock, Quentin Skinner, and Maurizio Viroli), it is essential that Machiavelli's soldiers be selflessly devoted to the common, republican good. But it is just as essential to the arguments of Leo Strauss, Harvey Mansfield, Vickie Sullivan, and others that Machiavelli be seen as having unleashed the self-regarding passions—even as he advocated a management of those very passions that serves the aggregate (not to say common) good. Mansfield is the only scholar to subject the *Art of War* to the kind of extended—albeit introductory—examination necessary to help decide this important question.[10] On the whole, however, those who take Baron's "civic humanist" approach have had more to say on the importance of the question of the military and civilian lives.

For Pocock the issue is especially important. The central thesis of his massive *Machiavellian Moment* is that Machiavelli somehow provides the essential link between ancient theories of political life and the later Atlantic republican tradition.[11] At a crucial step in his argument, Pocock asserts that human nature can be perfected by means of military virtue and announces the need to "understand the relations existing in Machiavelli's mind between the military and civic capacities of the individual—in shorter language, between the soldier and the citizen."[12] He takes this relation to be double: only a citizen can be a good soldier, and only a soldier can be a good citizen, which is to say that the soldier's

---

comprehensive books to the subject of conspiracies; see *The Prince* 19 and *Discourses on Livy* III 6. In the latter he suggests that experience in war is the only preparation for the psychological strain entailed in executing a conspiracy (*D* III 6.12).

10. Mansfield, *Machiavelli's Virtue*, 191–218.

11. J. G. A. Pocock, *The Machiavellian Moment: Florentine Political Thought and the Atlantic Republican Tradition* (Princeton: Princeton University Press, 1975), vii–viii, 183–218.

12. Ibid., 199.

dedication to the common good must be carried over into politics. Pocock argues that, for Machiavelli,

> [m]ilitary *virtù* necessitates political virtue because both can be presented in
> terms of the same end. The republic is the common good; the citizen, directing
> all his action toward that good, may be said to dedicate his life to the republic;
> the patriot warrior dedicates his death, and the two are alike in perfecting
> human nature by sacrificing particular goods to a universal end. It may be
> through military discipline that one learns to be a citizen and to display civic
> virtue.[13]

Pocock suggests that military discipline (with the help of civic religion) is *the*
mechanism by means of which man's "original nature" is irreversibly developed
and perfected.[14] He claims that Machiavelli's innovation was to show that human nature can be perfected by means of military virtue. For human nature
is perfected by dedication to the common good, a dedication nowhere more
clearly demanded and achieved than in military self-sacrifice.

Quentin Skinner shares Pocock's conviction that Machiavelli was committed to the humanist ideal of the citizen army and wholehearted service to the
community. Skinner emphasizes the willingness to sacrifice, patriotism, and
commitment to liberty he believes Machiavelli sought either to find within his
citizen army or to infuse into the polity by means of that army. Asserting an ultimate continuity between Machiavelli and the classical tradition, Skinner believes that writers such as Machiavelli bring the "Aristotelian figure of the armed
and independent citizen, willing to fight for his liberties . . . once again to the
centre of the political stage." This commitment to the humanist ideal was so
deep, believes Skinner, that it clouded Machiavelli's military and political judgment: he "resolutely refused to see that no amount of mustering of the most willing and patriotic citizenry could hope to make the small-scale principalities of
Italy any match for the vast national armies" of France, Germany, and Spain.
Skinner considers Machiavelli's efforts to raise a militia and his *Art of War* to be
evidence that his "continuing commitment to the ideal of a citizen soldier went
far beyond a mere repetition of . . . humanist common places."[15] More recently,

---

13. Ibid., 201.

14. Ibid., 184, 203; cf. Felix Gilbert, "Machiavelli: The Renaissance of the Art of War," in *The
Makers of Modern Strategy: From Machiavelli to the Nuclear Age,* ed. Peter Paret (Princeton: Princeton University Press, 1986), 26.

15. Quentin Skinner, *The Foundations of Modern Political Thought,* vol. 1 (Cambridge: Cambridge University Press, 1978), 173–75. Cf. Skinner's apparent application of his understanding of
Machiavelli to our own situation: "[A] leading theme of Book II of Machiavelli's *Discorsi*" is that "a

Maurizio Viroli has argued that what Machiavelli "wished to revive from classical politics is stated more clearly in *The Art of War* than in any other of his
works." Indeed, he asserts elsewhere that the *Art of War* provides the best evidence for his subordination of the Machiavellian Machiavelli to a republican
Machiavelli wedded to the "conventional image of the political man who benefits" the common good, the rule of law and civic equality.[16]

The proximate source of this civic humanist interpretation of Machiavelli
is the work of Hans Baron.[17] Baron too asserts the fundamental continuity of
Machiavelli's thought with that of the ancients. For Baron, Machiavelli is essentially at one with the fifteenth-century humanism of Leornardo Bruni, who in
turn was solidly ensconced in the classical and medieval Aristotelian tradition.
Referring to the *Art of War* in a telling passage, Baron asserts Machiavelli's agreement with the civic humanist "persuasion that political *virtù*, to achieve its full
growth, had always needed the active citizenship extant in small free states."
Such active citizenship, he goes on to argue, requires "reviving the citizen-army
of the medieval commune" and dismantling the predominant system of mercenary warfare.[18] On this reading, Machiavelli is entirely averse to any form of military professionalism, for professionals, like mercenaries, are presumed to be
motivated by the desire for personal profit. While Pocock, Skinner, and Viroli
each differ in various ways from Baron's full analysis, they all agree regarding
Machiavelli's unity with the humanism of his day, his related reverence for antiquity, and the centrality of the citizen-soldier as the bulwark of selfless or
wholehearted dedication to the common good.

---

willingness to cultivate the martial virtues, and to place them in the service of our community,
must be indispensable to the preservation of our own individual liberty as well as the independ-
ence of our native land" (Skinner, "The Republican Idea of Political Liberty," in *Machiavelli and
Republicanism*, ed. Gisela Bock, Quentin Skinner, and Maurizio Viroli [Cambridge: Cambridge
University Press, 1990], 303, 303 n. 40; cf. 308–9).

16. Viroli, *Niccolò's Smile*, 218; Maurizio Viroli, "Machiavelli and the Republican Idea of Politics," in *Machiavelli and Republicanism*, 168–69; cf. ibid., 152–61.

17. A less immediate—if not the ultimate—source is Hannah Arendt's understanding of the
vita activa; for Pocock's connection to Arendt, see Pocock, *Machiavellian Moment*, 516 n. 15, 550;
for Skinner's debt to Pocock, see Quentin Skinner, *Machiavelli* (New York: Hill and Wang, 1981), v–
vi; "The Republican Idea of Liberty," in *Machiavelli and Republicanism*, 300 n. 2; cf. ibid., 308 for
an explanation of his differences from Arendt; cf. also Viroli, "Machiavelli and the Republican Idea
of Politics," 144 n. 4.

18. Hans Baron, *The Crisis of the Early Italian Renaissance: Civic Humanism and Republican
Liberty in an Age of Classicism and Tyranny* (Princeton: Princeton University Press, 1966), 430–32;
for a recent reconsideration of Baron and his general thesis, see James Hankins, ed., *Renaissance
Civic Humanism: Reappraisals and Reflections* (Cambridge: Cambridge University Press, 2000);
Hankins, "The 'Baron Thesis' after Forty Years and Some Recent Studies of Leonardo Bruni,"
Journal of the History of Ideas 56 (1995): 309–38.

Aspects of this civic humanist understanding of Machiavelli have been challenged by a variety of scholars. Speaking of passages in the *Art of War* that might seem to support a civic humanist reading of that work, Felix Gilbert suggests that one should "doubt that these sentences reflect Machiavelli's true sentiments."[19] Peter Godman, basing his case on Machiavelli's preference for practical experience and his contempt for misguided bookishness, has recently argued that "antagonism" rather than "dependence characterized [Machiavelli's] relation to humanism."[20] But the most thoroughgoing opposition to the civic humanist understanding stems from the work of Leo Strauss. Far from providing a vital link to the classics, Machiavelli is represented by Strauss as having effected a radical break with antiquity, as having been the discoverer and communicator of the "new modes and orders" that would become the foundation of modernity in general and of acquisitive liberalism in particular.[21] For Strauss, Machiavelli's well-known praise of republics in no way entails a call for the wholehearted dedication to the common good implied by republican*ism*, a term never used by Machiavelli himself. Instead, citizens serve the public good because it serves their respective private goods; when such calculative reasoning fails, institutions with teeth in them work upon citizens' passions to ensure compliance with the demands of the common.[22] In war, the activity that would seem above all others to require selfless dedication, the soldier in the field—whether citizen of a republic or subject of a prince—is motivated by his captain's manipulation of his fear of death and hope for material reward. Similarly, captains themselves are motivated by a self-regarding desire for fame or glory.[23] On this reading, military professionalism as such would present no problem for Machiavelli; for the professional armies of the criminal tyrant Septimius Severus and the paid citizen-soldiers of the later Roman republic were models of an effective and well-controlled military force. The problem would

19. Gilbert, "Machiavelli," 24. For Gilbert's relationship to the civic humanist school, see William J. Connell, "The Republican Idea," in *Renaissance Civic Humanism*, 17–21.

20. Peter Godman, *From Poliziano to Machiavelli: Florentine Humanism in the High Renaissance* (Princeton: Princeton University Press, 1998), 261–62.

21. Leo Strauss, *Natural Right and History* (Chicago: University of Chicago Press, 1953), 178; Strauss, *Thoughts*, 231, 249, 264, 296–97; but compare ibid., 120–21 with Strauss, *Persecution and the Art of Writing* (Chicago: University of Chicago Press, 1952), 33, and *Natural Right*, 164; see also *Persecution*, 15; Strauss, *What Is Political Philosophy? and Other Studies* (Chicago: University of Chicago Press, 1959), 102–3; and compare *Thoughts*, 202–3 and *Studies*, 226 with *Studies*, 209.

22. Strauss, *Thoughts*, 262–65, 269–70, 281; *What Is Political Philosophy?* 43; cf. Mansfield, *Machiavelli's Virtue*, xv.

23. Strauss, *Thoughts*, 247–48, 278–82.

seem to be with mercenary or auxiliary forces, not professional forces paid and controlled by the political authorities (who may even be military authorities themselves).[24]

But considerations of actual combat and military organization are far from Strauss's chief interest in Machiavelli's military thought. Instead, Strauss traces to its ultimate conclusion the suggestion that "there is a certain similarity between warfare proper and spiritual warfare": Machiavelli himself waged a war against the entire tradition of political philosophy, making special use of propaganda, the favorite weapon of his most powerful enemy, Christianity.[25] Thus for Strauss the chief problem of the *Art of War* is less about the personal tension between the civilian and military lives as lived by the average civilian or soldier than it is about the political alternative offered by those two lives at the highest level: the alternative between the rule of priests and the rule of warriors, between that of the unarmed and that of the armed. Since for Strauss's Machiavelli to be armed means to be a knower of the art of war and of "the world," the question ultimately concerns the place of reason in human life.[26] Insofar as its ultimate purpose is to help recover the permanent problems or alternatives, *Thoughts on Machiavelli* may be said to be an extended inquiry into whether the alternative of priest versus warrior, properly elaborated, represents a fundamentally novel problem.[27] The novel problem could be a genuine one only if biblical religion (and perhaps Christianity in particular) had revealed in nature the presence of something that before had gone unrecognized, or that had at least not been given sufficient weight, namely, the malleability of human nature by human means.[28] The alternative recognized by Machiavelli concerned who would shape humanity, those who professed belief in the biblical revelation (and especially its counsel not to resist evil with evil)[29] or those who saw the truth of the modes and orders put forth by Machiavelli himself.

Many studies of Machiavelli have been inspired by the work of Strauss, most

24. Ibid., 309–10 n. 53 (note that even mercenaries can be well used if the captain has, like Hannibal, sufficient virtue).

25. Ibid., 35, 102, 106, 138, 171–72; cf. Ernst Cassirer, *The Myth of State* (New Haven: Yale University Press, 1946), 162, 173; Strauss, *What is Political Philosophy?* 45.

26. Ibid., 17–19, 155, 184; cf. 19, 144, 153–55, 162, 218, 223, 243–44.

27. Ibid., 14, 113–14, 184; cf. Strauss, *Persecution,* 168. Strauss's studies of Machiavelli concentrate on his two comprehensive works, *The Prince* and *Discourses on Livy;* however, he makes numerous references to the *Art of War* in *Thoughts on Machiavelli* and discusses its use of ancient sources in "Machiavelli and Classical Literature," *Review of National Literatures* 1 (1970): 7–25.

28. Strauss, *Thoughts,* 124, 184, 205, 232, 252–53, 278–80; but see also 283, 297.

29. Ibid., 180–85.

significantly those by Harvey Mansfield.[30] The contrast between this approach and the "civic humanist" interpretation could hardly be more pronounced. Indeed, prominent "Straussians" have pointedly criticized the three principal figures of the latter school. Vickie Sullivan has criticized Pocock's interpretation of the *Discourses on Livy* as a testament to wholehearted dedication to the common good,[31] Nathan Tarcov has dissected Skinner's methodology in general and his interpretation of *The Prince* in particular,[32] and Mansfield has recently offered a wholesale critique of Hans Baron's thesis and the very idea of civic humanism.[33]

This brief review of the secondary literature shows the intimate links between the three issues touched on so far: the relationship between the civilian and military lives, the connection between the *Art of War* and its humanist intellectual context, and Machiavelli's use of ancient sources. In the secondary literature, a stand on one issue entails a stand on the other two. Those who see self-sacrificing dedication as the moral-political teaching regarding war tend to think that Machiavelli's contemporary context and fidelity to antiquity determined his thought; those, on the other hand, who see the management of selfish passions at the moral-political core of his teaching hold that Machiavelli knew his context at least as well as we and sought to transform it by means of subtly co-opting his ancient sources. Thus the substantive question of what Machiavelli taught regarding war and politics is entwined with the historical or literary question of how to read his work. The only nonarbitrary manner to decide between the approaches spearheaded respectively by Baron and Strauss is through a careful interpretation of the dialogue, one that shows due deference

30. Most of Mansfield's writings on Machiavelli have been collected in *Machiavelli's Virtue;* for his commentary on Machiavelli's *Discourses on Livy,* see Harvey C. Mansfield, *Machiavelli's New Modes and Orders: A Study of the* Discourses on Livy (Chicago: University of Chicago Press, 2001).

31. More specifically, Sullivan judges Pocock's claim that human nature can be perfected by means of a dedication to the common good, fostered by military virtue, to be implausible; she makes the further point that Pocock assumes the truth of this crucial claim without proving it. Sullivan's arguments are based on an interpretation of *Discourses* I 16 and I 55. She does not directly address Pocock's treatment of the *Art of War* (cf. Paul Rahe, *Republics Ancient and Modern,* vol. 2, *New Modes and Orders in Early Modern Political Thought* [Chapel Hill: University of North Carolina Press, 1994], 323–24n).

32. Nathan Tarcov, "Quentin Skinner's Method and Machiavelli's Prince," *Ethics* 92 (1982): 692–709; see also Paul Rahe, "Situating Machiavelli," in *Renaissance Civic Humanism,* 270–308; W. R. Newell, "How Original is Machiavelli? A Consideration of Skinner's Interpretation of Virtue and Fortune," *Political Theory* 15 (1987): 612–34; Michael P. Zuckert, "Appropriation and Understanding in the History of Political Philosophy: On Quentin Skinner's Method," *Interpretation* 13 (1985): 403–24 (cf. Rahe, *Republics Ancient and Modern,* vol. 2, 328 n. 7).

33. Mansfield, "Bruni and Machiavelli on Civic Humanism," in *Renaissance Civic Humanism,* 223–46.

to Machiavelli's literary and philosophical greatness without forgetting the military, political, and intellectual context of the work. I attempt to supply such a treatment in the interpretive essay.

It is fitting to offer here a single bit of guidance on how to read the *Art of War*. Contrary to the standard assumption that Fabrizio is simply a mouthpiece for Machiavelli, as well as to Mansfield's far preferable understanding of Fabrizio as a representative of humanism whose position is undermined by the action of the dialogue,[34] I have concluded that the aging condottiere is a self-consciously restrained version of Machiavelli himself. Fabrizio's (and Machiavelli's) full understanding is brought partly to light by the questions put to him by the younger participants in the discussion. This is not to say that the younger participants can be identified (or even more closely aligned than Fabrizio) with Machiavelli;[35] rather, the dialogue as a whole displays how the demands of spirited youths can serve to remove the moral veil of wise political discourse. Up to Machiavelli's time, political philosophers had kept at arm's length the force and fraud endemic to political rule and especially to its founding moments. They did so by censuring or beautifying that force or fraud, or by placing its precepts in the mouths of unsavory characters; otherwise, they simply maintained a prudent silence concerning it. Early in the dialogue, Fabrizio continues this tradition of reticence. But in response to insistent if polite questioning, at *AW* II 81 he begins deftly to alter course in the direction of Machiavelli's own posthumous openness; by the end of the work he can be heard to recommend the imitation not of morally upstanding republican captains but of two of the chief exemplars of tyrannical cruelty and of fraud on nearly the grandest of scales, Alexander's father, Philip of Macedon, and Cyrus the Great (*AW* VII 204, 243; cf. *D* I 26, II 13). It is important to note, however, that Fabrizio merely begins down the path toward Machiavelli's openness. Nonetheless, by means of the dialogue's muted drama, Machiavelli stages this partial disclosure of the truth about politics, thereby highlighting what is perhaps the most salient aspect of the rhetoric of his posthumous comprehensive writings—its appeal to the coarser passions of the young. (*P* 25, end; *D* I 60, II pr.)[36]

In the *Art of War* itself, Fabrizio proclaims his warm hopes for a favorable reception of his military ideas among his young interlocutors: "For I believe that youth makes you more friendly to military things and more ready to believe what will be said by me. By already having white heads and ice in their veins . . .

---

34. Mansfield, *Machiavelli's Virtue*, 194–98, 202, 205–8; cf. ibid., 212, 217.

35. Ibid., 338 n. 33.

36. Cf. Strauss, *Thoughts*, 126–27; Strauss, *Studies*, 222, 225; Mansfield, *New Modes and Orders*, 177–89.

others are accustomed to being enemies of war" (*AW* I 47–48). Indeed, it must
not be forgotten that it is first and foremost a book about how to fight and win
wars. In this regard Machiavelli and his *Art of War* were influential throughout
Italy, Europe, and beyond. By the end of the sixteenth century, no less than
twenty Italian editions had been published, and translations or plagiarizations
had been made into Spanish, French, English, and Latin; the following centuries
saw translations into German, Russian, and other European languages.[37] Considered by Montaigne to be on a par with the war writings of Caesar and Polybius, Machiavelli's military writings continued to influence military thought
directly and indirectly through the works of Montecuccoli, Fourquevaux, Jus-
tus Lipsius, and others;[38] his teachings were applied to the great modern militaries of Maurice of Nassau and Gustavus Adolphus;[39] and the *Art of War* was
relied on in Marshal de Saxe's *Reveries on the Art of War,* was grudgingly acknowledged for its insight and impact by the likes of Voltaire, and is thought by
many to have influenced both Frederick the Great and Napoleon.[40] Clausewitz
himself held that Machiavelli "was a very sound judge of military matters."[41] The
effects of the *Art of War* can even be said to have reached across the Atlantic in
that Captain John Smith studied the 1560 Whitehorn translation,[42] Thomas Jef-
ferson owned a copy of the work, and an American edition of the 1775 Farneworth translation was brought out in the wake of the War of 1812.[43] Machiavelli's
influence was summed up by Felix Gilbert, the most widely read interpreter in
English of Machiavelli's military thought, with the statement that "military

---

37. Sergio Bertelli and Piero Innocenti, *Bibliografia Machiavelliana* (Verona: Edizioni Val-
donega, 1979), 363–77.

38. Montaigne, *Essays* II 34; Gunther D. Rothenberg, "Maurice of Nassau, Gustavus Adolphus, Raimondo Montecuccoli, and the 'Military Revolution' of the Seventeenth Century," in
Makers of Modern Strategy, 33–36; cf. Thomas M. Barker, *The Military Intellectual and Battle: Raimondo Montecuccoli and the Thirty Years War* (Albany: State University of New York Press, 1975),
56–57; Neal Wood, introduction to Niccolò Machiavelli, *The Art of War* (New York: Da Capo,
1965), xxx.

39. Rothenberg, "'Military Revolution' of the Seventeenth Century," 33–36.

40. Gilbert, "Machiavelli," 27; Voltaire, "Battalion," in *A Philosophical Dictionary* (New York:
E. R. DuMont, [1901]), 215–17; Francesco Algarotti, *Letters Military and Political* (London: T. Eger-
ton, 1782); cf. Wood, introduction to *Art of War*, xlii–xliv.

41. Carl von Clausewitz, *Historical and Political Writings,* ed. and trans. Peter Paret and
Daniel Moran (Princeton: Princeton University Press, 1992), 281.

42. John Smith, *The Complete Works of Captain John Smith* (Chapel Hill: University of North
Carolina Press, 1986), 156.

43. Gilbert, "Machiavelli," 27; *The Art of War. In Seven Books. Written by Nicholas Machiavel,
Secretary of State, to the Republic of Florence. To which is added, Hints Relative to Warfare, by a
Gentleman of the State of New York,* trans. Ellis Farneworth (New York: Henry C. Southwick, 1815).

thought since the sixteenth century proceeded on the foundations Machiavelli laid."[44] Even those who rail against his supposed errors or inveigh against his ahistorical rationalism agree that in terms of breadth of scope, fundamental principles, and strategic insight, Machiavelli began and perhaps framed the debates of subsequent military thought.[45] The *Art of War* provides unique access to both the military thought of his time and the origins of modern military thought itself.

This universal acknowledgment of the *Art of War*'s status as a classic of strategic thought is more than tempered by widespread criticism of its specific military analyses and prescriptions. Indeed, critics attribute to its author countless errors of military judgment, most of which relate to technology, battlefield tactics, and military professionalism. Virtually all of the criticisms are based on the assumption that Machiavelli was the unwitting victim of three related prejudices: an uncritical preference for all things ancient (and especially Roman), a dread of any form of military professionalism, and the quaint conviction that gunpowder technology—and technological innovation in general— was a factor of negligible significance or a pernicious trend to be resisted. I believe, however, that Machiavelli suffered from none of these prejudices. The above-mentioned division among scholars regarding Machiavelli's views on the ancients and professionalism raises the possibility, which I develop in the interpretive essay, that his vision of both was crystal clear. But what of his position regarding technological innovation in general and gunpowder technology in particular?

Contrary to nearly unanimous scholarly opinion, Machiavelli was very much in favor of both. In fact, he acknowledged that siege artillery had eclipsed all ancient ballistics and that field artillery allowed for significant improvements over ancient practices (*AW* VII 75–76; *D* II 17.3; cf. *AW* IV 26–31, VII 24, 139–40); he advocated—perhaps for the first time ever—universal training in the use of firearms (*AW* II 125–26); and he extolled technological innovation in war above nearly everything else (*AW* VII 190–93; *D* III 14). This case is developed fully in the first part of the interpretive essay, but it is useful to alert readers here to three factors contributing to the widespread misunderstanding of Machiavelli's true positions. The charge that Machaivelli failed to foresee rapid transformations in

44. Gilbert, "Machiavelli," 29–30.

45. Ibid., 30; Hans Delbrück, *The Dawn of Modern Warfare: History of the Art of War,* vol. 4, trans. Walter J. Renfroe Jr. (Lincoln: University of Nebraska Press, 1985), 293 (cf. 101–13); Sir Charles Oman, *A History of the Art of War in the Sixteenth Century* (New York: E. P. Dutton, 1979), 93; Azar Gat, *The Origins of Military Thought: From the Enlightenment to Clausewitz* (Oxford: Oxford University Press, 1991).

the conduct of war arising from gunpowder technology assumes both that rapid transformations actually occurred and that Machiavelli sought to predict the future of specific military developments. But no rapid change took place: gunpowder technology had been around for centuries by Machiavelli's day, and it would be more than another century before gunpowder brought about fundamental changes on the field of battle (as opposed to during sieges, where it had already wrought great changes).[46] More important, no direct or indirect source has ever been produced that would suggest that Machiavelli took himself to be in the business of military prognostication. Indeed, he is at pains to indicate that his specific prescriptions were intended to give his army the relative advantage over any army already in existence at his time in Europe (*AW* I 82, II 71, II 81, VII 182; cf. *P* 26.104–5 [in citations to *The Prince*, numbers that follow the chapter number and period refer to pages in the Mansfield translation]). The quotations that are generally produced as evidence of his short sightedness bring us to the second factor contributing to scholarly misunderstandings: the failure to disentangle his actual analyses and prescriptions from his flattery of the primary audience (the "lovers of ancient actions" [*AW* pr. 10]). To take a famous example from another work with a similar primary audience, in the treatment of artillery in the *Discourses on Livy* cited above, Machiavelli might seem at the opening of the chapter to side with ancient virtue over and against modern artillery. But the chapter as a whole in fact concludes that one can and must use both virtue *and* modern artillery, indicating at the same time that virtue will now have to be of a different quality from—and perhaps even superior to—ancient virtue in order to counter and incorporate modern artillery. Thus he starts off with sentiments most congenial to his primary humanist audience, refines them in a subtle treatment of the issue, and ends with a novel conclusion remarkable for both its insight and utility. If one is overwhelmed by the initial or general impression, one is likely to mistake Machiavelli's indulgence of his audience for his own considered opinion.

The failure to appreciate the subtlety of Machiavelli's rhetoric and conclusions has led most readers to overlook a piece of sobering advice at least as ap-

---

46. For the case that gunpowder technology evolved slowly and in turn caused less rapid changes than is usually imagined, see Bert S. Hall, *Weapons and Warfare in Renaissance Europe: Gunpowder, Technology, and Tactics* (Baltimore: Johns Hopkins University Press, 1997). Even those military historians who argue for a relatively rapid revolution in military affairs due to technological changes assume that changes took place over generations; for an overview and appraisal see Clifford J. Rogers, ed., *The Military Revolution Debate: Readings on the Military Transformation of Early Modern Europe* (Boulder: Westview Press, 1995); cf. David Eltis, *The Military Revolution in Sixteenth-Century Europe* (London: I. B. Tauris Publishers, 1995).

plicable to our own times as it was half a millennium ago. In the chapter of the *Discourses on Livy* just discussed, Machiavelli cautions against seeing technology as a military panacea, as a way of freeing warriors from the harsh realities of killing and the dangers of being killed, and from the discipline, skills, and qualities necessary for success on the field of battle. He offers similar advice in his discussions of the utility of fortresses (*AW* VII 1–152; *D* II 24). There he cautions that fortresses are no substitute for well-trained soldiers willing and able to fight at close quarters. These passages are frequently offered as evidence that Machiavelli wished to deny the reality of the need to defend against modern artillery. In fact, throughout his life he was at the cutting edge of siege and fortification technology, from his encounter with the innovative "double-Pisan ramparts" during his earliest military experiences to his final commission in 1527 to determine how to modernize Florence's defensive walls.[47] Thus, for Machiavelli, innovations in military technologies are useful and necessary, but they do not obviate the need for human excellence. One cannot help but think of the version of the fortress just over our own technological horizon: ballistic missile defense. Machiavelli can be likened to contemporary defense experts who are very much in favor of ballistic missile defense but who nonetheless warn against pursuing it at the expense of a solid force structure, effective recruitment and training, and sound strategic doctrine governing them all. Finally, Machiavelli's numerous attempts in the *Art of War* to discern the best combinations of weapons on the tactical level, and his measured embrace in all his major works of artillery and fortresses at the operational or strategic level, serve as a firm reminder to us today: strategy must drive the use of technology; technology must not determine strategy. Otherwise, means become ends and ends become means; moreover, the need for military excellence—or virtue as Machiavelli calls it—is imagined away.

Machiavelli was no enemy of technological innovation. He fully embraced it and can even be said to have prepared the way for the modern technological enterprise about to be launched by his greatest successors.[48] Once the critical assumptions regarding Machiavelli's understanding of war are seen to be mistaken, most of his supposed errors of military judgment melt away. His many

---

47. Compare Christopher Duffy, *Siege Warfare: The Fortress in the Early Modern World, 1494–1660* (London: Routledge and Kegan Paul, 1979), 15 with *AW* VII 135–38; see also J. R. Hale, "To Fortify or Not to Fortify? Machiavelli's Contribution to a Renaissance Debate," in *Renaissance War Studies* (London: Hambledon Press, 1983); Geoffrey Parker, "In Defense of *The Military Revolution*," in *Military Revolution Debate*, 345–46.

48. See Roger D. Masters, *Machiavelli, Leonardo, and the Science of Power* (Notre Dame: University of Notre Dame Press, 1996); cf. Strauss, *What Is Political Philosophy?* 286–90.

prescriptions and principles can be seen for what they are: the results of judicious mixtures of—or rhetorical compromises with—the military, political, and intellectual necessities of his time and place. The difficulty lies in seeing his teaching and intention through and within the rhetoric with which it is entwined.

The subtle rhetoric of the *Art of War* is better appreciated by Felix Gilbert, author of the influential essay on Machiavelli's military thought in Peter Paret's *The Makers of Modern Strategy: From Machiavelli to the Nuclear Age*. This treatment is outstanding in many ways. Gilbert's recognition that the *Art of War* made many compromises with the conventions of the day inoculates him against the more extreme misunderstandings of the work and its military prescriptions.[49] Furthermore, Gilbert accurately sketches the relation between Machiavelli's deeds as Florentine secretary and his later military and political writings. For these reasons alone his essay will remain a useful overview of Machiavelli's military thought. Nonetheless, the erroneous assumptions mentioned above would seem to be at the root of Gilbert's assessment of Machiavelli's "misjudgments" regarding important developments in the areas of military professionalism and artillery.[50] For all of his appreciation of Machiavelli's acumen, Gilbert ultimately concludes that Machiavelli can be easily snared by means of a straightforward historical critique.

Gilbert begins by sketching a balanced view of the relation between the long-term transformation of feudal militaries into professional armies and the development of gunpowder technology. He argues that the expense of the latter did not single-handedly bring about a sudden transformation from feudal to professional armies; instead it "accelerate[d] the tempo of the evolution" in the direction of the latter.[51] He then begins to turn the tables on Machiavelli, first by noting that Machiavelli himself was interested in the relation between the social changes and the military crisis of his day, and then by developing at some length the idea that Machiavelli analyzed that relationship fairly well. Gilbert concludes first that Fabrizio's and Machiavelli's advocacy of a part-time militia modeled on ancient city-states was inadequate for a territorial state such as Florence, and second that the future lay with professionals since the core of any army would consist of a small number of experts, difficult to train and expensive to equip. Together these developments point to the need for the large professional armies Machiavelli is presumed to have loathed.[52] Present in Gilbert's analysis are all the usual assumptions regarding Machiavelli's supposed errors. Gilbert incorrectly

49. Gilbert, "Machiavelli," 22, 24.   51. See note 46.
50. Ibid., 28.   52. Gilbert, "Machiavelli," 28

assumes that Machiavelli fails to see the importance and expense of field and siege artillery[53] and that the model of "ancient city-states" blinds him to the possibility of professional armies. In addition, Gilbert saddles him with the burden of predicting long-term trends in military technology and economics. But if these assumptions are incorrect, so too must be Gilbert's overall critique of Machiavelli.

The point here is not to quibble about which details Machiavelli got right or wrong; it is to gain from Machiavelli as much profit as one possibly can. Most treatments of Machiavelli on war—and not only on war—seek to cut him down to size by attempting to show that he was in the grips of his passions or his times—in a word, his prejudices. They often do so by appealing to *our* prejudices that current knowledge is necessarily superior to earlier claims to know and that no one, after all, really knows more than his own times allow. But what if Machiavelli knew his own times better than we? What if, in addition, he understood our own times better then we? The latter seemingly absurd suggestion could be true if he did in fact launch the modern enterprise of human freedom on the basis of the true understanding of "the things of the world" (*D* Dedicatory Letter, I 38.3, III 1.1, III 43). If he did, how much more might we have to learn from him than is commonly believed?

Although the scholarly assessment of Machiavelli's understanding of tactics and weaponry has been harsh, he has garnered high praise for what he says about military strategy at the highest level of command. His strategic thought is generally lauded for being "modern"—that is to say, Clausewitzean—in its emphasis on the people in arms, the ideal of victory by means of a decisive battle, and the understanding of war as a continuation of politics by other means. Insofar as Machiavelli's strategic thought is criticized, it is for not having shaken free of the constraints imposed by the antiquated ways of the condottiere warfare of his day. This latter type of warfare was practiced not by the people at large, but by skilled mercenaries leading hired hands; its ideal of victory was the bloodless checkmate rather than the decisive battle; and it served as a most unreliable instrument of politics. It is often thought that Machiavelli despised this condottiere warfare, but was so in the thrall of his times as to be unable to think his fundamental criticisms through to their Clausewitzean conclusions. Thus even while approving of Machiavelli's strategic thought, the secondary literature tends

---

53. He also seems to assume that portable firearms required more expertise to operate and money to produce than other weapons (ibid., 28). They actually required considerably less expertise to use than virtually any other weapon and less money to produce than their best alternative, the crossbow (Hall, *Weapons*, 16–20, 47–51).

to portray him as lacking adequate self-knowledge, as being torn between two historical epochs.[54] The possibility is never considered that Machiavelli deliberately and coherently combines these two apparently contradictory ways of war.[55]

Everyone knows that Machiavelli's used the Roman army as his model; but it is not as widely recognized that he was nonetheless deeply critical of that same army. Not only did its victories destroy freedom throughout the West, thereby preparing the West for future spiritual subjugation, but the Roman army was also acutely vulnerable to the non-Western militaries such as the Numidian horsemen of Africa and the Parthian military of Asia, by which Machiavelli meant regions including modern Iraq, Iran, and Afghanistan. (*AW* II 80 ff., 283–309, V 157–59; *D* I pr. 2, II pr. 2, II 2; compare *D* II 18.3 with III 12.2). Would Machiavelli slavishly imitate an army that wrought such pernicious effects and bore such fatal flaws? As I seek to show in the last section of the first part of the interpretive essay, Machiavelli's army amalgamates crucial elements of the non-Western armies with essential elements of the ancient Roman and Greek armies to establish an entirely new kind of army led by commanders who judiciously alternate between the Western and non-Western ways of war. Far from being the standard bearer of the traditional Western way of war, Machiavelli innovates under the cover provided by his apparent call to return to traditional ways.[56] Because of the unique combination entailed in this new army, the *Art of War* could be singularly useful for military theorists seeking both to understand the complex nature of war itself and to combine coherently such disparate ways of war.

The U.S. military has often hewn to the model of the "Western" or Clausewitzean war of annihilation. The emphasis has been on achieving decisive victories by fighting big and (when possible) short conflicts such as the Persian Gulf War. From this point of view, the use of small, light forces designed to hit an enemy's weak points or to counter similar forces was subordinated to the strategy of bringing overwhelming force to bear against the enemy's main military forces and, when necessary, the infrastructures that supported them. Failures like Vietnam and Somalia are thought to have resulted at least in part from the Ameri-

54. The most instructive example is Delbrück, *Dawn of Modern Warfare*, 107–12; cf. ibid., 293–318.

55. Though not a study of Machiavelli in particular, a notable exception is Michael Handel, *Masters of War: Classical Strategic Thought* (London: Frank Cass, 2001), 3–4; cf. esp. 170, 421–23.

56. Cf. Victor Davis Hanson, *Carnage and Culture: Landmark Battles in the Rise of Western Power* (New York: Doubleday, 2001), 129, 213. Machiavelli would have recognized the terms in which Hanson casts the history of Western warfare and would likely have agreed with many of Hanson's conclusions regarding its superiority to non-Western ways of war; elements of Hanson's persuasive historical analysis would require some modification if integrated with a periodization of the history of political philosophy that suggests a radical break between antiquity and modernity.

can departure from this "big-and-short" doctrine. But dating back to the hit-and-run methods of both Washington and Nathanael Greene during the Revolutionary War and all the way up to the Special Operations Forces currently in use in the war on terrorism, the American military has shown its willingness and ability to fight the "other" kind of war.[57] But can and should such forces be thoroughly integrated into the military as a whole? What would be the consequences and requirements—military, moral, and political—of such integration? Few writers can be of more use than Machiavelli when it comes to grappling with such urgent and fundamental military questions.

But Machiavelli's utility as a theorist of war is not the most important reason for studying the Art of War. Whether Machiavelli was merely present at the origins of "modernity" or was indeed its founder, the study of his works affords unique insight into what the modern West was in its beginnings and, therefore, what it has since become. There is a pervasive sense that it has a distinct identity, but one that is difficult to define and ambiguous, both morally and politically. Difficult to define because it is hard to know when modernity began, what its boundaries are, and what it is in itself. Ambiguous because the modern West seems to be the home of economic prosperity, political freedom, and religious toleration, and yet conservatives and liberals alike are apprehensive about its present and future. Conservatives sense that the longer the modern West endures, the more traditional virtues wane, while liberals view its global ascendancy as an unjust hegemony. Have either sufficiently reflected on whether and how both the fruits and the fears of modernity are rooted in its origins, and on whether and how those origins are in turn rooted in war? At the very least, the Art of War is a report from the front by a seasoned observer on an era in which Italy became the battlefield of the great European powers and Europe itself was poised to become the dominant world power. It may also have been the moment at which the West, at war with itself, forged a new understanding of humanity, of its nature and possibilities; an understanding that held and holds that man is not by nature a political animal, but is instead "without a city through nature rather than chance . . . 'without clan, without law, without hearth,' like the person reproved by Homer, for the one who is such by nature has by this fact a desire for war, as if he were an isolated piece in a game of chess."[58] Rejected by Aristotle and propagated by Machiavelli, this view of human nature was modified by

<hr>

57. Cf. Max Boot, The Savage Wars of Peace: Small Wars and the Rise of American Power (New York: Basic Books, 2002); Allan R. Millet and Peter Maslowski, For the Common Defense: A Military History of the United States of America, 2nd ed. (New York: Free Press, 1994); Russell F. Weigley, The American Way of War: A History of United States Military Strategy and Policy (New York: Macmillan, 1973).

58. Aristotle, The Politics, trans. Carnes Lord (Chicago: University of Chicago Press, 1984), 37.

Machiavelli's greatest successors. Their changes—especially those wrought by John Locke—have served to take the edge off modernity's sword, and still later changes were made in hopes that modernity might sheath its sword altogether. But however much these modifications of Machiavelli's enterprise have served to foster peace, prosperity, and toleration, we do well to remember that the enterprise itself was forged in thoughts of war.

SUGGESTED READINGS

Anglo, Sidney. *Machiavelli: A Dissection*. New York: Harcourt, Brace and World, 1969.

Baron, Hans. *The Crisis of the Early Italian Renaissance*. Rev. ed. Princeton: Princeton University Press, 1966.

Bayley, C. C. *War and Society in Renaissance Florence: The* De Militia *of Leonardo Bruni*. Toronto: University of Toronto Press, 1961.

Bruni, Leonardo. *De militia.* In *The Humanism of Leonardo Bruni: Selected Texts*. Edited and translated by Gordon Griffiths, James Hankins, and David Thompson. Binghamton, N.Y.: Medieval and Renaissance Texts and Studies, 1987.

Burd, L. Arthur. "Le fonti letterarie di Machiavelli nell'*Arte della guerra*," *Atti della Academia dei Lincei*, 5th ser., *Cl. di scienze morali, storiche, e filologiche* 4 (1896): 187–261.

Butters, H. C. *Governors and Government in Early Sixteenth-Century Florence, 1502–1519*. Oxford: Clarendon Press, 1985.

Colish, Marcia. "Machiavelli's 'Art of War': A Reconsideration." *Renaissance Quarterly* 51 (1998).

Delbrück, Hans. *The Dawn of Modern Warfare: History of the Art of War*, vol. 4. Translated by Walter J. Renfroe Jr. Lincoln: University of Nebraska Press, 1990.

Dionisotti, Carlo. "Machiavelli, Cesare Borgia e Don Michelotto." *Rivista storica italiana* 79 (1967).

Duffy, Christopher. *Siege Warfare: The Fortress in the Early Modern World, 1494–1660*. London: Routledge and Kegan Paul, 1979.

Eltis, David. *The Military Revolution in Sixteenth-Century Europe*. London: I. B. Tauris Publishers, 1995.

Feld, Maury. "Machiavelli's Militia and Machiavelli's Mercenaries." In *The Military, Militarism, and the Polity*. Edited by Michel Louis Martin and Ellen Stern McCrate, 79–92. New York: Free Press, 1984.

Frontinus. *Strategems*. Loeb Classical Library edition. Translated by Charles E. Bennett. Cambridge, Mass.: Harvard University Press, 1925; repr. 1950.

Gat, Azar. *The Origins of Military Thought from the Enlightenment to Clausewitz*. Oxford: Oxford University Press, 1989.

Gilbert, Felix. "Bernardo Rucellai and the Orti Oricellai: A Study on the Origins of Modern Political Thought." In *History: Choice and Commitment*. Cambridge, Mass.: Harvard University Press, 1977.

———. "Machiavelli: The Renaissance of the Art of War." In *The Makers of Modern Strategy: from Machiavelli to the Nuclear Age*. Princeton: Princeton University Press, 1986.

Godman, Peter. *From Poliziano to Machiavelli: Florentine Humanism in the High Renaissance*. Princeton: Princeton University Press, 1998.

Goffart, Walter. "The Date and Purpose of Vegetius' 'De re militari.'" *Traditio* 33 (1977): 58–100.

Guicciardini, Francesco. *The History of Italy*. Translated by Sidney Alexander. Princeton: Princeton University Press, 1969.

Hale, J. R. "A Humanistic Visual Aid. The Military Diagram in the Renaissance." *Renaissance Studies* 2 (1988): 280–98.

———. *War and Society in Renaissance Europe, 1450–1620*. Baltimore: Johns Hopkins University Press, 1985.

———. *Renaissance War Studies*. London: Hambledon Press, 1983.

Hall, Bert S. *Weapons and Warfare in Renaissance Europe: Gunpowder, Technology, and Tactics*. Baltimore: Johns Hopkins University Press, 1997.

Handel, Michael I. *Masters of War: Classical Strategic Thought*. 3rd ed. London: Frank Cass, 2001.

Hankins, James, ed. *Renaissance Civic Humanism: Reappraisals and Reflection*. Cambridge: Cambridge University Press, 2000.

Hassner, Pierre. *Violence and Peace: From the Atomic Bomb to Ethnic Cleansing*. Budapest: Central European University Press, 1997.

Hobohm, Martin. *Machiavellis Renaissance der Kriegskunst*. Berlin: Curtius, 1913.

Howard, Michael. *War in European History*. Oxford: Oxford University Press, 1976.

Hulliung, Mark. *Citizen Machiavelli*. Princeton: Princeton University Press, 1983.

Jahns, Max. *Geschichte der Kriegswissenschaften*. Munich: Oldenbourg, 1889–91.

Jones, Archer. *The Art of War in the Western World*. Oxford: Oxford University Press, 1987.

Livy. *The Early History of Rome: Books I–V of "The History of Rome from Its Foundation."* Translated by Aubrey de Selincourt. New York: Viking Penguin, 1960; repr. 1973.

———. *The War with Hannibal: Books XXI–XXX of "The History of Rome from Its Foundation."* Translated by Aubrey de Selincourt. Edited by Betty Radice. New York: Viking Penguin, 1965.

———. *Rome and the Mediterranean: Books XXXI–XLV of "The History of Rome from Its Foundation."* Translated by Henry Bettenson. New York: Viking Penguin, 1976.

———. *Rome and Italy: Books VI–X of "The History of Rome from Its Foundation."* Translated and annotated by Betty Radice. New York: Viking Penguin, 1982; repr. 1986.

Lord, Carnes. "Allegory in Machiavelli's *Mandragola*." In *Political Philosophy and the*

Human Soul: Essays in Memory of Allan Bloom. Edited by Michael Palmer and Thomas L. Pangle. London: Roman and Littlefield, 1995.

Machiavelli, Niccolò. *The Art of War.* Translated by Ellis Farneworth. Revised and introduced by Neal Wood. New York: Da Capo Press, 1965.

———. *The Prince.* Translated by Harvey C. Mansfield Jr. Chicago: University of Chicago Press, 1985.

———. *Florentine Histories.* Translated by Laura F. Banfield and Harvey C. Mansfield Jr. Princeton: Princeton University Press, 1988.

———. *The Chief Works and Others,* vol. 2. Translated by Allan Gilbert. Durham: Duke University Press, 1989.

———. *Tutte le opere.* Edited by Mario Martelli. Firenze: Sansoni, 1992.

———. *Discourses on Livy.* Translated by Harvey C. Mansfield and Nathan Tarcov. Chicago: University of Chicago Press, 1996.

———. *L'Arte della guerra; scritti politici minori.* Edited by Jean-Jacques Marchand, Denis Fachard, and Giorgio Masi. Roma: Salerno Editrice, 2001.

Mallett, Michael. *Mercenaries and Their Masters.* Totowa, N.J.: Rowan and Littlefield, 1974.

———. "The Theory and Practice of Warfare in Machiavelli's Republic." In *Machiavelli and Republicanism.* Edited by Gisela Bock, Quentin Skinner, and Maurizio Viroli. Cambridge: Cambridge University Press, 1990.

Mansfield, Harvey C., Jr. *Taming the Prince.* New York: Free Press, 1989.

———. *Machiavelli's Virtue.* Chicago: University of Chicago Press, 1996.

———. *Machiavelli's New Modes and Orders: A Study of the* Discourses on Livy. Chicago: University of Chicago Press, 2001.

Marchand, Jean-Jacques. *Niccolò Machiavelli, i primi scritti politici (1499–1512): nascita di un pensiero e di uno stile.* Padua: Editrice Antenore, 1975.

Masters, Roger D. *Machiavelli, Leonardo, and the Science of Power.* Notre Dame: University of Notre Dame Press, 1996.

Oman, Sir Charles. *A History of the Art of War in the Sixteenth Century.* New York: Dutton and Co., 1979.

Paret, Peter. *Clausewitz and the State.* New York: Oxford University Press, 1976.

Parker, Geoffrey. *The Military Revolution: Military Innovation and the Rise of the West, 1500–1800.* Cambridge: Cambridge University Press, 1988.

———. "In Defense of *The Military Revolution.*" In *The Military Revolution Debate: Readings on the Military Transformation of Early Modern Europe.* Edited by Clifford J. Rogers. Boulder: Westview Press, 1995.

Pesman Cooper, R. "Machiavelli, Francesco Soderini and Don Michelotto." *Nuova Rivista Storica* 66 (1982).

Pieri, Piero. *Il Rinascimento e la crisi militare italiana.* Turino: Giulio Einaudi, 1952.

———. *Guerra e politica negli scrittori italiani.* Milano: Riccardo Riccardi, 1955.

Pitkin, Hannah. *Fortune Is a Woman: Gender and Politics in the Thought of Niccolò Machiavelli.* Berkeley: University of California Press, 1984.

Pocock, J. G. A. *The Machiavellian Moment: Florentine Political Thought and the Atlantic Republican Tradition.* Princeton: Princeton University Press, 1975.

Polybius. *The Histories,* vol. 3. Loeb Classical Library edition. Translated by W. R. Paton. Cambridge, Mass.: Harvard University Press, 1923; repr. 1954.

Rahe, Paul A. *New Modes and Orders in Early Modern Political Thought,* vol. 2 of *Republics Ancient and Modern.* Chapel Hill: University of North Carolina Press, 1994.

Ridolfi, Roberto and Piero Ghiglieri. "I *Giribizzi* al Soderini." In *La Bibiliofilia* 72 (1970): 53–74.

Rubenstein, Nicolai. "Machiavelli and the World of Florentine Politics." In *Studies on Machiavelli.* Edited by Myron P. Gilmore. Florence: Sansoni, 1972.

Skinner, Quentin. *The Foundations of Modern Political Thought,* vol. 1. Cambridge: Cambridge University Press, 1978.

———. *Machiavelli.* New York: Hill and Wang, 1981.

———. "The Republican Idea of Political Liberty." In *Machiavelli and Republicanism.* Edited by Gisela Bock, Quentin Skinner, and Maurizio Viroli. Cambridge: Cambridge University Press, 1990.

Spackman, Barbara. "Politics on the Warpath: Machiavelli's *Art of War.*" In *Machiavelli and the Discourse of Literature.* Edited by Albert Russell Ascoli and Victoria Kahn. Ithaca, N.Y.: Cornell University Press, 1993.

Strauss, Leo. *Thoughts on Machiavelli.* Chicago: University of Chicago Press, 1958.

———. "Machiavelli and Classical Literature." *Review of National Literatures* 1 (1970): 7–25.

———. "Niccolò Machiavelli." In *Studies in Platonic Political Philosophy.* Chicago: University of Chicago Press, 1983.

Stephens, J. N. *The Fall of the Florentine Republic, 1512–1530.* Oxford: Clarendon Press, 1983.

Sullivan, Vickie B. "Machiavelli's Momentary 'Machiavellian Moment': A Reconsideration of Pocock's Treatment of the *Discourses.*" *Political Theory* 20 (1992): 309–18.

———. *Machiavelli's Three Romes: Religion, Human Liberty, and Politics Reformed.* De Kalb: University of Northern Illinois Press, 1996.

Tallet, Frank. *War and Society in Early-Modern Europe, 1495–1715.* London: Routledge, 1992.

Tarcov, Nathan. "Quentin Skinner's Method and Machiavelli's *Prince.*" *Ethics* 92 (1982): 692–709.

Viroli, Maurizio. *Niccolò's Smile: A Biography of Machiavelli.* Translated by Anthony Shugaar. New York: Farrar, Straus and Giroux, 2000.

———. "Machiavelli and the Republican Idea of Politics." In *Machiavelli and Republicanism.* Edited by Gisela Bock, Quentin Skinner, and Maurizio Viroli. Cambridge: Cambridge University Press, 1990.

Vegetius. *Epitome of Military Science.* Translated by N. P. Milner. Liverpool: Liverpool University Press, 1993.

Wood, Neal. Introduction to *The Art of War* by Niccolò Machiavelli. Translated by Ellis Farneworth. New York: Da Capo Press, 1965.

NOTE ON THE TRANSLATION

My goal in this book is to provide English-speaking readers with the closest possible approximation to Machiavelli's own presentation of his work. I have therefore translated the Italian as literally and consistently as is compatible with readable English, keeping at a minimum influences arising from my own judgments, opinions, and other limitations. Such influences are, of course, inevitable. The question one must ask concerns the translator's disposition toward this inevitability. Is it a fact to be struggled against, an occasion to display one's virtuosity and expertise, or a confirmation of the fundamental impossibility of translation? I have struggled against the inevitable influences as best I could, on the principle that I should—as much as possible—remove myself from between Machiavelli and his reader.

My first rule has been to render each Italian word by a single English word. Consistent translation allows the reader to concentrate on coming to terms, as it were, with Machiavelli. For example, Machiavelli chose time and again to use the term *"ordine"* (consistently translated here as "order") without specifying whether he meant "regulation," "arrangement," "organization," and so forth, all words often used to translate *ordine*. An over-eagerness on my part to make just the right choice among the thirteen or so most common English translations of *ordine* would, in effect, have drawn a veil between the reader and Machiavelli's frequent use of this key term. The result of unnecessary variation is that readers are denied the chance to discover for themselves what Machiavelli intended to teach—in each instance and overall—by means of such words and about such words. Consistency gives readers a fighting chance to discover for themselves Machiavelli's meanings. It also affords them the opportunity to notice lexical connections within and among Machiavelli's own works, as well as between his works and those of other Romance language and Latin authors. One drawback of this approach is that extended metaphors that are only slightly jarring in Italian can seem more so when rendered literally in English. For example, instead of using the more familiar "officer" and "enlisted men," I follow Machiavelli's bodily metaphor of "head" and "members." Another drawback is that certain words in English do not readily call to mind the wide range of meanings expressed in the Italian words they translate. To return to the word *"ordine,"* in addition to the English words already mentioned, readers should also consider the following as possible meanings of each occurrence of "order": categorization, classification, deployment, disposition, formation, grouping, layout, sequence, command, and association. Which of these many meanings conveys *ordine* in each case is rarely clear. It is possible that there are still other meanings; it is certain that Machiavelli invited his readers to think of the many meanings as—somehow—one.

In many cases, however, my preference for consistency and literalness was superseded by two pressing needs: accuracy and readability. I would have liked, for example, to translate *rispetto a* always as "respect for" or "respect to," but accuracy usually demanded "thanks to" (in the sense of "due to") or "compared to." I have sought in all similar cases to prevent my approach from leading to inaccuracies. Most exceptions to my general rule can be followed by referring to the glossary and to my notes to the translation indicating departures from literalness and consistency. Other exceptions require some explanation.

Ordinanza is almost always translated as "militia" even though it is only a very rough equivalent. *Ordinanza* is neutral with respect to political arrangements in that it can refer to an army composed of either a monarch's subjects or a republic's citizens. The hybrid "citizen-soldiery" is therefore too republican, and is perhaps the single most misleading term in other translations. Furthermore, an *ordinanza* can consist exclusively of soldiers with civilian occupations, as in the case of Florence's *ordinanza,* or it can include professional soldiers, as in the case of those who served the king of France (*AW* I 104); in both cases, the soldiers are paid by means of tax relief, cash, spoils, or some combination of the three. Finally, no English word refers, as does *ordinanza,* both to a document or decree (that is, an ordinance) establishing an army and to the army so established. Although our word "militia" conveys few of these nuances and has stronger republican connotations than *ordinanza,* it does less violence than the alternatives and is less awkward than leaving the term in the Italian.

Modo is translated as "mode" except when it occurs in the phrases *in modo che* and *di modo che,* when it is translated "so that" or "so." *Assaltare, assalire, combattere, offendere,* and *azzuffarsi* are respectively translated whenever possible by "assault," "assail," "fight," "harm" or "offend," and "fight," but considerable overlap was unavoidable; please consult the glossary for clarification. *Armare* and *armato* are usually translated as "arm" and "armed," but occasionally as "armor" and "armored." The verbs "exercise," "drill," and "train" translate *esercitare;* the nouns "exercise," "drill," and "training" usually translate *esercizio* (see the glossary for the few instances in which *esercizio* is translated by "career"); both of these Italian words are related to *esercito*, translated "army." *Uno* standing alone has been translated as "one individual"; "the one who" sometimes translates *quello che*. *Quello* is sometimes translated as "the" when to translate it as "that" would lead to a jarring "that . . . that" construction. *Cosa/e* ("thing/s") has sometimes been omitted from the translation. The *braccio* (pl. *braccia*), a unit of measurement used by Machiavelli, is equal to 22.84 inches; it has been left in the Italian and appears in nonitalicized script (though the plural form is used in the translation more frequently than in the original because numbers ending with *uno* [for example, *ventuno*, for twenty-one] in the original call for the singular form but will be given in the plural form in the translation). Arabic numerals translate Roman numerals. Roman military terms are left in the Latin original if Machiavelli himself left them so; English translations of Italian words for various weapons correspond when possible to Milner's renderings of Vegetius's Latin words for the same weapons (see Milner's translation of Vegetius's *Epitome of Military Science* in the suggested readings).

Finally, many of Machiavelli's longer sentences, so beguiling in Italian, are broken up for the sake of English readability; in many cases I have altered the sentence structure, sometimes considerably, for the same reason. The numbers inserted within the text in square brackets indicate the beginnings of Italian sentences in the edition of Marchand, Fachard, and Masi. Parentheses are added by me to make long sentences more intelligible; the note "Parentheses in original" indicates that either dashes or parentheses appear in the edition of Marchand et al. Commas are usually as they are in the Italian, but sometimes are added or removed to improve intelligibility; they are sometimes replaced by "and," which is also sometimes added or subtracted before the last item in a series of items separated by commas. Words in square brackets have been inserted by me; the only other insertions I have made are the subjects of verbs and participles when they can be safely inferred from the context and are required for intelligibility, and temporal or causal adverbs such as "while" and "since" before participles (for example, "while marching" instead of "marching" for *camminando* [II 204]) when required for intelligibility or readability. The word to which a pronoun refers is often put in brackets in place of the pronoun when the gender of the pronoun makes the reference clear; for readability, I have sometimes added the noun in brackets when context alone (rather than the gender of the pronoun) makes the reference clear. Also for readability, verbs usually translated as "to be," "to have," "to do," and "to make" are occasionally omitted from the translation or are translated by one of these other three English words. Instances of formal or plural and informal or singular address are not exhaustively distinguished in the notes; instead, see the glossary under "you" for all instances of the singular or informal "you." (When I have inserted "you" for clarification, it will not be found in the glossary; when an instance of the formal or plural "you" occurs within sentences containing instances of the informal or singular "you," the formal or plural instance is noted.) I have done my best to provide for all explicit internal references (for example, "as I mentioned before") to specific passages not in the immediate context; but I have not attempted to do so for those references that are to the general discussion.

In general, I have done my best to make the translation as smooth as possible without unnecessarily compromising my chief goal—admittedly unattained—of representing Machiavelli as he presented himself. This goal has been considerably facilitated by the most recent critical edition of the work, *L'Arte della guerra; scritti politici minori,* edited by Jean-Jacques Marchand, Denis Fachard, and Giorgio Masi (Rome: Salerno Editrice, 2001). This edition reconstitutes the original Florentine edition of 1521, carefully tracing and eliminating the many erroneous emendations offered and unknowingly reproduced by earlier critical editions and the translations based on them. It also notes and explains its few departures from the 1521 original. This translation, based initially on the Bertelli and Martelli editions, was complete by the time the new Italian edition came to my attention, but all important modifications have subsequently been made. Such modifications include restoring the proper titles to each of the books (see *L'Arte della guerra,* 48, 51, 95 n. 1), restoring and noting some of Machiavelli's supposed errors (for example, Titus Didius is called Titus Dimius at IV 83 and the Epidaurians are called Epidaunians at VI 227), and removing other errors introduced by earlier editions (for example, "those men who do" is changed to "those men who know" at II 160). I note the few cases in which the readings of Marchand and his colleagues seem debatable, offering alternative translations in the notes. For lists of the new edition's most significant discoveries, see *L'Arte della guerra,* 376–90.

The figures at the end of the work are photocopies of microfilm of the original 1521 edition. This is the only English translation to use the figures from the original edition. Later editions that have tried to improve upon Machiavelli's original figures have introduced omissions or errors of their own. The best such attempt is L. Arthur Burd's "Le fonti letterarie di Machavelli nell'*Arte della guerra,*" *Atti della Reale Academia dei Lincei,* 5th ser., *Cl. di scienze morali, storiche e filologiche* 4 (1896): 251–61; for some of the problems with Burd's figures, see Marchand, *L'Arte della guerra,* 302–11. Corrections of apparent errors in the original figures are noted on pages 176–77 below.

OUTLINE OF THE *ART OF WAR*

Ancient Italy:~

ALPS

LIGURIA

Adria·

AP PENIN

ADRIATIC SEA

Fiesole
Arno ·Florence
ETRURIA ·Arretium
Volterra·

UMBRIA

Epidaurus

TYRRHENIAN SEA

Clusium·
CIMINIAN FOREST
SABINES
Tiber Falerii
AEQUI
HERNICI
Rome | ·Sora
VOLSCI SIDICINUM
CAUDINE FORKS

SAMNIUM

Cannae

Fidenae·
Capenae· ·Tibur
Veii· Anio ·Praeneste
Rome· ·Alba
Ardea· Albanus ·Velitrae
Antium· ·Cercii

Privernum·
Minturnae·
Casilinum·

Nola·
Capua·

·Lucera
·Aquilionia

CAMPANIA
ES

Tarentum·

LUCANIA

MEDITERRANEAN SEA

LIPARI ISLANDS

SICILY

Messina· ·Rhegium

·Syracuse

0 50 100 150 200 kms

0   50   100   150 miles

ALPS

Arbedo
Brescia · Vicenza
Novara · Milan
Agnadello
LOMBARDY
Verona · Venice
Mantua
Po
Mirandola
Ferrara
Genoa
Bologna · Ravenna

Ravenna
Faenza
Forlì
Bersíghella

TUSCANY
Pisa · Florence · Castiglione
· Urbino
Volterra · Arezzo
Siena
· Camerino
MARCHES

LIGUREAN
SEA

Popolonia
Piombino
Perugia
UMBRIA

ADRIATIC SEA

Ragusa

TYRRHENIAN SEA

Tiber
Aquila
· Rome

Cerignuola · Barletta
· Nocera
· Naples

Pistoia · Casaglia
Lucca · Mugello
· Prato · Fiesole
Pisa · Arno
· Florence
· Cascina
· San Regolo

CALABRIA

SICILY

Italy in
Machiavelli's Time

R·WILLIAMS FECIT MXMXI

0 50   150 200 kms
0 50 100 150 miles

ART OF WAR

PREFACE

———— ❧ ————

by Niccolò Machiavegli,[1]
Florentine Citizen and Secretary,[2]
to his book on the art of war
to Lorenzo di Filippo Strozzi,[3] Florentine Patrician

[1] Many have held and hold this opinion, Lorenzo: that there are no things less in agreement with one another or so dissimilar as the civilian and military lives. [2] Hence it is often seen that if someone plans to succeed in the soldier's career,[4] he not only changes dress immediately, but also departs from every civilian practice[5] in his customs, usages, voice, and bearing. For he who wants to be unencumbered and ready for every [act of] violence does not believe he can wear civilian dress; nor can he, judging civilian customs to be effeminate and such usages to be unfavorable to his deeds, have those customs and usages; nor does maintaining his ordinary bearing and words appear fitting to him who wants to frighten other men with his beard and curses. In these times, this makes such an opinion very true. [3] But if ancient orders were considered, nothing would be found more united, more in conformity, and, of necessity, as much inclined

---

1. The Tuscan spelling of Machiavelli.

2. The title "Secretary" refers to Machiavelli's fourteen years of service to the Florentine republic, from 1498 to 1512, as secretary to the Second Chancery. Regarding his publisher's willingness to allow Machiavelli to use the title of which he had been stripped years earlier, see Peter Godman, *From Poliziano to Machiavelli: Florentine Humanism in the High Renaissance* (Princeton: Princeton University Press, 1998), 235–38.

3. Lorenzo di Filippo Strozzi (1482–1549) was a wealthy banker and a member of an influential family with complicated connections to the Medici family. Often rivals, the two families were nonetheless linked by bonds of marriage and finance, and even political alliances (most notably between Lorenzo de' Medici and Lorenzo Strozzi's brother, Filippo). Lorenzo Strozzi facilitated contact between Machiavelli and the Medici in March of 1520 and was an occasional visitor to the Orti Oricellari and a son-in-law of Bernardo Rucellai (see *AW* I, note 5).

4. Or: to take advantage of the business of money.

5. Lit.: use.

toward one another[6] as these. For all the arts that are ordered in a city[7] for the sake of the common good of men, all the orders made there for living in fear of the laws and of God, would be in vain if their defenses were not prepared. When these [defenses are] well ordered, they maintain the [arts and orders], even though the latter are not well ordered. [4] Thus, on the contrary, good orders without military help are disordered no differently than the rooms of a proud and regal palace when, by being uncovered, they have nothing that might defend them against the rain, even though [they are] ornamented with gems and gold. [5] And if in every other order of cities or kingdoms the utmost diligence was used to keep men faithful, peaceful, and full of the fear of God, in the military it was redoubled. For in what man should the fatherland look for greater faith than in him who has to promise to die for it? [6] In whom should there be more love of peace than in him who alone can be harmed by war? [7] In whom should there be more fear of God than in him who, submitting to infinite dangers everyday, has more need of His help? [8] This necessity, well considered both by those who gave laws to empires and by those who were put in charge of military training, made the soldiers' life praised by other men and followed and imitated with utmost attention. [9] But because military orders are altogether corrupt and separated by great lengths from ancient modes, these[8] sinister opinions regarding them have arisen that make [men] hate the military and flee association[9] with those who practice it. [10] And judging by what I have seen and read that it is not impossible to bring [the military] back to ancient modes and give it some form of past virtue, I decided, so as not to pass these my idle times without doing anything, to write what I understand about the art of war for the satisfaction of those who are lovers of ancient actions. [11] And although it is a spirited thing to deal with material of which one has not made a profession, nonetheless I do not believe it is an error to occupy with words a rank that many have, with greater presumption, occupied with deeds. For the errors I may make as I write[10] can be corrected without harm to anyone, but those that are made by them as they act cannot be known except with the ruin of empires. [12] Therefore, Lorenzo, you will consider the qualities of my efforts and give them that blame or praise which, according to your judgment, they will seem to have merited. [13] These I am sending to you, both to show myself [to be] grateful for the benefits I have received from you, even though my ability[11] does not measure up, and also be-

---

6. Lit.: that love one another as much.

7. Lit.: civility.

8. "These" seems to have no antecedent.

9. Lit. conversation.

10. Lit.: [while] writing; i.e., the personal pronoun "I" has been added.

11. Lit.: possibility.

cause (since it is customary to honor with similar works[12] those who are re-
splendent in nobility, wealth, talent, and liberality) I know in wealth and nobility you do not have many equals, in genius few, and in liberality none.

12. Here Machiavelli calls writings "works," while above he contrasts his writing to the "works" (translated as "deeds" or "act") of soldiers and military leaders.

BOOK ONE OF THE ART OF WAR

———— ❧ ————

by Niccolò Machiavegli,
Florentine Citizen and Secretary,
to Lorenzo di Filippo Strozzi,
Florentine Patrician[1]

[1] Because I believe that one can praise any man without reproach after his death, since every cause and suspicion of adulation have passed away, I will not hesitate to praise our Cosimo Rucellai,[2] whose name will never be recalled by me without tears, since I knew in him those things that can be desired by friends in a good friend and by his fatherland in a citizen. [2] For I do not know what was so much his (not even excepting his soul)[3] that it would not have been willingly spent by him for his friends; I do not know of any undertaking that would have frightened him wherein he had recognized the good of his fatherland. [3] And I confess freely that I have not found among the many men I have known and dealt with, a man in whom there was a spirit more on fire for great and magnificent things. [4] Nor in his death did he complain to his friends of anything else but of being born to die young in his own houses and unhonored without having been able, as accorded with his spirit, to help anyone. For he knew that nothing else could be said of him except that a good friend had died. [5] It does not stand because of this, however, that we, and anyone else who knew him as we did, cannot vouch for his praiseworthy qualities because his works did not appear. [6] It is true that fortune was not, however, so much an enemy to him that he did not leave any brief record of the dexterity of his talent, as some of his

1. For explanations of names and titles used in the title of book I, see *AW* pr., notes 1–3.

2. Cosimo Rucellai (1494–1519), a dedicatee of the *Discourses on Livy,* hosted a circle of prominent Florentines with literary and political interests frequented by Machiavelli and the young interlocutors of the *Art of War* (see note 8). The circle met on the same site and had some of the same participants as that begun by his grandfather, Bernardo Rucellai (see note 5).

3. Machiavelli's parentheses.

writings and compositions of love verses show. In these, although he had not been in love, he used to train himself in his youthful age so as not to consume his time in vain, until fortune had conducted him to higher thoughts. Therein one can clearly understand with how much felicity he would have described his concepts and how much he would have been honored in poetry if it had been practiced by him as his ultimate purpose. [7] Since, therefore, fortune has deprived us of the use of one [who was] so much a friend, it appears to me that one cannot make other remedies—the best that are possible for us to seek—than to enjoy his memory and repeat anything that may have been subtly said or wisely disputed by him. [8] And because nothing regarding him is more fresh than the discussion that Lord Fabrizio Colonna[4] had with him in his gardens[5] in recent times (where the things of war were disputed at length by that lord, both subtly and prudently questioned in good part by Cosimo), and having been present with some other friends of ours, it seemed [well] to me to recall it to memory so that by reading it the friends of Cosimo who convened there may refresh the memory of his virtue in their spirit, and others may, on the one hand, complain about not having been there and, on the other hand, learn many things useful not only for military but also civil life, wisely disputed by a very knowledgeable man.

[9] I say, therefore, that while returning from Lombardy, where he had soldiered for a long time for the Catholic King[6] to his own great glory, Fabrizio Colonna decided as he passed through Florence to stay in that city for some days

---

4. Fabrizio Colonna (1450–1520), a prominent mercenary captain, fought in the Italian Wars first for the French against Italian, papal, and Aragonese forces, and then for the papacy and the Spanish against the French. He had major roles in Charles VIII's invasion of Italy (1494) and at such battles as Cerignola (1503) and Ravenna (1512), where as cavalry commander on the Spanish side he was subjected to the first decidedly successful deployment of field artillery. In 1515 he became constable of the kingdom of Naples, in the northern region of which he had his estate at Tagliacozza. Several times between 1504 and 1505, Piero Soderini (1452–1522), leader of the Florentine republic and Machiavelli's political patron, championed hiring Fabrizio to lead Florence in its costly war to retake Pisa. Soderini's efforts to hire Fabrizio were unsuccessful in part because Fabrizio was then in the hire of Spain, the chief adversary of Florence's traditional ally, France.

5. The Orti Oricellari (the Rucellai family's gardens) were the meeting place of a literary circle of prominent intellectuals and politicians founded by Cosimo Rucellai's grandfather, Bernardo Rucellai (1448–1514), who was married to Nannina de' Medici (cf. *FH* VII 5), granddaughter of the great Medici ruler of Florence, Cosimo de' Medici (1389–1464). Bernardo was a proponent of an aristocratic or oligarchic republic and a bitter enemy of Piero Soderini and of what Bernardo took to be Soderini's excessively democratic republic. Bernardo withdrew into his literary circle and then into exile during Florence's republican years (1494–1512), returning to politics under the restored Medici only briefly before his death.

6. Ferdinand the Catholic (1452–1516), II king of Sicily, II of Aragon, III of Naples, and V of Castile. Ferdinand died some eight months before the supposed date of the setting of the dialogue (September 1516) and was succeeded by Charles I of Spain (1500–58), who in 1519 became Charles V of the Holy Roman Empire.

so as to visit His Excellency the Duke[7] and to see again some gentlemen with whom he had had some acquaintance in the past. [10] Hence it seemed [well] to Cosimo to invite him to a banquet in his gardens, not so much to use his liberality as to have cause to speak with him at length, and to understand and learn various things from him in accordance with what one can hope for from such a man, since it appeared to him to be an opportunity to spend a day discussing those matters that satisfied his spirit. [11] So according to his wish, Fabrizio came and was received by Cosimo together with some other of his trusted friends, among whom were Zanobi Buondelmonti, Batista della Palla, and Luigi Alamanni,[8] all youths loved by him and very ardent for the same studies, whose good qualities we will omit because every day and every hour they are their own praise. [12] Therefore, according to the times and the place, Fabrizio was honored by all of them with the greatest honors possible. But convivial pleasures passed, the tables cleared, and every order of celebration concluded—which are concluded promptly in the presence of great men who have turned their minds to honorable thoughts—since the days were long[9] and the heat great, Cosimo, so as better to satisfy his desire, judged that it would be well to go to the most secret and shady part of his garden, using the opportunity of fleeing the heat. [13] Having arrived there and taken seats, some on the grass, which is very fresh in that place, and some on the benches ordered in those parts under the shade of very tall trees, Fabrizio praised the place as delightful. And considering the trees individually[10] and not recognizing some of them, he stopped, his spirit uncertain.[11] [14] Having discerned this, Cosimo said: "You perhaps do not have knowledge of some of these trees. But do not marvel at this, for some of these are more celebrated by the ancients than by the common usage today." [15] And

7. Lorenzo di Piero di Lorenzo de' Medici (1492–1519), the dedicatee of *The Prince*, was made duke of Urbino in August 1516 by his uncle, Giovanni de' Medici (1475–1521), who had become Pope Leo X in 1513. Only by dint of heavy taxation (which earned him the resentment of many Florentines) was Lorenzo able to hold the duchy of Urbino against the attempts of his predecessor, Francesco Maria della Rovere, to retake it by force. Lorenzo had succeeded his uncle, Giuliano de' Medici, as the effective ruler of Florence in 1513 (while maintaining the pretense that Florence was still a republic) and had been named (contrary to the Florentine custom of naming only foreigners) captain general of Florence in 1515 and then captain general of the Church.

8. Zanobi Buondelmonti (1491–1527), a dedicatee of Machiavelli's *The Life of Castruccio Castracani of Lucca* and, along with Cosimo Rucellai, of his *Discourses on Livy;* Batista della Palla (d. 1530); Luigi (Ludovico di Piero) Alamanni (1495–1556), the other dedicatee of *The Life of Castruccio Castracani of Lucca.* In 1522, a year after the publication of the *Art of War,* all three men went into exile because of their involvement in a conspiracy with members of the Soderini family to topple the rule of Cardinal Giulio de' Medici.

9. Lit.: day was long, i.e., it was summertime.

10. Lit.: particularly.   11. Lit.: suspended, here and in *AW* I 16.

[Cosimo] having told him their names and how his grandfather Bernardo had exerted himself so much in cultivating them, Fabrizio replied: "I was thinking that what you say might be so; and this place and this study[12] were making me remember some princes of the Kingdom[13] who delight in these ancient growths and shades." [16] And at this, having stopped speaking and been for a while in reflection as if uncertain, he added: "If I did not believe I would offend, I would state my opinion; but I do not believe I would, since I am speaking with friends so as to dispute things and not to calumniate them.[14] [17] How much better they would have done, may it be said with everyone's leave,[15] to seek to be like the ancients in the strong and harsh things, not in the delicate and soft ones, and in those that they did under the sun, not in the shade, and to take up the modes of the true and perfect antiquity, not the false and corrupt one. For after these studies pleased my Romans, my fatherland went to ruin." [18] To which Cosimo responded . . . But so as to avoid the trouble of having to repeat many times "this one said" and "the other one added," only the names of the speakers will be noted, without recounting anything else. [19] Thus said

COSIMO. [20] You have opened the way to a discussion such as I was desiring, and I beg you to speak without respect, because I will question you without respect. If while questioning and replying I excuse or accuse someone, it will not be for the sake of excusing or accusing,[16] but for understanding from you the truth.

FABRIZIO. [21] And I will be very content to tell you what I understand of all that you will ask me; whether it will be true or not, I will refer to your judgment. [22] And I will be grateful for your questioning of me, because I am going to learn as much from your questioning me as you from me in responding to you. For many times a wise questioner makes one consider many things and recognize many others that one would never have recognized without having been asked.

COSIMO. [23] I want to return to what you said before: that my grandfather and those [princes] of yours[17] would have acted more wisely by being like the

---

12. In addition to its academic sense (as in "humanist studies" *[studio humanitatis]*), *studio* had the more general sense of prolonged attention, care, or cultivation.

13. "The Kingdom" customarily referred to that of Naples (cf. *FH* I 20).

14. "Them" refers to "things."   16. See *D* I 7–8 on accusation and excuse.

15. Lit.: with peace to all.

17. "Those [princes] of yours" seems to refer to the "princes of the Kingdom" mentioned in sentence 15.

ancients in harsh rather than in delicate things. I want to excuse my family[18] because the other I will leave to you to excuse. [24] I do not believe there was, in his times, a man who detested the soft life as much as he, and who was so much a lover of that harshness of life that you praise. Nonetheless, he recognized that he was not able to make use of it personally or with his own children,[19] since he had been born in an era of so much corruption, wherein one who wanted to part from the common usage would be defamed and vilified by everyone. [25] Because if in the summer, under the highest sun, an individual were to roll around naked on the sand, or on the snow in the winter in the frostiest months, as Diogenes[20] used to do, he would be held to be crazy. [26] If, like the Spartans, an individual were to raise his children in the country, make them sleep in the open, go with head and feet naked, and wash in cold water so as to harden them to be able to withstand evil and so as to make them love life less and fear death less, he would be jeered and held to be a beast rather than a man. [27] If one were also seen to eat vegetables and to despise gold, like Fabricius,[21] he would be praised by few and followed by no one. [28] So, frightened by these present modes of living, he left behind the ancients, and in that which he could with less amazement imitate antiquity, he did so.

FABRIZIO. [29] You have vigorously excused him in this regard, and certainly you speak the truth. But I was not speaking so much of those hard modes of living, as of other more humane modes and those that have more conformity with life today, which I do not believe would have been difficult to introduce for one who is numbered among the princes of a city. [30] I will never depart from my Romans as the example for anything. [31] If one were to consider their life and the order of that republic, one would see in it many things not impossible to introduce into a city[22] where there was still something good.

COSIMO. [32] What are these things, similar to the ancient ones, that you would like to introduce?

FABRIZIO. [33] To honor and reward the virtues, not to despise poverty, to esteem the modes and orders of military discipline, to constrain the citizens to love one another, to live without sects, to esteem the private less than the public, and other similar things that could easily accompany our times. [34] These modes

18. Lit.: my part.

19. Lit.: in his own person or in those of his children.

20. Diogenes the Cynic (ca. 400–325 B.C.). See Diogenes Laertius, *Lives of Eminent Philosophers* VI 2 23.

21. Gaius Luscinus Fabricius ("Fabrizio" in Italian), twice consul of the Roman republic (282, 278 B.C.) and famous for incorruptible moral rectitude. See *D* III 1.3, 20.

22. Lit.: civilization.

are not difficult to persuade [men of] when one thinks about them much and they are entered into by due degrees. For in them truth appears so much that every common talent can be capable of it. Whoever orders that thing plants trees under the shade of which one resides more happy and more glad than under this.

COSIMO. [35] I do not want to make any reply to what you have said; rather, I wish to allow the judgment of it to be given to these,[23] who can easily judge it. And thinking by this path to be more easily satisfied in my intention, I will turn[24] my speech to you, the accuser of those who are not imitators of the ancients in grave and great actions. [36] I would therefore like to know from you whence it arises that, on the one hand, you condemn those who are not like the ancients in their actions, and on the other, in war, which is your art and in which you are judged [to be] excellent, one does not see that you have used any ancient means or [ones] that bear any likeness to them.

FABRIZIO. [37] You have turned up exactly where I was expecting you, for my speech merited no other question, nor did I desire another. [38] And although I might save myself with an easy excuse, nonetheless, since the season allows it, I want to enter into a longer discussion for my and your greater satisfaction. [39] Men who want to do something must first prepare themselves with every industriousness to be set to satisfy that which they have set themselves to do when the opportunity comes. [40] And because when the preparations are made cautiously they are not recognized, one cannot accuse anyone of any negligence if it is not discovered before the opportunity. But after that, by his not taking action, one sees either that he did not prepare well enough or that he has not thought in any way of this. [41] And because no opportunity has come to me to make it possible to show the preparations made by me so as to be able to bring back the military to its ancient orders, if I have not brought it back, I cannot be blamed for it by you or others. [42] I believe that this excuse should be enough as a response to your accusation.

COSIMO. [43] It would be enough if I were certain that the opportunity had not come.

FABRIZIO. [44] But because I know that you can doubt whether or not this opportunity has come, I want to discourse at length, if you want to listen to me with patience, on what preparations are necessary to make before, what opportunity must arise, what difficulty impedes so that preparations do not help and so that the opportunity does not come, and how this thing is, though the terms seem contrary, at once[25] very difficult and very easy to do.

23. It is no clearer in Italian to whom "these" refers.
24. Or: vulgarize, i.e., speak in a common manner or speak in Italian rather than Latin.
25. Lit.: at a stroke.

COSIMO. [45] You cannot, both for me and for these others, do anything more welcome than this. And if speaking will not be tiresome to you, listening will never be tiresome to us. [46] And because this discussion must be long, with your permission I want help from these friends of mine. And they and I beg one thing of you, that you not be annoyed if sometimes we interrupt you with some importunate question.

FABRIZIO. [47] I am very content, Cosimo, that you with these other youths here should question me. For I believe that youth makes you more friendly to military things and more ready to believe what will be said by me. [48] By already having white heads and ice in their veins,[26] some of these others[27] are accustomed to being enemies of war; some [are] incorrigible, like those who believe that the times and not wicked modes constrain men to live thus. [49] So all of you, question me securely and without respect. I desire this both because it would be a little rest for me and because I will be pleased not to leave any doubt in your minds. [50] I want to begin from your words, where you said that in war, which is my art, I had not used any ancient means.[28] [51] About this I say that as this is an art by means of which men cannot live honestly in every time, it cannot be used as an art except by a republic or a kingdom. And the one and the other of these, when it was well ordered, never consented to any of its citizens or subjects using it as an art, nor did any good man ever prac- tice it as his particular art. [52] Because he will never be judged good who en- gages in a career in which, by wanting to draw utility from it in every time, he must be rapacious, fraudulent, violent, and have many qualities that of neces- sity make him not good. Nor can the men who use it as an art, the great as well as the small, be made otherwise, because this art does not nourish them in peace. Hence they are necessitated either to plan that there not be peace or to succeed so much in times of war that they can nourish themselves in peace. [53] And neither one of these two thoughts dwells in a good man. For from wanting to be able to nourish oneself in every time arise the robberies, the acts of vio- lence, and the assassinations that such soldiers do to friends as well as to ene- mies. And from not wanting peace come the deceptions that the captains use on those who hire them so that war may last. If peace does indeed come, often it happens that the heads, being deprived of their stipends and living, set up a flag of fortune[29] without restraint[30] and pillage a province without any mercy. [54] And do you not have in the memory of your things how, when many sol- diers found themselves in Italy without pay because the wars were finished, sev-

---

26. Lit.: being filled with frozen blood.

27. Referent unclear.

28. See AW I 36.

29. *Ventura,* not *fortuna.*

30. Lit.: licentiously.

eral groups, which were called Companies, gathered together and went about levying tribute on the towns and pillaging the country without one being able to make any remedy for it?[31] [55] Have you not read that the Carthaginian soldiers, having finished the first war with the Romans, made (under Matho and Spendius, the two they made their heads in a mutiny)[32] a war against the Carthaginians [that was] more dangerous than the one they had finished with the Romans?[33] [56] In the times of our fathers, Francesco Sforza, so as to be able to live honorably in times of peace, not only deceived the Milanese, whose soldier he was, but took away their liberty and became their prince.[34] [57] Similar to these have been all the other soldiers of Italy who have used the military as their particular art; and if they have not become dukes of Milan by means of their malefactions, so much more do they merit being blamed, because, if one were to see their lives, they all have the same faults[35] without so much utility. [58] Sforza, father of Francesco, having abandoned Queen Giovanna all of a sudden and left her unarmed in the middle of her enemies, constrained her to jump into the arms of the king of Aragon, only so as to vent his ambition either to levy a tribute against her or to take her kingdom.[36] [59] With the same devices Braccio sought to occupy the kingdom of Naples and, if he had not been routed and killed at Aquila,[37] would have succeeded. [60] Similar disorders arise from nothing other than there having been men who used the career of the soldier as their own art. [61] Do you not have a proverb that fortifies my reasons: "War makes thieves, and peace hangs them"? [62] For those who do not know how to live from another career and do not find someone to support

31. The Great Company, composed of nearly ten thousand men of many nationalities who had fought in the crusades or for the German emperor, marauded throughout Italy from 1338 to 1354. The White Company was formed in 1361 from soldiers of many nationalities who had been fighting in the Hundred Years War (1337–1453) by John Hawkwood (d. 1394), the English mercenary captain who was in the service of Florence from 1377 to 1393. The first Italian mercenary band was the "Company of St. George," formed by Alberigo da Barbiano, count of Conio (d. 1409). From Alberigo stem the condottieri who predominated in Italian warfare throughout the fifteenth century. See *P* 12.52–53; *FH* I 34; see also *FH* I 39, IV 6, V 2.

32. Lit.: their heads in a tumult. Regarding "tumults," see *D* I 4–5.

33. The First Punic War, between Rome and Carthage, ended in 241 B.C.; the subsequent mutiny or "tumult," led by the Lybians Matho and Spendius, and the ensuing Mercenary War (241–237 B.C.) are recounted in Polybius I 65–88. See also *P* 12.50; *D* III 32.

34. Francesco Sforza (1401–1466) seized Milan in 1450. See *FH* VI 18–22; *P* 7.26, 12.50; see also *P* 14.58, 20.87; *D* II 24.2.

35. Or: burdens.

36. Muzio Attendolo Sforza (1369–1424); Giovanna II, queen of Naples (1414–35); Alfonso V, king of Aragon (1416–58). See *P* 12.50; *FH* I 33, 38, 39, IV 7.

37. Andrea Fortebracci (1368–1424), known as Braccio da Montone, was killed by Francesco Sforza in 1424 at the town of Aquila in the Abruzzo region of Italy. See *FH* I 38.

them and do not have so much virtue that they know how to gather together to make an honorable wickedness,[38] are forced by necessity to take to the road,[39] and justice is forced to snuff them out.

COSIMO. [63] To me, you have made this soldier's art be worth almost nothing, and I had presupposed it the most excellent and most honorable that one could do; so if you do not explain it to me better, I remain dissatisfied. For if it is as you say, I do not know from where arises the glory of Caesar, Pompey, Scipio, Marcellus,[40] and so many Roman captains who are by fame celebrated as gods.

FABRIZIO. [64] I have not yet finished disputing all that I proposed, which was two things: the one, that a good man could not exercise this career[41] as his art; the other, that a well-ordered republic or kingdom never allowed its subjects or its citizens to use it as an art. [65] About the first I have spoken as much as has occurred to me; it remains for me to speak of the second, where I will come to responding to this last question of yours. And I say that Pompey and Caesar, and almost all those captains who were in Rome after the last Carthaginian war,[42] acquired fame as able, not as good, men; those who had lived before them acquired glory as able and good. [66] This arose because these men did not take the practice of war as their art, and those that I named first used it as their art. [67] And while that republic lived immaculately, never did any great citizen presume by means of such a practice to take advantage of the peace by breaking the laws, despoiling the provinces, usurping and tyrannizing the fatherland and taking advantage in every mode. Nor did anyone of obscure fortune think of violating the oath,[43] adhering to private men, not fearing the Senate, or pursuing any tyrannical insult so as to be able to live by the art of war in every time. [68] But those who were captains, contented with their triumph, used to return to private life with desire; and those who were members used to lay down their arms with a greater will than they picked them up. And everyone used to return to the art by means of which he had ordered his life;[44] nor was there ever anyone who hoped to be able to nourish himself with spoils and with this art.[45] [69] About this one can make an evident conjecture regarding the great citizens by means of Regulus Attilius, who, being captain of the Roman armies in Africa

---

38. Cf. the discussion of "honorably wicked men" in *D* I 27.

39. That is, become bandits.

40. Julius Caesar (100–44 B.C.); Pompey (106–48 B.C.); Scipio Africanus (236–182 B.C.); Marcus Claudius Marcellus (270–208 B.C.).

41. Lit.: exercise this exercise.

42. Third Punic War (149–146 B.C.).

43. See *AW* II 134–35 on the military oath.

44. That is, to his civilian occupation.

45. The art of war.

and having almost conquered the Carthaginians, asked the Senate for permission to return to his house to take care of his farms, which were being spoilt by his workers.[46] [70] From which it is clearer than the sun that if he had used war as his art and by means of it had thought to make use of it [for profit], he, having so many provinces as prey, would not have asked permission to return to care for his fields, for each day he would have acquired much more than the price of all of them. [71] But because these good men who do not use war as their art do not want to draw from it anything but toil, dangers, and glory, when they are sufficiently glorious they desire to return home and live from their art. [72] How much it is true of the base men and the common soldiers that they kept the same orders appears [from the facts] that each willingly withdrew from such a practice, and when he was not in the military he wanted not to be in the military,[47] and when he was in the military he would have wanted to be discharged.[48] [73] This agrees with many modes, especially seeing how among the first privileges that the Roman people gave to one of its citizens was that he would not be constrained to soldier against his will. [74] Therefore while Rome was well ordered (which was until the Gracchi),[49] it did not have any soldier who took this practice as an art; yet it had a few wicked ones and these were severely punished. [75] So a well-ordered city ought to want this study of war to be used in times of peace for training and in times of war for necessity and for glory, and the public alone left to use it as an art, as Rome did. [76] And any citizen who has another end in such a practice is not good; and any city governed otherwise is not well ordered.

COSIMO. [77] I remain very content and satisfied by what you have said up to now, and this conclusion you have made is very pleasing to me. And as far as a republic is concerned, I believe that it is true. But as to kings, I do not yet know. For I would believe that a king would want to have around him whoever particularly takes such a practice for his art.

FABRIZIO. [78] So much more ought a well-ordered kingdom to flee similar artifices, for these alone are the corruption of its king and are altogether the ministers of tyranny. [79] And do not allege to me any present kingdom to the contrary, because I will deny that these are well-ordered kingdoms. [80] For the kingdoms that have good orders do not give absolute rule to their kings ex-

46. See Valerius Maximus IV 4 6; Livy, *Summaries* XVIII; *D* III 25; see also Vegetius III pr.; Frontinus IV 3 3; *D* II 18.4, III 1.3.

47. Following the reading of Marchand et al.; but there is some support for the rendering: "when he was not in the military he would have wanted to be in the military."

48. Lit.: licensed.

49. Late-second-century B.C. reformers. See Plutarch, *Tiberius Gracchus* 9–21, *Caius Gracchus* 4–6, 9–17; cf. *D* I 37.2; see also *D* I 4, I 6.1.

cept in the armies; for in this place alone is a sudden decision necessary, and because of this there is only one power. [81] In other things he cannot do anything without counsel; and those who give him counsel have to fear that he may have someone near who in times of peace desires war because he cannot live without it. [82] But I want to stay a little longer on this, not to seek out a kingdom altogether good, but one similar to those that exist today, where those who take war for their art must be feared even by the king because the sinew of armies without any doubt is the infantry. [83] So if a king does not order himself so that his infantrymen may be content in time of peace to return home and to live from their arts, of necessity he must come to ruin, for a more dangerous infantry is not found than that which is composed of those who make war as their art. For you[50] are forced either to make war always or to pay them always or to bear the danger that they may take the kingdom from you. [84] To make war always is not possible and to pay them always one cannot do; thus of necessity one incurs the danger of losing one's state. [85] As I have said,[51] while my Romans were wise and good they never permitted their citizens to take this practice as their art, notwithstanding that they were able to nourish them in every time because they made war in every time. [86] But to flee the harm that this continual practice could do them, since the time did not vary, they varied the men, and they went on temporizing with their legions so that [every] fifteen years they had always renewed them. And thus they availed themselves of the men in the flower of their age, which is from 18 to 35 years, at which time the legs, the hands and the eyes respond to one another. Nor did they wait until strength decreased in them and malice increased, as it did later in corrupt times. [87] For first Octavius, and then Tiberius,[52] thinking more of their own power than of the public utility, began to disarm the Roman people so as to be able to command it more easily, and to keep those same armies continually at the frontiers of the Empire. [88] And because they still did not judge that this was enough to keep the Roman people and Senate in check, they ordered an army called Praetorian that stayed near the walls of Rome and was like a castle close by that city. [89] And because they then began freely to allow the men deputed in those armies to use the military for their art, their insolence suddenly arose from it, and they became formidable to the Senate and harmful to the emperor. Hence it resulted that many of them[53] died from their insolence because they gave the empire to, and

50. The first instance of the singular or informal "you;" see glossary for all later instances.

51. See *AW* I 64–74; cf. *AW* I 17.

52. Octavius (Augustus) (63 B.C.–A.D. 14), first Roman emperor (27 B.C.–A.D. 14); Tiberius (42 B.C.–A.D. 37), second Roman emperor (14 B.C.–A.D. 37).

53. "Them" appears to refer to the Roman emperors.

took it from, whomever they wished;[54] and sometimes it happened that at one and the same time there were many emperors created by various armies. [90] From which proceeded first the division of the Empire and ultimately its ruin. [91] If they want to live securely, kings must therefore have their infantries composed of men who, when it is time to make war, go to it willingly because of their love, and then when peace comes return home more willingly. [92] This always is [the case], when he chooses men who know how to live from another art than this. [93] And thus, peace having come, he ought to want his princes to return to govern their peoples, the gentlemen to the cultivation of their possessions, and the infantrymen to their particular arts; and [he ought to want] each of them to make war willingly so as to have peace, and not to seek to disturb the peace so as to have war.

COSIMO. [94] Truly this reasoning of yours appears to me well considered; nonetheless, this being almost the opposite of what I have thought about this until now, my spirit does not remain purged of every doubt, for I see many lords and gentlemen nourish themselves in time of peace by means of the studies of war, as do your peers who have provisions from princes and communities. [95] I also see almost all the men-of-arms remain with their provisions, and I see many infantrymen stay in the guard of cities and fortresses; so that it seems to me that there is a place for each in time of peace.

FABRIZIO. [96] I do not believe that you believe this, that in time of peace each and every one has a place. For supposing that no other reason can be adduced regarding this, the small number made up by all those, alleged by you, who remain in the places would respond to you: what proportion do the infantries that are needed in war have to those that are employed in peace? [97] For the fortresses and cities that are guarded in time of peace are guarded much more in war; to that are added the soldiers that are kept in the country, a large number who are all abandoned in peace. [98] And as to guards of states, which are a small number, Pope Julius[55] and you have shown to everyone how much are to be feared those who do not know how to do any art other than war. And for their insolence you have deprived them of [being] your guards and posted Swiss there, as [men] born and raised under the laws and selected by the community according to a true selection. So say no longer that in peace there is a place for every man. [99] As to the men-of-arms, since they all remain with their pay in peace, this solution seems more difficult; nonetheless, whoever considers everything well finds the response easy, for this mode of keeping men-of-arms

54. Lit.: whomever it seemed to them.
55. Julius II (Giuliano della Rovere) (1443–1513), pope (1503–13).

is a corrupt mode and not good. [100] The cause is that they are men who make it an art, and from them would arise a thousand inconveniences each day in the states where they were if they were accompanied by a sufficient company; but since they are few and cannot by themselves make an army, they cannot so often do grave harm. [101] Nonetheless, they have done it many times, as I said to you of Francesco and of Sforza, his father, and of Braccio of Perugia.[56] [102] So I do not approve this usage of keeping men-of-arms; it is corrupt and can make great inconveniences.

COSIMO. [103] Would you like to do without them?—or, keeping them, how would you keep them?

FABRIZIO. [104] By way of a militia; not similar to that of the king of France[57] because it is dangerous and insolent like ours, but similar to those of the ancients who used to create the cavalry from their subjects and, in times of peace, used to send them to their homes to live off their arts, as I will contend[58] at greater length before this discussion finishes. [105] So that now if this part of the army is able to live by such a practice even when there is peace, it arises from a corrupt order. [106] As to the provisions that are reserved for me and for other heads, I say to you that this likewise is a very corrupt order, for a wise republic ought not to give them to anyone; rather, it ought to use its citizens as heads in war, and in time of peace it ought to want them to return to their art. [107] Thus a wise king also ought not to give them, or, if he gives them the causes ought to be: either as a reward for some outstanding deed or because he wants to avail himself of one man in peace as well as in war. [108] And because you alleged me,[59] I want to use myself as an example. And I say I have never used war as an art, because my art is to govern my subjects and to defend them, and, so as to be able to defend them, to love peace and know how to make war. [109] And my king rewards and esteems me not so much because I understand war as because I also know how to counsel him in peace. [110] Hence any king, if he is wise and wants to govern prudently, ought not to want to have near him anyone who is so made. For if he has around him either too great lovers of peace or too great lovers of war they will make him err. [111] I cannot say anything else in this my first discussion and according to my proposals; and if this is not enough for you, you must seek out someone who may better satisfy you. [112] You can well have begun to understand how much difficulty there is in bringing back ancient modes

---

56. See *AW* I 56–59.
57. Francis I (1494–1547) had succeeded Louis XII as king in 1515; cf. note 82.
58. Lit.: dispute.   59. See *AW* I 94; cf. *AW* I 77.

in the present wars, and what preparations a wise man must make, and what opportunities one can hope for so as to be able to execute them. But little by little[60]
you will understand these things better if the discussion, conferring some part
of ancient orders on present modes, does not tire you out.

COSIMO. [113] If before we were desiring to hear you discuss these things,
truly what you have said up till now has redoubled the desire. Therefore, we
thank you for what we have had and we ask for the rest.

FABRIZIO. [114] Since this pleases you, I want to begin to treat this material
from the beginning so that it may be better understood, being enabled by that
mode to demonstrate at greater length. [115] The purpose of whoever wants to
make war is to be able to fight with any enemy in the field and to be able to win a
battle. [116] To want to do this, one must order an army. [117] To order the army,
one needs to find the men, arm them, order them, and train them in small and in
large orders, quarter them, and then present[61] them, either standing or marching,
to the enemy. [118] In these things consist all the industry of open-field warfare,
which is the most necessary and the most honored. [119] The other errors that he
may make in the handling of the war could be withstood by whoever knows well
how to present battle to the enemy. But whoever lacks this discipline, though he
be very worthy in other particulars, will never conduct a war with honor because
a battle that you win cancels any other bad action of yours. In the same way, by
losing one, all the good things worked by you before become vain. [120] Therefore, since it is necessary first to find the men, one must come to the levying[62]
of them, for so the ancients called it. We would call it a "draft;"[63] but so as to call
it by a more honored name, I want us to use the name of levy. [121] Those who
have given rules for war want men to be selected from the temperate countries,
so that they have spirit and prudence. For a warm country generates prudent and
not spirited [men], a cold one spirited and not prudent ones.[64] [122] This rule is
well given to one individual who is prince of all the world and, through this, is allowed to draw men from those places that look good to him. [123] But wanting to
give a rule about this that each can use, one must say that every republic and every
kingdom should choose its soldiers from its own countries, be they warm or cold
or temperate. [124] Through this one sees, by ancient examples, how with training good soldiers are made in every country. For where nature is lacking, indus-

---

60. Lit.: from hand to hand.   61. Lit.: represent.

62. "Levy" and "levying" translate *deletto*, from the Latin *delectus*.

63. *Scelta*, related to words translated elsewhere as "choose."

64. Vegetius I 2; cf. Aristotle, *Politics* 1327b.

try, which in this case[65] avails more than nature, provides. [125] And selecting them from other places cannot [truly] be called a levy, because a levy means to draw the best from a province and to have the power to select those who do not want to serve in the military as well as those who do want to. [126] Therefore, this levy cannot be made except in places subject to you. For from countries that are not yours you cannot draw whomever you want; rather, you need to take those who want [to serve in the military].

COSIMO. [127] But from among those who want to come, one can, of course, take some and leave some, and through this it can be called a levy.

FABRIZIO. [128] You speak the truth in a certain mode. But consider the defects that such a levy has in itself, for many times it still happens that it is not a levy. [129] First: those who are not your subjects and who are in the military voluntarily are not the best; rather, they are among the most wicked of a province. For if any are scandalous, idle, without restraint, without religion, fugitives from their fathers' rule,[66] blasphemers, gamblers, in every part badly raised, they are those who want to be in the military. These customs cannot be more contrary to a true and good military. [130] When so many of such men are offered to you that you exceed the number that you have planned, you can select them; but, since the matter is wicked, it is not possible that the levy be good. [131] But many times it happens that they are not enough to reach the number you need; such that, being forced to take them all, it arises that it can no longer be called a levy but a hiring[67] of infantrymen. [132] Today the armies of Italy and elsewhere, except Germany, are made with these disorders. For no one is hired at the prince's command, but according to the will of whoever wants to soldier. [133] So consider now which modes of those ancient armies can be introduced in an army of men put together in a similar way.

COSIMO. [134] What way would one have to take, then?

FABRIZIO. [135] The one I said:[68] pick them from one's own subjects and by the authority of the prince.

COSIMO. [136] In those thus chosen, would any ancient form be introduced?

FABRIZIO. [137] You know well that this is so, when whoever commands them is their prince or ordinary lord, when it is a principality; or, if it is a republic, as a citizen and, for that time, a captain. Otherwise, it is difficult to do anything good.

COSIMO. [138] Why?

65. Or: chance.
66. Lit.: empire.
67. *Soldare.*
68. See *AW* I 123–30.

FABRIZIO. [139] I will tell you in time;[69] for now I want this to be enough for you: that one cannot operate well by another way.

COSIMO. [140] Then, since one has to make this levy in one's own countries, from where do you judge it better to draw them, from the city or from the country?

FABRIZIO. [141] Those who have written about this are all in accord that it is better to select them from the country, since they are men used to hardship, raised amidst toils, accustomed to being in the sun, fleeing the shade, knowing how to work a tool, digging a hole, carrying a load, and being without astuteness or malice.[70] [142] But since there are two kinds of soldiers, on foot and on horse, in this part my opinion would be that those on foot should be selected from the country and those on horse from the cities.

COSIMO. [143] At what age would you take them?

FABRIZIO. [144] If I had to make a new military, I would take them from 17 to 40 years; if it were made and I had to restore it, always at 17.

COSIMO. [145] I don't understand this distinction well.

FABRIZIO. [146] I'll tell you. [147] If I had to order a military where there was none, it would be necessary to select all those men who were more fit and were also of military age so as to be able to instruct them, as will be said by me.[71] But if I had to make the levy in places where this military was [already] ordered, I would take them from 17 years so as to supplement it, because others with more time would [already] be chosen and enrolled.

COSIMO. [148] So you would want to make a militia similar to that which is in our countries.[72]

FABRIZIO. [149] You speak well. [150] It is true that I do not know whether you have ordered them in the mode in which I would arm, captain, train, and order them.

COSIMO. [151] Then you praise the militia?

FABRIZIO. [152] Why, do you want me to condemn it?

COSIMO. [153] Because many wise men have always blamed it.

FABRIZIO. [154] You say a contradictory thing, in saying that someone wise blames the militia, that he can be held wise and be shown to be wrong.

COSIMO. [155] The poor[73] showing that it has made will always make us have such an opinion.

---

69. See *AW* VII 208 ff.   71. See *AW* I 199 ff.

70. Vegetius I 3.

72. A reference to Machiavelli's own militia, the *ordinanza* of 1506, which was reconstituted by Lorenzo de' Medici in 1514.

73. The word can also mean wicked or naughty.

FABRIZIO. [156] Beware that the defect is not yours, rather than its; you will recognize this before this discussion is finished.

COSIMO. [157] You will do a very agreeable thing; however, I want to state that for which they accuse it, so that you can better justify it. [158] They say this: either it is useless, and entrusting ourselves to it will make us lose our state; or it is virtuous, and by its means whoever governs it will easily be able to take [our state]. [159] They allege the Romans, who by means of these very arms lost their liberty; they allege the Venetians and the king of France. The former of whom use the arms of others so as not to have to obey one of their own citizens; the king has disarmed his own people so as to command them more easily. [160] But they fear its uselessness even more than this. [161] They allege two principal reasons for this uselessness: one, through being inexperienced, the other, through having to serve in the military by force. For they say that things are not learned thoroughly, and that by force nothing is ever done well.

FABRIZIO. [162] All these reasons that you state are from men who recognize things nearby,[74] as I will openly show you.[75] [163] First, as to the uselessness, I say to you that one does not use a more useful military than one's very own, nor can one's very own military be ordered except in this mode. [164] And because this was not disputed, I do not want to lose time on it, for all the examples of ancient history are for us. [165] And because they allege inexperience and force, I tell them that it is true that inexperience makes for lack of spirit and force makes for discontent. But one makes them gain spirit and experience by the mode of arming them, training them, and ordering them, as you will see as this reasoning progresses. [166] But as to force, you have to understand that the men who are inducted into the military by commandment of the prince have to come to it neither altogether forced nor altogether willingly. For complete willingness would make for the inconveniences that I stated above: that it would not be a levy, and those that went would be few; and complete force would also carry wicked effects. [167] Therefore, one should take a middle way where there is neither complete force nor complete willingness; rather, they must be drawn through the respect that they have for the prince, where they fear his disdain more than present pain. And it will always happen that it is a force mixed with willingness, so that such discontent as to have bad effects will not be able to arise from it. [168] I do not at all say by this that it cannot be conquered. For the Roman armies were conquered many times, and the army of Hannibal was conquered, such that it can be seen that one cannot order an army that someone may promise cannot be beaten. [169] Therefore, these wise men of yours must

---

74. Lit.: little distant.

75. In the discussion immediately following.

not gauge this uselessness from its having lost one time;[76] rather, [they must] believe that just as one loses, so can one win and remedy the cause of the loss. [170] And if they were to seek this, they would find that it was not through a defect of the mode but of the order that it did not attain its own perfection. And as I have said,[77] they should have provided for it not by blaming the militia, but by correcting it. How that should be done you will understand little by little.[78] [171] As to the fear[79] that such an order may take away your state by means of the individual who is made its head, I respond that arms, given by the laws and by order, on the back of one's own citizens or subjects never do harm; rather, they are always useful, and cities more often maintain themselves immaculate by means of these arms than without them. [172] Rome remained free for 400 years and was armed; Sparta for 800; many other cities have been unarmed and they have been free less than forty. [173] For cities need arms; and when they do not have their own arms they hire foreigners. And foreign arms can do damage to the public good more quickly than one's own, because they become corrupt more easily and can be used more quickly by a citizen who has become powerful. And, in part, he has material that is easier to manage, since he has to oppress unarmed men. [174] Besides this, a city ought to fear two enemies more than one. [175] That which avails itself of foreign arms fears at a stroke the foreigner it hires and its citizen. [For evidence] that it should fear this, remember what I said about Francesco Sforza a little while ago.[80] [176] That [city] which uses its very own arms is not afraid except of its own citizen. [177] But of all the reasons one could give, I want to use this: never did anyone order any republic or kingdom who did not think that the same men who inhabited it had to defend it with their arms. [178] And if the Venetians had been wise in this as in all their other orders, they would have made a new monarchy in the world. [179] So much more do they merit blame, since they had been armed by their first lawgivers. [180] But not having dominion on land, they had been armed on the sea, where they waged their own wars virtuously and, with arms in hand, increased their fatherland. [181] But as the time came when they had to wage war on land to defend Vincenza, where they should have sent one of their citizens to fight on land, they hired the marquis of Mantua as their captain.[81] [182] This was the sinister policy that cut off their legs for leaping to heaven and expanding. [183] And if they

---

76. The Florentine militia, organized by Machiavelli himself, lost to the Spanish at Prato in 1512. This loss led directly to the end of the republican government in which Machiavelli had served and to the return of the Medici as rulers of Florence (see *D* II 27.3).

77. See *AW* I 156.   79. Lit.: doubt.

78. Lit.: from hand to hand.   80. See *AW* I 56 ff., I 101.

81. Gianfrancesco Gonzaga I (1366–1407) conquered Vincenza for Venice in 1404.

made [that policy] in the belief that they lacked confidence for waging war on land, although they knew how to wage it at sea, then it was an unwise lack of confidence. For a sea captain, who is used to fighting with the wind, water, and men, will more easily become a captain on land, where he fights with men alone, than [a captain] on land will become one at sea. [184] Knowing how to fight on land and not at sea, and coming to war with the Carthaginians who were powerful at sea, my Romans did not hire Greeks or Spaniards accustomed to the sea, but imposed that task on their own citizens whom they used to send out on land; and they won. [185] If they did it so that one of their citizens would not become tyrant, it was a fear lacking consideration. For besides those reasons which I stated to this purpose a little while ago, if one citizen with sea arms had never made a tyranny in a city placed on the sea, so much less would he have been able to do this with land arms. [186] And by this means, they should have seen that arms in their citizens' hands could not make them tyrants, but that evil orders of government make a city tyrannize. Since they had a good government, they did not have to fear their own arms. [187] However, they adopted an imprudent policy, which has been the cause of the loss of much glory and much happiness for them. [188] As to the error which the king of France makes in not keeping his peoples disciplined for war[82] (which those [men] of yours allege[83] as an example),[84] there is no one, having set aside any particular passion of his, who does not judge this defect to be in that kingdom and this negligence alone to make it weak. [189] But I have made too large a digression, and perhaps I have gone outside of my purpose; however, I did this so as to respond to you and to demonstrate to you that one cannot make a foundation on other arms than one's own and one cannot order one's own arms otherwise than by way of a militia, nor by other ways introduce forms of armies in any place, nor by another mode order a disciplined military. [190] If you read the orders that the first kings made in Rome, and especially Servius Tullius, you will find that the order of the classes is nothing other than a militia for the sake of being able immediately to put together an army for the defense of that city.[85] [191] But let us return to our levy. [192] I say anew that having to restore an old order, I would take them at 17 years;

---

82. By the mid-fifteenth century, Charles VII of France had organized a military that consisted of French subjects, a large portion of whom were civilians drawn from communities throughout the kingdom to serve as "free archers" (so called because they were exempted from taxation in recompense for weekly training and occasional combat service). Charles's successor, Louis XI, disbanded the free archers in 1474, hiring in their stead Swiss and German mercenaries; he was in turn succeeded by Louis XII. For the Venetians, see the following discussion.

83. See *AW* I 159.   84. Parentheses in the original.

85. Servius Tullius, the sixth king of Rome (578–535 B.C.). See Livy I 42–44; see also *D* II 3.

having to create a new one, I would take them from every age between 17 and 40, so as to enable me to use them immediately.

COSIMO. [193] Would you make a distinction in the arts from which you pick them?

FABRIZIO. [194] These writers do so[86] because they do not want fowlers, fishermen, cooks, pimps, and anyone who makes an art of amusement to be taken; but besides those who work the land, they want smiths, ferriers, carpenters, butchers, hunters, and the like, to be taken. [195] But with respect to conjecturing the goodness of the man from his art, I would make little distinction among them; yet I would definitely do so, so as to be able to use him with more utility. [196] And for this cause the peasants who are used to working the land are more useful than anyone. For of all the arts, this is used in armies more than the others. [197] After this are the smiths, carpenters, ferriers, and stone cutters. It is useful to have many of these because their art is quite worthwhile for many things, since it is a good thing to have one soldier from whom you take a double service.

COSIMO. [198] By what does one recognize those who are or are not fit to serve in the military?

FABRIZIO. [199] I want to speak of the mode of selecting a new militia so as to make an army of it later. For in part one also ends up reasoning about the selection that is made in the restoration of an old militia. [200] Therefore, I say that the goodness of one whom you have to select as a soldier is known either by experience through some outstanding deed of his or by conjecture. [201] Proof of virtue cannot be found in men who are being selected anew and who have never been selected before; and few or none [who have been chosen before] are found in a militia that is ordered anew. [202] Therefore, lacking this experience, it is necessary to recur to conjecture, which is made from his years, his art, and his bearing. [203] These first two have been reasoned about. It remains to speak of the third. Therefore, I say that some, among whom was Pyrrhus, have wanted the soldiers to be large; some others have selected them only from bodily vigor, as Caesar did. This vigor of body and spirit is conjectured from the composition of the members and from the grace of aspect.[87] [204] And therefore those who write of this say that he needs to have lively and bright eyes, a sinewy neck, a large chest, muscular arms, long fingers, a small belly, round flanks, and lean legs and feet.[88] These parts usually render the man agile and strong, which are the two

86. Vegetius I 7, with changes; cf. Cicero, *De Officiis* I 150.

87. The sources are unknown for Pyrrhus's and Caesar's preferences asserted here; cf. Vegetius I 5.

88. See Vegetius I 6.

things above all others that one seeks in a soldier. [205] One should above all look to his customs, and what in them is honest and shame-filled, otherwise one selects an instrument of scandal and a beginning of corruption. For there is no one who believes that any virtue that is in any part laudable can be known in a dishonest education and base spirit. [206] It does not seem superfluous to me; indeed, so that you may better understand the importance of this levy, I believe it is necessary to tell you the mode that the Roman consuls observed in selecting the Roman legions at the beginning of their magistracies. In that levy, because those whom they had to select were, thanks to continual wars, a mixture of veterans and new men, they were able to proceed by experience with the old and by conjecture with the new. [207] And this should be noted: that these levies were made either so as to use them right then or so as to train them right then and use them in time. [208] I have spoken and will speak of all that is ordered for using them in time, because my intention is to show you how one can order an army in countries where there was no military. In those countries one cannot have levies so as to use them right then; but in those where it is a custom to draw up armies, and [to do so] by the prince's way, one can well have them right then, as used to be observed in Rome and as is observed today among the Swiss. [209] For in these levies, if there are some new [men], there are also so many others accustomed to remain in the military orders, that the new and the old mixed together make a united and good body. Notwithstanding, when they began to keep the stations of the soldiers fixed, the emperors had a teacher put in charge of the new soldiers, whom they called Tironi, to train them, as is seen in the life of Emperor Maximinus.[89] [210] While Rome was free, this was ordered not in the armies but within the city. Since military drills in which the young were trained were customary there, it arose that when they were later chosen to go to war, they had been accustomed to the mock military, so that they could easily be used for the true one. [211] But since these emperors later eliminated these drills, they were necessitated to use the means I have demonstrated here. [212] Therefore, coming to the mode of the Roman levy,[90] I say that the Roman consuls, upon whom the care of war was placed, created 24 military tribunes, who did the office done today by those whom we call constables, and put six of them in each legion. [They did so] after they had taken over the magistracy [and] when they wanted to order their armies (for it was a custom that each of them had two Roman legions, which were the sinew of their armies).[91] [213] They then had all the

89. Julius Verus Maximinus, Roman emperor (235–38). See Herodian VI 8.2; cf. L. Arthur Burd, "Le fonti letterarie di Machavelli nell'*Arte della guerra*," *Atti della Reale Academia dei Lincei*, 5th ser., *Cl. di scienze morali, storiche e filologiche* 4 (1896): 191 n. 1.

90. See Polybius VI 19–20.   91. Parentheses in original.

Roman men fit to bear arms convene, and placed the tribunes of each legion separate from one another. [214] Then by lot they drew the tribes from which the selection first had to be made, and from the tribe [chosen first] they chose four of the best, and from [among] these [four] one was selected by the tribunes of the first legion; from the other three, one was selected by the tribunes of the second legion; from the other two, one was selected by the tribunes of the third; and the last one fell to the fourth legion. [215] After these, another four were chosen; from these, first, one of them was selected by the tribunes of the second legion; the second of these by the third; the third of these by the fourth; the fourth remained for the first. [216] Then another four were chosen: the third chose the first, the fourth the second, the first the third, and the fourth remained for the second; and thus this mode of selecting varied successively, so much so that the selection came out to be equal and the legions balanced one another. [217] And as we said above,[92] this levy could be made so as to use it right then, because it was made from men a good part of whom were experienced in the true military and all of whom were trained in the mock military; and this selection could be made by conjecture and experience. [218] But where one has to order a military anew, and therefore has to choose for a time [in the future], this levy cannot be done except by conjecture, which is made from their years and bearing.

COSIMO. [219] As much as has been said by you, I believe to be altogether true. [220] But before you pass to another reasoning, I want to ask you about one thing that you made me remember by saying that the levy which had to be made where there were no men used to soldiering would have to be made by conjecture. For I have heard our militia blamed in many parts, and especially as to the number, because many say that a smaller number should be taken. From this, one would take this fruit: that they would be better, and chosen better; one would not give so much hardship to the men; one would be able to give them some reward by means of which they would remain more content, and they could be better commanded. [221] Hence, I would like to understand your opinion in this part, and whether you would like a larger or a smaller number, and what mode you would take to select them for one and the other number.

FABRIZIO. [222] Without a doubt a large number is better and more necessary than a small one; indeed, it is better to say, where one cannot order a large quantity, one cannot order a perfect militia; and I will easily invalidate all the reasons allotted[93] by those [who blame the militia]. [223] Therefore, I say first that where there are many people, as there are in Tuscany, for example, the

92. See I 202 ff.

93. The metaphor is economic: the checks (i.e., reasons) written by the critics of the militia will be canceled by Fabrizio.

smaller number does not make you have better [men] or a better chosen levy. [224] For in selecting men, [although] wanting to judge by experience, one would find very few in that country whom experience made probable [choices], both because few have been in war and because among these few very few have given proof by means of which they merit being chosen before the others. So whoever has to select them in similar places must lay aside experience and take them by conjecture. [225] Hence, since others are reduced to such a necessity, I would like to understand by what rule I should take or leave anyone, if twenty youths of good bearing come before me. So without doubt, I believe that every man will confess that it is less an error to take them all so as to arm them and train them, since one cannot know which of them is better, and to reserve for later making a more certain levy once one recognizes, by testing them in training, those of more spirit and of more life. [226] So everything considered, in this case to choose few so as to make them better is altogether false. [227] As to giving less hardship to the country and to the men, I say that the militia, whether it be large or small, will not give any hardship. For this order does not take the men from any of their affairs, nor does it keep them from being able to go to do any of their business. For it obliges them to convene together for training only on holidays.[94] This does harm neither to the country nor to the men. Indeed, it would give a delight to the youths because on festival days when they stay idly in their retreats, they would go with pleasure to these drills. For, since the handling[95] of arms is a beautiful spectacle, it is delightful to young men. [228] As to being able to pay the smaller number and, because of this, to keep them more obedient and more content, I respond that one cannot make a militia of so few that they can be paid continuously such that the pay satisfies them. [229] For example, if one ordered a military of five thousand infantrymen, to want to pay them so that one would believe they would be contented one would have to give them at least ten thousand ducats a month. [230] First, this number of infantry is not enough to make an army; this payment is not supportable by one state and, on the other hand, it is not sufficient for keeping the men contented and obligated to enable one to use them in their post. [231] So that in doing this, one would spend more and have few forces, and they would not be sufficient either to defend you or to engage in any enterprise of yours. [232] If you gave them more, or took more of them, by so much more would it be impossible for you to pay them. [233] If you gave them less, or took less of them, by so much less would they be content, or by so much less would they bring utility to you. [234] Thus those who reason about making a militia and paying them while they remain at

94. Lit.: idle days.   95. Or: treatment.

home, reason of things either impossible or useless. [235] But it is very necessary to pay them when they are raised to remain at war. [236] Yet if such an order were to give some hardship (what [hardship], I do not see) to those enrolled in it in time of peace, as recompense for this there are all those goods which an ordered military brings to a country, because without that nothing is secure there. [237] I conclude that this is not understood by whoever wants a small number so as to be able to pay them, or for some other of the causes alleged by you. For my opinion is also supported [by the fact] that any number will always diminish in your hands because of the infinite impediments that men have, so that a small number would turn into nothing. [238] Besides, when you have a large militia, [through] your selection [of men] you can avail yourself of few or of many. [239] Beyond this, it has to serve you in fact and in reputation, and a large number will always give you more reputation. [240] Add to this that since the militia is made so as to keep the men trained, if you enlist[96] a small number in a large country, those enlisted are so distant from one another that you cannot, without very grave harm to them, collect them so as to train them; and without this training the militia is useless, as will be said in its place.

COSIMO. [241] You have said enough about this question of mine; but now I desire that you resolve another doubt for me. [242] These [men] say that such a multitude of armed [men] makes for confusion, scandal, and disorder in the country.

FABRIZIO. [243] I will tell you the cause why this is another vain opinion. [244] These [men] ordered for arms can cause disorder in two modes: either among themselves or against others. [245] One can easily avoid these things where the order by itself does not avoid them. For, as to the scandals among them, this order takes them away rather than nourishes them, because in ordering them you give them arms[97] and heads. [246] If the country where you order them is so unwarlike that there are not arms among its men, and so united that there are not heads there, this order makes them more ferocious against foreigners but does not make them in any mode more disunited. For well-ordered men, armed as well as unarmed, fear the laws. Nor can they rebel if the heads that you give them do not cause the rebellion. The mode to do this will now be told. [247] But if the country where you order them is armed and disunited, this order alone is the cause of uniting them. For they have arms and heads for themselves, but the arms are useless for war, and the heads are nurturers of scandals. [248] This order gives them arms useful for war and heads [that are] extinguishers of scandals. For in that country as soon as anyone is offended, he recurs

---

96. Lit.: write.

97. Weapons *(arme)*, not upper limbs *(braccia)*, here and in the following discussion.

to the head of his party who, to keep up reputation, encourages him to ven-
geance, not to peace. [249] The public head acts to the contrary so that by this
way the cause of scandals is taken away and that of union is prepared. The
united and effeminate provinces lose their vileness and maintain their union;
the disunited and scandalous ones unite, and that ferocity of theirs which usually works in a disordered manner is turned to the public utility. [250] As to
wanting them not to do harm to others, one should consider that they cannot
do this except by means of the heads that govern them. [251] To want the heads
not to make disorder, it is necessary to make sure that they not acquire too much
authority for themselves. [252] And you have to consider that this authority is
acquired either by nature or by accident. [253] And as to nature, one must provide that whoever is born in a place not be assigned to the men enrolled there,
but be made head in those places where he does not have any natural connection. [254] As to accident, one should order the thing in a mode that each year
the heads are changed from government to government; because the continued
authority over the same men generates among them so much union that it can
easily be converted to the prejudice of the prince. [255] How useful these changes
are to those who have used them and harmful to whoever has not observed them
can be recognized by the example of the kingdom of the Assyrians and of the
empire of the Romans. There one sees that that kingdom lasted a thousand years
without tumult and without any civil war, which did not proceed from anything
other than the changes that these captains, who had been assigned to the care of
the armies, made from place to place every year. [256] In the Roman Empire,
once the blood of Caesar was spent, so many civil wars among the captains of
the armies, and so many conspiracies of the aforementioned captains against
the emperors, arose from no other cause than from continually keeping those
captains fixed in the same government. [257] And if in some of those first emperors and those who then kept the empire with reputation, such as Hadrian,
Marcus, Severus,[98] and the like, it had been seen that they had introduced this
custom of changing the captains in that empire, without doubt they would have
made it more quiet and more durable. For the captains would have had less opportunity to tumult, the emperors less cause for fear, and the Senate, in the absence of successors, would have had more authority in the election of the emperor, and as a consequence it would have been better. [258] But wicked customs,
either because of the ignorance or little diligence of men, can be taken away neither by evil nor by good examples.

COSIMO. [259] I do not know whether with my questioning I have some-

98. Hadrian (emperor 117–38); Marcus Aurelius (emperor 161–80); Septimius Severus (emperor 193–211). See *P* 19 (esp. 81–82).

what taken you out of your order, because from the levy we have entered into another reasoning; and if I had not excused myself a little while ago,[99] I would believe that I merit some reprehension for it.

FABRIZIO. [260] Do not let this worry you. For all this reasoning was necessary [since we] wanted to reason about the militia, which, since many have blamed it, needed to be excused, [since we] wanted this first part of the levy to have a place here. [261] And before I descend to the other parts, I want to reason about the levy of the men for the cavalry. [262] According to the ancients, this was made from the wealthiest, having a regard for both years and the quality of the man. And they selected three hundred of them per legion, so that the Roman cavalry in every consular army did not pass the sum of six hundred.

COSIMO. [263] Would you make a cavalry militia to train them at home, and avail oneself of them in time?

FABRIZIO. [264] Indeed, it is necessary; and one cannot do otherwise, wanting to have arms that are one's own, and not wanting to have to draw from among those who make it an art.

COSIMO. [265] How would you select them?

FABRIZIO. [266] I would imitate the Romans. I would draw from the wealthiest, I would give them heads in the mode in which they are given to the others today, and I would arm and train them.

COSIMO. [267] Would it be well to give some provision to these?

FABRIZIO. [268] Indeed, but only as much as is necessary to feed their horses. For bringing expense to your subjects would enable them to complain of you. [269] But it would be necessary to pay for the horse and its expenses.

COSIMO. [270] What number would you make them, and how would you arm them?

FABRIZIO. [271] You are passing on to another reasoning. [272] I will tell you in its place,[100] which is when I will have told you how infantrymen should be armed, or how they are prepared to do battle.

---

99. See AW I 20, 45.   100. See AW II 67 ff.

BOOK TWO[1]

———— ◡◡◡ ————

[1] I believe that it is necessary, once the men have been found, to arm them; and wanting to do this, I believe it is necessary to examine the arms that the ancients used, and to select the best of these. [2] The Romans divided their infantries into heavy and light armed.[2] [3] Those with light arms they called by the one term *velites.* [4] Under this name are understood all those who shot with the sling, with the crossbow, and with darts. For their defense, the greater part of them had their heads covered and a kind of round shield on the arm. [5] These men fought outside of the orders and at a distance from the heavily armed. The latter[3] had a helmet that came down to the shoulders and a cuirass that came down to the knees with its layers; they had their legs and arms covered with greaves and arm plates and on their arms a shield two-braccia[4] long and one[-braccio] wide that had an iron rim on top so as to be able to sustain a blow, and another on the bottom, so that it was not worn out when it rubbed along the ground. [6] For offense they had a sword one-and-a-half-braccia long strapped to their left side and a dagger on their right side. [7] They had a spear in hand which they called a *pilum,* and at the outset of battle they threw it at the enemy. [8] This was the chief thing about[5] Roman arms, with which they occupied all the world. [9] And although some of the ancient writers give them, besides the aforesaid arms, a

---

1. The translation of the complete title of book II parallels that of book I: "Book Two of the Art of War by Niccolò Machiavegli, Florentine Citizen and Secretary, to Lorenzo di Filippo Strozzi, Florentine Patrician." The titles of books III and VII follow the same form.

2. For the following discussion of light arms, see Polybius VI 22; Vegetius I 20, II 2, IV 22; cf. Livy XXXI 34, XXXVIII 21; for that of heavy arms, see Polybius VI 23; Josephus III 5 5.

3. That is, the heavily armed soldiers.   5. Lit.: the importance of.

4. One braccio is equal to 22.84 inches.

spear in hand in the mode of a javelin,[6] I do not know how a heavy spear can be used by one who is holding a shield. For in managing it with two hands, the shield impedes him; with one, he can do no good because of its weight. [10] Besides this, to fight in crowds and in orders with a weapon on [the end of] a spear is useless, except in the first front where one has the free space to be able to extend the spear completely. One cannot do this in the orders within because the nature of the battalions is to tighten continually, as I will tell you[7] while ordering them. For although this is inconvenient, it is less feared than their widening, the danger of which is very evident. [11] Hence, all arms that exceed two braccia are useless in the constricted [orders]. For, supposing that the shield does not hinder you, if you have the spear and you want to use it with two hands, with it you cannot harm an enemy who is nearby you. [12] If you take the spear with one hand so as to use the shield, so much of the rear part sticks out, since you cannot hold it except in the middle, that those who are behind impede you in managing it. [13] And read all the battles celebrated by Titus Livy in his history [to see] that it is true either that the Romans did not have these spears or that, having them, they rarely availed themselves of them. In these you will see mention made of spears very few times; indeed, he always says that, the *pila* having been thrown, they put hands to swords. [14] But I want to leave these spears and, regarding the Romans, keep to the sword for offense and, for defense, to the shield and the other arms mentioned above. [15] The Greeks were not armed as heavily for defense as the Romans. But for offense they founded themselves more on the spear than on the sword, and especially the Macedonian phalangites, who carried spears a good ten-braccia long, called sarisses, with which they opened the enemy ranks and kept the orders in their own phalanxes.[8] [16] And although some writers say that they also had a shield,[9] I do not know how the sarisses and the shields could be together for the reasons given above. [17] Besides this, in the battle that Paulus Emilius had with King Perseus of Macedon, I do not recall that mention was made there of shields, but only of the sarisses and of the difficulty that the Roman army had in defeating them.[10] [18] So I conjecture that a Macedonian phalanx was not otherwise than is a battalion of Swiss today, who have all of their force and all of their power in their pikes. [19] Besides arms, the Romans ornamented their infantries with plumes, which things make the sight[11] of

6. *Spiedo,* a long, slender spear used for war and hunting and as a spit.

7. See *AW* III 156.

8. For a discussion of the Macedonian phalanx, see Polybius XXVIII 12–16.

9. See Plutarch, *Aemilius Paulus* 19–20; Livy XXXI 39.

10. The battle of Pydna (168 B.C.) See Livy XLIV 36–43; Plutarch, *Aemilius Paulus* 16–23. Both authors report that the Macedonians used shields.

11. Lit.: aspect.

an army beautiful to friends, terrible to enemies. [20] In that first Roman antiquity, the armor of the men on horseback was a round shield and they had their
heads covered; the rest was unarmored.[12] [21] They had a sword and a spear, long
and slender, with the iron on the front end only. Hence they ended up being
unable to steady the shield, and the spear was broken in the fray; and by being
unarmored, they were exposed to being wounded. [22] Then in time they were
armed like the infantrymen; but they had a shorter, square shield and a firmer
spear with two iron [spearheads] so that when one part came off they could avail
themselves of the other.[13] [23] With these arms, on foot as well as on horse, my
Romans occupied the whole world. And because of the fruit that was seen from
them, it is believable that they were the best armed armies that ever were. [24]
And Titus Livy vouches for this many times in his histories, when he comes to a
comparison with the enemy armies, where he says: "But the Romans, through
virtue, through the kind of arms and discipline, were superior."[14] And, therefore,
I have reasoned more particularly about the arms of the victors than of the van-
quished. [25] It seems well to me only to reason about the present mode of arming. [26] For their defense, the infantrymen have a breast[plate] of iron; and for
offense a lance nine-braccia long which they call a pike, and at their side a sword,
somewhat more round than sharp at the point. [27] This is the ordinary arming
of the infantries of today, for few of them have armored their backs and arms,
none the head. Instead of a pike, those few [who are in armor] carry a halberd
whose spear, as you know, is three-braccia long and has the iron retracted like
a hatchet. [28] They have among them arquebusiers, who, with the vehemence
of their fire, do the office that the slingers and crossbowmen did anciently.
[29] This mode of arming was discovered by the German peoples, especially the
Swiss. Since they were poor and wanted to live freely, they were and are necessitated to fight against the ambition of the princes of Germany; because [the lat-
ter] were rich, they were able to raise horses, which these peoples were not able
to do because of poverty. From this it arises that, since they were on foot and
wished to defend themselves from their enemy who was on horseback, they had
to search the ancient orders again and find arms that might defend them from
the fury of horse. [30] This necessity has made them either maintain or redis-
cover ancient orders, without which, as every prudent [man] affirms, infantry
is altogether useless. [31] They therefore took for arms these pikes, arms most
useful not only for withstanding cavalrymen, but for conquering them. [32] By

12. *Disarmato*, translated as either unarmed or unarmored, depending on context; see the
glossary.

13. Polybius VI 25.

14. Quotation not found. For related discussions, see Livy IX 17 and 18.

virtue of these arms and orders, the Germans have attained so much audacity that fifteen to twenty thousand of them would assault any number of cavalrymen, however large. During the past twenty-five years, many experiences of this have been seen here. [33] And there have been so many powerful examples of their virtue founded upon these arms and these orders, that when King Charles passed into Italy,[15] every nation imitated them; so much so that the Spanish armies have come into very great reputation.

COSIMO. [34] Which mode of arming is praised more by you, this German one or the ancient Roman?

FABRIZIO. [35] The Roman without a doubt; and I will tell you the good and the bad of the one and the other. [36] The German infantrymen thus armed can withstand and conquer; they are more expeditious on the road and in being ordered, because they are not laden with arms. [37] On the other hand, by being unarmored they are exposed to every blow, both distant and near. They are useless in battles against towns and in any fight where there is hardy resistance. [38] But like the former, the Romans withstood and conquered cavalrymen; they were secure against blows from near and far by being covered with armor; they could charge and were better able to withstand charges, since they had shields; they could more ably avail themselves of the sword at close quarters than the former [could avail themselves] of the pike; and if [the former] have a sword as well it becomes useless in such a case because they are without a shield. [39] They were able to assault towns securely, since their heads were covered and could be better covered with their shields. [40] Thus, they had no other inconvenience than the weight of their arms and the annoyance of having to carry them, which things they overcame by habituating the body to hardships and by hardening it to be able to endure fatigue. [41] And you know how men do not suffer from things [to which they are] accustomed. [42] And you have to understand this: infantries may have to fight against infantrymen and cavalrymen; and always will they be useless who are unable either to withstand cavalrymen or, being able to withstand them, nonetheless have to be afraid of infantries that are better armed and better ordered than they. [43] Now if you consider the German infantry and the Roman, you will find in the German the ability to beat cavalrymen, as we have said, but a great disadvantage when it fights with an infantry ordered like them and armed like the Roman. [44] Such that this will be the

15. Charles's invasion in 1494 marks the beginning of what came to be called the Italian Wars, in which Italy became the battlefield of various European powers, especially France and Spain, until 1559.

advantage of the one and the other: that the Romans will be able to overcome infantrymen and cavalrymen, the Germans only cavalrymen.

COSIMO. [45] I would desire that you come to some more particular example, so that we may better understand this.

FABRIZIO. [46] I say this: in many places of our histories you will find that the Roman infantries defeated innumerable cavalrymen, and never will you find that they have been defeated by men on foot either through a defect they may have had in arming or through an advantage their enemy had had in arms. [47] Because, if the mode of arming them had had a defect, it was necessary that one of two things happen. Finding that someone was better armed than they were, either they would not have gone any further with their acquisitions, or they would have taken up the foreign modes and left their own. [48] And because neither the one thing nor the other happened,[16] it arises that one can easily conjecture that their mode of arming was better than that of anyone else. [49] It has not yet happened with the German infantries. For one has seen them make a bad showing any time they have had to fight with men on foot ordered and obstinate like themselves. This arose from the advantage that they had encountered in the enemy arms. [50] Filippo Visconti, duke of Milan, being assaulted by eighteen thousand Swiss, sent against them Count Carmignuola,[17] who was then his captain. [51] With six thousand cavalrymen and a few infantrymen, he went to find them. Upon coming to blows with them, he was beaten back to his own very grave harm. [52] Then Carmignuola, as a prudent man, immediately recognized the power of the enemy arms—how much they prevailed against cavalrymen and the weakness of cavalrymen against [men] on foot so ordered. He put his men together again, went to find the Swiss again, and when he came near them made his men-at-arms get down from their horses. Fighting with them in such a manner, he killed all of them except for three thousand who, seeing themselves consumed without having a remedy, threw their arms to the ground and surrendered.[18]

COSIMO. [53] From what does so much disadvantage arise?

FABRIZIO. [54] I told you a little while ago;[19] but since you didn't under-

---

16. See Polybius VI 25 for the Roman discovery of the superiority of Greek arms and their subsequent imitation of them.

17. Filippo Maria Visconti, duke of Milan (1412–47); Francesco Bussone (1390–1432), count of Carmignuola. Filippo Visconti figures prominently in the *Florentine Histories,* especially Books IV–VI; for Carmignuola, see *P* 12.51; *D* II 18.4.

18. The battle of Arbedo (1422); cf. *D* II 18.4.   19. Presumably at *AW* II 34–44.

stand, I will repeat it for you. [55] As you were told a little while ago, the German infantries, almost without armor for defending themselves, have the pike and the sword for offense. [56] They come with these arms and in their order to find the enemy, who comes with his sword and in his orders to find them if he is well armored for defense, as were Carmignuola's men-at-arms who were made to get down on foot. And he has no other difficulty than getting near enough to the Swiss to join them with his sword, since he fights them securely once he has joined them. For a German[20] cannot stick an enemy who is close to him with his pike because of the length of his spear, and he must put his hand to his sword, which is useless to him since he is unarmored and has to meet an enemy who is completely armored. [57] So whoever considers the advantage and the disadvantage of the one and of the other will see how the unarmored [man] has no remedy at all for this; and winning the first clash and passing the first pike points is not very difficult, if whoever fights them is well armored. For the battalions advance (you will better understand how once I have shown you how they are put together),[21] and while advancing of necessity they draw near to one another so that their chests hit; and if anyone is killed or thrown to the ground by the pikes, those that remain on foot are more than enough for victory. [58] From this it arose that Carmignuola won with so much slaughter of the Swiss and so little loss of his own.[22]

COSIMO. [59] You observe[23] that Carmignuola's men were men-at-arms who, although they were on foot, were completely covered with iron and were therefore able to pass the test they passed. So I think that one needs to arm infantry like them, if one wants to pass the same test.

FABRIZIO. [60] If you recalled how I said the Romans were armed, you would not think so. For an infantryman who has his head covered with iron, his chest defended by a cuirass and a shield, his legs and arms armored, is much more able to defend himself against pikes and to enter among them than is a man-at-arms on foot. [61] I want to give you a brief modern example.[24] [62] The Spanish infantries had gone from Sicily to the kingdom of Naples so as to go to find Gonsalo,[25] who was besieged at Barletta by the French. [63] Against [the

---

20. Machiavelli alternates between discussing the Swiss and the Germans, who used similar armaments and tactics. The Swiss are sometimes treated as a subset of the Germans.

21. Parentheses in the original.

22. Cf. *D* II 18 for another account of Carmignuola.

23. Lit.: consider.   24. Lit.: a little of a modern example.

25. Gonzalo Fernández de Córdoba (1453–1515) (see *D* I 29.2). At the battle described below, known as that of Cerignuola or Seminara (1503), Fabrizio Colonna fought on the Spanish side.

Spanish] were Monsieur d'Aubigny[26] with his men-at-arms and with around four thousand German infantrymen. [64] [The Spanish] came to blows[27] with the Germans. [65] With their pikes low, [the Germans] opened up the Spanish infantries. But the latter, helped by their bucklers and by the agility of their bodies,[28] so mixed themselves with the Germans that they were able to join them with their swords. From this arose the death of almost all [the Germans] and the victory of the Spanish. [66] Everyone knows how many German infantrymen died in the battle of Ravenna,[29] which arose from the same causes. For the Spanish infantries had drawn to within sword-range of the German infantries and would have completely consumed them if the German infantrymen had not been aided by the French cavalrymen. Nonetheless, the Spanish, having drawn together, retired to a secure place. [67] I conclude, therefore, that good infantry must not only be able to withstand cavalrymen, but it must not be afraid of infantrymen. As I have said many times, this proceeds from arms and orders.

COSIMO. [68] Then say how you would arm them.

FABRIZIO. [69] I would take from the Romans and from the Germans, and I would want half to be armed like the Romans and the other half like the Germans. [70] For if among six thousand infantrymen, as I will tell you a little later,[30] I had three thousand infantrymen with shields like the Romans' and two thousand pikes and a thousand arquebusiers like the Germans', they would be enough for me. For I would place the pikes either in the front of the battalion or where I most feared cavalrymen; and those with shield and sword I would use to back up the pikes and to win the battle, as I will show you.[31] [71] Hence I believe that an infantry so ordered would today overcome any other infantry.

COSIMO. [72] What you have just said is enough for us as to infantries, but as to cavalrymen we desire to understand which seems to you more hardily armed, ours or the ancient?

FABRIZIO. [73] I believe that, in these times, on account of[32] the arched saddles and the stirrups not used by the ancients, one remains more firmly on horseback than then. [74] I believe that one is also more safe, such that today a

---

26. Robert Stuart D'Aubigny (1470–1544).

27. Lit.: hands.   28. Or: body.

29. The battle of Ravenna (April 11, 1512). After losing many of his men to field artillery in this battle, Fabrizio was taken prisoner by the French. The Spanish went on from this loss to the victory over Machiavelli's militia at Prato, leading to the reinstallation of the Medici in Florence. For the battle of Ravenna, see *P* 13.54, 26.105; *D* I 12.2, II 16.2, 17.3, 17.4.

30. This relatively high one-to-five ratio of arquebus to other weapons is not repeated when Fabrizio discusses the composition of his forces at *AW* II 147 ff.

31. See *AW* III 90–96.   32. Lit.: with respect to.

squadron of men-at-arms, by weighing so much, is resisted with more difficulty than were ancient cavalrymen. [75] With all of this, nonetheless, I judge that one should not set more store by horse than was set by it in antiquity. For, as was said above,[33] they have been put to shame many times in our times by infantrymen, and they will always be put to shame if they encounter infantry armed and ordered as above. [76] Against a Roman army whose captain was Lucullus, Tigranes, king of Armenia, had 150 thousand cavalrymen, among whom very many, called cataphracts, were armed like our men-at-arms. On the other side, the Roman [cavalrymen] did not reach six thousand, with 25 thousand infantrymen, such that Tigranes, upon seeing the enemy's army, said: "These are cavalrymen enough for an embassy."[34] Nonetheless, having come to blows, he was beaten. [77] He who writes of that battle deprecates these cataphracts by showing their uselessness. For he says that by having their faces covered they were hardly able to see and to harm the enemy, and by being weighed down by arms, they could not get up once they had fallen nor avail themselves of their bodies[35] in any manner. [78] I say, therefore, that those peoples and kings who esteem cavalry more than infantry must always be weak and exposed to every ruin, as has been seen in our times in Italy, which has been plundered, ruined, and overrun by foreigners for no other sin than having taken little care of the military on foot and having put all of its soldiers on horses.[36] [79] One should indeed have cavalrymen, but as the second and not as the first foundation of one's army. For they are necessary and very useful for scouting, overrunning and wasting the enemy's country, keeping his army worried and harassed and always under arms, and cutting off his provisions. But as to the battle and the open-field fight, which are the important thing[37] in war and the end for which armies are ordered, they are more useful for following the enemy once he is beaten than for doing anything else one does with them. And in virtue they are very much inferior to foot soldiers.

COSIMO. [80] Two doubts occur to me: one is that I know that the Parthians used nothing other than cavalrymen in war, and yet they divided the world

33. See *AW* II 29–58.

34. Lucius Licinius Lucullus (110–56 B.C.) in the battle of Tigranocerta (69 B.C.) during the Romans' Third Mithridatic War (74–63 B.C.) defeated Tigranes (94–56 B.C.). See Plutarch, *Lucullus* 26 ff., where Tigranes is said to have had one hundred fifty thousand heavy infantry and fifty-five thousand cavalry, Lucullus approximately ten thousand heavy infantry and one thousand cavalry. Tigranes says of Lucullus's troops as a whole that they are too many for ambassadors, and too few for soldiers. Cf. *D* II 19.1.

35. Lit.: of their person.   37. Lit.: the importance.
36. Cf. *D* II 18; *P* 12.

with the Romans. The other is that I would like you to tell me how cavalry can be withstood by infantrymen, and from what the virtue of the latter and the weakness of the former arise.

FABRIZIO. [81] Either I told you[38] or I meant to tell you that my discussion[39] of the things of war does not exceed the limits of Europe. [82] When it does so, I am not obligated to give reasons for what is customary in Asia. [83] However, I have to say this: the Parthians' military was entirely contrary to that of the Romans, because the Parthians all soldiered on horseback, and in fighting they proceeded confused and dispersed. It was an unstable mode of fighting and was full of uncertainty. [84] The Romans were, it can be said, almost all on foot and fought together, tight and solid. One or the other alternately won according to whether the site was wide or tight. For in the latter the Romans were superior; in the former, the Parthians. [The Parthians] were able to make a great showing with that military thanks to[40] the region they had to defend, which was very wide because it had seas a thousand miles[41] apart, rivers two or three days from one another, and towns as well as inhabitants dispersed. So a Roman army, heavy and slow because of its arms and orders, was not able to cross it without heavy harm, as he who defended it was on horseback and very rapid, so that one day it was in one place and the next it was fifty miles away. From this it arose that the Parthians were able to prevail with cavalry alone, both to the ruin of the army of Crassus and to the peril of that of Marc Antony.[42] [85] But, as I told you,[43] I do not intend this discussion[44] of mine to speak of the military outside of Europe. Therefore, I want to remain with what the Romans and the Greeks ordered in the past, and what the Germans do today. [86] But let's come to the other question of yours, where you desire to understand what order or what natural virtue makes infantrymen surpass cavalry. [87] And I say to you, first, that cavalrymen cannot go every place like infantrymen. [88] They are slower to obey than infantrymen when their orders happen to vary. For if while they are going forward

---

38. Fabrizio does not speak of this limitation earlier. On the contrary, the discussion at *AW* I 121–23 would seem to presume that his reasoning would apply outside of Europe (cf. that earlier discussion with *AW* VI 162–63).

39. Lit.: reasoning.   40. Lit.: respect to.

41. The Tuscan and ancient Roman mile was slightly shorter than ours. The seas referred to are the Caspian Sea to the north and the Persian Gulf and the Gulf of Oman to the south. The territory of ancient Parthia roughly corresponds to contemporary Syria, Iraq, and Iran. Judea, on the other hand, was successfully conquered by Rome.

42. Marcus Lucinius Crassus (115–53 B.C.) was defeated by the Parthians in 53 B.C. In 36 B.C. Mark Antony (ca. 83–32 B.C.) led an expedition against the Parthians, which concluded with a disastrous retreat. See Plutarch, *Crassus* 16 ff., and *Mark Antony* 37–52; cf. *D* II 18.3, III 12.2.

43. See *AW* II 81.   44. Lit.: reasoning.

they need to move back, or while moving back they need to go forward, or they need to move when they are standing still, or when they are going they need to stop, without doubt cavalrymen cannot do so as precisely as infantrymen. [89] If they have been disordered by some thrust, even once that thrust is over, cavalrymen cannot return to their orders except with difficulty. Infantrymen do this very rapidly. [90] Besides this, many times it happens that a spirited man will be on a vile horse or a vile [man] on a spirited [horse]. Hence these disparities of spirit must make for disorder. [91] Nor may anyone marvel that a maniple[45] of infantrymen withstands every thrust of cavalrymen. For a horse is a feeling animal and recognizes the dangers and enters them unwillingly. [92] And if you will consider which forces make it go forward and which keep it back, without doubt you will see that those which keep it back are greater than those which push it on. For the spur makes it go ahead, and, on the other side, either the sword or the pike keep it back, [93] such that a maniple of infantrymen is seen through ancient and through modern experiences to be very secure, indeed insuperable, against cavalrymen. [94] And if against this you argue that the impetus with which it comes makes it more furious in charging whoever wants to withstand it, and makes it esteem the pike less than the spur, I say that if the horse begins to see from afar that it has to hit the points of the pikes, either it checks its course on its own, so that as it feels itself pricked it will stop entirely, or as it approaches them it will turn to the right or left. [95] If you want to make an experiment of this, try to run a horse into a wall with whatever impetus you want: rarely will you find that it goes into it. [96] Caesar, having to fight with the Swiss in France, got down and made each individual get down on foot and remove the horses from the line, as more apt to flee than to fight.[46] [97] But, notwithstanding these natural impediments that horses have, the captain who leads infantrymen should select ways that have the most impediments they can for horses; rarely will it happen that a man will be unable to secure himself through the quality of the country. [98] For if one walks through the hills, the site will free you from the charges that you[47] fear.[48] If one goes through a plain, there are few plains that do not secure you with cultivation and with woods. For every marsh, every embankment however weak, prevents that charge, and every cultivation, where there are vines and other trees, impedes horses. [99] And if

---

45. The maniple roughly corresponds to our company and consisted of two centuries of sixty men each.

46. See Caesar, *Gallic War* I 25.

47. The only formal or plural "you" in the Italian sentence.

48. Lit.: doubt.

you come to battle, the same thing happens for you as when you are marching, because every little impediment that a horse has takes away its impetus. [100] I nonetheless do not want to forget to tell you one thing: so much did the Romans esteem their orders and so much did they trust in their arms, that if they had to choose either a place so rough—so as to guard against cavalrymen—that they were not able to deploy their orders, or one where they had more fear of cavalrymen but were able to spread out, they always took the latter and let the former go. [101] But because it is time to pass to their training, having armed these infantries according to ancient and modern usage, we should see what training the Romans made them do before the infantries are led to do battle. [102] Even though they are well selected and better armed, they must train with very great attention,[49] for without this training no soldier was ever good. [103] These drills[50] must have three parts: one, to harden the body and make it fit for hardship and faster and more dexterous; next, to learn to use arms; third, to learn to observe the orders of the army, as much in marching as in fighting and encamping. [104] These are the three principal actions that an army makes. For if an army marches, encamps, and fights in an ordered and practiced way, the captain retains his honor therein, even if the battle does not have a good end. [105] All ancient republics provided for these drills so that through custom and through law not any part of them was left behind.[51] [106] Thus they used to drill their youths to make them fast in running, to make them dexterous in jumping, and to make them strong in heaving the post and in wrestling. [107] And these three qualities are virtually necessary for a soldier, because speed makes him fit to occupy places before the enemy, to come upon him unhoped for and unexpected, and to follow him when he is beaten. [108] Dexterity makes him fit to dodge a blow, to jump a ditch, and to get over an embankment. [109] Strength makes him carry his arms, hurt the enemy, and withstand a thrust better. [110] And above all, to make his body more fit for hardship, they got used to carrying great weights. [111] This custom is necessary because in difficult expeditions many times a soldier must carry, in addition to his arms, supplies for extra days; and if he were not accustomed to this trouble he wouldn't be able to do so, and through this he would be unable to flee a danger or to acquire a victory with fame. [112] As to learning how to use arms, they trained him in this mode. [113] They wanted the youths to wear arms that weighed more than double the true ones, and for a

49. Lit.: study.

50. The words translated as "drill," "train," "exercise," and "army" have the same root.

51. For the following discussion of infantry training, see Vegetius I 9, 11–16; cf. Vegetius I 1, III 4.

sword they gave them a lead-weighted club which was very heavy in comparison to the former.⁵² [114] They had each of them drive a post into the ground three-braccia high and in such a strong mode that blows would not pierce it or knock it to the ground. Against this post, as if against an enemy, the young man drilled himself with his shield and club: sometimes he stabbed it as if he wanted to wound the head or the face, sometimes as if he wanted to hit it in the side, sometimes in the legs, sometimes he drew back, sometimes he moved forward. [115] In this exercise they had this purpose: to make themselves fit to cover themselves and to strike the enemy; and by having very heavy fake arms, the true ones seemed lighter after those. [116] The Romans wanted their soldiers to strike with the point and not with the edge, both because the blow is more deadly and there is less defense against it, and because he who strikes [with the point] exposes himself less and is more able to strike again than he is with the edge. [117] Do not marvel that those ancients thought about these little things, considering⁵³ that every little advantage is of great moment when men have to come to blows.⁵⁴ And I remind you of what the writers say of this, rather than teach it to you myself. [118] Nor did the ancients esteem anything to be happier in a republic than for there to be many men in it trained in arms; for the splendor of gems and gold does not make your enemies submit themselves to you, but only the fear of arms. [119] Then the errors that are made in other things can at some time be corrected, but those that are made in war cannot be amended, since the penalty happens immediately. [120] Besides this, knowing how to fight made men more bold, because no one fears doing what it seems to him he has learned to do. [121] Therefore, the ancients wanted their citizens to be trained in every warlike action, and had them throw darts heavier than the true ones against the post. Besides making men expert in throwing, this drill also makes the arms⁵⁵ looser and stronger. [122] They also taught them to shoot with the bow and the sling. And over all of these things they had placed teachers so that later, when they were selected to go to war, they already had spirit and a soldierly disposition. [123] Nothing remained for them to learn other than to move in their orders and to maintain themselves in them, whether marching or fighting; they learned this easily, since they were mixed with those who knew how to stay in their orders through having soldiered longer.

COSIMO. [124] What drills would you make them do at present?

FABRIZIO. [125] Many of those that were mentioned, like running and having them wrestle, having them jump, having them toil under arms heavier than

---

52. That is, in comparison to a real sword.

53. Lit.: reasons.   55. Upper limbs, not weapons.

54. Lit.: hands.

the ordinary ones, having them shoot with the bow and the crossbow. To this I would add the arquebus, a new instrument, as you know, and a necessary one. And I would accustom all the youths of my state to these drills, but with greater industry and more solicitude for that part I had designated as military. And they would always be trained on holidays. [126] I would also want them to learn to swim, which is very useful because there are not always bridges over rivers, nor are there always ships at the ready, such that if your army does not know how to swim, it is left deprived of many advantages, and many opportunities for doing good are taken from you. [127] The Romans ordered that the young men be trained in the Campus Martius for nothing else if not [these things]: because, having been exhausted in drills on land, they were able to refresh themselves in the water since it was near the Tibur and, on the other hand, to train themselves in swimming.[56] [128] I would also, like the ancients, train those who soldier on horseback. This is very necessary, for besides knowing how to ride, they must know how to handle themselves on horseback. [129] For this they had ordered wooden horses upon which they made themselves adroit by jumping on them armed and unarmed, without any help from any hand. This made it that at a stroke and at a sign from the captain the cavalry was on foot, and likewise at a sign it remounted its horses. [130] And as such drills, both on foot and on horse, were easy then, so now they would not be difficult for that republic and that prince which wants to make its youth put them into practice, as is seen by experience in some cities of the West[57] in which they keep alive similar modes with this order. [131] They divide all of their inhabitants into various parts, and they name every part by the kind of arms they use in war. [132] And because they use pikes, halberds, bows, and arquebuses, they call them pikers, halberdiers, arquebusiers and archers. [133] Thus, every inhabitant must declare the order in which he wants to be enrolled. [134] And because through old age or through other impediments not everyone is fit for war, they make a levy from each order and call them the Sworn. On holidays they are obligated to train with those arms for which they are named. [135] And each has his place, designated by the public, where such training should be done. Those who are of that order but are not among the Sworn contribute money for those expenses that are necessary in such training. [136] Therefore, what they do, we could do. But our lack of prudence does not allow us to take any good policy. [137] From these drills it arose that the ancients had good infantries and that now those of the West have better

56. See Vegetius I 10.

57. It is not clear to which cities Machiavelli refers. Perhaps it is to German and Swiss cities (see Machiavelli's *Rapporto delle cose della Magna,* in *Tutte le opere,* ed. Mario Martelli [Firenze: Sansoni, 1992] , p. 65).

infantrymen than ours. For the ancients trained them either at home, as the republics did, or in the armies, as the emperors did, for the causes spoken of above. [138] But we do not train them at home; in camp, we cannot because they are not our subjects and we can oblige them to do only those drills that they themselves want to do. [139] This cause has made first the drills and then the orders to be neglected, and [made] kingdoms and republics, especially Italian ones, live in so much weakness. [140] But let's return to our order. Following this matter of drills, I say that to make good armies it is not enough to have hardened the men, to have made them hardy, fast, and dexterous; there is also the need for them to learn to be in their orders, to obey the signals by sound and at the words[58] of the captain and, while standing, withdrawing, going forward, fighting, and marching, to know how to maintain them. For without this discipline, observed and practiced with utmost care [and] diligence, never was an army good. [141] And without doubt, ferocious and disordered men are much weaker than timid and ordered ones. For order chases fear from men and disorder lessens ferocity.[59] [142] So that[60] you may better understand what will be said below,[61] you have to understand that in ordering its men for war every nation has made one principal group[62] within its army or its military. If they have varied its name, they have varied its number of men little. For all have composed it of six to eight thousand men. [143] This group was called legion by the Romans, phalanx by the Greeks, and caterva by the French.[63] [144] In our times the Swiss, who alone retain some shadow of the ancient military, call this same thing in their language what in ours signifies brigade. [145] It is true that each has then divided it into various battalions and has ordered it to its purpose. [146] It seems [well] to me that we base our discussion[64] on this name as better known and then, as well as is possible, order it according to ancient and modern orders. [147] And because the Romans divided their legion, which was composed of five to six thousand men, into ten cohorts, I want us to divide our brigade into ten battalions and compose it of six thousand men on foot. And we should give to each battalion 450 men, of whom 400 should be armed with heavy arms and fifty with light arms. [148] The heavy arms should be 300 shields with swords, and they should be called shieldmen; one hundred with pikes, and they should be called ordinary pikes; and the light arms should be fifty infantrymen armed with ar-

---

58. Lit.: voice.   60. Or: because.

59. Cf. *D* III 36.

61. Presumably Fabrizio refers to the discussions of the ordering of the army in books II and III.

62. Lit.: member (here and below).   64. Lit.: found our discussion.

63. See Vegetius II 2.

quebuses, crossbows, and partisans and bucklers; and these should be called by the ancient name of ordinary velites. [149] Therefore, altogether the ten battalions end up having three thousand shieldmen, one thousand ordinary pikes, and 500 ordinary velites; which all together make the number of four thousand five hundred infantrymen. [150] And we say that we want to make a brigade of six thousand. So we must add one thousand five hundred infantrymen, of which I would have one thousand with pikes, which would be called extraordinary pikes, and five hundred armed lightly, which I would call extraordinary velites. [151] Thus, my infantries, according to what was just said, would end up being composed half of shields and half of pikes and other arms. [152] I would place a constable, four centurions, and forty decurions[65] over each battalion; and in addition, a head over the ordinary velites, with five decurions [per battalion]. [153] I would give three constables, ten centurions, and one hundred decurions to the one thousand extraordinary pikes; to the extraordinary velites, two constables, five centurions, and fifty decurions. [154] I would then order a head-general of the entire brigade. [155] I would want each constable to have a flag and music. [156] Therefore, one brigade of ten battalions would be composed of three thousand shieldmen, one thousand ordinary and one thousand extraordinary pikes, five hundred ordinary and five hundred extraordinary velites. So they would end up having six thousand infantrymen, among whom would be six hundred decurions[66] and, in addition, fifteen constables with fifteen musicians and fifteen flag-bearers, fifty-five centurions, ten heads of ordinary velites, and one captain of the entire brigade with his own flag and his own music. [157] And I have gladly[67] repeated this order to you a number of times so that later you will not get confused when I show you the modes of ordering the battalions and armies. [158] Therefore, I say that that king or republic which wants to order its subjects in arms should order them with these arms and with these parts, and should make as many brigades as its country is capable of. [159] And when he has ordered them according to the above-mentioned distributions, if he wishes to exercise them in their orders, it would be enough to exercise them battalion by battalion. [160] And although the number of men in each of these cannot by itself form a complete army,[68] nonetheless, each man can learn to do what pertains to him particularly. For in the armies one observes two orders: one, what the men in each battalion must do; the other, what the battalion must then do

---

65. Lit.: heads of ten.

66. The first edition (1521) gives fifteen hundred, but Marchand et al. follow the two manuscripts that give six hundred.

67. Lit.: willingly.   68. Lit.: make the form of a just army.

when it is with the others in one army. [161] And those men who know the first well observe the second easily; but without knowing how to do the former, one can never reach the discipline of the second. [162] Thus, as I have said,[69] each of these battalions can by itself learn to keep the order of its files in every quality of motion and rest[70] and then, so as to learn to know how to put itself together, to understand the music by means of which it is commanded in battle. From the latter, like a galley oarsman from the whistle,[71] they learn to know how to recognize what they have to do, whether they have to stand firm, or go ahead, or turn back, or where to turn their arms and faces. [163] So since they know how to keep their files such that neither rest nor motion disorders them, and since they understand well the commands of the head by means of the music, and they know how to return to their place immediately, when many are put together, these battalions can then, as I said,[72] easily learn to do what their entire body is obliged to do together with the other battalions in a complete[73] army. [164] And because such general practice is also of no small esteem, one could bring together the whole brigade once or twice a year when there is peace, and give it the form of one entire army, drilling it some days as if it had to do battle, putting the front, sides, and followers in their places. [165] And because a captain orders his army for battle either on account of an enemy he sees or for one of which he is afraid without seeing it,[74] he should train his army in the one mode and in the other, and instruct it so that it can march and, if need be,[75] to fight, showing your[76] soldiers how they have to govern themselves when they are assaulted by the latter or by the former band. [166] And when he instructs it in fighting against an enemy they see, he shows them how to join battle, where they have to retreat if they are repelled, who has to follow in their place, and what signs, what sounds, and what words[77] they must obey, and to practice them thus so that by fake battles and assaults they have to desire true ones. [167] For a spirited army is not made so by having spirited men in it but by having well-ordered orders. For if I am among the first combatants, and I know where I have to retreat once I have been overcome and who has to follow in my place, I will always fight with spirit, see-

69. See *AW* II 123; cf. *AW* II 88–89.

70. Lit.: place (here and in the next sentence).

71. Cf. Dante, *Paradiso* XXV 133–35.   73. Lit.: just.

72. See *AW* II 160–61.

74. For training to fight an unseen but always feared enemy, see *D* III 38.

75. Lit.: if the need were to seek [the army] out.

76. Fabrizio switches to the familiar second person in the midst of repeated use of the third person.

77. Lit.: voices.

ing succor nearby. [168] If I am among the second combatants, when the first
ones are pushed and repelled I will not be afraid, because I will have presupposed that it can be so and I will have desired it so as to be the one who gives victory to my master, and not they. [169] These exercises are very necessary where
one makes a new army; and where an old army is, they are necessary. For even
though the Romans knew the orders of their armies from childhood, nonetheless one sees how those captains continually exercised them in them. [170] And
Josephus in his history says that the continual exercises of the Roman armies
made it that the whole mob that follows the camp so as to profit was useful in
battles.[78] For they all knew how to stay in their orders and to fight while keeping
them. [171] But in armies of new men, either those you put together to fight then
or those you make into a militia so as to fight in time, nothing is done without
these exercises, as much for a battalion by itself as for a whole army. For since
orders are necessary, one must show them with a double industry and effort to
those who do not know them and maintain them with those who do know them,
as one sees that by maintaining them and by teaching them many excellent captains have exhausted themselves without any hesitation.[79]

COSIMO. [172] It seems to me that this reasoning has somehow transported
you. For, having not yet described the modes in which the battalions are trained,
you have reasoned about the entire army and about battles.

FABRIZIO. [173] You speak the truth; and truly the cause of this has been the
affection I bear for these orders, and the sadness I feel at seeing that they are not
put into action. Nonetheless, do not doubt that I will return to the mark. [174]
As I said to you,[80] to know how to keep files well is of the first importance in
training a battalion. [175] To do this it is necessary to exercise them in the orders
they call the snails. [176] And because I told you that one of these battalions
should be of 400 infantrymen armed with heavy arms, I will stay with this number. [177] They must therefore be arranged in 80 files of five per file. [178] Then,
going either quickly or slowly, one must knot them together and open them out;
how one does this I can demonstrate more with deeds than with words. [179]
Then it is less necessary, because each one who is experienced[81] in armies knows
how this order proceeds, which is good only for accustoming soldiers to keep
their files. [180] But let's put together one of these battalions. [181] I say that one
gives them three principal forms. [182] The first, and the most useful, is to make
it altogether solid and to give it the form of two squares;[82] the second is to make

---

78. See Josephus, *The Jewish War* III 4 69 to 5 71, where the military training of slaves rather
than camp followers is discussed.

79. Lit.: respect.   81. Lit.: practiced.

80. See *AW* II 162 and note 69.   82. See figure 1, page 169.

the square with the horned front;[83] the third is to make it with a vacuum in the middle, which they call a piazza.[84] [183] The mode of putting together the first form[85] can be of two kinds. [184] One is to make the files double. That is, the second file enters into the first, the forth into the third, the sixth into the fifth, and so on successively; so that where there used to be eighty files of five per file, they become forty files of ten per file. [185] Then make them double another time in the same mode, by joining them together, one file into the other; and so there are twenty files of twenty men per file. [186] This makes about two squares.[86] For even though there are as many men on one side as on the other, nonetheless, on the side [on which] the heads are conjoined, one side touches the other, but on the other side, they are at least two braccia distant from one another, of a quality that the square is longer from back to front than from one flank to the other. [187] And because today we have to speak many times of the part in front, behind, and on the side of these battalions and of the whole army together, know that when I say either head or front, I mean the parts in front; when I say back, the part behind; when I say flanks, the parts on the side. [188] The fifty ordinary velites of the battalion are not mixed with the other files; rather, when the battalion is formed, they are extended along its flanks. [189] The other mode of putting together the battalion is this—and because it is better than the first, I wish to put before your eyes exactly how it should be ordered. [190] I believe that you remember the number of men, the heads it is composed of, and the arms it is armed with. [191] Thus, as I said,[87] the form that this battalion should have is of twenty files with twenty men per file: five files of pikes in front and fifteen files of shields in back. Two centurions are at the front and two behind at the back who do the office of those whom the ancients called *tergiduttori*. The constable with the flag and music is in the space that is between the five files of pikes and the fifteen of shields. One of the decurions is on each flank of the file so that each has his men at his side; those that will be on the left-hand side [of the file have their men] on their right-hand side, those that are on the right-hand side [of the file have their men] on their left-hand side. [192] The fifty velites are on the flanks and at the back of the battalion. [193] To want this battalion now to be put together in this form while the infantrymen are going ordinarily, it must be ordered thus: have the infantrymen be arranged in eighty files of five per file, as we said a little while ago,[88] leaving the velites either at the head or at the tail, still staying outside of this order; and it should be ordered so that each centurion has

83. See figure 2, top, page 170.
84. See figure 3, bottom, page 171.
85. See figure 1, page 169.

86. That is, a rectangle.
87. See *AW* II 185.
88. See *AW* II 177.

behind his back twenty files, and immediately behind each centurion are five files of pikes, and the rest are shields. [194] The constable is with the music and with the flag in the space that is between the pikes and the shields of the second centurion, and occupying the places of three shieldmen. [195] Of the decurions, twenty of them are on the flanks of the files of the first centurion, on their left-hand side, and twenty of them are on the flanks of the files of the last centurion, on their right-hand side. [196] And you have to understand that the decurions that guide the pikes should have a pike, and those that guide the shields should have similar arms. [197] Thus, having arranged the files in this order and wanting to arrange them on the march in a battalion so as to make a front, you have to make the first centurion stop with the first twenty files, and the second continue to march and, turning around to the right, go along the flanks of the twenty stopped files, so that he comes abreast of[89] the other centurion, where he stops as well. The third centurion continues to march and, turning to his right as well and along the flanks of the stopped files, marches so that he comes abreast of the other two centurions. When he too stops, the other centurion continues with his files, turning to his right along the flanks of the stopped files as well, so that he arrives at the front with the others, and then stops. At once two of the centurions leave the front alone and go to the rear of the battalion, which is made in the mode and with the exact order that we demonstrated a little while ago.[90] [198] The velites are extended along its flanks, according to the first mode [in which] it is arranged. The latter mode is called doubling by line; the former is said [to be] doubling by flank. [199] That first mode is easier. The latter is more orderly and comes out more exact and you are more able to correct it in your own mode. For in the former, one must obey the numbers, because you make five ten, ten twenty, twenty forty, such that, by doubling directly you cannot make a front of fifteen or of twenty five, nor of thirty or thirty five, but you need to go where that number leads you. [200] However, in particular actions it happens everyday that one must make a front with sixty or eighty infantrymen, so that doubling by straight line would disorder you. [201] Therefore, I like the latter one better; and the greater difficulty that it gives you must be made easy with practice and with training. [202] Therefore, I tell you that it is more important than anything to have soldiers who know how to put themselves in their orders quickly. And it is necessary to keep them in these battalions, to train them in them, and to make them go quickly either forward or backward, and to pass

89. Lit.: makes a head with. In its transitive form, this verb, which Machiavelli uses again later in this sentence, means "attest to, certify, witness."
90. See *AW* II 191.

through difficult places without disturbing their order. For soldiers who know how to do this well are practiced soldiers, and even though they have never seen the enemy face to face, they can be called old soldiers. [203] And those, on the contrary, who do not know how to keep these orders would always be esteemed as new soldiers [even] if they found themselves in a thousand wars. [204] This is with regard to putting them together when they are in small files while marching. [205] But having been put [together], and then, having been broken by some accident that arises either from the site or from the enemy, the important thing and the difficulty is to have them reorder themselves at once; this is where much training and much practice are needed, and where the ancients used to put forth much attention.[91] [206] It is therefore necessary to do two things: first, to have this battalion full of markers; the other, always to keep this order: that the same infantrymen always stay in the same files. [207] For instance, if one individual began standing in the second [file], he then always remains in that one; and not only in that same file, but in that same place; and to observe this, as I have said,[92] many markers are necessary. [208] First, it is necessary that the flag be marked so that when it comes together with the other battalions it is recognized by them. [209] Second, that the constable and the centurions have different and recognizable crests on their heads; and, what is more important, to order it that the decurions be recognized. [210] The ancients gave so much care to this that they even used to write the number on the helmet, calling them first, second, third, forth, etc. [211] And they were not content even with this, for each of the soldiers used to write on his shield the number of his file and the number of the place that he had in that file.[93] [212] So if the men are marked in this way and accustomed to stay within these limits, it is an easy thing immediately to reorder all of them when they have been disordered. For when the flag is firm, the centurions and the decurions can judge their place by eye; and the left ones having arranged themselves on the left and the right ones on the right at their accustomed distances, the infantrymen, guided by their rule and from the different markers, can be in their own places immediately. [This is] not otherwise than when you disconnect the staves of a barrel that you have first marked: you reorder it with very great ease; [but] having not marked it, it is impossible to reorder it. [213] With diligence and with training these things are quickly taught and quickly learned, and having been learned, are forgotten with difficulty. For the new men are guided by the old ones, and with these drills a province would in time become altogether practiced in war. [214] It is also necessary to teach them to turn themselves around and, if need be, to make the front with their

91. Lit.: study.   93. Vegetius II 13, 18.
92. See *AW* II 206.

flanks and their back, and the flanks and the back from their front. [215] This is very easy, because it is enough that each man turn his person toward the part he is commanded; and where they turn their faces ends up being the front. [216] It is true that when they turn to the flank, the orders go out of proportion, because from chest to back it is a small distance, and from one side to the other it is a long distance, which is altogether against the ordinary order of the battalion. [217] Therefore, practice and discretion must rearrange them. [218] But this is a small disorder because they remedy it easily by themselves. [219] But what is more important, and where more practice is needed, is when one wants a battalion to turn around altogether as if it were a solid body. [220] Here much practice and much discretion are needed. For wanting to turn to the left, for instance, the left horn[94] needs to stop, and those who are nearer to whomever [it is that] is standing still walk so slowly that those who are on the right do not have to run; otherwise, everything would be confounded.

[221] But because it always happens, when an army marches from place to place, that the battalions which are not posted in the front have to fight not at the head but at the flank or the back, so that a battalion at once has to make the front from the flank or from the back (and wanting battalions like these in such a case to keep their proportion, according to what was demonstrated above,[95] it is necessary that they have the pikes on the flank that has to be the head, and the decurions, centurions, and constables, balanced with it in their places)—to want to do this, in putting them together you therefore need to order the eighty files of five per file thus:[96] put all the pikes in the first twenty files, and put five of their decurions in the first place and five of them in the last place. The other sixty files, which come behind, are all shields that come to be three centuries. [222] Thus one wants the first and the last file of each century to be decurions, the constable with the flag and with the music to be in the middle of the first century of shields, and the centurions to be at the head of each century. [223] Ordered thus, if you want the pikes to come to the left flank, you have to double them century by century on the right flank;[97] if you want them to come on the right flank, you have to double them on the left. [224] So this battalion winds up with its pikes on one flank, with the decurions at the head and at the back, with the centurions along the head, and the constable in the middle. [225] It keeps that form while on the go; but as the enemy, as well as the time at which it wants to make

94. That is, the left wing, as in figure 3, page 171, where each wing protrudes.

95. See *AW* II 214–17.   96. See figure 2, page 170.

97. That is, each century stops in turn and the following one moves around to the left of the stopped one as described in *AW* II 197.

its flank its head, approach, it has nothing to do except to turn the faces of all the soldiers toward the flank where the pikes are. And then the battalion winds up with the files and with the heads in the mode [in which] it was ordered above. For all, except the centurions, are in their places, and the centurions at once and without difficulty enter theirs.

[226] But when it has to fight at its back while marching ahead, in putting them into a battalion, one must order the files so that the pikes come along behind. To do this, one does not have to keep another order, except that where, in ordering the battalion, every century ordinarily has five files of pikes in front, it has them in back; and in all the other parts [one has] to observe the order that I mentioned first.[98]

COSIMO. [227] You said, if I remember well, that this mode of training is for being able to order these battalions together into one army later, and that this practice serves to enable them to order themselves into the latter. [228] But if it were to happen that these 450 infantrymen had to make a separate action, how would you order them?

FABRIZIO. [229] Then whoever guides them must judge where he wants to locate the pikes and put them there. [230] This is not inconsistent in any part with the order written above.[99] For even though that is the mode that is observed for doing battle together with the other battalions, it is nonetheless not a rule that is of use for all those modes in which you may happen to have to manage. [231] But in showing you the other two modes of ordering the battalions I placed, I will satisfy your question even more. For either they are never used or they are used when a battalion is alone and not in the company of others. [232] And so as to come to the mode of ordering it with two horns,[100] I say that you must order the 80 files of five per file in this mode: put a centurion there in the middle, and after him, 25 files that have two pikes on the left and three shields on the right. And after the first five, twenty decurions are placed in the following twenty [files], all between the pikes and the shields, except for those that carry pikes, who can stay with the pikes. [233] After these 25 files so ordered, another centurion is placed who has behind him 15 files of shields. [234] The constable, between the music and the flag, [is placed] after these. He also has behind him another 15 files of shields. [235] After these is placed the third centurion, and he has behind him 25 files. In every one of the latter are three shields on the left and two pikes on the right; and after the first five files [of this last group of twenty-five files] are twenty decurions posted between the pikes and the shields. [236]

98. See AW II 191 ff.

99. Apparently a reference to figure 1, page 169.

100. See figure 3, top, page 171.

After these files is the fourth centurion. [237] Therefore, in wanting to make a battalion with two horns from these files so ordered, the first centurion has to stop with the 25 files that are in back. [238] Then the second centurion has to move with the 15 shieldmen files that are at his back, and has to turn around to the right hand [of the first twenty-five files] and go along the right flank of the twenty-five files until it arrives at the fifteenth file, and has to stop here. [239] Then, with the fifteen files of shields that are behind him, the constable has to move; and turning to the right as well, he marches along the right flank of the fifteen files first moved, until he arrives at their head, and stops here. [240] Then the third centurion moves with his twenty-five files and with the fourth centurion that was in back, and turning to the right as well, marches along the right flank of the last fifteen files of shieldmen, and does not stop when he is at its head but continues marching until the last of the twenty-five files is even with its last file. [241] And, having done this, the centurion who was the head of the first fifteen files of shieldmen leaves where he was and goes to the back on the left corner. [242] So a battalion will wind up with 15[101] firm files of twenty infantrymen per file, with two horns, one on each side of the front. And each [horn] will have ten files of five per file, and between the two horns a space will remain that is as much as ten men take up who turn their sides to one another. [243] The captain will be between the two horns; [and] one centurion [will be] on each point of a horn. [244] Also, on each side of the back will be one centurion. [245] Two files of pikes and twenty decurions are on each flank. [246] These two horns serve to keep between them the artillery, when this battalion has it with it, and the wagons. [247] The velites have to remain in place on the flanks along the pikes. [248] But to want to arrange this horned battalion into a piazza,[102] one needs to do nothing other than to take 8 of the 15 files of 20 per file and put them on the points of the two horns, which, from [being] horns, then become the back of the piazza. [249] In this piazza the wagons are kept and the captain and the flag stay there, but no longer the artillery, which is put either in the front or along the flanks. [250] These are the modes of a battalion that one can keep when it must pass alone through suspected places. [251] Nonetheless, the solid battalion, without horns and without a piazza, is better. [252] However, if you wish to secure the unarmed, the horned one is necessary.

[253] The Swiss make many forms of the battalion as well. Among these they make one in the mode of a cross. For in the spaces that are between its arms,[103]

---

101. Following Marchand et al. and figure 3 rather than the text of the original 1521 edition, which gives the number twenty-five.

102. See figure 3, bottom, page 171.

103. *Ramo*, neither weapons *(arme)* nor the upper limbs of the body *(braccia)*.

they keep their arquebusiers from the charge of the enemy. [254] But because battalions like these are good for fighting by themselves, and my intention is to show how several united battalions fight together against the enemy, I do not want otherwise to fatigue myself in demonstrating them.

COSIMO. [255] It seems to me that I have understood very well the mode that one must hold to train men in these battalions. But if I remember well, you said[104] that besides the ten battalions you would add to the brigade a thousand extraordinary pikes and 500 extraordinary velites. [256] Wouldn't you want to conscript and train these?

FABRIZIO. [257] I would, and with very great diligence. [258] And the pikes at least I would exercise flag by flag in the orders of their battalion, like the others. For I would make use of these more than of the ordinary battalions in all particular actions, such as escorting, plundering, and similar things. [259] But the velites I would train at home without bringing them together. For since it is their office to fight scattered, it is not necessary that they come together with the others in the common drills. So it would be enough to train them well in their particular drills. [260] Thus, as I said at first[105]—and it does not seem tiresome to me to repeat it now—one must make one's men train in these battalions, so that they know how to keep their files, to recognize their places, and to return to them at once when either the enemy or the site perturbs them. For when one knows how to do this, one then easily learns the place that a battalion has to keep and what its own office in the army is. [261] And when a prince or a republic endures exertion and puts diligence into these orders and these drills, it will always happen that the soldiers in his country will be good, and they will be superior to their neighbors and will be those who give laws and not those who receive them from other men. [262] But, as I have said to you,[106] the disorder in which one lives [today] makes it that these things are not cared for and are not esteemed. And, therefore, our armies are not good. And even if there were heads or members naturally virtuous, they could not demonstrate it.

COSIMO. [263] What wagons would you want each of these battalions to have?

FABRIZIO. [264] First, I would want neither centurions nor decurions to have to go on horseback. And if the constable wants to ride, I would want him to have a mule and not a horse. [265] I would, indeed, allow two wagons for him and one for each centurion and two for every three decurions. For we quarter that many in the encampment, as we will say in its place,[107] such that each bat-

104. See AW II 150.   106. See AW I 132, II 137–39.
105. See AW II 140 ff.; cf. AW II 123.
107. No mention is made of wagons in the discussion of the encampment at AW VI 8 ff.

talion would come to have 36 wagons. Of necessity, these I would want to carry the tents, the cooking vessels, hatchets, and enough iron stakes to make the camps, and then, if they can, other [things] for their comfort.

COSIMO. [266] I believe that the heads ordered by you in each of these battalions are necessary; nonetheless, I would doubt that so many commanders would not confuse one another.

FABRIZIO. [267] This would be so if they were not responsible to one individual; but since they are responsible, they make order. Indeed, without them it is impossible to stand firm. For a wall that leans in every part wants many and frequent supports, even if they are not so strong, rather than a few, even if hardy. For the virtue of one alone cannot remedy its ruin at a distance. [268] Therefore, in the armies, and among every ten men, there must be one of more life, of more heart, or at least of more authority, who with his spirit, with his words, and with his example keeps the others firm and disposed to fight. [269] And one sees that we have in our armies the things said by me to be necessary in an army, like heads, flags, and musicians. But no one does his office. [270] First, to want decurions to do that for which they are ordered, it is necessary, as I said, that each one have his own distinct men, lodge with them, take actions and be in the orders with them. For, located in their places, they are like a line and a guide[108] to maintain the files straight and firm. And it is impossible that they disorder them or, being disordered, that they not rearrange them in their places. [271] But we do not use them today except to give them more money than the others and to have them take particular actions. [272] The same thing happens with the flags, for they are held to make a beautiful show rather than for another military use. [273] But the ancients used them as a guide and for reordering. For when the flag had stopped, each knew the place that he kept near his flag and always returned there. [274] [Each] also knew that, when it moved or[109] stood still, they had to stop or to move. [275] Therefore, it is necessary that there be many bodies in an army, and that each body have its own flag and its own guide. For having this, it must have many souls and, as a consequence, many lives. [276] Thus the infantrymen must march according to the flag, and the flag move according to the music. The music, having been well ordered, commands the army, which, while going with steps that correspond to its time, ends up keeping the orders easily. [277] This is why the ancients had pipes, fifes, and perfectly modulated instruments. For just as he who dances proceeds with the time of the music and while going with it does not err, so an army, while obeying that music in moving, does not get disordered. [278] And, therefore, they used to vary the music in

---

108. Or: a staff and a timbre.   109. Lit.: and.

accord with how they wanted to vary the motion, and in accord with how they wanted to enflame or quiet or firm up the spirits of the men. [279] And as the music varied, they used to name them variously. [280] The Dorian music generated constancy, the Phrygian, fury; hence they say that while Alexander was at table and one individual played Phrygian music, it so inflamed his spirit that he put his hand to his arms.[110] [281] It would be necessary to find all of these modes again, and if this were difficult, one would at least not want to leave behind those that teach the soldier to obey. Each can vary and order these to his own mode, as long as with practice he accustoms the ears of his soldiers to recognize them. [282] But today for the most part no fruit is gained from this music other than the making of the noise.

COSIMO. [283] I would like to understand from you, if you yourself have ever discoursed on it, from where so much vileness and so much disorder and so much neglect of this training arise in these times.

FABRIZIO. [284] I will willingly tell you what I think about this. [285] Of the many men excellent in war, you know how there have been many so named in Europe, few in Africa, and less in Asia. [286] This arises because these last two parts of the world have had one or two principalities and few republics; but Europe alone has had several kingdoms and infinite republics. [287] Men become excellent and show their virtue according to [whether] they are used and brought forth by their prince, be he a republic or a king. [288] Therefore, where there are many powers, many valiant men must spring up; where there are few of them, few. [289] In Asia one finds Ninus, Cyrus, Artaxerxes, and Mithridates,[111] and very few others who keep company with these. [290] In Africa, leaving Egyptian antiquity be, Massinissa, Jugurtha,[112] and those captains who were raised by the Carthaginian republic are named. These too, with respect to those of Europe, are very few. For in Europe there are excellent men without number, and there would be many more if together with them the others were named who have been extinguished by the malignity of time. For the world has been more virtuous where there have been more states that have favored virtue, either by necessity or by another human passion. [291] Thus, few men sprang up in Asia, because that province was altogether under one kingdom in which, due to

---

110. See Seneca II 2; Roberto Valturio, *De Rei Militari* II 3.

111. Ninus is the legendary founder of the Assyrian empire (cf. *L'Asino*, lines 88 ff.); Cyrus (559–486 B.C.) was the founder of the Persian Empire and the subject of Xenophon's *Education of Cyrus* (cf. *P* 6.22–23, 24, 14.60, 16.64, 26.102; *D* II 12.1, 13.1, III 20, 22.4, 22.5, 39.1); the reference is most likely to Artaxerxes II, king of Persia (404–359 B.C.) and the subject of Plutarch's *Artaxerxes;* Mithridates VI was king of Pontus (ca. 132–63) (cf. *D* III 13.3, *AW* IV 68).

112. Massinissa was king of Numidia (213–206) and an ally of Rome during the Second Punic War (218–201 B.C.) (cf. *D* II 1.3, 30.2); Jugurtha was king of Numidia (118–103 B.C.) (cf. *D* II 8.1).

the magnitude [of the province of Asia], men excellent in their deeds could not arise, since [that kingdom] was idle most of the time. [292] The same happened in Africa. If it raised more of them there, however, it is on account of[113] the Carthaginian republic. [293] For excellent men come from republics more than from kingdoms, because in the former most of the time virtue is honored; in kingdoms it is feared. From this it arises that, in the one, virtuous men are born, in the other, they are extinguished. [294] Thus, whoever considers the case of Europe will find it to have been full of republics or principalities which, through the fear that one had of the other, were constrained to keep military orders alive and to honor those who most prevailed in them. [295] For in Greece, besides the kingdom of the Macedonians, there were many republics, and in each of these very excellent men arose. [296] In Italy were the Romans, the Samnites, the Tuscans, and the Cisalpine Gauls. [297] France and Germany were[114] full of republics and princes; Spain, the same. [298] And although compared to the Romans one can name few others, this arises from the malignity of the writers, who follow fortune, and for them most of the time it is enough to honor the victors. [299] But it is not reasonable that among the Samnites and the Tuscans, who fought for a hundred and fifty years with the Roman people before they were conquered, very many excellent men did not arise. [300] And, likewise, so [it is] in France and Spain. [301] But that virtue which the writers do not celebrate in particular men, they celebrate in peoples, where they exalt all the way to the stars the obstinacy that was in them for defending their liberty.[115] [302] Since it is true that where there are more empires, more valiant men spring up, it follows of necessity that, when the former are extinguished, virtue is extinguished little by little, since the causes that make men virtuous come less. [303] Therefore, when the Roman Empire later grew, and when it had extinguished all the republics and principalities of Europe and of Africa and the greater part of those of Asia, it did not leave any way to virtue, except Rome. [304] From this it arose that virtuous men began to be as few in Europe as in Asia. That virtue then came to ultimate decline. For, when all virtue was brought to Rome, as it was corrupt, almost all the world ended up being corrupt. And the Scythian peoples were able to come to prey upon the empire that had extinguished the virtue of the others and did not know how to maintain its own. [305] And although that empire was then divided in several parts through the inundation of these barbarians, this virtue was not reborn there. One reason for this is that[116] one suffers a bit to recover orders when they are spoiled; the other reason is that[117] today's mode of living, on

---

113. Lit.: with respect to.
114. The verb is singular in Italian.
115. Cf. *D* II 2.

116. Lit.: one, because.
117. Lit.: the other, because.

account of[118] the Christian religion, does not impose that necessity to defend oneself that there was in antiquity. For then, men conquered in war were either killed or remained in perpetual slavery, where they led their lives miserably. Their conquered towns were either dissolved or, their goods taken, the inhabitants were driven out and sent dispersed throughout the world. So those overcome in war suffered every last misery. [306] Frightened by this fear, men kept military training alive and honored whoever was excellent in it. [307] But today this fear is for the most part lost. Of the conquered, few of them are killed; no one is kept in prison for long, because they are freed with ease. [308] Even though they have rebelled a thousand times, cities are not demolished and men are left with their goods, so that the greatest evil that is feared is a ransom. So men do not want to submit themselves to military orders and to struggle along beneath them so as to flee those dangers they little fear. [309] These provinces of Europe are then under very few heads, as compared to[119] before. For all France obeys one king, all Spain another, and Italy is in few parts, so that the weak cities defend themselves by siding with whoever wins, and the hardy states, for the causes mentioned, do not fear an ultimate ruin.

COSIMO. [310] However, during the last twenty-five years[120] one has seen many towns put to sack here, as well as the loss of kingdoms. That example should teach the others how to live and recover some of the ancient orders.

FABRIZIO. [311] It is as you say; but if you note which towns have been put to sack, you will find that they are not the heads of states but among their members, as one sees that Tortona was sacked and not Milan, Capua and not Naples, Brescia and not Venice, Ravenna and not Rome.[121] [312] These examples do not make whoever governs change their presupposition. Indeed, it makes them stay more in their opinion of being able to buy themselves back with ransoms; and because of this they do not want to undergo the exertions of the training for war, since, on the one hand, it seems to them unnecessary and, on the other hand, a tangle they do not understand. [313] Those others who are servants, whom such examples should make afraid, do not have the power to remedy things. The latter princes have no more time through having lost their states; and those that have [time], do not know how and do not want [to remedy things]. For they want to remain without any hardship by fortune and not by their own virtue.

---

118. Lit.: with respect to.   119. Lit.: respect to.

120. Twenty-five years before the time of the narration of the dialogue would be 1494, the year that Charles VIII invaded Italy; twenty-five years before the apparent time of the setting of the dialogue would be 1491; see the introduction, pages xvii–xviii.

121. The French sacked Tortona in 1499, Capua in 1501, and Brescia and Ravenna in 1512 (for Capua, see P 25.104; for Brescia, see D II 17.1, 24.3, III 44.3; and for Ravenna, see note 29).

For they see that, through there being little virtue here, fortune governs everything, and they want it to be the lord of them, not themselves to be the lord of it.
[314] [As evidence] that what I have discussed[122] is true, consider Germany: in it
there is much virtue through there being many principalities and republics, and
all that is good in the present military depends on the example of those peoples,
who, since they are altogether jealous of their states and since they fear servitude
(which is not feared elsewhere),[123] all maintain themselves lords and honored.
[315] I want having said this to be enough to show the causes of the present vileness, according to my opinion. [316] I do not know if it seems the same to you,
or if some doubt arose in you though this reasoning.

COSIMO. [317] None. Indeed, I understand everything very well. [318] Returning to our principal matter, I desire only to understand from you how you
would order the cavalrymen in these battalions, and how many [they would be]
and how [they would be] captained and how [they would be] armed.

FABRIZIO. [319] Perhaps it seems to you that I have left them behind. Do
not marvel at that, for I am speaking little about it for two reasons: one, because
the sinew and the important thing about the army is the infantry; the other, because this part of the military is less corrupt than that of the infantrymen. For if
it is not stronger than the ancient [cavalry], it is equal. [320] Also, the mode of
exercising them was mentioned a little earlier.[124] [321] And as to arming them,
I would arm them as is done at present, the light cavalrymen as well as the
men-at-arms. [322] But I would want all the light cavalrymen to be crossbowmen
with some arquebusiers among them who, although in the other managements
of war are not very useful, are very useful in this: frightening peasants and removing them from a pass that had been guarded by them. For one arquebusier
will make them more afraid than twenty other armed [men]. [323] But coming
to their number, and having taken the Roman military to imitate, I say that I
would not order more than three hundred useful cavalrymen for each battalion.
Of these, I would want 150 to be men-at-arms and 150 to be light cavalrymen.
And I would give one head to each of these parts, making then 15 decurions per
band among them, giving to each one musician[125] and one flag. [324] I would
want every ten men-at-arms to have five wagons and every ten light cavalrymen
two, which, like those of the infantrymen, carry tents, vessels, and axes and
stakes, and other tools of theirs, if [room] is left over. [325] And do not believe
that this is disorderly, seeing how the men-at-arms nowadays have four horses

---

122. Lit.: discoursed about.   124. See *AW* II 128–29.

123. Parentheses in original.

125. Lit.: one sound; translated elsewhere as "music."

in their service. For such a thing is a corruption. For in Germany one sees those men-at-arms alone with their own horses, every twenty having only one wagon that carries behind them their necessary things. [326] The cavalrymen of the Romans were likewise alone. It is true that the *triarii* lodged near by the cavalry and were obliged to administer aid to it in the governance of the horses. This can be easily imitated by us, as will be shown to you in the distribution of the encampments.[126] [327] Thus, what the Romans did and what the Germans do today, we too can do. Indeed, by not doing it, one errs. [328] These cavalrymen, ordered and conscripted together with the brigade, could sometimes be put together when the battalion is assembled, and made to make some show[127] of a fight between them; this would be more for them to get to know one another than for another necessity. [329] But enough has now been said of this part. Let us descend to give form to an army so as to be able to present battle to the enemy and hope to conquer him, which thing is the end for which the military is ordered and for which so much study is put into it.

126. See *AW* VI 8 ff.   127. Lit.: sight.

BOOK THREE

COSIMO. [1] Since we are changing the discussion, I want the questioner to be changed, for I would not want to be held presumptuous—something I have always blamed in others. [2] Therefore, I put down the dictatorship and give this authority to whichever of these other friends of mine wants it.

ZANOBI. [3] It would be very gratifying for us were you to continue. But since you do not want to, at least say which of us must succeed to your place.

COSIMO. [4] I want to give this burden to the lord.

FABRIZIO. [5] I am content to take it, and I want us to follow the Venetian custom [according to which] the youngest speaks first. For since this training is for the young, I am persuaded that the young are more fit to reason about it, as they are more quick to execute it.

COSIMO. [6] Then it's your turn, Luigi. [7] And I am as pleased with such a successor, as you will be satisfied with such a questioner. [8] Therefore, I beg[1] that we return to the material and not lose more time.

FABRIZIO. [9] I am certain that in wanting to demonstrate well how one orders an army to do battle, it would be necessary to tell how the Greeks and the Romans used to order the lines in their armies. [10] Nonetheless, since you yourselves can read and consider these things by means of the ancient writers, I will leave many particulars behind and adduce only those things about them that seem to me necessary to imitate, wanting in our times to give to our military some parts of perfection. [11] This will make me show at one time how one may order an army for battle, how one may engage in true fights, and how one may train it in fake ones. [12] The greatest disorder that those who order an army for battle make is to give it only one front and obligate it to one thrust and one

---

1. Lit.: pray.

fortune. [13] This arises from having lost the mode that the ancients had of receiving one line into the other. For without this mode, one cannot assist the first
[men], or defend them, or follow in their place in the fight; this had been observed by the Romans in the best way. [14] Wanting to show this mode, I say that
the Romans used to divide each legion into three parts—into *hastati, principes,*
and *triarii.* Of these, the *hastati* were put in the first front of the army with dense
and firm orders. Behind these were the *principes,* but placed with their orders
more spaced. After these they put the *triarii* with orders so spaced that when
needed they were able to receive between them the *principes* and the *hastati.*
[15] Besides these, they had slingers and crossbowmen and others lightly armed
who did not stay in these orders; rather, they located them at the head of the
army between the cavalrymen and the infantrymen. [16] These lightly armed
[men], then, joined the fight; if they won, which occurred rarely, they pursued
the victory; if they were repulsed, they withdrew along the flanks of the army
or through the intervals ordered to such an effect, and they arranged themselves among the unarmed.[2] [17] After their departure, the *hastati* came to hands
with the enemy. If these were seen to be overcome, they withdrew little by little
through the spaces in the orders between the *principes* and together with these
they renewed the fight. [18] If these too were forced [back], they all withdrew
into the spaces in the orders of the *triarii* and, having made one mass, they
recommenced the fight all together. If these lost, there was no more remedy for
them because no further mode of remaking themselves remained for them.[3] [19]
The cavalrymen, placed like two wings on a body, stayed on the sides of the
army; at one moment they fought with the cavalrymen, at another they helped
the infantrymen, as need demanded.[4] [20] This mode of remaking themselves
three times is almost impossible to overcome, for fortune needs to abandon you
three times and the enemy to have so much virtue that he beats you three times.[5]
[21] The Greeks with their phalanxes did not have this mode of remaking themselves; and although in the latter there were many heads and many orders,
nonetheless they made one body, or rather, one head. [22] The mode that they
held to in assisting one another was not to withdraw one order into the other,
like the Romans, but for one man to enter the place of the other. [23] They did
so in this mode: their phalanx was arranged in files; and let us suppose that they

2. See Vegetius II 17.

3. See Livy VIII 8; cf. *D* II 16. Against Livy's account, Piero Pieri makes a strong case that the
maneuvers described above were not performed on the battlefield, but were instead training exercises only (Piero Pieri, *Guerra e politica negli scrittori italiani* (Milan: Riccardo Riccardi, 1955),
31–36).

4. See Vegetius II 15.   5. See Livy VIII 8.

placed fifty men in each file, coming then with their head against the enemy; of all the files, the first six were able to fight, for their lances, which they called sarisses, were so long that the sixth file passed beyond the first file with the point of their own lances. [24] Thus, while fighting, if someone from the first [file] fell dead or wounded, the one who was behind in the second file immediately entered in his place. And into the place that was empty in the second [file], that [man who] was behind in the third [file] entered. Thus, the files behind at once successively restored the defects of those in front, so that the files always remained entire and no place was empty of combatants, except the last file, which came to be consumed by not having behind its back anyone who would restore it. So the harms that the first files suffered consumed the last, and the first always remained entire. Thus, these phalanxes, through their order, could be consumed rather than broken, for their thick body made them more immobile.[6] [25] In the beginning, the Romans used phalanxes, and they instructed their legions to be like them. [26] Later, they did not like this order, and they divided the legions into more bodies; that is, into cohorts and maniples.[7] For as I said a little while ago,[8] they judged that that body had more life which had more souls and was composed of more parts, so that each stood firm.[9] [27] In these times, the brigades of the Swiss use all the modes of the phalanx, as much in ordering themselves in mass and as a whole, as in assisting one another. And in doing battle, they put one brigade on the flank of the other; if they put one behind the other, they have no mode by which the first, when it withdraws, can be received by the second. Instead, so as to be able to assist one another, they keep this order: they put one brigade in front and another behind it on its right hand, such that if the first has need of help, the other can go ahead and give it aid. [28] The third brigade they put behind these, but at a distance of one arquebus shot. [29] They do this because, if the former two are repulsed, the latter can go ahead, and they have space for it; and the repulsed ones and those that are put ahead avoid charging into one another. For a large multitude cannot be received like a small body, and therefore the small and distinct bodies that were in a Roman legion could be located so that they could be received among them and assist each other with ease. [30] And many examples of the Roman legions demonstrate that this order of the Swiss is not as good as the ancient Roman one when they fought with the Greek phalanxes. The latter were always consumed by the former for, as

6. See Polybius XVIII 28–30 and Livy IX 19 for the most detailed ancient discussions of the Macedonian phalanx.

7. Livy VIII 8.   9. Or: rule itself (reggersi).

8. See AW II 275.

I said before, this kind of arms and this mode of remaking themselves could do more than the solidity of the phalanxes. [31] Thus, having to order an army according to[10] these examples, to me it seems [well] to retain the arms and modes of the Greek phalanxes, on the one hand, and of the Roman legions, on the other. Therefore, in one brigade I said[11] I wanted two thousand pikes, which are the arms of the Macedonian phalanxes, and three thousand shields with swords, which are the arms of the Romans. [32] I divided the brigade into ten battalions, like the Romans, whose legion [was divided] into ten cohorts. [33] I ordered the velites, that is, the light armed [troops], to join the fight like them. [34] And because the orders should also partake of [those of] one nation and the other, just as the arms are mixed and partake of[12] [both] of them, I ordered each battalion to have five files of pikes in front and the rest to be shields, so as to be able to withstand cavalrymen at the front and enter easily into the battalions of the enemy on foot, having the pikes in the first encounter, like the enemy. I want them to be enough to withstand him, and the shields then to beat him. [35] And if you observe the virtue of this order, you will see all of these arms doing their offices entirely. For the pikes are useful against cavalrymen, and when they come against infantrymen, they do their office well before the fight is joined. For once it is joined, they become useless. [36] Hence, the Swiss, so as to flee this inconvenience, put a file of halberds after every three files of pikes. They do this to give the pikes space, which is not as much as is needed. [37] Our pikes being placed ahead and our shields behind thus end up withstanding cavalrymen and, in joining the fight, open[13] and molest the infantrymen. But after the battle is joined,[14] and they become useless, the shields and swords, which can manage in any narrowness, follow.

LUIGI [38] We are now waiting with desire to understand how you would order the army for battle with these arms and with these orders.

FABRIZIO. [39] I now want to show you nothing but this. [40] You have to understand how in an ordinary Roman army, which they called a consular army, there were not more than two legions of Roman citizens [each of] which had six hundred cavalrymen and around eleven thousand infantrymen. [41] They then had as many cavalrymen and infantrymen sent to them by their friends and confederates, which they divided in two parts. They called one the right horn and the other the left horn. Nor did they ever permit these auxiliary infantrymen to pass beyond the number of infantrymen of their legions. They were quite con-

10. Lit.: with.
11. See *AW* II 70.
12. Lit.: participate in, here and below.
13. That is, break up the ordered ranks and files of the infantrymen.
14. Lit.: tightened.

tent that the number of cavalrymen be more. [42] With this army, which had 22 thousand infantrymen and around two thousand useful cavalrymen, one consul took every action and went on every campaign.[15] [43] However, when there was a need to oppose greater forces, they brought together two consuls with two armies. [44] You should also notice that ordinarily in all three of the armies' principal actions, that is, marching, encamping, and fighting, they put the legions in the middle.[16] For they wanted the virtue in which they had more confidence to be more united, as will be shown to you in the reasoning about all three of these actions. [45] These auxiliary infantrymen, through the practice that they had with the legionary infantrymen, were as useful as the latter. For, like them, they were disciplined, and therefore in ordering for battle they ordered them in a like mode. [46] So anyone who knows how the Romans arranged one legion of the army for battle knows how they arranged the whole. [47] Therefore, since I have told you[17] how they divided one legion into three lines, and how the one line received the other, I have ended up having to tell you how the whole army is ordered in a battle.

[48] Therefore, since I want to order a battle as the Romans [did], I will take two brigades just as they had two legions, and having placed these, the disposition of one whole army will be understood. For in adding more men, one will have to do nothing other than enlarge the orders. [49] I do not believe that I need to remind you how many infantrymen one brigade has, how it has ten battalions, what the heads of a battalion are, what arms they have, what the ordinary pikes and velites are, and what the extraordinary ones are. For I told you distinctly a little while ago, and reminded you to commit it to memory as a thing necessary for [one] wanting to understand all of the other orders.[18] I will therefore come to the demonstration of the order without repeating anything else.[19]
[50] It seems [well] to me that the ten battalions of one brigade be put on the left flank and the other ten from the other on the right. [51] Those on the left are ordered in this mode: five battalions are placed from one side of the front to the other, such that between one and the other a space of four braccia remains, so that they come to occupy 141 braccia of ground in width and 40 in length. [52] Behind these five battalions I would put three others in a straight line from the first at a distance of 40 braccia. Two of these should come in a straight line

---

15. See Polybius VI 26, where it is said that the Roman infantry usually equaled the infantry of their allies; cf. Livy XL 36, where it is said that the allies always had fifteen thousand infantry, considerably more than the Roman infantry.

16. See Polybius VI 26.   18. See *AW* II 157.

17. See *AW* III 14–20.

19. For the following discussion, see figure 4, page 172.

behind the extreme [left and right] of the [first five battalions], and the other should take the space in the middle. [53] And thus, in width and length, these three would come to occupy the same space as the five [in front]. But where the [first] five have a distance of four braccia between one and the other, these [three] would have [a distance] of 33. [54] After these I would likewise put the last two battalions behind the three [middle battalions], in a straight line and at a distance of 40 braccia from the three [middle battalions]. And I would put each one of these behind the extreme [right and left] of the three, such that the space that remains between the one and the other would be 91 braccia. [55] All of these battalions so ordered would be 141 braccia in width and 200 in length. [56] I would extend the extraordinary pikes along the flanks of the left side of these battalions, 20 braccia distant from the latter, making them 143 files of 7 per file, so that with their length they would cover the whole left side of the battalions ordered in the mode stated by me. And that would leave forty files to guard the wagons and the unarmed who would remain at the tail of the army, distributing the decurions and the centurions in their places. Of the three constables, I would put one of them at the head, the other in the middle, and the third in the last file, which does the office of *tergiduttore*,[20] for so the ancients called him who was posted at the back of the army. [57] But returning to the head of the army, I say that I would locate the extraordinary velites, which you know are 500, next to the extraordinary pikes, and I would give them a space of 40 braccia. [58] To the side of these, again on the left hand, I would put the men-at-arms, and I would want them to have a space of 150 braccia. [59] After these, [I would place] the light cavalrymen, which I would give the same space as the men-at-arms. [60] The ordinary velites, which would stay in the spaces that I put between one battalion and another, I would leave around their own battalions so that they would be like ministers of the latter, if it should not yet seem [well] to me to put them under the extraordinary pikes. I would do this, or not, according to what turns out to be more to my purpose. [61] The head-general of the whole brigade I would put in the space that is between the first and second orders of the battalions, or else at the head and in the space that is between the last battalion of the first five and the extraordinary pikes, according to what turns out to be more to my purpose, with 30 or 40 men around, chosen because they are known for prudence in executing a commission and for strength in withstanding a thrust; and he too is in the middle of the music and the flag. [62] This is the order in which I would arrange one brigade on the left part, which would be the disposition of half of the army. It would take up 511 braccia in width, and in length as much as was said

20. Rearguard.

above, not counting the space, which would be around one hundred braccia, taken up by that part of the extraordinary pikes which makes a shield for the unarmed. [63] The other brigade I would arrange on the right side, in the exact mode in which I have arranged the one on the left, leaving a space of 30 braccia between the one brigade and the other. At the head of this space I would put some artillery carts, behind which would be the captain-general of the whole army. He would have around him, with the music and the flag captain, at least 200 selected men, for the most part on foot, among whom would be ten or more fit to execute any commandment, and [who] would be on horseback and armed so that they would be able to be on horseback or on foot, as the need may require. [64] [As to] the artillery of the army, ten cannons, whose [ordnance] does not exceed fifty pounds of weight, are enough for storming towns. In the field I would use these more for the defense of the encampment than for making battle; [the ordnance of] all of the other artillery would weigh ten rather than fifteen pounds. [65] I would put this at the front of the whole army, unless of course the land[21] lies so that I can locate it along the flank in a secure place where it cannot be charged by the enemy. [66] This form of the army so ordered can keep the order of the phalanxes and of the Roman legions while fighting. For in the front are the pikes, and all the infantrymen are ordered in files so that when they join with the enemy and withstand him, they can restore the first files with those behind in the manner of the phalanxes. [67] On the other hand, if they are charged so that they are necessitated to break orders and withdraw, they are able to enter the intervals of the second battalions which are behind, to unite with them, and having made a mass anew, to withstand the enemy and fight him [68] And when this is not enough, they can withdraw in the same mode a second time, and fight a third, so that in fighting in this order there is remaking both according to the Greek mode and according to the Roman. [69] As to the strength of the army, it cannot be ordered stronger. For one and the other horn is very well provided with heads and with arms.[22] Nor is the rest weak except the part behind the unarmed; and even that has its flanks covered by the extraordinary pikes. [70] Nor can the enemy assault any part that he does not find ordered. And the part behind cannot be assaulted because there cannot be an enemy who has so many forces that he can assail you equally on every side. For if he has them, you do not have to put yourself in the field against him. [71] But when he is a third more than you and, like you, [is] well ordered, and if he weakens himself so as to assault you in more places and you break one part of him, all

---

21. *Paese*, usually translated "country."
22. Weapons *(arme)*, not upper limbs *(braccia)*.

goes badly [for him]. [72] You are very secure against cavalrymen, when they are more than yours. For the orders of pikes that cover you defend you from their every thrust, even when your cavalrymen have been repulsed. [73] Besides this, the heads are arranged in a place that they can easily command and obey. [74] The spaces that are between one battalion and another and one order and the other serve not only to enable one to receive the other, but also to give room to the messengers that go and come by order of the captain. [75] And, as I told you before,[23] [since] the Romans had around 24 thousand men for an army, this one should be so as well. And as the other soldiers took the mode of fighting and the form of the army from the legions, so those soldiers that you add to your two brigades would have to take the form and order of the latter. [76] Since one has an example of these things, it is an easy thing to imitate. For by increasing the army by two brigades, or by as many as there are of these other soldiers,[24] one has to do nothing else with them but duplicate the orders; and where ten battalions were placed on the left part, you put twenty of them, either enlarging or extending the orders as the place or the enemy command you.

LUIGI. [77] Truly, Lord, I imagine this army so that I already see it, and I burn with a desire to see it attack. [78] And I would not for anything in the world want you to become a Fabius Maximus, giving thought to keeping the enemy at bay and deferring battle, for I would speak worse of you than the Roman people spoke of him.[25]

FABRIZIO. [79] Doubt not. [80] Don't you hear [the sound of] artillery? [81] Ours has already fired, but it barely harmed the enemy. Together with the light cavalry, the extraordinary velites leave their places and, dispersed and with as much fury and as much clamor as they are able, they assault the enemy, whose artillery has unloaded one time and has passed over the heads of our infantrymen without doing them any harm. [82] And so that[26] it cannot fire a second time, see how our velites and cavalrymen have already occupied it, and how the enemy, so as to defend it, has been put ahead; such that that of friend and enemy can do its office no more. [83] See with how much virtue our [men] fight, and with how much discipline, through the training that has made them do so by habit and the confidence they have in the army that you see march ordered, at its

---

23. See *AW* III 42.

24. "These others" refers to the already existing brigades.

25. Quintus Fabius Maximus (275–203 B.C.), known as Cunctator (the Delayer). See Livy XXII 12–18; 23–30; cf. *AW* IV 116–32; *D* I 53.2, III 9.4, 10.1-3; see also *D* I 53.4, II 24.3, III 9.1, 34.4, 40.1, *P* 17.68. (Fabius Cunctator also was the nickname of Prospero Colonna, a mercenary captain more famous than his cousin Fabrizio Colonna, the participant in the *Art of War*.)

26. Lit.: because.

own pace and with its men-at-arms nearby to join with the adversary. [84] See how our artillery, so as to give them room and leave the space free for them, is withdrawn through that space where the velites had gone out. [85] See how the captain inspirits them and shows them certain victory. [86] See how the velites and the light cavalrymen are spread out and returned to the flanks of the army to see whether they can do any injury to their adversaries on the flank. [87] Behold how the armies attack one another. [88] Look with how much virtue they have withstood the thrust of the enemy, and with how much silence, and how the captain commands his men-at-arms to withstand [the enemy's thrust] and not to charge, and not to separate themselves from the order of their infantries. [89] See how our light cavalrymen went to charge a band of enemy arquebusiers who wanted to wound the flank, and how the enemy cavalrymen have helped them; such that, enveloped between one cavalry and the other, they cannot fire and withdraw behind their battalions. [90] See with what fury our pikes are attacked, and how the infantrymen are already so near to one another that the pikes can no longer be managed, so that, according to the discipline learned from us, the pikes are withdrawn among the shields little by little. [91] Look how a thick band of enemy men-at-arms have in the meantime pushed back our men-at-arms on the left, and how ours have withdrawn beneath the extraordinary pikes according to discipline and, having remade a front with their help, they have repulsed their adversaries and killed a good part of them. [92] Meanwhile, all of the ordinary pikes of the first battalion have hidden themselves among the orders of shields and left the fight to the shieldmen. Look with how much virtue, security, and calm[27] they kill the enemy. [93] Don't you see that while fighting their orders have contracted so much that [only] with trouble can they wield their swords? [94] Look with how much fury the enemies die. [95] For, armed with the pike, which is useless since it is too long, and with their own sword, which [is useless] since the enemy is too well armored, some [of the enemy] fall wounded or dead, some flee. [96] See them fleeing from the right side; they flee from the left as well; behold, the victory is ours. [97] Have we not won a battle very happily? [98] But with greater happiness would it be won, if making it fit were conceded to me. [99] And see how availing themselves either of the second or of the third order was not needed. For our first front was enough to overcome them. [100] In this part I have nothing else to say, except to dispel any doubt that occurs to you.

LUIGI. [101] You have won this battle with so much fury that I remain altogether amazed and so stupefied that I don't believe I'm able to explain well if any doubt remains in my spirit. [102] However, entrusting myself to your prudence,

27. *Ozio,* translated elsewhere as "idle."

I will take heart[28] and say what I think.[29] [103] First, tell me: Why did you not have your artillery fire more than once? [104] And why did you immediately have it withdraw behind the army, and then make no mention of it? [105] It also seems to me that you set the artillery of the enemy high and ordered it in our own mode, which can very well be [the case]. [106] However, when it happens, and I believe that it happens often, that they hit the lines, what remedy do you give for that? [107] And since I have begun with artillery, I want to offer this whole question, so as not to have to reason about it anymore. [108] I have heard many disparage the arms and the orders of the ancient armies, arguing that to-day they would be capable of little, or rather, would be completely useless on account of[30] the fury of artillery. For it breaks the orders and passes through the armor so that it seems crazy to them to make an order that cannot be kept, and to endure toil in carrying armor that cannot defend you.

FABRIZIO. [109] This question of yours needs a long response because it has many heads. [110] It is true that I did not fire the artillery more than one time, and I was in doubt even of that one. [111] The cause is that[31] it is more important for one[32] to guard against being hit than it is important to hit the enemy. [112] You have to understand that [if you] want an artillery piece not to harm you, it is necessary either to stay where it does not reach you or put oneself behind a wall or behind an embankment. [113] There is nothing else that keeps it away; but both need to be very strong. [114] Those captains who have arranged themselves to do battle cannot stay behind their walls or their embankments, nor where they are not reached. [115] Thus, since they cannot find a mode that defends them, they need to find the one by which they are least hurt; nor can they find another mode than occupying [the enemy artillery] immediately. [116] The mode of occupying it is to go to find it quickly and [in] broken [order], not slowly and in mass. For by speed, one doesn't let them redouble the blow, and since [you are] scattered, it is able to hurt a smaller number of men. [117] A band of ordered men cannot do this. For if it marches rapidly, it disorders itself; if it goes sparsely, to break it gives the enemy no trouble because it breaks by itself. [118] Therefore, I would order the army so that it can do the one thing and the other. For, having put a thousand velites on its horns, I would order it that they go out together with the light cavalry and occupy the enemy artillery after our

---

28. *Animo,* translated elsewhere as "spirit."

29. Lit.: confiding myself to your prudence, I will take spirit and say what I intend.

30. Lit.: with respect to.   31. *Perchè,* usually translated as "because."

32. *Uno,* usually translated as "one individual."

artillery has fired. [119] Therefore, I did not have my artillery fire again so as not to give the enemy time. For space cannot be given to me and taken from the others. [120] And for [the same] cause for which I did not have it fire a second time, I was not going to let them fire the first, so that the enemy would be unable to fire even the first time. [121] For to want the enemy artillery to be useless, there is no other remedy than to assault it. For if the enemies abandon it, you occupy it; if they want to defend it, they need to leave it behind [their own lines from the beginning], so that occupied by enemies and by friends, it cannot fire. [122] I would believe that without examples these reasons would be enough for you; however, being able to give them from the ancients, I want to do so. [123] Coming to battle with the Parthians, whose virtue consisted in large part in their bows and arrows, Ventidius let them come almost beneath his encampments before he took his army out. He did this only so as to be able to occupy them quickly and not give them space to fire.[33] [124] Caesar reports that in making a battle with his enemies in France he was assaulted by them with so much fury that his [men] did not have time to throw their darts according to the Roman custom.[34] [125] Therefore, one sees that in wanting a thing that fires far not to offend you while you are in the field, there is no other remedy than to occupy it with as much speed as you can. [126] Another cause also moved me to do without firing the artillery, at which you will perhaps laugh; however, I don't judge it to be [something to be] despised. [127] There's nothing that makes greater confusion in an army than obstructing its view. Hence, many very hardy armies have been beaten by their sight having been obstructed either by dust or by the sun. [128] And there's also nothing that obstructs the view more than the smoke that artillery makes in firing. Therefore, I would believe that there is more prudence in letting the enemy blind himself than for you, blind, wanting to go to find him. [129] Therefore, either I would not fire it or (because this would not be approved on account of[35] the reputation that artillery has)[36] I would put it on the horns of the army, so that in firing it does not blind the front of the latter with its smoke. This is the important thing for my men. [130] And [as evidence] that obstructing the enemy's view is a useful thing, one can adduce the example of Epaminondas. So as to blind the enemy army that came to make battle with him, he had his light cavalrymen run before the enemies' front because they raised the dust high and obstructed their view. This gave him the victory in the

---

33. Publius Bassus Ventidius at the battle of Gindarus in 38 B.C.; see Frontinus II 2.5.

34. Caesar, *Gallic War* I 52; Caesar was fighting the German troops of Ariovistus in 58 B.C.

35. Lit.: with respect to. 36. Parentheses in original.

battle.[37] [131] As to it seeming to you that I guided the shots of the artillery in my own mode, making them pass over the heads of the infantrymen, I respond to you that without comparison there are many more times that heavy artillery does not hit infantries than those that it does hit [them]. Because the infantry is so low and [the artillery] is so difficult to fire that if you raise it even a little, it passes over the heads of the infantrymen; and if you lower it, it harms the ground, and the shot does not reach them. [132] The inequality of the terrain also saves them because every little wrinkle and rise that is between the infantrymen and it impedes it. [133] As to cavalrymen, and especially the men-at-arms, since they have to be more confined than the light [cavalrymen] and can the better be hit through being taller, one can keep them at the tail of the army until the artillery is fired. [134] It is true that the arquebuses and the small artillery do much more harm than the [heavy artillery]. The best remedy for these is to come to hands quickly; and if in the first assault some die, some always die. And a good captain and a good army do not have to fear a harm that is particular, but a general one. They imitate the Swiss, who never shun battle for fear of artillery; indeed, they punish by capital punishment those who from fear of it either leave their file or show any sign of fear with their bodies.[38] [135] Once it had been fired, I had it withdraw into the army, for they left a free passage in the battalions. [136] As a thing useless once the fight has been joined, I made no more mention of it. [137] You also said that on account of[39] the fury of this instrument, many judge the arms and orders of the ancients to be useless. From this speech of yours it seems the moderns have found orders and arms that are useful against artillery. [138] If you know about this, I will cherish your teaching it to me, because up to this point I'm unaware of seeing any of them, nor do I believe one can find them. [139] So I would like to understand from them for what causes the foot soldiers of our times wear the breast[plates] and iron corselets and those on horseback go entirely covered in armor. For since they condemn ancient arming as useless on account of[40] artillery, they should flee these as well. [140] I would also want to understand through what cause the Swiss make a tight battalion of six or eight thousand infantrymen similar to the ancient orders; and for what cause all have imitated them, since this order bears the same danger on account of[41] artillery that those others would were they imitated from antiquity. [141] I believe that they would not know what to respond. But if you were to ask the soldiers that have some judgment, they would respond, first, that although

---

37. Epaminondas (ca. 418–362 B.C.) was a great Theban general. Frontinus II 2.12; cf. *AW* III 103, VII 204, 243; *D* I 17.3, 21.3, III 13.3, 18.1, 38.1; *P* 12.50.

38. Lit.: person.   40. Lit.: with respect to.

39. Lit.: with respect to.   41. Lit.: with respect to.

those arms do not defend them from artillery, they go armored because they do defend them from crossbows, pikes, swords, stones, and every other harm that comes from their enemies. [142] They would also respond that they come tight together like the Swiss so as to charge infantrymen more easily, so as to be better able to withstand cavalrymen, and so as to give more difficulty to the enemy in breaking them. [143] So one sees that the soldiers have to fear many other things besides artillery, from which things they are defended by arms and by orders. [144] From this it follows that by however much an army is better armored, and by however much it has its orders closer and stronger, by so much is it more secure. [145] Such that whoever is of the opinion that you stated must either have little prudence or have thought very little about these things. For if we see that the small part of the ancient mode of arming that is used today, which is the pike, and the small part of their orders, which are the battalions of the Swiss, do us so much good and give so much strength to our armies, why don't we have to believe that the other arms and the other orders that have been left are useful? [146] Then, if we do not have regard for artillery in putting ourselves close together like the Swiss, what other orders can make us more afraid of it? [147] With that being the case, no one order can make us fear it as much as those that constrict the men together. [148] Besides this, if the enemies' artillery does not frighten me from putting myself in the field by a town where it harms me from its own more secure [position] (since I cannot occupy it since it is defended by walls; indeed, only with time can my artillery impede theirs from being able to redouble its shots in its own mode),[42] why do I have to fear it on the field, where I can occupy it quickly? [149] So I conclude with this: that artillery, according to my opinion, does not impede one from being able to use the ancient modes and to show ancient virtue. [150] And if I had not spoken with you about this another time, I would expatiate more here; but I wish to put forth again what I said about it then.[43]

LUIGI. [151] We can understand very well as much as you have discussed[44] concerning artillery. In sum, it seems to me that you have shown that occupying it quickly is the best remedy one has for it, if one is on the field and faces an opposing army. [152] A doubt occurs to me concerning this: for it seems to me that the enemy could locate [his artillery] in a place within his army where it could offend you and would be guarded by infantrymen so that it could not be occupied. [153] If I remember well, in ordering your army for battle you have made intervals of four braccia between one battalion and the other, and of 20 between the battalions and the extraordinary pikes. [154] If the enemy ordered his army

42. Parentheses in original.   44. Lit.: discoursed.
43. Cf. D II 17.

similarly to yours, and put his artillery far back in those intervals, I believe that it could offend you with very great security for itself, because one could not enter into the forces of the enemy to occupy it.

FABRIZIO. [155] You doubt very prudently, and I will strive either to resolve your doubt or to offer a remedy. [156] I told you[45] that these battalions are continually in motion whether marching or fighting, and by nature always come to be constricted, so that if you make the intervals in which you put the artillery of little width, in a short time they are constricted so that the artillery will no longer be able to do its own office. If you make them wide so as to flee this danger, you will run into a greater one. For with these intervals you make it easy for the enemy not only to occupy your artillery but to break you. [157] But you have to know that it is impossible to keep the artillery between the lines, especially that which comes on wagons. For the artillery marches in one direction and fires in the other. So if it has to march and to fire, before firing it is necessary for it to turn around and, in turning, it requires so much space that fifty artillery wagons would disorder any army. [158] Therefore, it is necessary to keep it outside of the lines, where it can be fought in the mode that we demonstrated a little while ago.[46] [159] But let's set it down that they can be kept [within the orders] and that one can find a middle way of [such] a quality that, while being constricted, it does not impede the artillery and is not so open as to give passage[47] to the enemy. I say that this is easily remedied by opposing intervals in your army that give free passage to the shots of artillery. Thus, its fury will turn out to be in vain. [160] This can be done very easily. For since the enemy wants his artillery to remain secure, he must put it in back in the last part of the intervals. And since he wants them not to hurt his own [men], its shots must always pass along the same straight line. Therefore, by giving [the artillery shots] their place, they can easily be fled. For this is a general rule: that one has to give way to those things which cannot be withstood, as the ancients did with elephants and scythed chariots.[48] [161] I believe, indeed I am more than certain, that it seems to you that I have adjusted a battle to my own mode and won. Nonetheless, if what I have said up to this point is not enough, I reply to you with this: that it would be impossible for an army so ordered and armed not to overcome in the first encounter every other army that is ordered as modern armies are ordered. [162] Most of the time these make but one front, have no shields, and are unarmed in such a way[49] that they cannot defend themselves from a nearby enemy. And they are ordered so that if they put their battalions with the flank of one along that of the other, they

45. See *AW* II 10.
46. See *AW* III 64–65.
47. *Via*, translated elsewhere as "way."

48. See Polybius XV 9; cf. Vegetius III 24.
49. Lit.: of a quality.

make their army thin; if they put one behind the other, they make it confused and apt to be easily disturbed, having no mode for one to receive the other. [163] And although they give three names to their arms and divide them in three lines, vanguard, battalion, and rearguard, nonetheless, they use them for nothing other than marching and distinguishing encampments. But in battle all are obliged to one initial thrust and one initial fortune.

LUIGI. [164] I also noticed that in making your battle your cavalry was repulsed by the enemy cavalrymen, so that it [was] withdrawn among the extraordinary pikes. From this it arose that with their help it withstood and turned back the enemies. [165] I believe that pikes can withstand cavalrymen, as you say, but in a thick and solid brigade such as the Swiss make. But in your army you have five orders of pikes along the head and, along the side, seven, so that I do not know how they may be able to withstand them.

FABRIZIO. [166] Although I told you[50] that six files at a time[51] were used in the Macedonian phalanxes, you nonetheless have to understand that one brigade of Swiss, if it were composed of a thousand files, can use but four of them or, at most, five. For the pikes are nine braccia long. One and a half braccia are occupied by the hands, so in the first file, seven and a half braccia of pike remain free. [167] The second file, besides what it occupies with the hands, consumes one and a half braccia with the space that remains between one file and the other, so that only six useful braccia of pike remain. [168] To the third file, for these same reasons, four and a half braccia remain; to the forth, three; to the fifth, one and a half braccia. [169] The other files are useless for wounding [the enemy], but serve to restore these first files, as we had said,[52] and to act as a barbican for these five. [170] Thus, if five of their files can resist cavalrymen, why can't five of ours resist them? These also do not lack files behind, which sustain them and give them the same support, even though they do not have pikes like the former. [171] And if the extraordinary pikes that are posted on the flanks seem thin to you, they could be arranged in a square and put along the flank of the two battalions that I put in the last line of the army. From that place, all together could easily protect[53] the front and the back of the army and lend help to the cavalrymen, as need requires.

LUIGI. [172] Would you always use this form of order when you want to do battle?

FABRIZIO. [173] Not in any mode. For you have to vary the form of the army according to the quality of the site and the quality and quantity of the enemy, as will be shown by some examples before this reasoning is finished. [174] But

---

50. See *AW* III 23.
51. Or: at a stroke.

52. See *AW* III 21–24.
53. Lit.: favor.

this form was given to you not so much as being hardier than the others, though truly it is very hardy, as because you may take from it one rule and one order to know how to recognize the modes of ordering the others. For every science has its generalities upon which it is in good part founded. [175] Of one thing alone I remind you: never order an army so that whoever fights ahead cannot be assisted by those posted behind. For whoever makes this error renders the greatest part of his army useless, and he cannot win if he encounters any virtue.

LUIGI. [176] A doubt has occurred to me over this. [177] I saw that in the arrangement of the battalions you make the front from five [battalions] in a line, the middle from three, and the last parts from two. I would believe that it is better to order them oppositely, because I think that an army can be broken with more difficulty when whoever charges finds it harder the more he penetrates it. And the order made by you seems to me to make it that the more one enters it the weaker one finds it.

FABRIZIO. [178] If you were to remember that the *triarii*, which were the third order of the Roman legions, were not assigned more than six hundred men, you would doubt less, having understood that they were posted in the last line. For you would see how I, moved by this example, posted in the last line two battalions of nine hundred infantrymen.[54] So that, going by the Roman order, I end up erring by having taken too many rather than too few of them. [179] And although this example should be enough, I want to tell you the reason for it. [180] It is this: the first front of the army is made solid and dense because it has to withstand the thrust of enemies and does not have to receive into itself any of its friends. And for this it must abound in men, for few men would make it weak either through sparsity or in number. [181] But because it has to receive its friends before withstanding the enemy, the second line must have large intervals, and for this it must have a smaller number than the first. For if it had a greater or equal number, it would be necessary[55] either not to leave intervals there, which would be a disorder, or, if they are left there, to pass beyond the ends of the first one, which would make the form of the army imperfect. [182] And what you say is not true, that the more the enemy enters into the brigade the more he finds it weak. For the enemy can never fight with the second order unless the first has joined with it, so that [the enemy] ends up finding the middle of the brigade hardier and not weaker, since it has to fight with the first and the second orders together. [183] The same happens when the enemy reaches the third line. For there he has to fight not with the two fresh battalions that he finds there, but with the whole brigade. [184] And because this

54. See Polybius VI 21.   55. *Convenire*

last part has to receive more men, the spaces must be bigger, and whoever receives them [must] be less numerous.

LUIGI. [185] I like what you have said. But answer this for me as well: if the first five battalions withdraw among the second three, and then those eight among the third two, it doesn't seem possible, once the eight are arranged together and then the ten [are arranged] together, that they, either when they are eight or when they are ten, would take up[56] the same [amount of] space that the [first] five took up.

FABRIZIO. [186] The first answer I give you is that it is not the same [amount of] space. For the [first] five have four spaces in between which they occupy while withdrawing among the three [in the second line] and among the two [in the third line]. Then there is the space that is between one brigade and another and between the battalions and the extraordinary pikes, which spaces all make room. [187] Add to this that the battalions take up a different space when they are in their orders without being altered than when they are altered. For in altering they either constrict or widen the orders. [188] They widen them when they are so afraid that they are put to flight; they constrict them when they fear in such a mode as[57] to seek to secure themselves not with flight but with defense, such that in this case they would end up being constricted and not being widened. [189] Add to this that the five files of pikes that are in front, once they have joined the battle, have to be withdrawn among their battalions to the back of the army so as to give place to the shieldmen, who are able to fight. [190] And the former, by going to the back of the army, can attend to what the captain judges it is well for them to do; whereas in front they would be altogether useless once the fight is joined. [191] And through this, the ordered spaces end up being very capacious for the remaining troops. [192] However, when these spaces are not enough, the flanks on the side are men, not walls. By yielding and widening themselves, they can make a space of enough capacity to be sufficient to receive them.

LUIGI. [193] Do you want the files of extraordinary pikes, which you place on the flanks of the army when the first battalions withdraw into the second, to stay solid and remain as the two horns of the army, or do you want them as well to withdraw together with the battalions? [194] I don't see how they can do so when they have to, since they do not have battalions behind them with thin intervals to receive them.

FABRIZIO. [195] If the enemy does not fight them when he forces the bat-

56. *Capere*, related to the words translated as "grasp," "understand," "capable," "capacity," and "capacious."

57. *In modo che*, usually translated "so that."

talions to withdraw, they can stay solid in their orders and wound the enemy on the flanks, once the first battalions have been withdrawn. But they too must withdraw if he fights them as well, as seems reasonable, since he is so powerful that he is able to force the others. [196] They can do this very well, even though they do not have anyone behind who receives them. For by the previous means they can double by right [lines], the one file entering into the other in the mode that we discussed when the order of doubling was spoken of.[58] [197] It is true that in wanting to withdraw by doubling, a mode must be kept other than that which I showed you. For I said to you that the second file had to enter into the first, the forth into the third, and so on.[59] In this case, one would not have to start from the front, but from behind, so that in doubling the files they end up withdrawing backward, not going forward. [198] But so as to respond to everything that can be asked by you about this battle shown by me, I tell you anew that I have ordered this army and shown this battle for two causes: the one, so as to show you how it is ordered; the other, so as to show you how it is trained. [199] I believe that you grasp the order very well; and as to the training, I say to you that one must put them together in these forms as many times as one can. For the heads learn to keep their battalions in these orders. [200] Because it belongs to the particular soldiers to keep the orders of each battalion well, it belongs to the heads of the battalions to keep them in each order of the army well and to know how to obey the commandment of the captain-general. [201] Therefore, they must know how to conjoin one battalion with the other [and] know how to take their places at a stroke. The flag of each battalion must, therefore, have its number written in an obvious place so that they can be commanded and because the captain and the soldiers may recognize them more easily by that number. [202] The brigades must also be numbered and have the number on their principal flag. [203] Thus, one must know what number the brigade posted on the left or on the right is, what number the battalions posted on the front and in the middle are, and so on, one after the other.[60] [204] One also wants these numbers to ascend by the ranks of the honors of the armies. For instance, the first rank to be the decurion; the second, the head of the fifty ordinary velites; the third, the centurion; the forth, the head of the first battalion; the fifth, [the head] of the second; the sixth, [the head] of the third; and, from one to the other,[61] up to the tenth battalion, [whose head] would be honored in the second place after the head-general of a brigade. Nor could anyone end up as that head unless he had climbed there through all of these ranks. [205] And because besides[62] these heads

---

58. See *AW* II 183 ff.
59. Lit.: from hand to hand.
60. Lit.: from hand to hand.

61. Lit.: from hand to hand.
62. Lit.: outside of.

there are the three constables of the extraordinary pikes and the two of the extraordinary velites, I would want them to be of the [same] rank as the constable
of the first battalion.[63] Nor would I care that six men would be of equal rank, so
that each of them would be in competition for being promoted to the second
battalion. [206] So since each one of these heads knows in which place his battalion has to be located, it would follow from this of necessity that at the sound
of the trumpet, the captain's flag being raised, the whole army would be in their
places. [207] And this is the first exercise to which an army should be accustomed, that is, being put together quickly. And so as to do this, one must order
it and disorder it everyday, and many times in one day.

LUIGI. [208] What sign would you want the flags of the whole army to have,
besides the number?

FABRIZIO. [209] That of the captain-general is to have the sign of the prince
of the army. The others would be able to have the same sign and to vary by
camps, or to vary by signs, as may seem better to the lord of the army. For this is
of little importance, as long as the effect arises from it that they recognize one
another. [210] But let's pass to the other training in which an army should be
trained. This is to have it move and go with a fitting pace, and see that it maintain its orders while moving. [211] The third drill is [to have] it learn to manage
itself in that mode in which it later has to manage itself in battle: to have it fire
the artillery and withdraw it; to have the extraordinary velites go out and, after
seeming to attack, to withdraw them; to have the first battalions, as if they were
pushed back, retire into the sparsity of the second, and then all into the third,
and from there each return to his place; and to accustom them to this drill, so
that everything is noted and familiar to each. With practice and familiarity this
is performed very quickly. [212] The fourth drill is [to have] them learn to recognize the commandment of their captain by virtue of his musical instrument
and flags. For they will understand without another commandment what is ut-
tered to them by voice. [213] And because the important thing about this commandment must arise from the musical instrument, I will tell you those musical instruments which the ancients used. [214] As Thucydides affirms, flutes
were used by the Lacedemonians in their armies. For they judged that this har-
mony was more apt to make their army proceed with gravity and not with fury.[64]
[215] Moved by this same reason, the Carthaginians used the cythera in the first
assault.[65] [216] Halyattes, king of Lydia, used the cythera and flutes in war. But

63. See Vegetius II 21.   64. See Thucydides V 70.

65. The source for this passage would seem to be Aulus Gellius I 11, in which case Machiavelli
has replaced Cretans with Carthaginians. No ancient source asserts that the Carthaginians used
cytheras (see L. Arthur Burd, "Le fonti letterarie di Machiavelli nell'*Arte della guerra*," *Atti della
Reale Academia dei Lincei*, 5th ser., *Cl. di scienze morali, storiche e filologiche* 4 (1896): 208–9).

Alexander the Great and the Romans used horns and trumpets,[66] as they thought that by virtue of such instruments they were more able to inflame the spirits of the soldiers and make them fight more hardily. [217] But just as we, in arming the army, have taken the Greek and Roman mode, so in distributing the musical instruments we use the customs of the one and the other nation. [218] Therefore, I would have the trumpets stay near the captain-general, not only as a musical instrument fit to inflame the army but more fit than any other musical instrument to be heard amidst every noise. [219] I would want all the other musical instruments that were around the constables and the heads of the brigades[67] to be little drums and loud flutes played not as they are now, but as is customary in playing at banquets. [220] With the trumpet, the captain thus shows when one has to stop or go forward or turn backward, when the artillery has to fire, when the extraordinary velites have to move, and, with the variation of such musical instruments, he shows the army all those motions that can be shown generally. Those trumpets would then be followed by drums. [221] His army would indeed have to train in this drill, for it is very important. [222] As to the cavalry, one would likewise want to use trumpets, but with less volume and with a different sound[68] from those of the captain. [223] This is as much as occurs to me about the order of the army and about its training.

LUIGI. [224] I pray that clarifying something else for me is not a burden[69] for you: for what cause did you have the light cavalrymen and extraordinary velites move with cries and noise and fury when they attacked, and then, in engaging the rest of the army, you showed that the affair continued in very great silence? [225] And because I do not understand the cause of this variety, I would desire that you clarify it for me.

FABRIZIO. [226] There have been various opinions among the ancient captains about coming to blows: whether one should accelerate the pace with noise or go slowly in silence. [227] This last mode helps in keeping the order firmer and in understanding better the commandments of the captain; the first helps more in inflaming the spirits of the men. [228] And because I believe that one must have respect for the one and the other of these two things, I had some move with noise and others in silence. [229] Nor does it seem to me that continual noises are to the purpose, because they impede the commandments, which is a very pernicious thing. [230] Nor is it reasonable [to suppose] that the Romans con-

---

66. Halyattes, king of Lydia. See Herodotus I 17; Vegetius II 22; cf. Xenophon, *Anabasis* II 2.4.

67. *Battaglione* where one would expect *battaglie.*

68. Lit.: voice.   69. Lit.: heavy.

tinued making noise after[70] the first assault. For it is seen to have happened many times in their histories that soldiers who were fleeing were stopped by the speeches and encouragements[71] of the captain, and in various modes their orders were varied by his own commandments. This would not have happened if their noises had overcome his voice.

70. Lit.: outside of.   71. Lit.: comfortings.

BOOK FOUR

LUIGI. [1] Since under my rule a battle has been won so honorably, I think it is well that I no longer tempt fortune, knowing how much it is variable and unstable. [2] Therefore, I desire to put down the dictatorship and for Zanobi now to carry on this office of questioning, wanting to follow the order that proceeds by the youngest. [3] And I know that he will not refuse this honor or, we mean to say, this trouble, both so as to please me and also through being naturally more spirited than I; nor will it bring him fear to have to enter into these travails, wherein he can just as well be conquered as conquer.

ZANOBI. [4] I'm going to stay wherever you put me, even though I would more gladly keep listening. For up to this point, your questions have satisfied me more than those have pleased me which have occurred to me while listening to your reasonings. [5] But I believe it is well, Lord, that you press on[1] and have patience if we tire you with these ceremonies of ours.

FABRIZIO. [6] Indeed, you give me pleasure. For this variation of questioners allows me to know your various talents and various appetites. [7] But does anything remain that seems [well] to you to add to the material discussed?[2]

ZANOBI. [8] I desire two things before moving on to another part: one is that you show me whether another form of ordering armies occurs to you; the other, those considerations[3] a captain ought to make before he goes to battle, and, if any accident arises in it, what remedies he can use.

FABRIZIO. [9] I will do my utmost[4] to satisfy you. [10] I will not really respond distinctly to your questions, for while I respond to one, many times another will end up being responded to. [11] I have told you how I proposed one

1. Lit.: spare time.
2. Lit.: reasoned.
3. Lit.: respects.
4. *Sforzarmi.*

form of an army for you, so that according to it, he[5] could give it all those forms that the enemy and the site require. For in this case one proceeds both according to the site and according to the enemy. [12] But note this: that there is no more dangerous form than to extend the front of your army greatly, if you do not already have a very hardy and very great army. Otherwise, you have to make it thick and not very wide rather than very wide and thin. [13] For when you have few men in comparison to the enemy, you must search for other remedies, such as ordering your army so that you are covered on one side either by a river or by a marsh, so that you cannot be surrounded;[6] or covering yourself on the flanks with ditches, as Caesar did in France.[7] [14] And in this case you have to take up this generality: to extend yourself or constrict yourself on the front according to your number and that of the enemy. And if the enemy has a smaller number, you must seek wide places, especially if you have disciplined your troops, so that you can not only surround the enemy, but extend your orders. For in harsh and difficult places you end up having no advantage since you cannot avail yourself of your orders. [15] Hence it arose that the Romans almost always sought open fields and fled difficult [ones]. [16] You must do the contrary, as I said,[8] if you have few or badly disciplined men. For you have to seek places where the small number is saved or where the lack of experience does not hurt you. [17] You also ought to select a high place so as to be able to charge [the enemy] more easily.[9] [18] Nonetheless, one ought to take this precaution: do not order your army on a sloping hill or a place near its bases, where the enemy army can come. For in this case the higher place brings you disadvantage on account of[10] artillery. For you could always conveniently be hurt by the enemy artillery without being able to make any remedy, and you could not easily offend it, being impeded by your own [men]. [19] Whoever orders an army for battle also ought to take account of[11] the sun and the wind, that the one and the other do not hit you in the front. For the one and the other obstruct your vision, the one with its rays, the other with dust. [20] And the more the wind is unfavorable to the arms that are shot at the enemy, the more it weakens their blows. [21] And as to the sun, it is not enough to take care that it not hit you in the face right then. Rather, one must see to it that as the day goes on it does not offend you. [22] And for this, in ordering the troops, it would have to be altogether at the back, so that much time

---

5. The subject of this clause seems to be the captain mentioned above in sentence 8; but there is support for the impersonal rendering "one could give."

6. See Vegetius III 20.   9. See Vegetius III 13.

7. See Caesar, *Gallic War* II 8, VII 72.   10. Lit.: with respect to.

8. See *AW* IV 13–14.   11. Lit.: have respect for.

would have to pass for it to arrive in front of you.[12] [23] This mode was observed by Hannibal at Cannae[13] and by Marius against the Cimbri.[14] [24] If you are much inferior in cavalrymen, order your army amidst vines and trees and similar impediments, as the Spaniards did in our times, when they broke the French in the Kingdom at Cerignuola.[15] [25] And it is seen many times how from losing one becomes victorious with the same soldiers by varying only the orders and the place. So it happened with the Carthaginians, who, having been conquered by Marcus Regulus many times, were then victorious through the counsel of the Lacedeamonian Xantippus. He had them descend into the plain where they were able to overcome the Romans by virtue of the cavalrymen and the elephants.[16] [26] It seems to me that according to the ancient examples almost all the excellent captains did not oppose the strongest part but the weakest when they knew that the enemy had made one side of the battalion strong. And the other stronger part they opposed to the weakest. Then, in joining battle, they commanded their hardiest part only to withstand the enemy and not to extinguish him, and the weakest to allow itself to be conquered and to retire into the last line of the army. [27] This produces two great disorders for the enemy: the first, that he finds his strongest part surrounded; the second is that when it seems to him that he has an immediate victory, rare are the times that he is not disordered. His own immediate loss arises from this. [28] Cornelius Scipio, being in Spain against the Carthaginian Hasdrubal, knew Hasdrubal had noticed that in ordering his army he used to put his legions—the strongest part of his own army—in the middle, and through this [Scipio knew] that Hasdrubal had to proceed with similar orders when he later came to battle; [so Scipio] changed order and put his legions on the horns of the army, and in the middle he put all of his weakest men. [29] Then, coming to hands, he suddenly had the men posted in the middle walk slowly, and the horns of the army were made to advance with celerity, so that the horns of the one and the other army fought, and the lines in the middle, by being distant from one another, did not join one another. So the hardiest part of

12. See Vegetius III 14.

13. The battle of Cannae (216 B.C.); see Livy XXII 43.

14. Gaius Marius (ca. 157–186 B.C.) at the battle of Vercellae (101 B.C.); see Plutarch, *Marius* 26; Frontinus II 2.7; cf. *D* II 8.1, III 37.4; Augustine, *City of God* V 26.

15. The battle of Cerignuola (1503) between French and Spanish forces in the kingdom of Naples. Fabrizio is reported to have said of this battle (in which he participated on the Spain side) that the Spanish victory was due neither to the valor of their captain Gonzalo (see *AW* II 62, note 25) nor to the courage of Spanish troops, but to the small dirt wall behind which the Spanish arquebuses hid as they fired on their enemies. Cf. *D* II 17.4.

16. In 255 B.C.; see Polybius I 32–35; cf. *D* II 18.4.

Scipio's [army] ended up fighting with the weakest of Hasdrubal's. And he conquered him.[17] [30] That mode was useful then. But today, on account of[18] artillery, it could not be used. For the space that would remain in the middle, between one army and the other, would give time for it to be able to fire, which is very pernicious, as we said above.[19] [31] Therefore, one must leave this mode aside, and [instead of] it, use [the mode] of having the whole army join and the weakest part yield, as I said a little while ago.[20] [32] When a captain finds he has a larger army than that of the enemy, and wants to surround it without it foreseeing this, he orders his army with a front equal to that of his adversary. Then, the battle having been joined, little by little he has the front withdraw and the flanks extend themselves. And, unless he notices it, it will always happen that the enemy will find himself surrounded. [33] When a captain wants to fight with near certainty[21] that he cannot be beaten, he orders his army in a place where it has a nearby and secure refuge, either amidst marshes or amidst mountains or in a powerful city. For in this case he cannot be followed by the enemy and the enemy can be followed by him. [34] These means were[22] used by Hannibal, when fortune began to turn against him and he feared[23] the valor of Marcus Marcellus.[24] [35] So as to disturb the orders of the enemy, some have commanded those that were lightly armed to join the battle and, having joined it, to withdraw among the orders. And when the armies later came together head to head and the front of each was occupied with fighting, they had them go out along the flanks of the battalions, and disturb and beat him. [36] If someone finds himself inferior in cavalrymen, he can, besides the modes mentioned, put a battalion of pikes behind his cavalrymen and, in fighting, order that they give way to the pikes. And he will always remain superior. [37] Many were in the habit[25] of accustoming some lightly armed infantrymen to fight among the cavalrymen, which was of very great help to the cavalry.[26] [38] Of all those who have ordered armies for battle, the most lauded are Hannibal and Scipio when they fought in Africa. Because Hannibal had composed his army of Carthaginians and of auxiliaries of various kinds, he put eighty elephants in the first front; next he located the auxiliaries; after these he put his own Carthaginians. In the last place he put the Italians, in whom he had little confidence. [39] He so ordered these things

---

17. In 206 B.C.; see Livy XXVIII 14, Polybius XI 22.

18. Lit.: with respect to.   21. Lit.: secure.

19. Cf. *AW* III 101 ff.   22. Lit.: This end was.

20. See *AW* IV 26.   23. Lit.: doubted.

24. At the battle of Nola (215 B.C.); see Livy XXIII 16, XXVII 12, 14.

25. *Consueto,* usually translated as "accustomed."

26. See Vegetius III 16.

because the auxiliaries could not flee, since they had the enemy in front and were blocked from behind by his own [men]. Since they were necessitated to fight, they conquered or tired out the Romans. He thought then [he could] easily overcome the already tired Romans with his own fresh and virtuous troop[s]. [40] Against this order, Scipio placed the *hastati*, the *principes*, and the *triarii* in the accustomed mode of one being able to receive the other and one being able to help the other. [41] He made the front of the army full of intervals. And so that it would not be transparent, but rather would seem united, he filled them with velites. He commanded, as soon as the elephants came, that the [velites] yield, and enter among the legions through the ordinary spaces and leave the way open for the elephants. Thus, he ended up rendering the impetus of the latter vain, so that, having come to hands, he was superior.[27]

ZANOBI. [42] You have made me remember, in alleging this battle to me, how in fighting Scipio did not have the *hastati* withdraw into the order of the *principes*, but divided them and had them withdraw to the horns of the army, so that they gave place to the *principes*, when he wanted them to push them ahead. Therefore, I would like you to tell me what cause moved him not to use the accustomed order.

FABRIZIO. [43] I will tell you. [44] Hannibal had posted all of the virtue of his army in the second line. Hence, so as to oppose similar virtue to the latter, Scipio collected the *principes* and the *triarii* together, such that since the intervals of the *principes* were occupied by the *triarii*, there was no room where the *hastati* could be received. [45] And therefore he had the *hastati* divide and go to the horns of the army, and not withdraw among the *principes*. [46] But note that one cannot use this mode of opening the first line so as to give place to the second except when one is otherwise superior.[28] For then one has the convenience of being able to do it, as Scipio was able to. [47] But being inferior and having been repulsed, you cannot do it except with your own manifest ruin. Therefore, there must be orders behind that receive you. [48] But let us return to our reasoning. [49] Among other things thought up to offend their enemies, the ancient Asiatics used chariots that had several scythes on the sides, such that they not only served to open the lines with their thrust, but also killed their adversaries with the scythes.[29] [50] These thrusts were provided against in three modes: either they were withstood with the density of the orders, or they were received into the lines like the elephants, or some hardy resistance was made

27. At the battle of Zama (202 B.C.); see Frontinus II 3.16; Livy XXX 33, 35; Polybius XV 9, 11; cf. *D* II 27.4.

28. Or: is superior to others.

29. See Vegetius III 24, Livy XXXVII 41; cf. Xenophon, *Education of Cyrus* VI 1.29.

with art, as the Roman Sulla did against Archelaus. The latter had many of these chariots which they called scythed, so that he drove many pikes into the ground after the first lines so as to withstand them. Having been withstood by them, the chariots lost their impetus. [51] And the new mode that Sulla took against them in ordering his army is to be noted. For he put the velites and the cavalrymen behind and all of the heavily armed ahead, leaving many intervals so as to be able to send ahead those from behind when the necessity required it. Hence, the fight having been joined, he had the victory with the help of the cavalrymen to whom he had given a way.[30] [52] To want to disturb the enemy army in a fight, one must make something that frightens him arise, either by announcing new supports that are coming, or by showing things that represent them, in such a way that the enemies, deceived by that appearance, are frightened and being afraid, can easily be conquered.[31] [53] The Roman consuls Minucius Rufus[32] and Acilius Glabrio[33] held to these modes. [54] Gaius Sulpitius also put many bags on mules and other animals useless in war, but ordered [them] so that they represented men-at-arms. He commanded that they appear on a hill while they were at hands with the French. His victory arose from this.[34] [55] Marius did the same when he fought against the Germans.[35] [56] As feigned assaults are thus very valuable while the battle goes on, it must be that true ones are much more helpful, especially if by improvising in the middle of the fight one can assault the enemy from behind or on the side. [57] This can be done [only] with difficulty if the country does not help you. For when it is open, part of your troops cannot be concealed, as they must be in such enterprises. But in places wooded and mountainous, and thus fit for ambushes, part of your troops can be hidden well, so as to be able to assault the enemy at once contrary to his expectation.[36] This thing will always be cause for giving you the victory. [58] Sometimes it has been of great moment, while the fight is going on, to disseminate words that pro-

30. At the battle of Cheronea (86 b.c.), Lucius Sulla (ca. 138–178 b.c.) fought Archelaus, a general of Mithridates VI (132–163), king of Pontus; see Frontinus II 3.17; Plutarch, *Sulla* 15–19.

31. Cf. *D* III 14.

32. Marcus Minucius Rufus against the Sordiscans and Dacians in 109 b.c.; see Frontinus II 4.3.

33. In 191 b.c., at the Pass of Thermopylae, Marcus Porcius Cato, the Elder (234–149 b.c.), surprised and defeated Antiochus III of Syria while fighting for Manius Acilius Glabrio. There is no record of the ruse reported by Fabrizio; see Frontinus II 4.4; Livy XXXVI 18; Plutarch, *Marcus Cato* 12.

34. In 358 b.c., Gaius Sulpicius Peticus as dictator; see Frontinus II 4.5; cf. Livy VII 12–15; *D* III 14.3; cf. also *D* III 10.

35. Gaius Marius (157–186 b.c.) against the Teutons at Aquae Sextiae in 102 b.c.; see Frontinus II 4.6; cf. *D* II 8.1.

36. Lit.: outside of his opinion.

nounce the enemies' captain to be dead, or to have been conquered by another part of the army. Many times this has given victory to him who used it. [59] One easily disturbs the enemy cavalry by unusual forms or noises. Croesus, who opposed camels to the cavalrymen of his adversaries, did so.[37] And to the Roman cavalry Pyrrhus opposed elephants, whose aspect disturbed it and disordered it.[38] [60] In our times, the Turk beat the Sophy in Persia and the Sultan in Syria with nothing but the noise of their arquebuses, which confused the cavalry with their unusual noises, so that the Turk could easily conquer it.[39] [61] The Spanish, so as to beat the army of Hamilcar, put in the first front wagons full of brushwood pulled by oxen and, coming to hands, set fire to them. From this the oxen, wanting to flee the fire, charged into the army of Hamilcar and opened it up.[40] [62] It is customary, as we said,[41] to deceive enemies while fighting, drawing them into ambushes, where the country is convenient. But when it is open and wide, many were used to making ditches, and then covering them lightly with brush and earth and leaving some solid spaces between them to enable them to withdraw. Then, the fight having been joined, they have retired through them. When the enemy follows, he is ruined in them. [63] If in the fight it happens to you that some accident frightens your soldiers, knowing how to dissimulate it and pervert it for good is a very prudent thing, as did Tullus Hostilius and Lucius Sulla. The former, seeing how, while fighting, one part of his troops had gone over to the side of the enemy, and how that thing had frightened his own [men] very much, he had the whole army understand immediately that everything happened by his order. This not only did not disturb the army, but it increased its spirit so much that it remained victorious.[42] [64] It also happened to Sulla that since certain soldiers whom he sent to do some business had been killed, he said, so that his army would not be frightened, that he had them sent into the hands of their enemies by art because he had found out that they lacked

37. See Frontinus II 4.12–13. Near Sardis in 546 B.C., Croesus, king of Lydia (560–546 B.C.), fought Cyrus the Great, king of Persia (559–529 B.C.). See Frontinus II 4.12; but cf. Herodotus I 80 and Xenophon, *Cyropaedia* VII 1.27, 48–49, where it is Cyrus who uses this stratagem against Croesus.

38. At the battle of Heraclea (280 B.C.) between Pyrrhus, king of Epirus (297–272 B.C.), and Rome; see Frontinus II 4.13; Plutarch, *Pyrrhus* 17.

39. Selim I, sultan of Turkey (1512–20), the "Grand Turk," defeated Ismail I, the shah of Persia, in 1514 and the Mameluke dynasty in 1517. Cf. *D* II 17.5; cf. also *D* I 1.4, 19.2, 30.1, III 35.1.

40. In 229 B.C., Hamilcar Barca, father of Hannibal, conquered much of Spain for the Carthaginians from 238–229 B.C.; see Frontinus II 4.17; Polybius II 1.

41. See *AW* IV 57.

42. In 658 B.C. near Rome, Tullus Hostilius, Rome's third king (672–640 B.C.), was deserted by the Albans while preparing to fight the Veii and Fidenae. See Frontinus II 7.1 and Livy I 27, where the Albans do not go over to the enemy, but withdraw to nearby hills; cf. *D* I 22.

faith.[43] [65] Sertorius, doing battle in Spain, killed one who indicated to him the death of one of his own officers[44] for fear that he would frighten them if he said the same to others.[45] [66] It is a very difficult thing to stop an army and return it to battle once it has already moved to flee. [67] And you have to make this distinction: either the whole has moved, and then it is impossible to return it; or a part of it has moved, and then there is some remedy. [68] Many Roman captains, by getting in front of those who were fleeing, have stopped them, making them ashamed of their flight, as did Lucius Sulla. As part of his legions were already turning around having been chased by the troops of Mithridates, he put himself in front with a sword in hand, crying: "If anyone asks where you left your captain, say: We left him in Boeotia, fighting."[46] [69] The consul Attilius opposed those who were fleeing with those who were not fleeing, and made them understand that if they did not turn around they would be killed by their friends and by their enemies.[47] [70] Philip of Macedon, understanding that his own [men] feared the Scythian soldiers, put some of his most faithful cavalrymen behind his army, and commissioned them to kill anyone who fled. Hence his own [men] won, wanting to die fighting rather than fleeing.[48] [71] Not so much to stop a flight as to give opportunity to their own [men] for making a greater force, many Romans have taken a flag from the hands of their own [men] while they were fighting and thrown it amidst the enemies and proposed rewards to whoever regained it. [72] I do not believe that it is outside of the purpose to add to this reasoning those things that happen after the fight, especially since these things are brief and not to be left behind and conform well to this reasoning. [73] I say, therefore, that battles are lost or won. [74] When one wins, one must follow up the victory with utmost speed and in this case imitate Caesar and not Hannibal, who, by staying put after he had beaten the Romans at Cannae,[49] lost the empire of Rome. [75] The former never paused after a victory, but followed the beaten enemy with greater impetus and fury than [when] he had assaulted it in its entirety. [76] But when one loses, a captain must see if from his loss anything can

43. See Frontinus II 7.2–3.   44. Lit.: heads.

45. In 75 B.C., upon hearing of the death of Hirtuleius who had been killed by Quintus Caecilius Metellus Pius; see Frontinus II 7.5.

46. At the battle of Orchomenus (85 B.C.); see Frontinus II 8.12; Plutarch, *Sulla* 21.

47. In 294 B.C., during the Samnite Wars, Marcus Atilius Regulus; see Frontinus II 8.11, IV 1.29; cf. Livy X 36.

48. In 339 B.C. against the Scythians, Philip II, king of Macedon (359–336 B.C.), father of Alexander the Great; see Frontinus II 8.14.

49. At the battle of Cannae (216 B.C.).

arise for his own utility, especially if any residue of this army has remained with him. [77] The convenience can arise from the lack of caution of the enemy, who most of the time after a victory has become careless and gives you the opportunity to oppress him, as the Roman Martius oppressed the Carthaginian armies. The latter, having killed the two Scipios and beaten their armies [and] not esteeming that remnant of the troops that had remained alive with Martius, were assaulted and beaten by him.[50] [78] By this one sees that there is nothing as likely to succeed as what the enemy believes you cannot attempt, because most of the time men are hurt more where they fear[51] less. [79] Therefore, when he cannot do this, a captain should at least contrive with industry that the loss be less harmful. [80] To do this it is necessary for you to hold modes that do not enable the enemy to follow you with ease, or give him causes that have to delay him. [81] In the first case, after they recognize that they have lost, some ordered their heads to flee to diverse parts and by diverse ways, having given orders [as to] where they had to assemble later. That made it so that the enemy, fearing to divide his army, let all or the greater part of them go safely. [82] In the second case, many have thrown their dearest things in front of the enemy, so that having been delayed by the prey, he affords them more space for their flight. [83] Titus Dimius used no lack of astuteness so as to hide the harm that he had received in the fight; for, having fought until night with much loss of his own, at night he had most of them buried. Hence, seeing in the morning so many of their own dead and so few of the Romans, [and] believing they were at a disadvantage, the enemies fled.[52] [84] I believe I have thus haphazardly, as I said,[53] satisfied your question in good part. [85] Concerning the form of the armies, it's true that it remains for me to tell you how at times it was customary for some captain to make them with the front in the shape[54] of a wedge, judging that in such a way he could more easily open the enemy army. [86] Against this form, they used to make a form in the shape of a scissors so as to be able to receive the wedge between the opening[55] and to surround and fight it from every part.[56] [87] In regard to this I want you to take this general rule: the greatest remedy that is used against a plan of the en-

---

50. In 211 or 212 B.C.; cf. Frontinus II 10.2 on Titus Martius and Livy XXV 37 on Lucius Martius. The two Scipios, the father and the uncle of the Scipio who defeated Hannibal, are Publius Cornelius Scipio and Gnaeus Cornelius Scipo Calvus, respectively.

51. Lit.: doubt.

52. See Frontinus II 10.1 for a nearly identical strategem used by Titus Didius (not Dimius, as Fabrizio calls him), consul (98 B.C.), who fought in Spain 98–93 B.C. See AW VI 195 for evidence that Machiavelli was aware of the correct spelling.

53. See AW IV 10.   55. Lit.: vacuum.

54. Uso here and in the next sentence.   56. See Vegetius III 19.

emy is to do voluntarily what he plans that you do by force. For, by doing it voluntarily, you do it with order and to your advantage and his disadvantage. If you did it having been forced, it would be your ruin. [88] As fortification of this, I will not mind replying to you with something already said. [89] Does your adversary make a wedge so as to open your lines? [90] If you go with these opened, you disorder him and he does not disorder you. [91] Hannibal put elephants in the front of his army so as to open the army of Scipio with them. Scipio went with it opened and it was the cause both of his victory and of the ruin of the former.[57] [92] Hasdrubal put his hardiest troops in the middle of the front of his army, so as to push back the troops of Scipio. Scipio commanded that they themselves be withdrawn, and he beat him.[58] [93] Similar designs, when they are foreseen,[59] are the cause of the victory of those against whom they are ordered. [94] It also remains for me, if I remember well, to tell you what respects a captain ought to have before he goes to the fight. [95] Of this I have to tell you, first, that a captain is never to do battle unless he has the advantage, or unless he is necessitated. [96] The advantage arises from the site, from order, or from having either more or better troops. [97] Necessity arises when you see that by not fighting you must lose in any mode; as when you are lacking money and because of this your army has to be dissolved in any mode; through hunger assaulting you; when the enemy waits to be enlarged by new troops. [98] In these cases, you must always fight, even at your own disadvantage. For it is much better to tempt fortune where it can favor you than to see your certain ruin by not tempting it. [99] And in this case, not fighting is as grave a sin in a captain as having had the opportunity to win and either not to have recognized it through ignorance or to have let it go through vileness.[60] [100] Sometimes the enemy gives you advantages, and sometimes your own prudence [does so]. [101] In crossing rivers many have been beaten by a shrewd enemy of theirs who has waited until they were half on each side, and then he has assaulted him,[61] as Caesar did to the Swiss. He consumed a quarter part of them, through their having been divided by a river.[62] [102] Sometimes your enemy finds himself tired through having followed you too thoughtlessly. Finding yourself fresh and rested, you must not let such an opportunity pass. [103] Besides this, if the enemy presents battle to you at an early[63] hour of the morning, you can defer going out of your encampments for many hours. When he has been under arms enough and he has lost that first ardor with which he came, you can then fight with him. [104] Scipio and Metel-

---

57. At Zama in 202 B.C.; see Livy XXX 32 ff.

58. At Becula in 208 B.C.   61. Change from plural to singular.

59. *Presentire.*   62. In 58 B.C.; see Caesar, *Gallic War* I 12.

60. Cf. *D* III 10.2.   63. Lit.: good.

lus kept this mode in Spain, the one against Hasdrubal, the other against Serto-rius.⁶⁴ [105] If the enemy is diminished in forces, either through having divided his armies like the Scipios in Spain, or through some other cause, you must tempt chance. [106] The greater part of prudent captains receive the thrust of their enemies rather than go to assault them with a thrust. For fury is easily with-stood by firm and solid men; and fury easily withstood is converted into vile-ness.⁶⁵ [107] Fabius did so against the Samnites and against the Gauls, and he was victorious, and his colleague Decius remained there dead.⁶⁶ [108] Some who have feared the virtue of their enemy have begun the fight at an hour near night, so that when they were beaten, their own [men], defended by its darkness, were able to save themselves.⁶⁷ [109] Having recognized that the enemy army is over-come by a certain superstition of not fighting at some time, some have selected that time for the fight, and won. [110] Caesar obeyed⁶⁸ this in France against Ar-iovistus,⁶⁹ and Vespasian in Syria against the Jews.⁷⁰ [111] The greatest and most important precaution that a captain ought to take⁷¹ is to have nearby him faith-ful men, very expert in war and prudent, with whom he continually takes coun-sel.⁷² With them he reasons about his troops and about those of the enemy: which is the greater number; which is better armed or better on horseback or better trained; which are more fit to endure necessity; in which may he have more confidence, in the infantrymen or the cavalrymen. [112] Then they might consider the place where they are, and whether it is more to the purpose for the enemy or for him;⁷³ who may get provisions for themselves more easily; whether it is well to defer battle or make it; what good can time give to or take away from him; for many times soldiers, having seen the war drag on, become annoyed and, worn out by fatigue and tedium, they abandon you. [113] Above all it is impor-tant to know the enemies' captain and who he has around him; whether he is temerarious or cautious, whether timid or audacious. [114] [It is important] to

64. In 206 B.C., Scipio Africanus defeated Hasdrubal, son of Gisco; see Frontinus II 1.1.; cf. Livy XXVIII 15. The other incident occurred in 75 B.C., when Quintus Caecilius Metellus Pius fought against Hirtuleius rather then Sertorius; see Frontinus II 1.2. Sertorius is mentioned in the succeeding paragraph of Frontinus (II 1.3).

65. Cf. *D* III 11.

66. The battle of Sentinum (295 B.C.). Quintus Fabius Maximus Rullianus (dictator in 315 B.C.) and Publius Decius Mus, the Younger; see Frontinus II 1.8; cf. Livy X 28; *D* III 11, 45.

67. See Frontinus II 1.13.   68. Lit.: observed.

69. In 58 B.C.; see Frontinus II 1.16; cf. Caesar, *Gallic War* I 50.

70. In 70 A.D., the emperor Vespasian (69–79); see Frontinus II 1.17; cf. *D* I 29.2.

71. For the following, see Vegetius III 19.   73. Change from plural to singular.

72. Cf. *P* 14.59–60.

see whether you can trust the auxiliary soldiers. [115] And above all you ought to guard against leading an army to fight that is afraid or that is not confident[74] of victory. For the greatest sign of [an impending] loss is when one does not believe one can win. [116] In this case you ought therefore to flee battle, either by acting like Fabius Maximus who by encamping in strong places did not give Hannibal the spirit to go to find him, or—when you believe that the enemy may come to find you even in strong places—leaving the country and dividing your troops throughout your own towns, so that the tedium of storming them tires [out the enemy].

ZANOBI. [117] Can one not flee battle otherwise than by dividing into more parts and entering into one's towns?

FABRIZIO. [118] I believe I have reasoned with some of you another time[75] that he who stays in the country cannot flee the battle when he has an enemy who wishes to fight in any mode. He has only one remedy: placing himself with his army at least fifty miles distant from his adversary, so as to have time to get out of his way before he goes to find it. [119] And Fabius Maximus never fled from battle with Hannibal, but wanted to make it to his own advantage; and Hannibal did not presume that he was able to conquer him by going to find him in the places where he was encamped. For if he had presupposed himself capable of conquering him, Fabius would have had to do battle with him in any mode, or flee. [120] In coming to war with the Romans, Philip, king of Macedon, the one who was father of Perseus, put his own encampments on a very high mountain so as not to do battle with them. But the Romans went to find him upon that mountain and beat him.[76] [121] So as not to have to do battle with Caesar, who contrary to[77] his own opinion had crossed a river, Cingetorix, captain of the French, went with his own men to a distance of many miles.[78] [122] In our times, if the Venetians did not want to come to battle with the king of France, they should not have waited for the French army to cross the Adda,[79] but [should have instead] distanced themselves from it, like Cingetorix. [123] Hence it is that having waited, they did not know how to seize the opportunity of the crossing of the troops to do battle, nor to flee it. For the French, since they were nearby,

---

74. Lit.: is diffident.   75. See *D* III 10.

76. At the battle of Cynocephalae (197 B.C.); see Polybius XVIII 7; Livy XXXIII 7–10.

77. Lit.: outside of.

78. See Caesar, *Gallic War* VII 35, where Caesar uses the name Vercingetorix rather than Cingetorix for the leader of the Gauls and king of the Averni.

79. In 1509, at the battle of Agnadello between Venice and France. The latter was fighting as part of the Holy League, an alliance of the major Italian powers against Venice.

assaulted and beat the Venetians as they were decamping.[80] [124] So it is that one cannot flee battle when the enemy wishes to do [battle] in any mode. [125] Nor can anyone allege Fabius, because in that case he wanted to flee battle as much as Hannibal did. [126] It happens many times that your soldiers are eager[81] to fight; yet because you know you are at a disadvantage because of the numbers and the site or for some other cause, you desire to remove this desire from them. [127] It also happens that necessity or the opportunity constrains you to the battle, and that your soldiers lack confidence and are little disposed to fight. Hence it is necessary for you in the one case to frighten them and in the other to enflame them. [128] In the first case, when persuasions are not enough, there is no better mode than giving a part of them as prey to the enemy, so that those who have fought and those who have not believe you. [129] And you can very well do with art what happened to Fabius Maximus by chance. [130] As you know, the army of Fabius desired to fight with the army of Hannibal. His own master of horse had the same desire, but it did not seem [well] to Fabius to attempt a fight; so much so, that because of such disparity he had to divide the army. [131] Fabius kept his own [portion of the troops] in the encampments; the [master of horse] fought, and having ended up in great danger, would have been beaten if Fabius had not helped him. [132] Through this example, the master of horse, together with the whole army, knew that it was a wise policy to obey Fabius.[82] [133] As to inflaming them to fight, it is well to make them indignant toward their enemies, showing that they speak ignominious words about them; to show that you have communication[83] with them and have corrupted a part of them; to lodge in a place so that they see their enemies and make some light fight[s] with them, for the things that are seen daily are despised with more ease;[84] to show oneself to be indignant and, with an oration to that purpose, to reprimand them for their sloth and, so as to make them ashamed, to speak of wanting to fight alone if they do not want to remain in your company. [134] And you must, above everything, take this precaution in wanting to make your soldiery obstinate in the fight: do not permit them to send any of their property[85] home or to put it in some place until the war has ended, so that they understand

---

80. At the battle of Agnadello (1509), also called Vailà; see *P* 12.52, 20.84, 26.102; *D* I 6, 53, II 10, III 31.3; *Florentine Histories* I 29; *Second Decannale* lines 175–93.

81. Or: willing.

82. In 217 B.C.; see Livy XXII 24 ff.; cf. *D* I 53.2.

83. Lit.: intelligence.   84. See Vegetius III 12; Plutarch, *Marius* 16.

85. *Facultà*.

that if in fleeing they save their lives, they do not save their possessions, the love of which is no less a ground for rendering men obstinate in defense.

ZANOBI. [135] You have said[86] how one can make fleeing soldiers[87] fight by speaking to them. [136] Do you mean by this that one has to speak to the army, or to its heads?

FABRIZIO. [137] To persuade or dissuade a few of a thing is very easy. For if words are not enough, you can then use authority or force. But the difficulty is in removing from the multitude a sinister opinion that is also contrary either to the common good or to your opinion. There one can use only words that are heard by all, wishing to persuade all of them together. [138] For this, excellent captains needed to be orators, because without knowing how to speak to the whole army, [only] with difficulty can one do anything good. This is cast off altogether in these times of ours. [139] Read the life of Alexander the Great, and see how many times it was necessary for him to harangue and to speak publicly to the army. Otherwise, since it had become rich and full of prey, he would never have led it through the deserts of Arabia and into India to its own hardship and annoyance. For infinite times things arise by means of which an army falls to ruin, when the captain either does not know how or is not used to speaking to it. For this speaking takes away fear, inflames spirits, increases obstinacy, uncovers deceptions, promises rewards, shows dangers and the way to flee them, fills with hope, praises, vituperates, and does all of those things by which the human passions are extinguished or inflamed. [140] Hence that prince or republic which designs to make a new military and give reputation to this training ought to accustom its own soldiers to hear the captain speaking and the captain to know how to speak to them. [141] Religion, and the oath that was given to them when they went to serve in the military, was very valuable in keeping the ancient soldiers [well] disposed. For in each of their errors they were menaced not only by those evils that they could fear from men, but by those that they could expect from God. [142] Mixed with other religious modes, that thing many times made every enterprise easy for ancient captains, and it would always do so where religion is feared and observed. [143] Sertorius availed himself of this, by showing he spoke with a deer that, on behalf of God, promised him victory. [144] Sulla said he spoke with an image that he had taken from the temple of Apollo.[88] [145] Many have said that God, who admonished them to fight, appeared to them in a dream. [146] In the times of our fathers, Charles VII, king of France, in the war that he made against the English, said he held counsel with a young girl sent by

86. See *AW* IV 66–70; see also *AW* III 230.
87. *Soldati volti,* soldiers who have turned away from the enemy in order to flee.
88. See Frontinus I 11.13, 11.12; cf. Plutarch, *Sertorius* 11, 20; *Sulla* 29.

God, who was called by all the Virgin of France.[89] That was the cause of his victory. [147] You can also keep modes that make your own [men] prize the enemy little, like those kept by the Spartan Agesilaus, who showed to his soldiers some naked Persians, so that having seen their delicate members, they would have no cause to fear them.[90] [148] Some have constrained them to fight by necessity, taking away from them every hope of saving themselves, outside of winning. That is the most hardy and the best provision that one, wanting to make his own soldiery obstinate, can make. [149] That obstinacy is increased by confidence and by the love of the captain or of the country. [150] Confidence is caused by arms, and by order, fresh victories, and the reputation[91] of the captain. [151] Love of country is caused by nature; that of the captain, by virtue more than by any other benefit. [152] Necessities can be many, but the one that is stronger is that which constrains you to win or to die.

89. St. Joan of Arc (1412–31).

90. At Sardis (395 B.C.), Agesilaus II, king of Sparta (398–360 B.C.), defeated the Persians; see Frontinus I 11.17; Plutarch, *Agesilaus* 9; Xenophon, *Hellenica* III 4.19.

91. Lit.: opinion.

BOOK FIVE

———— ❦ ————

[1] I have shown you how one orders an army so as to do battle with another army that one sees placed against oneself, and have told you how one wins that [battle], and then the many circumstances for the various accidents that can happen in [the battle]. So now it seems to me to be time to show you how one orders an army against that enemy which others do not see,[1] but which, it is continually feared, may assault you. [2] This happens when one marches through enemy or suspect country. [3] And first you have to understand that ordinarily a Roman army always sent ahead some groups of cavalrymen as explorers[2] of the road. [4] Then the right horn followed. [5] After this came all of the wagons that belonged to it. [6] After these came one legion; after it, its wagons; after these, another legion and, after that, its wagons; after these came the left horn with its wagons behind and, in the last part, the remainder of the cavalry followed. [7] This in effect was the mode in which it marched ordinarily. [8] And if on the march it turned out that the army was assaulted in front or in back, at a stroke they had all of the wagons withdraw either to the right or to the left, according to need or as best one could do with respect to the site. And all of the troops together, free from their impediments, made a front on the side where the enemy came. [9] If they were assaulted on the flank, the wagons were withdrawn toward the part that was secure, and [opposite] from the others made a front. [10] It seems to me it would be well to imitate this mode, since it is good and prudently governed, by sending the light cavalrymen ahead as explorers[3] of the country, then, having four brigades, to have them march in a file, each with its own

1. Or: which no one sees.
2. Lit.: herds of horses as speculators; for the marching order of the Romans, see Polybius VI 40.
3. Lit.: speculators.

wagons behind. [11] And because there are two types of wagons, that pertaining to particular soldiers and that pertaining to public use by the whole camp, I would divide the public wagons into four parts, and to each brigade I would assign their own part of them by also dividing the artillery and all of the unarmed in four, so that each number of armed [men] had their own impediments equally. [12] But because it sometimes happens that one marches through a country not only suspect, but so hostile that you fear being assailed any hour, you are necessitated, so as to go more securely, to change the form of the march and to go in an ordered mode, so that neither the peasants nor the army can offend you, finding you unprepared.[4] [13] In such a case the ancient captains usually went with the army squared (so they called this form, not because it was altogether square, but through its being able to fight on four sides)[5] and they said that they went prepared both for marching and for fighting. I do not want to distance myself from that mode, and to this effect[6] I want to order my own two brigades, which I have taken as a general rule. [14] Therefore, wanting to march securely through enemy country and to be able to respond on any side when assaulted unexpectedly,[7] and wanting, according to the ancients, to arrange it in a square whose opening is a 212-braccia space on each side, I would plan to make a square in this mode: I would first place the flanks 212 braccia distant from one another, and I would put five battalions on the flank lengthwise and three braccia distant from one another. Since each battalion occupies 40 braccia, these would occupy 212 braccia with their spaces. [15] Between the fronts and between the tails of these two flanks I would then put the other ten battalions, five on each side, so that four are close to the right flank along the front, and four [are close] to the left flank along the tail, leaving between each one an interval of three braccia. One, then, is near to the left flank along the front and to the right flank along the tail. [16] And because the opening from one flank to the other is 212 braccia, and these battalions, which are posted alongside one another by width and not by length, would occupy 134 braccia with their intervals, a space of 78 braccia would end up remaining between the four battalions placed on the front on the right flank and the one placed on [the front] on the left. And that same space would end up remaining in the battalions placed on the rear part. Nor would there be any other difference except that one space would end up on the back part and toward the right horn, the other would end up on the front part toward the left horn. [17] In the space of 78 braccia in front, I would place all of the or-

---

4. Lit.: unforeseen.
5. Parentheses in original; "squared" translates *quadrato,* "square" *quadra,* and "four" *quattro.*
6. See figure 5, page 173.   7. Lit.: unforeseen.

dinary velites; in that behind, the extraordinary [velites], which would end up being one thousand per space. [18] And wanting the space that is inside the army to be 212 braccia in every direction, it would be necessary for the five battalions that are placed at the front, and those that are placed at the tail, not to occupy any part of the space that the flanks take. It would therefore be necessary for the battalions behind to touch the tail of the flanks with their front, and for those in front to touch [the flanks'] front with their tail, so that in every corner of this army a space would be left for receiving another battalion. [19] And because there are four spaces, I would take four bands from the extraordinary pikes, and I would put one of them in every corner. In the middle of the vacancy of this army, I would put, as one battalion in a square, the two bands[8] of the said pikes that remain to me. At their front would be the captain-general with his own men around him. [20] Because these battalions so ordered all march in one direction but do not all fight in one direction, in placing them together one has to order for fighting those sides that are not guarded by other battalions. [21] One must therefore consider that the five battalions that are in front guard all the other parts except those in front, and ordinarily these have to be put together there, with the pikes forward. [22] The five battalions that are behind are guarded on all their sides except the side behind. One must therefore put these together so that the pikes end up behind, as we showed in its place.[9] [23] The five battalions that are on the right flank are guarded on all their sides except the right flank. [24] The five that are on the left are covered on all their sides except the left flank. Therefore, in ordering the battalions, one must make the pikes turn to the flank that remains uncovered. [25] Because the decurions end up along the front and along the tail, so that if they have to fight all of the arms and members are in their own places, the mode of doing this was mentioned when we reasoned about the modes of ordering the battalions.[10] [26] I would divide the artillery. I would put one part of it outside on the right flank and the other [outside] on the left. [27] The light cavalrymen I would send ahead to scout the country. [28] I would place the men-at-arms behind, part on the right corner and part on the left, forty braccia distant from the battalions. [29] In any mode you order an army, you have to take this generality regarding cavalry: it always has to be placed either behind or on the flanks. [30] And whoever puts them ahead, directly in front of the army, must do one of two things. Either put them so far ahead that, if they are repulsed, they have enough space to give them time to be able to get out of the way of your infantrymen and not to charge them. Or order them with so many intervals that the cavalrymen can enter through them without disor-

8. Lit.: flags.   10. See ibid.
9. See *AW* II 221–26.

dering the [infantrymen]. [31] And do not let anyone fail to esteem this reminder. For many have been ruined by not having heeded it, and have been disordered and broken by their very own [cavalrymen]. [32] The wagons and the
unarmed men are put in the piazza that is left inside the army, and are divided
so that they easily give passage[11] to anyone wanting to go either from one side of
the army to the other or from one front to the other. [33] In every direction from
the outer side, these battalions occupy two hundred and eighty-two braccia of
space,[12] without the artillery and the cavalrymen. [34] And because this square
is composed of two brigades, one must divide that part which makes one brigade
from that [which makes] the other. [35] And because the brigades are named by
their number, and each of them, as you know, has ten battalions and one head-
general, I would have the first brigade place its first five battalions on the front
and the other five on the left flank, and the head stand on the left corner of the
front. [36] [I would] then [have] the second brigade put its first five battalions
on the right flank, and the other five on the tail, and the head would be on the
right corner, which would end up doing the office of the *tergiduttore*. [37] Having ordered the army in this mode, one has to make it move and, while going,
observe this order completely. And without doubt, it is secure against all the tumults of the peasants. [38] Nor need the captain make any other provision
against tumultuous assaults than sometimes to give to some cavalryman or band
of velites a commission to push them back. [39] Nor will it ever happen that
these tumultuous troops end up finding you within range of sword or pike. For
unordered troops fear ordered ones, and it will always be seen that they make a
great assault with cries and with noises without otherwise getting near, just like
snapping dogs around a mastiff. [40] When he came to harm the Romans in
Italy, Hannibal passed through all of France and always took little account of the
tumultuous French.[13] [41] In wanting to march, one must have levelers and sap-
pers ahead who make the road for you. They will be guarded by those cavalrymen who are sent ahead to scout. [42] In this order, an army will march ten miles
a day, and enough of the sun will be left for it to encamp and eat, for ordinarily
an army marches twenty miles. [43] If it ends up being assaulted by an ordered
army, this assault cannot arise at once. For an ordered army comes at your pace,
so that you know in time to reorder yourself for battle and arrange yourself
quickly in the form, or similar to the form, of the army that was shown to you

11. Lit.: a way.

12. Here Fabrizio seems to contradict his earlier claim (see *AW* II 186) that a battalion will not
be square but rectangular, such that five battalions put together front-to-back would be considerably longer than five put together from side-to-side.

13. See Polybius III 51.

above.[14] [44] For if you are assaulted on the part ahead, you have nothing to do but to make the artillery that is on the flanks and the cavalrymen that are behind come ahead, and place them in those places and at that distance spoken of above.[15] [45] The thousand velites that are ahead go out of their places and divide themselves in five hundred per part, and enter into their places between the cavalrymen and the horns of the army. [46] In the opening that they leave, the two bands of extraordinary pikes, which I placed in the middle of the piazza of the army, will then enter. [47] The thousand velites that I placed behind leave that place and divide themselves along the flanks of the battalions as fortification for them, and through the opening that they leave, all of the wagons and the unarmed go out and are put at the back of the battalions. [48] Thus, the piazza being empty and each man having gone to his place, the five battalions that I placed behind come forward through the opening that is between one flank and the other, and march toward the front battalions. Three [of the five battalions that are coming forward] stop forty braccia from the [five battalions in front], with equal intervals between one [battalion and] another [from side to side]; and the [other] two [battalions] remain behind at a distance of forty braccia [from the three that have just moved ahead]. [49] That form can be ordered at once, and it ends up being almost the same as the first arrangement of the army that we showed.[16] And if it ends up more narrow in front, it ends up more thick on the flanks; which does not give them less strength. [50] But because the five battalions that are at the tail have pikes on the rear part, for the causes that I mentioned before,[17] it is necessary to have them come to the part ahead, wanting them to make the back into the front of the army. Therefore, one must either have it turn around battalion by battalion as a solid body, or have them enter at once between the orders of the shields, and go ahead. The latter mode is more rapid and less disorderly than making them turn around. [51] You must do this for all those that remain behind, in every quality of assault, as I will show you. [52] If one senses that the enemy will come on the rear part, one first has to make each one turn his face where he had his back, and immediately the army ends up having made its head into a tail and its tail into a head. [53] One must then keep all those modes of ordering the front that I speak of above. [54] If the enemy ends up attacking the right flank, one should make the whole army turn its face toward that side, then do all those things in the fortification of the front that are spoken of

---

14. The arrangement Fabrizio is about to show is represented in figure 6, page 174. The arrangement of the "army shown above" is represented in figure 4 and is described at *AW* III 48 ff.

15. For the placement of the artillery, see *AW* III 64–65; for that of cavalry, see *AW* III 19, 58–59.

16. Cf. figures 4 and 6, pages 172 and 174.   17. See *AW* V 22.

above, such that the cavalrymen, the velites, and the artillery are in places that conform to this front. [55] Here there is only this difference: that in varying the fronts of those that are switched, some have to go less [distance] and others more. [56] It is very true that in making a front from the right flank, the velites that had to enter into the intervals that are between the horns of the armies and the cavalrymen would be those that were nearer to the left flank. In their place, the two bands of extraordinary pikes would have to enter, posted in the middle. [57] But before they entered there, the wagons and the unarmed would clear out the piazza through the opening and withdraw behind the left flank; which would then end up being the tail of the army. [58] The other velites that had been posted on the tail according to the principal ordering would not change in this case, because that place, which from the tail would end up being the flank, would not remain open. [59] All of the other things must be done in the first front as spoken of. [60] What was said about making the right flank into a front is [also] understood to have been said about making the left flank into [a front]. For one must observe the same order. [61] If the enemy comes thick and ordered so as to assault you on two sides, the two sides that he comes to assault must be made strong with the two that are not assaulted by doubling the orders in each one and by dividing the artillery, the velites and the cavalrymen for each part. [62] If he comes on three or four sides, it is necessary that either you or he lack prudence. For if you are wise, you will never put yourself in a place in which the enemy can assault you on three or four sides with thick and ordered troops. For in wanting to offend you securely he must be so thick that he assaults you on every side with almost as many troops as your whole army has. [63] And if you are so lacking prudence that you enter into the lands and forces of an enemy that has three times more ordered troops than you, you can complain only about yourself if you end badly. [64] If this happens not through your fault, but through some misfortune,[18] it will be harm without shame, and will happen to you as to the Scipios in Spain and to Hasdrubal in Italy.[19] [65] But if the enemy does not have many more troops than you, and wants to assault you from more sides so as to disorder you, it will be his foolishness and your fortune.[20] For to do this he must thin himself out so that you can easily charge him on one side and sustain him on another, and in a brief time ruin him. [66] This mode of ordering an army is necessary against an enemy that one does not see but that one fears. It is a very useful thing to accustom your soldiers to put themselves together and march in such an order and, while marching, to order themselves so as to fight according

18. *Sventura*, not *sfortuna*.
19. For the two Scipios, see note to *AW* IV 77; for Hasdrubal, see Livy XXVII 39 ff.
20. *Ventura*, not *fortuna*.

to the first front, and then to return to the form in which they march, and from that, to make their tail and then their flank into a front, and from these to return to the first form. [67] These drills and accustomings are necessary when wanting to have a disciplined and practiced army. [68] In these things captains and princes have to exert themselves. Military discipline is nothing other than knowing how to command and execute them well; a disciplined army is nothing other than an army that is well practiced in these orders; and it would not be possible that whoever used similar discipline would ever, in these times, be beaten. [69] And if this squared form that I have shown you is somewhat difficult, such difficulty is necessary, and to be handled through training. For knowing well how to order and to maintain oneself in it, one will then know how to stay more easily in those that do not have so much difficulty.

ZANOBI. [70] I believe, as you say, that these orders are very necessary, and for my part, I would not know what to add or take away. [71] It is true that I desire to know two things from you: one, when you want to make the tail or the flank into the front, and you want to have them turn, whether this is commanded with the voice or with music; the other, whether those whom you send ahead to level the roads so as to make a way for the army must be among the same soldiers from your own battalions, or other vile troops deputed for a like exercise.

FABRIZIO. [72] Your first question is very important, for many times captains' armies have been disordered by their commandments not being understood well or interpreted badly. Therefore, amidst dangers, the words[21] with which one commands must be clear and sharp. [73] And if you command with music, one mode must be made so different from the other that they are not mistaken for each other. If you command with words, you must take the precaution of fleeing general words, and [must] use particular ones and flee those among the particular ones that can be interpreted sinisterly. [74] Many times the saying "Back! Back!" has made an army come to ruin.[22] Therefore, one must flee this word and use "Withdraw!" in its place. [75] If you want to turn them so as to change a front into either a flank or a back, never use: "Turn!" but say, "To the left! To the right! To the rear! To the front!" [76] All the other words have to be simple and sharp as well, like, "Close ranks! Stand strong! Forward! Retreat!" [77] And all those things that can be done with the voice are done [with the voice]; the other things are done with music. [78] As to the levelers, which is your second question, I would have my very own soldiers do this office, both because in the ancient military it was so done, and also so that there may be fewer un-

---

21. Lit.: voice. In sentences 71–77, *voce* is translated as "word" and "voice." *Parola*, also translated as "word" but never as "voice," does not occur in these sentences.

22. Cf. *D* III 14.1.

armed people and fewer impediments in the army. I would draw the needed number from every battalion, and I would have them take instruments fit for leveling and leave their arms with those files that were nearest to them, which would carry them for them. When the enemy came, they would not have to do anything but take them again and return to their orders.

ZANOBI. [79] Who would carry the instruments for leveling?

FABRIZIO. [80] The wagons deputed for carrying such[23] instruments.

ZANOBI. [81] I doubt that you would ever get these soldiers of yours to dig.

FABRIZIO. [82] Everything will be reasoned about in its place;[24] now I want to let this part be and to reason about the army's mode of living. For having so exhausted it, it seems to me to be time to refresh it and restore it with food. [83] You have to understand that a prince should order his army to be as unencumbered as possible and take away from it all those things that add a burden to it and make enterprises more difficult for it. [84] Among those that increase the difficulty more is having to keep the army provided with wine and with cooked bread. [85] The ancients did not think of wine. For, lacking it, they drank water tinged with a little vinegar to give it taste. So among the army's food supplies there was vinegar and not wine. [86] They did not cook their bread in ovens, as is done in the cities,[25] but they did provide flour, and with it every soldier satisfied himself in his own mode, having lard and fat as condiments that gave taste to the bread they made and maintained their strength. So the food provisions for the army were flour, vinegar, lard and fat, and for the horses, orzo. [87] Ordinarily, they had big and small herds of animals that followed the army and did not give much impediment since they did not need to be carried. [88] From this order it arose that an ancient army sometimes marched many days through isolated and difficult places without suffering the hardships of foraging, because they lived on things that could be pulled behind them easily. [89] The contrary happens in modern armies. Not wanting to do without wine and eating bread cooked in those modes in which [it is cooked] when they are at home, and not being able to make provision for this for long, they are often starved, or if they are indeed provided for, it is done with hardship and at very great expense. [90] Therefore, I would withdraw my army from this form of living, nor would I want them to eat bread other than that which they have cooked themselves. [91] As to wine, I would not prohibit drinking it or some of it coming along with the army,

---

23. A *simile*.   24. See *AW* VII 214.

25. *Cittadi*, coined in antiquity for a free city with its own name and emblem, can mean a "real city" or "principal city" as well as simply "city."

but I would not use either industry or any trouble so as to have it. And in other provisions I would govern myself altogether like the ancients. [92] If you would consider these things well, you would see how much difficulty is taken out of the way, and how many worries and hardships an army and a captain are deprived of, and how much convenience will be given to whatever enterprise one wants to make.

ZANOBI. [93] We have conquered the enemy in the field and marched upon his country. It is reasonable[26] that spoils be had, towns made to pay tribute, and prisoners taken. I would therefore want to know how the ancients governed themselves in these things.

FABRIZIO. [94] Here I will satisfy you. [95] Because I have reasoned about this with some of you another time,[27] I believe[28] that you have considered how present wars impoverish the lords that win as much as those that lose. For if the one loses his state, the other loses his money and his belongings. This was not so anciently, for the winner of wars got rich. [96] This arises from not taking account of spoils in these times, as was done anciently, but leaving everything to the discretion of the soldiers. [97] This mode makes two very great disorders: one, I have stated;[29] the other, that the soldiery becomes more greedy for spoils and less observant of orders. Many times it has been seen that greed for spoils has made the one who had been victorious lose. [98] Therefore, the Romans, who were the princes of this exercise,[30] provided for one and the other of these inconveniences by ordering it that all the spoils belong to the public, and that the public then dispense it as seemed [best] to it. [99] Therefore, they had questors in the armies, who were bursars, as we said.[31] All the tribute and spoils were located next to them. The consul used this to give the ordinary pay to the soldiers, to help the wounded and the sick, and for the other needs of the army. [100] The consul was very able, and often did, use it to yield spoils to the soldiers. But this concession did not make disorder. For having beaten the army, all the spoils were put in the middle and distributed by head, according to the qualities of each. [101] This mode made the soldiers attend to winning and not to robbing. And the Roman legions used to conquer the enemy and not follow him, because they never departed from their orders. Only the cavalry followed him with those

26. Lit.: Reason wants.   27. See *D* II 6; cf. *FH* VI 1.

28. In Italian, "I believe" begins the sentence.

29. Presumably immediately above in *AW* V 95.

30. For the Romans' management of spoils, see Polybius X 16, 17; Livy IV 53, V 20, X 46, XXXVII 57.

31. There seems to be no such previous discussion.

lightly armed and, if there were [any heavily armed soldiers, they were] soldiers other than legionaries. [102] For if the spoils had belonged to him who gained them, it would not have been possible or reasonable to keep the legions firm; and many dangers would have been borne. [103] Therefore, from this it arose that the public got rich, and at their own triumphs every consul carried into the treasury much treasure, all of which was from tributes and spoils. [104] The ancients considered another thing well:[32] they wanted each soldier to deposit a third of the money that they gave him next to the one who carried the flag of his battalion, who never reconsigned it to him unless the war was finished. [105] They did this for two reasons. First, because the soldiery made capital from its money; for since the greater part were young and negligent, they spent as much as they had without necessity. Second, because they knew that their belongings were next to the flag, they were forced to take more care of it and defend it with more obstinacy. Thus, this mode made them savers and hardy. [106] It is necessary to observe all of these things in wanting to return the military to its limits.

ZANOBI. [107] I believe that it is not possible that dangerous accidents not befall an army while it marches from place to place, wherein the industry of the captain and the virtue of the soldiers are needed if it wants to evade them. Therefore, I would value it[33] were you to relate any that occur to you.

FABRIZIO.[108] I will gladly[34] content you, it being especially necessary, and since I want to provide perfect knowledge[35] of this exercise. [109] While they are with the army, captains must guard themselves against ambushes above every other thing. One runs into these in two modes: either you enter them while marching, or by the art of the enemy you are drawn in, without your anticipating it. [110] Wanting to avoid the first case, it is necessary to send ahead double guards that scout the country. You should use more diligence the more the country is fit for ambushes, as are wooded and mountainous countries, because they are always put in a forest or behind a hill. [111] And just as an ambush ruins you when you don't foresee it, so you are not harmed[36] when you do foresee it. [112] Birds and dust have uncovered the enemy many times. For when the enemy comes to find you, he will always make a great deal of dust that will signal to you

---

32. For this discussion, see Vegetius II 20, who says, "It was a divinely inspired institution of the ancients to deposit ʿwith the standards' half the donative that the soldiers received" (Vegetius, *Epitome of Military Science*, trans. N. P. Milner [Liverpool: Liverpool University Press, 1993], 53). The donative, which far exceeded the soldiers' regular pay, consisted of bounty distributed on imperial birthdays and accession days (ibid., 53 n. 6).

33. Lit.: hold it dear.   35. Lit.: science.
34. Lit.: voluntarily.   36. Lit.: offended.

his approach. [113] A captain, by seeing doves and other birds that fly in formation[37] take off and circle around and not land in places where he should pass, has many times recognized an ambush of the enemy to be there, and has sent his troops ahead. Having recognized it, he has saved himself and harmed his enemy. [114] As to the second case of being drawn in, which we call being drawn in by a tug, you must be shrewd about easily believing those things that lack the reasonableness they have.[38] For instance, if the enemy puts spoils in front of you, you must believe that in them is a hook, and that a deception is hidden within. [115] If many enemies are chased by few of your [men], if few enemies assault many of your [men], if the enemies make a sudden and unreasonable retreat, you must always fear a deception in such cases. [116] And you must never believe that the enemy does not know how to conduct his own affairs. Indeed, if you want to be deceived less and want to bear less danger, the more the enemy is weak [or] the less the enemy is cautious, so much more must you esteem him. [117] And in this you have to use two diverse means, for you have to fear him in thought and in order, but with words and with other extrinsic demonstrations, show that you despise him. For this last mode makes your soldiers hope more to have victory; the other one makes you more cautious and less apt to be deceived. [118] And you have to understand that when one marches through enemy country, one bears more and greater dangers than in doing battle. Therefore, while marching, the captain must redouble his diligence.[39] The first thing he must do is to have the whole country through which he is marching described and depicted,[40] so that he knows the places, the number, the distances, the roads, the rivers, the marshes, and all of their qualities. To get to know this, he must have with him, diversely and in diverse modes, those who know the places, and question them with diligence, and compare what they say and, according to the comparisons, take note. [119] He ought to send cavalrymen ahead, and with them prudent heads, not so much to discover the enemy as to contemplate[41] the country, to see whether it compares with the design and with the notes that he has made of it. [120] He also ought to send guides guarded by the hope of reward and fear of penalty. Above all, he should have the army not know to what action he guides it. For there is nothing more useful in war than keeping silent the things that have to be done. [121] And you ought to warn your own soldiers to be prepared with their arms so that[42] a sudden assault does not disturb them. For

37. Or: line.   38. "They" refers to "things."

39. For the following discussion (*AW* V 118–26), see Vegetius III 6.

40. That is, he should have maps made.   42. Lit.: because.

41. Lit.: speculate; cf. *AW* V 3, 10.

things foreseen offend less. [122] To flee the confusions of the march, many have put the wagons and the unarmed under flags, and commanded them to follow them, so that if they have to stop or withdraw while marching, they can do it more easily. I much approve of this as something useful. [123] In marching one should also beware that one part of the army does not come unstuck from the other, or that by one going quickly and the other slowly, the army does not thin itself out. These things are cause for disorder. [124] Therefore, he needs to locate the heads in a place in which they maintain a uniform pace, holding back those who have sped up too much and speeding up the late ones. This pace cannot be better regulated than by music. [125] One ought also to widen the roads, so that a battalion can almost always go in order.[43] [126] One ought to consider the custom and the qualities of the enemy, and whether he usually assaults you in the morning or at midday or in the evening, and whether he is more powerful with his infantrymen or with his cavalrymen; and to order yourself and to prepare yourself according to your understanding. [127] But let us come to some particular accidents. [128] Removing yourself from before the enemy because you judge yourself inferior and, through this, not wanting to do battle with him, it sometimes happens as he comes behind you that you arrive at the bank of a river which takes you time to cross, so that the enemy is about to overtake and fight you. [129] Some who have found themselves in such a danger have enclosed their army on the rear part with a ditch, and filled it with brushwood and set it on fire, then crossed with the army without being able to be impeded by the enemy, as he was held back by the fire that was in the middle.

ZANOBI. [130] It is hard for me to believe that this fire could hold them back, especially because I recall having heard how Hanno the Carthaginian, as he was being besieged by the enemy, enclosed himself with timber on the part through which he wanted to break, and set it on fire. From this, since his enemy didn't know on which part to guard him, he had his army pass over those flames, by having each one keep his shield over his face so as to defend himself from the fire and from the smoke.[44]

FABRIZIO. [131] You speak well. But consider what I have said and what Hanno did. For I said that they made a ditch and filled it with brushwood, so that whoever wanted to pass through had to contend with the ditch and the fire. [132] Hanno made the fire without the ditch. And because he wanted to pass through it, he must not have made it hardy. For even without the ditch it would have hindered him. [133] Don't you know that Nabis the Spartan, besieged in Sparta by

---

43. *Ordinanza,* usually translated "militia."   44. See Frontinus I 5.27.

the Romans, set fire to a part of his town so as to impede the pace of the Romans, who had already entered inside? [134] And by means of the flames, he not only impeded their pace, but pushed them back outside.[45] [135] But let us return to our material. [136] Quintus Latatius, the Roman, having the Cimbri at his back and having arrived at a river, showed that he was giving time to the enemy to fight him so that[46] the enemy would give him time to cross. He therefore feigned wanting to camp there, had ditches made and some tents pitched, and sent some cavalrymen through the field foraging so that the Cimbri, believing that he was encamping, encamped as well and divided themselves in several parts to provide for food. By being crafty about this, he crossed the river without their being able to impede [him].[47] [137] To cross a river with no bridge, some have diverted it and drawn off part of it behind their back; and the other, having then become lower, was crossed with ease. [138] When wanting infantrymen more securely to cross rivers that are rapid, one puts part of the heaviest cavalrymen up [stream] to withstand the water, and the other part, down [stream] to help the infantrymen if some of them are conquered by the river while crossing.[48] [139] Rivers that one does not ford are also crossed with bridges, boats, and [floating] bags. It is therefore well for your armies to have the aptitude for being able to do all of these things. [140] Sometimes it happens that the enemy, opposed on the other bank, impedes you from crossing a river. [141] In wanting to conquer this difficulty there is no example better for imitating than that of Caesar. Having his army on the bank of a river in France, and his crossing impeded by Vercingetorix, the Frenchman, who had his troops on the other part of the river, he marched for several days along the river, and the enemy did likewise. [142] Having made an encampment in a wooded place fit for hiding troops, Caesar drew off three cohorts from each legion and had them stop in that place, commanding that once he had departed, they throw a bridge up and fortify it. With his other troops he continued the march. [143] Hence, upon seeing the number of legions and believing that no part had remained behind, Vercingetorix also followed him on the march. But Caesar, when he believed that the bridge was done, turned back around and, having found everything in order, crossed the river without difficulty.[49]

ZANOBI. [144] Do you have any rule for recognizing fords?

45. Nabis, tyrant of Sparta (207–192 B.C.), in 195 B.C.; see Livy XXXIV 39, who says that it was due solely to Pythagoras, a Spartan commander, that the city was saved by this stratagem while Nabis looked about in fear for a way to escape.

46. Lit.: because.

47. In 102 B.C., Quintus Lutatius Catulus.

48. See Vegetius III 7.

49. See Caesar, *Gallic War* VII 34–35.

FABRIZIO. [145] Yes, we have. [146] Between the stagnant and the running water, in the part which seems[50] like a ridge to him who looks at it, the river is always less deep. It is a place more fit to be forded than elsewhere. For the river has always deposited more in that place, and has collected more of that material that the deep [part of the river] takes with it. [147] Because it has been tested[51] many times, this is something very true.

ZANOBI. [148] If it ends up that the river has deepened the ford, such that the cavalrymen sink there, what remedy do you give for that?

FABRIZIO. [149] To make grates of timber and put them on the bottom of the river and cross on them. [150] But let's continue our reasoning. [151] If it happens that a captain goes[52] with his army between two mountains that have only two roads, the one ahead or the one behind, for saving oneself, and these are occupied by his enemies, as a remedy he has to do that what someone has done before him. This is to make a great and difficult-to-cross ditch on his rear part, and show the enemy that he wants to hold him back with it, so as to be able to force all of his forces through the road that remains open ahead without having any fear from behind. [152] Once the enemies believe this, they make themselves strong toward the open part and abandon the closed. He then throws a bridge of timber ordered to such an effect over the ditch, and on that part without any impediment he crosses and frees himself from the hands of the enemy. [153] Lucius Minucius, the Roman consul, was in Liguria with his armies, and had been closed up by his enemies between certain mountains from which he could not get out. [154] Therefore, on horseback he sent some Numidian soldiers he had in his army, who were badly armed and on little skinny horses, toward the places that had been guarded by the enemies. On first appearance, they made the enemies get together to defend the pass. But when they saw these badly ordered and, according to them, badly horsed troops, they widened the orders of their guard, esteeming them little. [155] When the Numidians perceived this, having spurred their horses and made a thrust upon them, they passed through without their being able to make any remedy. By wasting and plundering the country, those that passed through constrained the enemy to leave the pass free to the army of Lucius.[53] [156] Any captain who has found himself assaulted by a great multitude of enemies, has drawn himself together and given the enemy the ability to surround him entirely. Then, he has forced the part that he has recognized [to be] the weakest, and through that way has had room made, and saved himself. [157]

---

50. Lit.: makes.   52. *Condursi.*

51. Or: experienced; lit.: experimented.

53. In 193 B.C.; cf. Frontinus I 5.16, who incorrectly names Lucius Manucius, with Livy XXXV 11, who correctly names Quintus Minucius Thermus.

Marc Antony, retreating before the army of the Parthians, noticed how everyday when he moved at daybreak, the enemy assaulted him and harassed him for the whole march. So he took the policy of not leaving before midday. [158] So the Parthians, believing that he did not want to decamp for that day, returned to their quarters. And Marc Antony was then able to march the whole rest of the day without any molestation.[54] [159] This same [man], to flee the arrows of the Parthians, commanded his troops to go down on their knees when the Parthians came toward them, and the second file of the battalion to place its shields on the head of the first, the third on the second, the forth on the third, and so on successively. So that the whole army ended up being as if under a roof and defended from the enemy arrows.[55] [160] This is as much as occurs to me to tell you about what can happen to an army while marching. Therefore, if nothing else occurs to you, I will pass to another part.

54. In 36 B.C.; see Frontinus II 13.7.

55. See Frontinus II 3.15.

BOOK SIX

———— ∾ ————

ZANOBI. [1] I believe that it is well, since the reasoning must be changed, that Batista take up his office and I put down mine. And in this case we will end up imitating the good captains, according to what I have just understood here from the lord. They put the best soldiers ahead and behind the army, since it seemed necessary to them to have ahead whoever joins the fight hardily and behind whoever sustains it hardily. [2] Therefore, Cosimo began this reasoning prudently, and Batista will finish it prudently. [3] Luigi and I have carried it on in these middle [parts]. [4] And just as each of us has taken his own part willingly, so I do not believe that Batista is going to refuse his.

BATISTA. [5] I have let myself be governed up to here; so am I going to let myself in the future. [6] Therefore, Lord, I would be content to follow your reasonings, and, if we interrupt you with these practices, may you excuse us.

FABRIZIO. [7] As I told you already, you've done something very gratifying. For your interrupting me does not take away my fancy,[1] indeed it refreshes it in me. [8] But wanting to follow our material, I say that it is now time that we encamp this army of ours. For you know that everything desires rest, as well as security, for to rest and not to rest securely is not perfect rest. [9] I very much fear[2] you desired me first to encamp it, then have [it] march, and, lastly, [have it] fight.[3] And we have done the contrary. [10] We were led to this by necessity. For wanting to show, while marching, how an army was arranged from the form of marching into that of fighting, it was necessary first to have shown how it was ordered for a fight. [11] But to return to our material, I say that in wanting the

---

1. *Fantasia* (cf. *D* III 6.12).   2. Lit.: doubt.
3. Cf. *AW* III 44; Polybius VI 26; and the beginning of Vegetius III 8.

encampment to be secure, it must be strong and ordered. [12] The industry of the captain makes it ordered, the site or art makes it strong. [13] The Greeks used to seek strong sites, and would never have put themselves where there was not a ditch or a riverbank or a multitude of trees, or another natural shelter that might defend them. [14] But the Romans encamped securely not so much from the site as from art. Nor would they ever have encamped in places where they would not have been able to extend all of their men according to their discipline. [15] From this it arose that the Romans were able to keep one form of encampment, for they wanted the site to obey them, not they the site. [16] The Greeks could not observe this. For since they obeyed the site, and sites vary in form, they also had to vary their mode of encamping and the form of their encampment. [17] Thus, where the site lacked strength, the Romans supplied it with art and with industry.[4] [18] And because in this narration of mine I have wanted to imitate the Romans, I will not depart from them in their mode of encamping. Though I do not therefore observe their orders in everything, but take that part of them that seems to me to suit the present times. [19] I have said several times[5] that in their consular armies the Romans had two legions of Roman men, which [together] were around eleven thousand infantrymen and 600 cavalrymen. And they had another eleven thousand infantrymen more from troops sent by friends to help them. Nor did they ever have more foreign than Roman soldiers in their armies, except for cavalrymen. They did not care if the latter exceeded[6] the number in their own legions.[7] And, as in all of their actions, they put the legions in the middle and the auxiliaries on the sides. [20] They observed that mode when encamping as well, as you yourselves could have read in those who write on their affairs. Therefore, I am not going to narrate to you exactly how they encamped, but am going to tell you only with what orders I would at present encamp my army, and you will then recognize which part I have taken from Roman modes. [21] You know that, in contrast to[8] the two Roman legions, I took two brigades of infantrymen, of six thousand infantrymen and three hundred useful cavalrymen per brigade, and [you know] into what battalions, with what arms, and with what names I divided them. [22] You know how in ordering the army for marching and for fighting, I did not make mention of other troops, but have only shown how, in doubling the troops, one did nothing but double the orders.[9] [23] But wanting at present to show you the mode of encamping, it seems [well] to me not to remain with only two brigades, but to put together one whole[10]

---

4. See Polybius VI 42.

5. See *AW* III 40–43.

6. Lit.: passed.

7. Cf. *AW* III note 15.

8. Or: corresponding to.

9. See *AW* III 43–48, 76.

10. Lit.: just.

army composed, like the Roman, of two brigades and of as many auxiliary troops. [24] I do this because the form of the encampment is more perfect by encamping a perfect army. This did not appear necessary to me in the other demonstrations. [25] So wanting to encamp a whole[11] army of 24 thousand infantrymen and of two thousand useful cavalrymen, since they are divided in four brigades, two of our very own troops and two of foreign ones, I would take this mode.[12] [26] Having found the site where I want to encamp, I would raise the captain-flag, and around it I would describe a square that has each face fifty-braccia distant from it, each one of which looks to one of the four regions of heaven, that is, East, West, South, and North. I would want the encampment of the captain to be within that space. [27] And because I believe that it is prudent, and because the Romans did so in good part, I would divide the armed from the unarmed and I would separate the impeded from the unimpeded men. [28] I would encamp all or the better part of the armed on the Eastern part, and the unarmed and the impeded on the Western part, making the East the front[13] and the West the back of the encampment, and the South and the North would be the flanks. [29] And so as to distinguish the encampments of the armed, I would take this mode: I would make[14] a line from the captain-flag and would guide it toward the East for a space of 680 braccia. [30] I would then make two other [parallel] lines that have the former [line] in between them and are the [same] length as that one, but each one fifteen braccia distant from it. At the extremity of these I would want the East gate to be, and the space that is between the two extreme lines would be a street[15] that goes from the gate to the captain's encampment. It would end up being thirty-braccia wide and 630 long (because the encampment of the captain would occupy fifty braccia of it) and this would be called Captain Street. I would then make one street from the South gate all the way to the North gate, and it would pass through the front of Captain Street and graze the captain's encampment toward the East. It would be 1,250 braccia long (because it would occupy the whole width of the encampment)[16] and it also would be thirty-braccia wide and would be called Cross Street. [31] So having drawn what would be the captain's encampment and these two streets, one would begin to draw the encampments of our own two brigades. One of them I

11. Lit.: just.

12. See figure 7, page 175. For the discussion of the making of the encampment, see Polybius VI 27–32; cf. Vegetius III 8; Xenophon, *Education of Cyrus* VIII 5.1–16.

13. See Xenophon, *Education of Cyrus* VIII 5.3; cf. Vegetius I 23; Polybius VI 27.

14. Lit.: move.

15. Lit.: way, throughout the discussion of the encampment.

16. Parentheses in original.

would encamp on the right side of Captain Street, and one on the left. [32] Therefore, having crossed the space taken by the width of Cross Street, I would place thirty-two encampments on the left side of Captain Street and thirty-two on the right side, leaving between the sixteenth and seventeenth encampments a space of thirty braccia, which serves as a traverse street that would traverse all the encampments of the brigades, as will be seen in their distribution. [33] I would encamp the heads of the men-at-arms in the first [encampment], which would end up being joined to Cross Street, at the front of these two orders of [fifteen encampments]. In the fifteen encampments that follow after [the first encampments] on each side [of Captain Street], [I would encamp] the men-at-arms themselves. Since each brigade has 150 men-at-arms, they would come out to ten men-at-arms per encampment. [34] The spaces of the encampments of the heads would be forty braccia in width and ten in length. [35] And let it be noted that, anytime I say width, I mean the space from the South to the North, and when I say length, that from the West to the East. [36] Those of the men-at-arms would be fifteen braccia in length and thirty in width. [37] In the other fifteen encampments that follow on each side (those whose beginning crossed Traverse Street and had the same space as those of the men-at-arms), I would encamp the light cavalrymen. Being 150, they would come out to ten cavalrymen per encampment. And in the sixteenth [encampment] that remains, I would encamp their head, giving to him that same space that is given to the head of the men-at-arms. [38] Thus, the encampments of the cavalrymen of the two brigades would end up putting Captain Street in between [them] and give a rule to the encampments of the infantries, as I will narrate. [39] You have noticed how I encamped the 300 cavalrymen of each brigade, with their heads, in thirty-two encampments placed on Captain Street and beginning from Cross Street; how from the sixteenth to the seventeenth remains a space of thirty braccia to make a Traverse Street. [40] Therefore, wanting to encamp the twenty battalions that the two ordinary brigades have, I would put the encampments of every two battalions behind the encampments of the cavalrymen. These would each be 15 braccia in length and, in width, 30, like those of the cavalrymen, and would be joined at the rear part, so that the one touched the other. [41] And on each side, in every first encampment that is joined to Cross Street, I would encamp the constable of one battalion. This encampment would end up corresponding to the encampment of the head of the men-at-arms and would have only 20 braccia of space in width, and ten in length. [42] In the other fifteen encampments that follow after these on each side up to Traverse Street, I would encamp one battalion of infantrymen on each side. Since they are 450, they would come out to 30 per encampment. [43] I would place the other 15 encampments contiguous with those of the light cavalry on each side, with the same [sized] spaces, in which I would encamp another battalion of infantrymen on each side. [44] And in the last encampment I would put on each side the constable of a battalion, who would end up being joined to that of the head of the light cavalry, with a space of ten braccia in length and twenty in width. [45] So these two first orders of encampments would consist half of cavalrymen and half of infantrymen. [46] And because I want all the cavalrymen to be useful, as I told you in its place,[17] and since through this they do not have attendants who assist them in governing the horses or in the other necessary things, I would want these infantrymen who encamp behind the cavalrymen to be obliged to help their masters provide for and govern them, and for this they would be exempt from the other actions of the camp. This mode was observed by the Romans. [47] Then, on each side having left after these encampments a space of 30 braccia that makes a street, the one called First Street on the Right Hand, and the other, First Street on the Left, I would put on each side another order of 32 double encampments. They would turn their rear parts to one another, with the same [sized] spaces that I have mentioned, and be divided in the same mode after the sixteenth [encampment] so as to make Traverse Street. There I would encamp on each side four battalions of infantrymen with their constables on the ends[18] at the foot and at the head. [48] Having then left on each side another thirty-braccia space that makes a street that on one side is called the Second Street on the Right Hand and, on the other side, the Second Street on the Left, I would put on each side another order of thirty-two double encampments with the same distance and divisions. There I would encamp on each side another four battalions with their constables. [49] And thus the cavalrymen and the battalions of the two ordinary brigades would come to be encamped in three orders of encampments per side, and would have Captain Street in between [them]. [50] Because I had them composed of the very same men,[19] I would encamp the two auxiliary brigades on each side of these two ordinary brigades, with the same orders of double encampments, first putting one order of double encampments where they would encamp half cavalrymen and half infantrymen, thirty braccia distant from the others, so as to make a street, one of which is called Third Street on the Right Hand, and the other, Third Street on the Left. [51] And then I would make two other orders of encampments on each side, distinct and ordered in the same mode as the ordinary brigades, which would make two other streets. All of them would be called by the number and the side where they would be located. [52] So all of these bands of the army would end up being encamped in twelve orders of double

---

17. See *AW* II 322–26; cf. *AW* III 42.   18. *Testa*, usually translated "front."

19. That is, of troops carrying the same types and numbers of weapons.

encampments, and on thirteen streets, counting Captain Street and Cross [Street]. [53] From the encampments to the ditch, I would want a space to remain of one hundred braccia all around. [54] And if you calculate all of these spaces, you will see that from the middle of the encampment of the captain to the East gate [there] are 680 braccia. [55] There now remain two spaces, one of which is from the encampment of the captain to the South gate, the other [of which] is from the former to the North gate. So that by measuring from the point in the middle, each ends up being 625 braccia. [56] Then, taking from each of these the fifty braccia that the encampment of the captain occupies, the 45 braccia for the piazza that I want to give on each side, the 30 braccia of the street that divides each of the mentioned spaces in the middle, and the hundred braccia that are left on each part between the encampments and the ditch, a space remains on each side [of the captain's quarters] for encampments 400-braccia wide and one hundred long, measuring the length by the space that the captain's encampment takes.[20] [57] Hence, by dividing the said length through the middle, one would make on each side of the captain 40 encampments [that are] fifty-braccia long and 20 wide, which would end up being 80 encampments in all. In these would be encamped the head-general of the brigades, the bursars, the quartermasters,[21] and all of those who would hold office in the army, leaving some empty for the foreigners who come and for those who serve in the military by favor of the captain. [58] On the side behind the captain's encampment, I would make[22] a street, 31-braccia wide, from the South to the North, and it would be called Front Street. It would end up being placed along the 80 encampments mentioned, because this street and Cross Street have between them the captain's encampment and the 80 encampments that would be on its flanks. [59] From this Front Street, and on the side opposite the captain's encampment, I would make[23] another street, also 30-braccia wide, that would go from it to the West gate. It would correspond in site and in length to Captain Street and would be called Piazza Street. [60] Having placed these two streets, I would order the piazza where the market is held. I would place [the piazza] at the head[24] of Piazza Street, opposite the captain's encampment and adjoining Front Street. I would want it to be a square,[25] and would assign 96 braccia per side.[26] [61] On the right hand and the left hand of the said piazza, I would make two orders of encampments, so that each order would have 8 double encampments that would occupy

20. Thus, the "length" from East to West is shorter than the "width" from North to South.

21. Lit.: "masters of the camps."   23. Lit.: move.

22. Lit.: move.   24. *Testa,* usually translated "front."

25. The piazza depicted in figure 7, page 175, is rectangular rather than square.

26. Lit.: square.

12 braccia in length and 30 in width. So 16 encampments would end up being on each side[27] of the piazza, which would be in the middle, so that there would be 32 [encampments] in all. In these I would encamp those cavalrymen left over from the auxiliary brigades. And if these were not enough, I would assign them some of those encampments that have the captain in between them, and especially those that look out toward the ditches. [62] It now remains to encamp the pikes and the extraordinary velites that each brigade has. You know that each [brigade], according to our order, has a thousand extraordinary pikes and five hundred velites besides the ten battalions. So our own brigades have two thousand extraordinary pikes and a thousand extraordinary velites and the auxiliary [brigades have] as many of these. So one ends up having to encamp another six thousand infantrymen, all of which I would encamp in the part toward the West and along the ditches. [63] From the end of Front Street and toward the North, leaving a space of a hundred braccia from these to the ditch, I would place one order of five double encampments that all take up 75 braccia in length and sixty in width. Such that, having divided the width, each encampment would come out to fifteen braccia in length and 30 in width. [64] And because there would be ten encampments, they would encamp three hundred infantrymen, every encampment coming out to 30 infantrymen. [65] Then, leaving a space of 31 braccia, I would place in like modes and in like spaces another order of five double encampments, and then another, so that there would be five orders of five double encampments. So fifty encampments would end up being placed along a straight line on the North, all one hundred braccia distant from the ditches. They would encamp one thousand five hundred infantrymen. [66] Turning then to the left side[28] toward the West gate, in that whole tract that would go from [the fifty encampments just discussed] to the said gate, I would place five other orders of double encampments with the very same spaces and with the very same modes. It is true that from one order to the other there would not be more than fifteen braccia of space, in which a thousand infantrymen would again be encamped. And thus from the North gate to that of the West, as they turn around the ditches in one hundred encampments, partitioned in ten orders of five double encampments per order, would be encamped all the extraordinary pikes and velites of our own brigades. [67] Thus from the West gate to that of the South, as they turn around the ditches in the exact same mode, in another ten orders of ten encampments per order, would be encamped the extraordinary pikes and velites of the auxiliary brigades. [68] Their heads or constables could pick those encampments that seemed most convenient to them on the side

27. Lit.: hand.   28. Lit.: hand.

toward the ditches. [69] The artillery I would arrange all along the embankments of the ditches. And in all of the other space that remains toward the West, I would encamp all the unarmed and all the impediments of the camp. [70] And one has to understand that under this name of impediments, as you know, the ancients understood that whole train and all those things, besides the soldiers, that are necessary to an army, such as carpenters, smiths, horseshoers, stone-cutters, engineers, bombardiers (even though these could be numbered among the armed),[29] herdsmen with their herds of geldings and cattle that they need for the army to live, and then workers[30] of every art, together with the public wagons for the public supplies pertaining to living and arming. [71] Nor would I distinguish these encampments individually.[31] I would only draw the streets that they must not occupy. Then to all the said impediments I would assign the other spaces by kind, which would be four, that would remain between the streets; that is, one [space] to the herdsmen, another to the artisans and workmen, another to the public wagons for provisions, the fourth to those for arming. [72] The streets, which I would want left unoccupied, would be Piazza Street, Front Street, and then a street called Middle Street. It would depart from the North and go toward the South and pass through the middle of Piazza Street. It would make that effect on the West part which Traverse Street [makes] on the East part; [73] and, besides this, a street that turns around the inside part, along the encampments of the pikes and the extraordinary velites. [74] And all these streets would be 30-braccia wide. [75] And the artillery I would arrange along the ditches of the camp on the inside part.

BATISTA. [76] I confess that I do not understand this. Nor do I even believe that for me to say so is shameful, since this is not my training. [77] Nonetheless, this order pleases me much. I would only want you to resolve these doubts for me: first, why you make the streets and the spaces around so wide; the other, which gives me more concern, is how these spaces that you drew for the encampments have to be used.

FABRIZIO. [78] Know that I make all the streets thirty-braccia wide so that a battalion of ordered[32] infantry can go through them. I told you,[33] if you remember well, that each of these takes up 25 to 30 braccia in width. [79] It is necessary that the space between the ditch and encampments be a hundred braccia because one can manage the battalions and the artillery there, lead the spoils through it, and, if needed, have space to withdraw with new ditches and new em-

---

29. Parentheses in original.   31. Lit.: particularly.

30. Or: masters.

32. *Ordinanza*, usually translated as "militia."

33. See *AW* VI 74; cf. *AW* VI 30, 59.

bankments. [80] It is also better for the encampments to be very distant from the ditches, so as to be more distant from the fire and the other things that the enemy can throw to hurt them. [81] As to your second question, my intention is not that every space drawn by me be covered by one shelter only, but [that it] be used as proves convenient to those who encamp there, with either more or fewer tents, so long as one does not go beyond its limits. [82] And to draw up these encampments, there must be very practiced men and excellent architects, who, immediately after the captain has selected the place, know how to give it form and distribute it, distinguishing the streets, dividing the encampments with ropes and with spears so that they are ordered and divided practically at once. [83] And so that no confusion arises, the camp must always wind up in the very same mode so that each one knows on which street and in which space he has to find his encampment. [84] And one must observe this every time and in every place, so that it may seem a mobile city that carries with it the same streets, the same houses, and the same aspect wherever it goes. Those seeking strong sites who have to change form according to the variation of site cannot observe this thing. [85] But the Romans used to make the place strong with ditches, with ramparts, and with embankments, for they used to make a palisade around the camp and, in front of that, a ditch, ordinarily six-braccia wide and three deep. These spaces grew according to [how much] they wanted to stay in one place and according to [how much] they feared the enemy. [86] I for my part would not at present make the palisade, unless I wanted to winter in a place. [87] I would definitely make the ditch and the embankment not less than but greater said, according to necessity. [88] On account of[34] artillery, I would also make a ditch in a partial[35] circle on each corner of the encampment. From it, the artillery could hit the flank of anyone who came to attack the ditches. [89] One must also drill the soldiers in this drill of knowing how to order an encampment, and with that [drill] make the ministers ready to draw it up and the soldiers quick to know their places. [90] Nor is anything difficult, as will be said in its place.[36] [91] For I now want to pass to the guards of the camp, because without the distribution of guards all the other troubles would be vain.

BATISTA. [92] Before you pass to the guards, I would like you to tell me: when someone wants to put the encampments near to the enemy, what mode is taken? For I do not know how there is time to order them without danger.

FABRIZIO. [93] You have to know this: no captain encamps near to the enemy, unless the former is arranged to do battle any time the enemy wants.

---

34. Lit.: with respect to.   35. Lit.: half.

36. Perhaps a reference to the discussion beginning at *AW* VII 199 and promised at *AW* I 44.

[94] When someone is so arranged, there is no danger but the ordinary one. For two parts of the army are ordered to do battle, and the other part makes the encampments. [95] In this case, the Romans gave the task[37] of fortifying the encampments to the *triarii,* and the *principes* and the *hastati* stayed in arms. [96] They did this because if the enemy came, since the *triarii* are the last to fight, they had time to leave their work and take up their arms and enter their places.[38] [97] In imitation of the Romans, you would have to have the encampments made by the battalions that you want to put in the last part of the army in the place of the *triarii.* [98] But let's return to reasoning about the guards. [99] It does not seem to me that I have found, among the ancients, that they kept guards, which they [now] call sentinels, outside of the ditches at a distance so as to guard the camp at night, as is done today.[39] [100] They did this, I believe, thinking that the army could easily remain deceived through the difficulty that there is in inspecting[40] them, and through their being able to be either corrupted or oppressed by the enemy. So they judged trusting in them [to be] dangerous, either in part or entirely. [101] Therefore, the whole guard force was inside the ditches. They did this with diligence and with very great order, punishing capitally anyone who deviated from such an order. [102] How it was ordered by them I will not otherwise tell you, so as not to bore you, since you can see it yourselves if, up to now, you have not seen it.[41] [103] I will only briefly tell you what would be done by me. [104] I would ordinarily have a third of the army stay armed every night, and of that, a fourth part always on foot. That [part] would be distributed along all of the embankments and through all the army, with double guards placed on every corner. Of these, part would stay put, part would continually go from on side of the encampment to the other. [105] And during the day, if I had the enemy near, I would also observe this order that I mention. [106] As to giving out the password[42] and renewing it every evening, and doing other things that are used by similar guards, I will not otherwise speak of, as being things [that are] known.[43] [107] I will recall only one thing as being very important and which produces much good when it is observed and much bad when not observed. It is that great diligence be used toward anyone who does not encamp inside the camp at night

37. Lit.: way.

38. Cf. Vegetius I 25, III 8; Xenophon, *Education of Cyrus* VIII 5.9.

39. Lit.: is used today; see Vegetius III 8, near the end, for the assertion that the cavalry was responsible for nighttime patrols outside the camp.

40. Lit.: seeing them again.

41. For the following discussion, see Polybius VI 35.

42. Lit.: name.   43. See Polybius VI 34.

and toward anyone new who comes there. [108] And it is an easy thing to in-spect[44] anyone who encamps in the order that we have drawn. For since every encampment has the number of its men determined, it is an easy thing to see if there are men missing or if there is a surplus. And when some are missing with-out permission,[45] [it is easy] to punish them as fugitives and, if there is a surplus, to understand who they are, what they are doing, and their other conditions. [109] This diligence makes it so that the enemy cannot, except with difficulty, do business[46] with your heads and be knowledgeable of your counsels. [110] If this thing had not been observed with diligence by the Romans, Claudius Nero, when he had Hannibal nearby, could not have departed from his own encamp-ments that he had in Lucania, and gone to and returned from the Marches, with-out Hannibal having had presentiment of anything.[47] [111] But it is not enough to make these orders good unless one makes them be observed with great sever-ity. For in an army there is nothing that needs[48] as much observance as is re-quired [for this]. [112] Therefore, the laws for its fortification must be harsh and hard, and the executor very hard. [113] The Romans punished with capital pun-ishment anyone who failed on guard, anyone who abandoned the place he had been given to fight, anyone who carried any concealed thing outside of the en-campments, if anyone said he had done something outstanding in the fight and had not done it, if some had fought contrary to[49] the commandment of the cap-tain, and if anyone had thrown away his arms in fear.[50] [114] And when it hap-pened that a cohort or an entire legion had made a similar error, so as not to have all of them die, they put all [of their names] in a bag, drew out a tenth part, and killed them.[51] [115] This punishment was used[52] so that if each did not feel it, each nonetheless feared it. [116] And because where there are great punishments, there should also be rewards. To have the men fear and hope at one stroke, they had rewards offered for every outstanding deed: to him who saved the life of one of his fellow[53] citizens while fighting, to him who first jumped over the wall of the enemy town, to him who first entered the encampments of the enemies, to

44. Lit.: see again.   46. Lit.: practice.

45. Lit.: license.

47. In 207 B.C.; see Frontinus I 1.9; Livy XXVII 43–47.

48. Lit.: wants.   49. Lit.: outside of.

50. See Polybius VI 37. Not all proscribed acts mentioned in Polybius are named by Machi-avelli, and Polybius mentions neither the offense of taking concealed things out of the camp nor that of fighting against the order of the commander (for the latter see Livy VIII 6–8; *D* II 16.1, III 1.3, 22.4, 34.2.).

51. See Polybius VI 38.   53. Lit.: own.

52. Lit.: done or made.

him who had wounded or killed the enemy while fighting, to him who had
thrown [the enemy] from his horse.[54] [117] And thus every virtuous act was
recognized and rewarded by the consuls and publicly praised by each. And besides the glory and the fame they acquired among the soldiers, those who received gifts for any of these things showed them with solemn pomp and with great
demonstrations among their friends and relatives when they had returned to
their fatherland. [118] Thus, it is not marvelous if that people acquired so much
empire, since it paid so much attention to the punishment and reward of[55] those
who merited either praise or blame, either through their good or through their
evil doings. The greater part of these things would have to be observed. [119] Nor
does it seem [well] to me to be silent about the mode of punishment observed
by them. It was that when the wicked [man] was convicted[56] before a tribune or
consul, he was hit by him lightly with a rod. After that hit, the wicked [man] was
allowed to flee and all the soldiers to kill him. So that at once each threw either
stones or darts, or hit him with other arms, in such a manner[57] that he went
along barely alive, and very rarely did they escape. And such as did escape, were
not allowed to return home, except with so many disadvantages and ignominies
that it was much better to die.[58] [120] One sees this mode is almost observed by
the Swiss, who have the condemned killed popularly by the other soldiers. [121]
This is well considered and optimally[59] done. For to want one individual not to
be a defender of someone wicked, the best remedy that is found is to make him
the punisher of the latter. For he favors him with a different respect and he longs
for his punishment with a different desire when he himself is the executioner
than when the execution belongs to another. [122] Thus, to want one individual
not to be favored in his errors by the people, a great remedy is to make the people
have to judge him. [123] As fortification of this, one can adduce the example of
Manlius Capitolinus, who, having been accused by the senate, was defended by
the people up until it became the judge of him. But having become arbiter of his
cause, it condemned him to death.[60] [124] Therefore, this is a mode of punishing

---

54. See Polybius VI 39, where entering the enemies' encampments is not mentioned.

55. Lit.: having so much observance of punishment and of merit toward.

56. *Convinto*, usually translated as "conquered."

57. Lit.: of a quality.   58. See Polybius VI 37.

59. *Ottimamente* is juxtaposed to *popolarmente* [popularly] above. In Florentine parlance and
politics, the *ottimati* or *grandi* constituted the upper crust of the political class, while the *popolari*
constituted its lower rungs (though the term could be applied to the political class as a whole).
Machiavelli refers to the people and the great as the two most important "humors" (see *P* 9; *D* I
4.1; *FH* II 12, III 1; cf. *P* 19.76–77).

60. See Livy VI 19–20; cf. *D* III 8.1.

that takes away tumults and makes justice be observed. [125] And because to check armed men neither the fear of the laws nor that of men is enough,[61] the ancients added the authority of God. And therefore with very great ceremony they made their soldiers swear to the observance of military discipline, so that if they acted against it, they not only had to fear the laws and men, but God. [126] And they used every industry to rule them with religion.

BATISTA. [127] Did the Romans permit women to be in their armies, or the use of those idle games that are used today?

FABRIZIO. [128] They prohibited the one and the other. [129] And this prohibition was not very difficult. For there were so many exercises in which they kept the soldiers, both individually[62] and generally, occupied everyday, that no time was left to them for thinking or for Love[63] or for games, nor for other things that seditious and useless soldiers do.

BATISTA. [130] That pleases me. [131] But tell me: when the army had to decamp,[64] what order did they keep?[65]

FABRIZIO. [132] The captain's trumpet was sounded three times. [133] At the first sound, the tents were taken away and the packs were made; at the second, the baggage was loaded; at the third, every armed part moved in the mode that I mentioned above,[66] with the impediments [coming] after and the legions in the middle. [134] You[67] would therefore have to have one auxiliary brigade move and, after that, their particular impediments, and with those, a fourth part of the public impediments, which would be all of those that had been lodged in one of the squares that we demonstrated a little while ago.[68] [135] It would therefore be necessary to have each one of these assigned to one brigade, so that when the army is moved, each one knows which place for marching is his. [136] And thus every brigade ought to move out[69] with its own impediments, and with a fourth part of the public [impediments] at its back, in the mode in which we demonstrated the Roman army marched.[70]

BATISTA. [137] In placing the encampment did they consider[71] other [things] than the ones you have mentioned?

---

61. Cf. *AW* I 246.

62. Lit.: particularly.

63. Lit.: Venus.

64. Lit.: rise up.

65. See Polybius VI 40.

66. See *AW* V 2–11.

67. An unusual instance of the formal or plural second person in that this seems to be advice to a practicing or would-be prince (which advice is elsewhere given in the familiar *tu* form) rather than to those reasoning with Fabrizio.

68. See *AW* VI 69–71; cf. figure 7, page 175.

69. Lit.: go away.

70. See *AW* V 2–11.

71. Lit.: have respects.

FABRIZIO. [138] I tell you anew that in encamping the Romans wanted to be able to keep to the accustomed form in their own mode. So as to observe this, they did not have any respect. [139] But as to other considerations,[72] they had two principal ones: one, to put themselves in a healthy place; the other, to put themselves where the enemy could not besiege [the encampment] and cut off the way to water and to food supplies. [140] So as to flee infirmity, they fled marshy places or those exposed to noxious winds. [141] They recognized this not so much from the quality of the site as from the faces of the inhabitants. When they looked badly colored or winded or full of another infection, they did not lodge there. [142] As to the other part [of your question] about not being besieged, one must consider the nature of the place, [as well as] where friends are posted and where enemies. From this, [you must] make your conjecture as to whether you can be besieged or not. [143] Therefore, the captain must be very expert about the sites of countries, and have around many who have the same expertise.[73] [144] Sickness and hunger are also fled by not having the army disordered. For to want to maintain it healthy, it must be worked out that the soldiers sleep under the tents, that one encamps where there are trees that make shade, where there is wood to be able to cook the food, and that it not march in the heat. [145] Therefore, in the summer, one needs to take it from the encampment before day, and in the winter, to beware that it not march through the snow and through ice without the convenience of a fire, and [that it] not lack the necessary clothing and not drink bad water. [146] Have doctors cure those who get sick by chance. For a captain has no remedy when he has to fight with sickness and the enemy. [147] But nothing is so useful in maintaining the army healthy as is exercise. And therefore the ancients had them exercise each day. [148] From this it is seen how much this exercise is worth. For in encampments, it makes you healthy, and in fights, victorious. [149] As to hunger,[74] not only is it necessary to see that the enemy not impede your food supplies, but to foresee from where you have to get them, and to see that what you have is not lost. [150] Therefore, you must always have a one-month supply [of provisions] with the army, and then tax your nearby friends to provide them to you daily. [You must] put supplies of them in some strong place and, above all, dispense them with care,[75] giving to each a reasonable measure every day. And [you must] observe this part so that it does not disorder you. For in war, every other thing can in time be conquered,

72. For the following discussion of the troops' health and the nature of the site, see Vegetius III 2; cf. Xenophon, *Education of Cyrus* I 6.16–17.

73. Cf. *D* III 39; *P* 14.

74. For the following discussion of supplying the army, see Vegetius III 3.

75. Lit.: diligence.

this alone in time conquers you. [151] Nor will any enemy of yours who can over-come you with hunger ever seek to conquer you with iron. For if the victory is not as honorable, it is more secure and more certain. [152] Thus, that army can-not flee hunger which does not observe justice and which licentiously consumes whatever it wishes.[76] For the one disorder makes food supplies not come to it; the other [makes] what has come be consumed uselessly. [153] Therefore, the an-cients ordered it that what they gave out be consumed, and at the time they wanted [it to be]. For no soldier ate except when the captain [did so]. [154] How much this is observed by modern armies each knows, and they cannot de-servedly be called ordered and sober like the ancients, but licentious and drunk.

BATISTA. [155] At the beginning of ordering the encampment, you said[77] that you did not want to stay in two brigades only, but that you wanted to take four, so as to show how a complete[78] army is encamped. [156] Therefore, I would like you to tell me two things: one, when I have more or fewer men, how do I have to encamp them; [157] the other, what number of soldiers would be enough to fight against any enemy whatsoever?

FABRIZIO. [158] As to the first question, I respond to you that if the army has more or less than four or six thousand[79] soldiers, one takes away or adds as many orders of encampments as suffice. And with this mode, it can be increased or decreased infinitely. [159] Nonetheless, the Romans, when they joined two consular armies together, made two encampments and turned the unarmed parts toward one another.[80] [160] As to the second question, I reply to you that the ordinary Roman army was around 24 thousand soldiers. But when a greater force pressed them, the most that they put together was fifty thousand. [161] With this number they opposed the French, who assaulted them after the first war that they had with the Carthaginians.[81] [162] With the same they opposed Hannibal. And you have to note that the Romans and the Greeks made war with few, fortified by order and by art. The occidentals and orientals made it with a multitude. But one of these nations, the occidentals, used natural fury; the other [used] the great obedience that those men had for their king. [163] But in Greece and in Italy, since there is not natural fury or natural reverence toward their king, it has been necessary to turn to discipline, which is of so much force that it has made it that the few have been able to conquer the fury and the natural

---

76. Lit.: that which seems [good] to it.   78. Lit.: just.

77. See *AW* VI 23–25.

79. That is, less than four thousand or more than six thousand.

80. Cf. Polybius VI 32.

81. The attacks of the "French" on Rome culminated in their defeat at Telamon in 225 B.C. They were entirely repelled by 222 B.C.; see Polybius II 22 ff.

obstinacy of the many.[82] [164] Therefore, wanting to imitate the Romans and the
Greeks, I say that the number of fifty thousand soldiers ought not to be passed,
indeed even fewer of them [ought to be] taken. For more make confusion, nor
do they let discipline and learned orders be observed. [165] And Pyrrhus used to
say that with fifteen thousand men he wanted to assail the world.[83] [166] But let
us pass to another part. We have had this army of ours win a battle, and shown
the travails that can occur in that fight. We have had it march, and narrated those
impediments by which it can be surrounded while marching. And in the end we
have encamped it where it must not only take a little rest[84] from its passed
troubles, but also think of how it must finish the war. For in the encampments
many things are managed, especially when enemies in the country and suspect
towns still remain for you, against which it is well to be secure, and to storm
those that are enemies. [167] Therefore, it is necessary to come to these demonstrations and to cross these difficulties with that glory with which we have served
in the military till now. [168] Therefore, descending to particulars, I say that if
you should need many men or many people to do a thing that would be useful
to you and of great harm to them (for instance, either undoing the walls of their
city or sending many of them into exile),[85] it is necessary for you either to deceive
them so that each believes only what touches him, so that by not assisting one
another, they all later find themselves oppressed without remedy; or, on one and
the same day, command to all what they must do, so that since each one believes
himself to be the only one to whom the commandment was made, [each] thinks
of obeying and not of remedies. And so it is that without tumult your commandment is executed by each. [169] If you had suspected the faith of a certain
people and wanted to secure yourself against it and occupy it unforeseen, so as
to be able to color your plan more easily, you cannot do better than to communicate to it some plan of yours, requesting help from it and showing that you
want to do another enterprise and have a spirit alien to any thought of [the suspected people]. This will make them not think of its defense, not believing that
you think of harming it, and it will give you the convenience of easily being able
to satisfy your desire. [170] When you sense[86] that there is in your army someone
who keeps your enemy advised as to your plans, so as to make use of his wicked
spirit, you cannot do better than to communicate to him those things that you
do not want to do and to keep quiet those that you want to do, and say you fear[87]
the things that you do not fear and hide those that you do fear. Since he believes

82. See Aristotle, *Politics* 1327b20–38; cf. *AW* I 121–23, II 81.
83. Source unknown.
84. Lit.: requiem.
85. Parentheses in original.
86. Lit.: [have a] presentiment.
87. Lit.: doubt, throughout this sentence.

he knows your plans, it will make him make some enterprise wherein you would easily be able to deceive and oppress him. [171] If you should plan, as did Claudius Nero, to diminish your army by sending help to some friend and that the enemy not be aware of it, it is necessary not to diminish the encampments, but to maintain the signs and orders entirely, everywhere making the same fires and the same guards.[88] [172] Thus, if new troops are conjoined with your army and you want the enemy not to know that you have been fattened, it is necessary not to increase the encampments. For to keep your actions and plans secret [would] always be very useful. [173] Hence, while with his army in Spain, Metellus responded to one individual who asked him what he would do the next day, that if his own shirt knew, he would burn it.[89] [174] Marcus Crassius, said to one individual who asked him when he would move the army, "Do you believe you may be the only one not to hear the trumpet?"[90] [175] If you should desire to understand the secrets of your enemy and to know his orders, some were used to sending ambassadors and, with them, men very expert in war in the clothes of attendants. The latter, having taken the opportunity to see the enemy army and to consider its strengths and its weaknesses, gave them the opportunity to overcome him.[91] [176] Some have sent into exile one individual intimate with them, and by means of that one, known the plans of his adversary.[92] [177] One also understands similar secrets from enemies, when one takes prisoners from them to this effect.[93] [178] In the war Marius made with the Cimbri, so as to know the faith of those Frenchmen who inhabited Lombardy and were confederated with the Roman people, he sent them opened and sealed letters. In the open ones, he wrote that they not open the sealed ones except at such and such a time. Before that time, by asking for them back and finding them opened, he knew their faith not to be entire.[94] [179] Having been assaulted, some captains have not wanted to go to find the enemy, but have gone to assail his country and constrained him

---

88. See *AW* VI 110 and note 47.

89. In 79 B.C., Quintus Caecilius Metellus Pius was made proconsul in Spain, where he fought Sertorius from 79–72 B.C.; see Frontinus I 1.12.

90. Marcus Lucinius Crassus (115–53 B.C.); see Frontinus I 1.13; cf. Plutarch, *Demetrius* 28.

91. See Frontinus I 2.1, where Scipio Africanus is said to have used this means in 203 B.C. against Syphax, king of the Maesulii; cf. Livy XXX 4.

92. See Frontinus I 2.3, where it is said that the Carthaginians, afraid that Alexander the Great would invade Africa, pretended to send Hamilcar Rhodinus into exile in 331 B.C. so as to learn Alexander's plans; cf. Xenophon, *Education of Cyrus* VI 1.

93. See Frontinus I 2.5, where Marcus Cato (the Elder) is said to have staged an attack while in Spain in order to seize a prisoner who was then tortured for secret information.

94. In 104 B.C.; see Frontinus I 2.6, where the war is said also to have been against the Teutons and the faith of the Ligurians also to have been tested.

to return to defend his own house.[95] [180] That has gone well many times. For your own soldiers begin to conquer, to fill themselves with spoils and confidence; those of the enemy are afraid, since it seems to them that from [being] victors they have become losers. [181] So for him who has made this diversion, many times it has gone well. [182] But it can be done only by him whose country is stronger than is that of the enemy. For if it were otherwise, he would end up losing. [183] It has often been something useful to a captain that finds himself besieged in his encampments by the enemy, to start a negotiation for an accord and make a truce with him for some day[s]. This only makes the enemies more negligent in every action, such that by making use of their negligence, you can easily have the opportunity to get out of their hands. [184] In this way Sulla freed himself two times from his enemies. With this same deception Hasdrubal in Spain got away from the forces of Claudius Nero that had besieged him.[96] [185] In freeing oneself from the forces of the enemy, it is also well, beside what was said, to do something that makes him delay. [186] One does this in two modes. Either assault him with part of your forces, so that he, intent on that fight, makes it convenient for the rest of your troops to be able to save themselves. Or, make some new accident arise that, by the novelty of the thing, makes him marvel and, through this cause, remain in doubt and stalled, as you know Hannibal did. Being closed in by Fabius Maximus, he put small, lighted lamps between the horns of many oxen so that Fabius, made uncertain[97] by this novelty, did not think to impede his passage otherwise.[98] [187] Among all his other actions, a captain ought with every art to contrive to divide the forces of his enemy, either by making him suspect his own men in whom he confides, or by giving him a cause that has him separate his own troops and, through this, become weaker. [188] The first mode is done by taking care of the things of someone of those whom [the enemy] has near him, such as preserving his troops and his possessions during the war, [or] giving him his children or his other necessities of his without ransom. [189] You know that Hannibal, having burned all the fields around Rome, allowed only those of Fabius Maximus to be saved.[99] [190] You know that Coriolanus, coming with the army to Rome, conserved the possessions of the nobles,

95. See Frontinus I 3.8, where Scipio is said to have sent troops to Africa so as to force Hannibal to leave Italy (204 B.C.); cf. Livy XXVIII 40 ff.

96. Sulla in 90 B.C. during the civil wars and two years earlier in Cappadoccia against Archelaus, a general of Mithridates; Hasdrubal in 211 B.C. in Spain against Claudius Nero; see Frontinus I 5.17–19.

97. Lit.: suspended.

98. In 217 B.C.; see Frontinus I 5.28; cf. Livy XXII 16, 17; Polybius III 93, 94; D III 40.1.

99. In 217 B.C.; see Frontinus I 8.2; cf. Livy XXII 23.

and those of the plebs he burned and sacked.[100] [191] All the ambassadors that Jugurtha had sent to Metellus while he had the army against Jugurtha were asked by him to give Jugurtha to him [as] a prisoner. And by later writing letters to these same men about the same matter, he worked it out so that in a small time Jugurtha was suspicious of all of his own counselors and eliminated them by diverse modes.[101] [192] When he was taking refuge with Antiochus, the Roman ambassadors dealt so familiarly with Hannibal that Antiochus, having become suspicious of him, soon after no longer trusted his counsels.[102] [193] As to dividing the enemy troops, there is no more certain mode than to have the country of part of them assaulted, so that having been constrained to defend it, they abandon the war. [194] Fabius kept this mode while encountering the forces of the French and of the Tuscans, Umbrians, and Samnites with his army.[103] [195] Titus Didius, had few troops compared to[104] those of his enemies and was awaiting a legion from Rome that the enemies wanted to go and oppose. So that they would not go there, he let it be known[105] throughout all his army that he wanted to do battle with the enemies on the next day. He then saw to it[106] that some of the prisoners that he had, had the opportunity to flee. By reporting the consul's order to fight the next day, they made the enemies not go to encounter that legion so as not to diminish their own forces. And by this way it conducted itself to safety.[107] This mode did not serve to divide the forces of the enemies, but to double his own. [196] So as to divide [the enemy's] own forces, some used to allow him to enter into their own country and, as proof, allowed him to take many towns, so that by putting guards in them he might diminish his own forces. Having made him weak in this way, [they have] assaulted him and won. [197] Wanting to go into a province, some others have feigned wanting to assault another and used so much industry that, having suddenly entered [the province] where it was not feared they would enter, they have conquered it before the enemy has had time to succor it. [198] For your enemy, not being certain whether you are going to go back to the place first threatened by you, is constrained not to abandon one place and help the other. Thus, he often defends neither the one nor the

---

100. In 491 B.C.; see Frontinus I 8.1; cf. Livy II 39; D I 7.1.

101. In 108 B.C.; see Frontinus I 8.8; cf. Sallust, *Jugurthine War* 61, 62, 70–72.

102. In 191 B.C., Antiochus III of Syria; see Frontinus I 8.7; cf. Livy XXXV 13.

103. During the fifth consulship of Quintus Fabius Maximus Rullianus (295 B.C.), these peoples allied against Rome; Frontinus I 8.3; cf. Livy X 27.

104. Lit.: respect to.   106. Lit.: kept the mode.

105. Lit.: gave voice.

107. While Titus was in Spain (98–93 B.C.).

other.[108] [199] Besides the things said, if sedition or discord arises among his soldiers, it is important for a captain to know how to extinguish them with art. [200] The best mode is to punish the heads of the errors. But do it so that you oppress them before they have been able to notice it. [201] The mode is: if they are distant from you, do not call only the guilty, but all the others together with them, so that, not believing that it is for the cause of punishing them, they do not become contumacious but make it convenient to punishment [them]. [202] When they are present, one must make oneself strong with those who are not culpable and, by means of their help, punish them. [203] When there is discord among them, the best mode is to put them in danger; this fear alone always makes them be united.[109] [204] But that which above every other thing keeps the army united is the reputation of the captain, which arises through his virtue alone. For neither blood nor authority ever gave it without virtue.[110] [205] And the first thing that a captain is expected to do is to keep his soldiers punished and paid. For whenever he lacks payment, he must lack punishment. For you cannot punish a soldier who robs if you do not pay him or who, wanting to live, cannot abstain from robbing. [206] But if you pay him and do not punish him, he becomes insolent in every mode. For you become of small esteem. Whoever arrives there cannot maintain the dignity of his rank, and by not maintaining it, tumult and discord, which are the ruin of an army, follow of necessity. [207] The ancient captains had a vexation[111] from which present ones are almost free. It was that of interpreting sinister auguries to their purpose. For if a bolt [of lighting] fell upon an army, if the sun or the moon was eclipsed, if an earthquake came, if the captain, either mounting or dismounting his horse, fell, it was interpreted by the soldiers in a sinister way, and generated in them so much fear that if they came to battle, they would easily lose it. [208] Therefore, as soon as a similar accident arose, the ancient captains either showed the cause of it and reduced it to a natural cause, or interpreted it to their purpose. [209] Caesar, falling in Africa while leaving a ship, said: "Africa I have taken you."[112] [210] And many have given the cause of an eclipse of the moon, and of earthquakes. These things in our times cannot happen, both through there not being so much superstition in our men, and because our religion completely removes such opinions from itself. [211]

108. Cf. *AW* VII 97.   110. Cf. *D* I 58.1, 58.4, 60; *AW* IV 137.

109. See Frontinus I 9.

111. *Molestia*, translated as "molestation" at *AW* V 158.

112. See Suetonius, *Julius Caesar* 59, where Caesar is also said to have mocked the prophesy that the Scipios would always be successful in Africa; cf. Frontinus I 12.1, where the same story is told of Scipio Africanus, who says, "Congratulate me, soldiers! I have hit Africa hard;" see also Frontinus I 12.2, where Caesar, who slips while embarking, says, "I seize you, Mother Earth."

However, when they should occur, one must imitate the orders of the ancients.
[212] When either hunger or other natural necessity or human passion has led
your enemy to ultimate desperation and, chased by that, he comes to fight with
you, you must stay inside your encampments and as much as is in your power
flee the fight. [213] The Lacedaemonians did so against the Messenians; Caesar
did so against Afranius and Petreius.[113] [214] While he was consul against the
Cimbri, for many continuous days Fulvius had his cavalry assault the enemies.
And he considered how they left their encampments so as to follow them. Thus,
he put an ambush behind the encampments of the Cimbri and, having had the
cavalry assault them, and the Cimbri leaving their encampments so as to follow
them, Fulvius occupied them and sacked them.[114] [215] It has been of great utility to a certain[115] captain, while near the enemy army, to send his own troops
with the enemy insignia to rob and burn their very own country. Hence the enemies have believed that they were troops coming to help them, and they too
have run to help them get spoils. By this they have disordered themselves and
given their adversary ease in beating them. [216] Alexander of Epirus used this
means while fighting against the Illyrians, and Leptine the Syracusan [did so]
against the Carthaginians.[116] For both the one and the other, the plan easily succeeded. [217] By simulating being afraid and leaving their own encampments
full of wine and herds, many have beaten the enemy by making it easy for him to
eat and drink to excess.[117] As he was filled with these beyond any natural use,
they have assaulted him and, to his own harm, beaten him. [218] Tamirus did
so against Cyrus,[118] and Tiberius Gracchus against the Spaniards.[119] [219] Some
have poisoned the wine and the other things for eating so as to be able to beat
him more easily.[120] [220] I said a little while ago[121] that I did not find that the
ancients kept night sentinels outside, and I reckoned that they did this so as to

113. The Spartans fought the Messenians sometime after 650 B.C.; see Frontinus II 1.10. In 49
B.C., during the civil wars, Caesar starved into submission forces led by Marcus Petreius and Lu-
cius Afranius, Pompey's lieutenants in Spain from 55–49 B.C.; see Frontinus II 1.11; cf. Caesar, *Civil
War* I 81–82.

114. In 181 B.C., Quintus Fulvius Flaccus fought in Spain against the Celtiberi rather than the
Cimbri; see Frontinus II 5.8; Livy XL 30–32.

115. Lit.: some.

116. Alexander II, king of Epirus (336–326 B.C.); Leptine, brother of Dionysius I (405–367
B.C.), tyrant of Syracuse; see Frontinus II 5.10–11.

117. Lit.: outside of mode.

118. Herodotus I 211 and Justin I 8 assert that Cyrus used this stratagem against forces lead by
Spargapises, son of Tomyris, queen of the Massagetae; cf. Polyaenus VIII 28.

119. Tiberius Sempronius Gracchus in Spain in 179 B.C.; see Frontinus II 5.14.

120. See Frontinus II 5.12.   121. See *AW* VI 99–101.

shun the evils that could arise from it. For one finds that even the lookouts[122] that
they post in the day to be on the look out for the enemy, have been the causes
of the ruin of those who post them. For having been taken, many times it happens that by force they have been made to make the signal with which they
had to call their own troops. Upon coming to the call,[123] they have been killed or
taken.[124] [221] To deceive the enemy, sometimes it is well to vary one of your habits. By founding himself upon it, he is ruined. One captain once did this. At the
coming of the enemy, he customarily had his own [troops] make a sign with
fire at night, with smoke by day. He commanded that without any intermission
smoke and fire be made, and then that it be stopped as the enemy came up. Believing he was coming without being seen, since he did not see signs made of [his]
being discovered, he made victory easier for his adversary by going forth disordered.[125] [222] Memnon of Rhodes, wanting to draw the enemy army out of his
strongholds, sent out one individual under the color of a fugitive who asserted
that his own army was in discord and that the greater part of it was departing. So
as to lend faith to this thing, he had certain tumults among the encampments
made as proof. Hence, the enemy, thinking himself able to break him, was broken when he assaulted him.[126] [223] One ought, besides the things said, to have
regard for not leading the enemy to ultimate desperation. Caesar had regard for
this while fighting with the Germans. He opened the way for them, seeing that
since they were not able to flee, necessity made them hardy. He wanted the
trouble of following them when they were fleeing rather than the danger of conquering them when they were defending themselves.[127] [224] Seeing some cavalrymen from Macedonia that were with him going to the side of the enemy, Lucullus immediately made the signal[128] for battle and commanded that the other
men follow him. Hence, the enemies, believing that Lucullus wanted to join
battle, went to charge the Macedonians with such impetus that they were constrained to defend themselves.[129] And thus from fugitives they became combatants against their will. [225] It is also important to know how to make sure of a
town when you doubt its faith, once you have conquered it in battle, or before.
Some ancient examples will teach you this. [226] Doubting the Catinensians,
Pompey begged them to be content to accept some of the sick that he had in his

122. Or: veils.   124. Cf. Frontinus II 5.15.
123. Lit.: sign.
125. See Frontinus II 5.16, where this stratagem is attributed to the Arabs.
126. See Frontinus II 5.18; cf. Polyaenus V 44.2.
127. Caesar invaded Germany in 55 B.C.; see Frontinus II 6.3, cf. IV 7.16; see also Vegetius III 21.
128. Lit.: sound.
129. Lucius Lucullus between 74–66 B.C.; see Frontinus II 7.8.

army. Having sent very robust men disguised as[130] sick [men], he occupied the town.[131] [227] Fearing the faith of the Epidaunians, Publius Valerius had, as we would say, an indulgence come to a church outside of the town. When all the people had gone for the indulgence, he closed the gate and then received inside none except those whom he trusted.[132] [228] Wanting to go to Asia and to make sure of Thrace, Alexander the Great brought with him all the princes of that province and gave them provisions. Over the people of Thrace he put vile men. Thus, he made the princes content by paying them, and the people quiet by not having heads that would disquiet them.[133] [229] But among all the things with which captains gain peoples to themselves, are examples of chastity and of justice, like that of Scipio in Spain when he gave that young girl of very beautiful body to her father and her husband. This did more for him than arms to gain Spain.[134] [230] By having payment made for the wood he had used to make the palisade around his army in France, Caesar gained for himself such a name for justice that he made the acquisition of that province easy.[135] [231] I don't know what else remains for me to say about these accidents. Nor does there remain any part about this material that has not been disputed by us. [232] There is only the need[136] to speak of the mode of besieging and defending towns. I will gladly do so, if you really don't mind.

BATISTA. [233] Your humanity is so much that it has us follow our desires without being afraid of being held presumptuous, since you freely offer us what we would be ashamed to ask of you. [234] Therefore, we say only this to you: you cannot do us a greater or more pleasant benefit, than to finish this reasoning. [235] But before you pass to that other matter, resolve one doubt for us: whether it is better to continue a war even in winter, as is done today, or to make it only in summer, and to go to quarters in the winter, like the ancients.

130. Lit.: under the dress.

131. Between 76 and 72 B.C.; see Frontinus II 11.2.

132. Cf. Frontinus II 11.1, where Publius Valerius is said to have closed the gates behind the Epidaurians—not the Epidaunians (*Epidauni*) as Fabrizio would have it—as they went to see an athletic contest he had prepared outside the city, refusing to allow their return until he had taken hostages from among their most important men.

133. In 334 B.C.; see Frontinus II 11.3.

134. See Frontinus II 11.5, where Scipio is said to have returned the girl to her betrothed, Alicius, along with the gold that her parents had given as a ransom; cf. Livy XXVI 49–50; see also *D* III 20, 34.3.

135. Frontinus II 11.7, where Caesar Augustus Germanicus (i.e., the Emperor Domitian [81–96]) is said to have won the faith of all through the fame of his justice gained by his compensation of the Cubii for the crops he had included within his fortifications during the conquest of the Germans (83 A.D.).

136. Lit.: lack.

FABRIZIO. [236] Behold; if it were not for the prudence of the questioner, a part that merits consideration would have remained behind. [237] I tell you anew that the ancients did everything better and with greater prudence than we. And if in other things some errors are made, in the things of war all are made. [238] There is nothing more imprudent or more dangerous to a captain than to make war in winter, and he who makes it bears much more danger than he who waits for it.[137] [239] The reason is this: all the industry that is used in military discipline is used so as to be ordered to do battle with your enemy. For this is the end to which a captain must proceed, because the battle gives you the war, won and lost. [240] Thus, whoever knows how to order it better, whoever has the better disciplined army, has more advantage in [battle] and can hope more to win it. [241] On the other side, nothing is more inimical to orders than are harsh sites or cold and wet weather. For a harsh site does not allow you to extend yourself fully according to discipline, cold and wet weather do not let you keep the troops together, nor can you present yourself to the enemy united. Rather, you must of necessity lodge disunited and without order since you have to obey the castles, neighborhoods, and villages that receive you, so that[138] all the trouble used by you so as to discipline your army is in vain. [242] And do not marvel if today they make war in the winter. For since the armies are without discipline, they do not recognize the harm that not lodging united does them. For it does not bother them not to be able to keep those orders and observe that discipline they do not have. [243] Therefore, they ought to see how campaigning in the winter has been the cause of many harms, and to remember how the French, in the year 1503, were beaten at Garigliano by the winter and not by the Spanish.[139] [244] For as I have told you,[140] whoever assaults has even more disadvantage. For the bad weather hurts him more, since the others are at home and he wants to make war. Hence he is necessitated either to sustain the inconvenience of the wet[141] and the cold so as to stay together, or to divide his troops so as to flee it. [245] But he who waits can select the place in his own mode and await him with his own fresh troops. These can at once unite and go to find a band of the enemy troops, which

137. Cf. *P* 12.53, where the unwillingness of condottieri to campaign in winter is listed as one of their many faults.

138. Lit.: in the manner.

139. On December 28, 1503, Gonzalo de Cordoba surprised and beat the French who had dispersed their numerically superior forces throughout the surrounding towns and castles to seek shelter from the winter weather. This victory was quickly followed by the capitulation of the French at Gaeta and Spanish control of southern Italy; cf. *Ritratto di cose di Francia,* in *Tutte le opera,* ed. Mario Martelli (Firenze: Sansoni, 1992), 57.

140. Presumably at *AW* VI 238.   141. Lit.: water.

cannot resist their thrust. [246] The French were beaten thus, and so those will always be beaten who in winter assault an enemy who has prudence in him. [247] So whoever does not in any part want to make use of forces, orders, discipline, and virtue, makes war on campaign in the winter. [248] And because the Romans wanted to make use of all those things into which they put so much industry, they fled the winter no less than harsh alps and difficult places and any other thing that impeded them from being able to show their art and virtue. [249] So this is enough for your question, and we come to treating the defense and attack of towns, and sites and their construction.

BOOK SEVEN

———— ✦ ————

[1] You ought to know that towns and citadels can be strong either by nature or by industry. [2] Those are strong by nature which are surrounded by rivers or by swamps,¹ as are Mantua and Ferrara, or which are placed on a cliff or on a steep mountain, like Monaco and Saint Leo.² For those posted on mountains that are not very difficult to climb are very weak today, on account of³ artilleries and mines. [3] Therefore, most of the time one seeks a plain for building today, so as to make it strong with industry. [4] The first industry is to make the walls twisted and full of turns and recesses. This makes it so that the enemy cannot approach them, since he can easily be wounded not only in front but on the flank.⁴ [5] If the walls are made high, they are too exposed to the blows of artillery; if they are made low, they are very easy to scale. [6] If you make ditches in front of them so as to make it difficult for ladders, if it ends up that the enemy fills them (which a large army can easily do), the wall is left as prey for the enemy. [7] Therefore, I believe (barring⁵ as always a better judgment)⁶ that to want to provide for the one and the other inconvenience, one should make the wall high and with ditches inside and not outside. [8] This is the strongest mode of building that may be used, because you defend against artillery and ladders, and it does not make filling the ditch easy for the enemy. [9] Thus the wall ought to be as tall as

---

1. See Vegetius IV 1.

2. Monaco refers to the present-day kingdom on the French Riviera. Saint Leo is the fortress by means of which Lorenzo de' Medici (1492–1519) maintained his control of the duchy of Urbino against attempts to retake it by his more popular predecessor, Francesco Maria della Rovere; cf. *AW* I 9, note 7; *D* II 10.1.

3. Lit.: with respect to.   5. Lit.: save.

4. See Vegetius IV 2.

6. Parentheses in original here and in sentence 6 above.

the height that seems high [enough] to you, and no less than three-braccia thick, so as to render putting them to ruin more difficult. [10] It ought to have the towers placed at intervals of 200 braccia; the ditch inside ought to be at least 30-braccia long and 12 deep. All the earth that is dug to make the ditch is to be thrown toward the city and is to be held up by a wall that starts from the bottom of the ditch and goes high enough above the earth for a man to be covered behind it. This will make the depth of the ditch greater. [11] At the bottom of the ditch, every 200 braccia there needs to be a casemate from which the artillery harms anyone who may descend into it. [12] The heavy artillery that defends the city is placed inside the wall that encloses the ditch. For to defend the front wall, since it is high, nothing other than the small or medium [artillery] can be used conveniently. [13] If the enemy comes to scale you, the height of the first wall easily defends you. [14] If he comes with artillery, he must first beat down the first wall. But having beaten it down, because the nature of all batteries is to make the wall fall toward the part hit, the rubble[7] of the wall ends up redoubling the depth of the ditch, since [the rubble does] not find a ditch that receives and hides it. So passing further ahead is not possible for you, since [you] find rubble that keeps you back, a ditch that impedes you, and enemy artillery that securely kills you from the wall of the ditch. [15] There is only this remedy for you: to fill the ditch. That is very difficult, both because its capacity is great and through the difficulty there is for you in approaching, since the walls are sinuous and concave. For the reasons mentioned, one can enter among them [only] with difficulty. Then, with equipment[8] on, [you] have to climb through a ruin that gives you very great difficulty. So I hold[9] a city so ordered [to be] altogether impregnable.

BATISTA. [16] If[10] besides the ditch inside, a ditch were also made outside, would it not be stronger?

FABRIZIO. [17] It would be, without doubt. But my reasoning is that when one wants to make one ditch only, it is better inside than outside.

BATISTA. [18] Would you want water to be in the ditches, or would you like[11] them dry?

FABRIZIO. [19] There are diverse opinions. For ditches full of water guard you from underground mines; ditches without water make filling them more difficult. [20] But having considered everything, I would make them without

7. Lit.: ruin (throughout sentence 14).

8. Lit.: material, apparently the fascines or other devices used to cross the ditch once it is reached.

9. Lit.: make.

10. Lit.: when.

11. Or: to love or be fond of.

water because they are more secure. And in winter one has seen the ditches freeze and make easy the storming of a city, as happened to Mirandola, when Pope Julius was campaigning there.[12] [21] And to guard myself against mines, I would make them so deep that whoever wanted to go under would find water. [22] I would also build strongholds, as much in the ditches as on the walls and in a similar mode, so that there would be a similar difficulty in storming them. [23] One thing I want much to remind anyone who defends cities is this, that they not make bastions that are outside of and distant from their walls; another, to anyone who makes castles, is this, that he not make any redoubt in them into which whoever is inside can withdraw, having lost the first wall. [24] What makes me give the first counsel is that no one should do a thing by means of which you begin, without remedy, to lose your earlier reputation, the losing of which makes your other orders less esteemed and dismays those who have taken up your defense. And what I say will always happen to you, when outside of town you make bastions that you have to defend. For you will always lose them, since today little things cannot be defended when they are exposed to the furor of artillery. So by losing them they will be the beginning and cause of your ruin. [25] When it rebelled from King Louis of France, Genoa made some bastions upon the hills around it. When they were lost (and they were lost immediately), they made the city be lost as well.[13] [26] As to the second counsel, I affirm nothing to be more dangerous for a castle than to have redoubts in it enabling one to withdraw. For the hope that men have in abandoning one place makes it be lost, and that loss makes the whole castle be lost. [27] A fresh example of this is the loss of the castle of Forlì, when the Contessa Caterina[14] was defending it against Cesare Borgia, son of Pope Alexander VI, who had led the army of the king of France. [28] The whole fortress was full of places for withdrawing from one to another. For first there was the citadel. From it to the castle, there was a ditch, so that one passed over a drawbridge. The castle was divided into three parts, and every part was divided from the next by ditches and water, and one passed by bridges from one place to the other. [29] Hence the duke battered one of those parts of the

---

12. In his efforts to oust the French from Italy in 1511, Pope Julius II joined the siege and, aided in part by the frozen ditches, forced the surrender of the fortress of Mirandola, key to the duchy of Ferrara held by Alfonso d'Este who had remained loyal to the French. This action marks the climax of Julius's reputation as the warrior pope in that he personally and energetically directed papal and Venetian forces against another Christian city, "something unheard of throughout the centuries" (Francesco Guicciardini, *History of Italy,* trans. Sidney Alexander [Princeton: Princeton University Press, 1969] , 212; cf. *P* 2.7, 11.47, 13.54.

13. Genoa rebelled in 1506 and was recaptured by Louis XII 1507; cf. *P* 3.13, 26.104; cf. *D* I 23, II 21, 24.2, 24.3.

14. Caterina Sforza Riario in 1500.

castle with artillery and opened part of the wall. Messer Giovanni of Casale,[15] who had been posted at that watch, did not think of defending that opening, but abandoned it by withdrawing into the other places. Such that the troops of the duke, having entered that part without opposition, took the whole at once because they became lords of the bridges that went from one member to another. [30] It had been held that this castle could not be stormed, but it was taken through two defects: the one, by having so many redoubts; the other, by each redoubt not being lord of its own bridges. [31] The badly built fortress and the lack of prudence of him who was defending it thus brought shame to the magnanimous enterprise of the Contessa, who had had the spirit to wait for an army that neither the king of Naples[16] nor the duke of Milan waited for. [32] And although her efforts did not have a good end, she nonetheless received the honor that her virtue had merited. [33] This was testified to in those times by the many epigrams written[17] in her praise. [34] Therefore, if I were to build castles, I would make their walls hardy and the ditches in the mode we have discussed.[18] I would make nothing inside them other than houses for living. And I would make those weak and low so that they may not impede the view of all the walls to anyone who might stand in the middle of the piazza, so that the captain might be able to see by eye where he might be able to help, and so that each may understand that having lost the walls and the ditch, the castle would be lost. [35] And therefore if I were to make any redoubt there, I would divide the bridges in such a mode that, by ordering them to come down on their own posts in the middle of the ditch, each part would be lord of the bridges on his own side.

BATISTA. [36] You have said[19] that little things cannot be defended today. It seems to me that I have heard[20] the contrary: that the smaller a thing was, the better it was defended.

FABRIZIO. [37] You have not understood well. For today one cannot call that place strong where whoever defends it does not have space to withdraw to new ditches and to new shelters, [both] because the fury of artillery is so much that he who founds himself on the protection[21] of one wall and of one shelter alone deceives himself, and because bastions (since one wants them not to pass

---

15. Giovanni of Casale was then employed by Ludovico Sforza, the duke of Milan mentioned in *AW* VII 31.

16. Alfonso II of Aragon (1448–95).

17. Lit.: made.

18. Lit.: reasoned. The explicit reference would seem to be to the immediately preceding passages, *AW* VII 4–30; but cf. *D* II 24.

19. See *AW* VII 24.

20. Or: understood.

21. Lit.: guard.

their ordinary measure, because they would then be towns and castles) are lost immediately because they are not made so that one can withdraw there. [38] It is thus a wise policy to let go of these outside bastions and to fortify the entrances of the towns and cover their gates with ravelins,[22] so that one neither enters nor exits the gate in a straight line, and [so that] from the ravelin to the gate there is a ditch with one bridge. [39] The gates are also fortified with portcullises; this is to enable one to put one's own men inside when they have gone outside to fight and, if it happens that the enemies chase them, to avoid their entering inside mixed up with them. [40] And therefore one finds these [portcullises], which the ancients called *cataractae*.[23] When they are let down, they exclude enemies and save friends. For in such a case one cannot use either the bridges or the gate, since the one and the other is occupied by the throng.

BATISTA. [41] I have seen these portcullises of which you speak, made in Germany from beams in the form of an iron grating, and ours, made from planks, are completely solid. [42] I would desire to understand from where this difference arises and which are hardier.

FABRIZIO. [43] I tell you anew that the modes and orders of war in all the world, as compared to those of the ancients, are extinguished. But in Italy, they are altogether lost. And if there is something here a bit more hardy, it is born of the example of the ultramontanes. [44] You are able to have heard, and these others are able to remember, with how much weakness one used to build before King Charles of France passed into Italy in 1494. [45] The merlons were made narrow, a half braccio; the embrasures for crossbows and bombards were made with a small opening outside and a large one inside; and many other defects that I will leave aside so as not to be tedious. For defenses of narrow merlons are easily removed, and embrasures for bombards built in that mode are easily opened. [46] From the French one has now learned to make merlons long and thick, and that even the embrasures for bombards are to be large at the inner part and tighten toward the middle of the wall and then enlarge again toward the outer crust. This makes it so that [only] with trouble can artillery raise the defenses. [47] The French, however, have many other orders like these which, by not having been seen by our [men], have not been considered. [48] Among them is this mode of portcullises made like grating, which is far and away a better mode than ours. For if you have a solid portcullis like ours to shelter a gate, by letting it down you close yourself inside and are not able to offend the enemy through it, such that he can fight you in security with hatchets and with fire. [49] But if it is

22. To cover a gate with a ravelin would be to block direct entry by building a defensive outwork in front of the gate.

23. See Vegetius IV 4; cf. Livy XXVII 28.

made like[24] a grating, when it is let down, you can defend it through those slats and intervals with lances, crossbows, and any other kind of arms.

BATISTA. [50] I have seen another ultramontane usage in Italy, and this is to make artillery wagons with the spokes of the wheels inclined toward the ends of the axles. [51] I would like to know why they make them so, since it seems to me that straight ones, like those on our wheels, must be stronger.

FABRIZIO. [52] Never believe that the things that depart from the ordinary modes are done by chance; and if you were to believe that they do so to be more beautiful, you would err. For where strength is necessary, one does not take account of beauty, but all [these departures] arise because they [make them] more secure and more hardy than yours. [53] The reason is this: the wagon, when it is laden, either goes evenly, or it leans to the right or to the left side. [54] When it goes evenly, the wheels sustain the weight equally, which, since it is divided equally between them, does not weigh them down much. But while leaning, it ends up having all the weight of the wagon on the wheel toward which it leans. [55] If its spokes are straight, they can easily break. For when the wheel leans, the spokes also end up leaning and not withstanding the weight through their straightness. [56] And thus when the wagon goes evenly and when they have less weight, they end up being stronger; when the wagon goes at an angle[25] and they end taking more weight, they are weaker. [57] Exactly the opposite happens with the inclined spokes of the French wagons. For when the wagon, leaning to one side, pushes down on them, through being inclined ordinarily, they then end up being straight and able hardily to withstand all the weight; when the wagon goes evenly and they are inclined, they sustain half of it. [58] But let us go back to our city and castle. [59] For more security for the gates of their towns, and to be able in sieges to put in and take out troops more easily, the French, besides the things said, also used another order of which I have not yet seen any example in Italy. This is that they erect two pillars on the outer edge of a drawbridge, and on each of them they balance a beam, so that half of [each beam] comes over the bridge, and the other half beyond. [60] Then all of the part that ends up outside, they join with joists, which they weave from one beam to the other like a grating, and they attach a chain to the end of the inside part of each beam. [61] When they then want to close the bridge on the outer edge, they slacken the chains and let fall the whole part with grating that closes the bridge as it lowers. And when they want to open it, they draw in the chains, and it ends up being raised. It can be raised so that a man and not a horse may pass under it, and so that a horse and a man may pass; and it can also be closed entirely, because it is lowered and

---

24. Lit.: in the use of.   25. *Torto*, crookedly or wrongly.

raised like the shelter of a merlon.[26] [62] This order is more secure than the portcullis. For [only] with difficulty can it be impeded by the enemy so that it doesn't fall, since it doesn't fall in a straight line like a portcullis which can easily be propped open. [63] Hence, those who want to make a city must see to the ordering of all the said things. And then, for at least a mile[27] around the walls, one would need[28] to allow neither cultivation nor walls; rather, it would be all country in which there would be no thicket or embankment or trees or houses that might impede the view and give aid to the encamped enemy. [64] And note that a town that has ditches outside with embankments higher than the ground is very weak. For they provide shelter to the enemy who assaults you, and they do not impede him in harming you because they can easily be opened and give place to his artillery. [65] But let us pass inside the town. [66] I do not want to lose much time showing you how one must, besides the things said before, have supplies to live on and to fight. For these are things that everyone understands himself, and without them, every other provision is vain. [67] Generally, two things must be done: provide for oneself and take from the enemy the convenience of availing himself of things in your country. [68] Therefore, the straw, the animals, and the grain that you cannot receive within[29] must be destroyed. [69] Whoever defends a town should also provide that nothing be done tumultuously and without order, and keep modes so that in every accident everyone knows what he has to do. [70] The mode is this: that the women, the elderly, the children, and the weak stay at home and leave the town free to the young and the hardy; the armed are distributed for defense, some staying on the walls, some at the gates, some at the principal places of the city, so as to remedy those inconveniences that can arise within. Another part is not obligated to any place, but is prepared to give succor to all, as need requires. [71] And things being ordered thus, tumults that disorder you arise with difficulty. [72] I also want to note this in regard to the attack and defense of cities: nothing gives to the enemy as much hope of being able to occupy a town as the knowledge that it is not accustomed to seeing the enemy. For many times cities are lost through fear alone, without any other experience of force. [73] Therefore, when he assaults a similar city, an individual should make all of his displays terrible. [74] On the other side, in that part where the enemy fights, whoever is assaulted should put strong men whom arms rather than opinions frighten. For if the first attempt proves to be vain, the

26. Tables of wood, placed horizontally between two merlons, which could be raised and lowered as needed.

27. A Tuscan mile is slightly less than ours.

28. Lit.: would want.   29. Lit.: at home.

spirit of the besieged grows, and then the enemy is forced to overcome with virtue, and not with reputation, anyone who is inside.[30] [75] The instruments with which the ancients used to defend their towns were many, like catapults, mangonels, tiny and thin darts, crossbows, sling-staves, and slings;[31] and there were also many with which they assaulted them, like rams, towers, mantelets, screens, penthouses, siege-hooks, and tortoises.[32] [76] Instead of these things, today there is artillery, which serves anyone who attacks[33] and anyone who defends. Therefore I will not otherwise speak of them. [77] But let us return to our reasoning and come to particular attacks. [78] One should take care that one cannot be taken by hunger and that one not be forced by assault. [79] As to hunger, it was said that one needs to be well supplied with food before the siege comes. [80] But when this is lacking because of the length of the siege, one has sometimes been seen to use some extraordinary mode for being provisioned by friends who would like to save you, especially if a river runs through the middle of the besieged city. The Romans did so while their castle at Casalino was being besieged by Hannibal. Not being able to send them anything else by river, they threw into it a great quantity of nuts, which could not be stopped; carried by the river, they fed the Casalinesi for a longer time.[34] [81] Having been besieged, some, so as to show the enemy they have surplus grain and [thus] make him despair of being able to besiege them through hunger, have either thrown bread outside the walls or given a steer grain to eat and then allowed it to be taken so that when [the steer] is killed and found full of grain, it shows what abundance they have.[35] [82] On the other side, excellent captains have used various means for starving the enemy. [83] Fabius allowed the Campanians to sow so that they would lack the grain that they sowed.[36] [84] Dionysius, being encamped at Reggio, feigned wanting to make an accord with them, and during the proceedings had himself provided with food. Then when he had emptied them of grain, he tightened around them and starved them.[37] [85] Alexander the Great, wanting to storm Leucadia, stormed all the castles around it, and allowed their men to

---

30. See Vegetius IV 12.

31. See Vegetius IV 22; cf. IV 8; these English terms follow Milner's translations of Vegetius's Latin.

32. See Vegetius IV 13–17; these English terms follow Milner's translations of Vegetius's Latin.

33. *Offendere,* usually translated "harm" or "offend."

34. In 216 B.C.; see Frontinus III 14.2; cf. Livy XXIII 19.

35. See Frontinus III 15.1 where it is said that when the capitol was besieged by the Gauls in 390 B.C., the Romans threw bread over the walls (cf. Livy V 48), and III 15.5, where the Thracians used sheep for this ruse.

36. Fabius Maximus Cuntator in 215 B.C.; see Frontinus III 4.1; cf. Livy XXIII 46, 48.

37. In 391 B.C.; see Frontinus III 4.3.

take refuge in it. Thus, with a large multitude suddenly coming, he starved it.[38]
[86] As to assaults, it has been said[39] that one ought to guard against the first
thrust. Many times the Romans occupied many towns with this, assaulting them
at a stroke and from every side and calling it "*Aggredi urbem corona.*"[40] Scipio did
this when he occupied New Carthage in Spain.[41] [87] If that thrust is withstood,
you are then overcome with difficulty. [88] If it should happen, however, that the
enemy were to enter inside the city by having forced the walls, the townspeople
still have some remedy other than abandoning themselves. For many armies
have been repelled or killed once they have entered a town. [89] The remedy is
that the townspeople maintain themselves in high places and fight them from
the houses and towers. [90] Those who have entered cities have contrived to defeat this in two modes: one, by opening the gates of the city and making a way
for the townspeople so that they are able to flee in security; the other, by making
a proclamation[42] that signifies that none but the armed are to be offended and
that whoever throws his arms to the ground is to be pardoned.[43] [91] This thing
has rendered easy the conquest of many cities. [92] Besides this, cities are easily
stormed if you come upon them unforeseen. This is done when you are found
to be far away with the army so that it is not believed either that you want to attack or that you can do so without being exposed by the distance of the place.
[93] Hence it is that if you secretly and promptly assault them, you will almost
always succeed in bringing back the victory. [94] I reason unwillingly[44] about
things that happen in our times. For it would be a burden to reason about myself and my own; I would not know what to say about others. [95] Nonetheless,
I cannot to this purpose not adduce the example of Cesare Borgia, called Duke
Valentino. Finding himself at Nocera with his own troops, under the color of going to harm Camerino, he turned toward the state of Urbino and occupied in
one day and without any trouble a state that another would hardly have occu-

38. See Frontinus III 4.5, where it is Alexander I, king of Epirus.

39. Cf. *D* III 11.

40. Attacking the city with a crown, i.e., on all sides at once.

41. See Livy XXVI 44–46, where attacking on all sides at once all but fails Scipio until he gains
access to a portion of the wall left undefended because it had been deemed unreachable; cf. Polybius X 12–15; *D* II 32.1.

42. Lit.: sending out a voice.

43. See Vegetius IV 25; Frontinus II 6.9. Neither source mentions the second mode of offering
to pardon the unarmed. On the contrary, in the passages cited above for the immediately preceding episode (see *AW* VII 86, note 41), both Livy and Polybius state and illustrate the Roman policy
of slaughtering every living thing (Polybius X 15) or every human adult (Livy XXVI 46) up to the
moment that the order to begin pillaging is given.

44. *Male volentieri.*

pied with much time and expense.[45] [96] Those who are besieged must also guard themselves against the deceptions and tricks of the enemy. And therefore the besieged ought not to trust anything that they see the enemy do continually, rather they [should] always believe a deception is beneath it and that it can vary to their harm.[46] [97] When besieging a town, Domitius Calvinus made it his custom to circle its walls everyday with a good part of his troops. [98] Hence the townspeople, believing he did so for training, slackened their guard. When Domitius noticed this, he assaulted and stormed them.[47] [99] Some captains, understanding that help should be coming to the besieged, have dressed their soldiers in the insignias of those who should be coming. Having been admitted, they occupied the town.[48] [100] One night Cimon the Athenian set fire to a temple that was outside the town. The townspeople, going to aid it, thus left the town to the enemy as prey.[49] [101] Some have killed those from the besieged castle who went to forage and then dressed their own soldiers in the clothes of the foragers, who then gave them the town.[50] [102] Ancient captains have also used various means to despoil the guards of the towns they wanted to seize. [103] Scipio, being in Africa and desiring to occupy some castles in which guards had been placed by the Carthaginians, pretended to want to assault them several times, but then not only to abstain through fear but to distance himself from them. [104] Believing this to be true, Hannibal, so as to be able to oppress him more easily, withdrew all of the guards from [the castles]. Having recognized this, Scipio sent his own captain Massanissa to storm them.[51] [105] While making war in Schiavonia against a capitol[52] city in that country, in which many troops had been placed as guards, Pyrrhus feigned despairing of being able to storm it. Having turned toward other places, he made it empty itself of guards to help them; and

45. On June 21, 1502; cf. *AW* VI 194–95. This passage seems to allude to several significant facts. The ruler of Urbino overthrown by Cesare was a close friend of Fabrizio. The year before, Fabrizio himself had been imprisoned after the fall of Capua, in which he had had a significant role, to French forces accompanied by Cesare. Lorenzo de' Medici (1492–1519) poured considerable time and expense into occupying Urbino in 1516. Finally, it was shortly after Cesare's seizure of Urbino that Machiavelli was sent by Florence for an extended stay in Cesare's court at Imola.

46. Cf. *D* III 48.

47. Domitius Calvinus (consul in 53 and 42 B.C.); see Frontinus III 2.1.

48. See Frontinus III 2.4, where the Arcadians are said to use a version of this ruse against the Messenians.

49. See Frontinus III 2.5, where Cimon is said to set fire to a grove in addition to the temple of Diana outside a city in Caria in Asia Minor (ca. 470 B.C.).

50. See Frontinus III 2.9, where Antiochus does this while besieging Suenda in Cappadocia.

51. In 202 B.C.; see Frontinus III 6.1.   52. *Capo.*

it became easy to overpower.[53] [106] Many have poisoned[54] the water and diverted rivers so as to take towns, even though it was not successful for you.[55] [107] One also easily makes the besieged surrender through frightening them by making known to them that a victory has been had or that new troops are coming to their disadvantage.[56] [108] Ancient captains have sought to occupy towns by treachery, corrupting someone inside, but they have used diverse modes. [109] Someone has sent one individual of his who, under the name of fugitive, gets authority and trust with the enemies that he then uses to his benefit. [110] Someone by this route has learned the guards' mode and, by means of this knowledge, taken the town.[57] [111] Someone has by some ruse blocked the gate with a wagon or with beams so that it cannot be closed, and in this mode made entering it easy for the enemy.[58] [112] Hannibal persuaded one individual to give him a castle of the Romans and to feign to go hunting at night; [he was] to make a show of not being able to go by day for fear of the enemies, and, returning later with his game, to get some of [Hannibal's] men in with him, and, upon having killed the guard, to give him the gate.[59] [113] One also deceives the besieged by making a show of fleeing when they assault you, thereby drawing them out of the town and away from it. Many, among whom was Hannibal, have even allowed their encampments to be taken so as to have the opportunity to put themselves in between [the town and its inhabitants] and take the town from them.[60] [114] One also deceives them by feigning to leave, as Phormio the Athenian did. Having preyed upon the country of the Chalcidians, he then received their ambassadors, filling their city with security and with good promises under which they, as men lacking caution, were a little later oppressed by

53. Schiavonia roughly corresponds to ancient Illyria and contemporary Slovenia; see Frontinus III 6.3.

54. Lit.: corrupted.

55. See Frontinus III 7, where all stratagems involving the divergence of water ways are successful. For two unsuccessful Florentine attempts, consider Brunelleschi's efforts to flood Lucca with the waters of the Serchio (*FH* IV 23) and Machiavelli's own to divert the Arno in order to cut Pisa off from the sea (*Decennale primo* vv. 502–4; cf. Roger Masters, *Machiavelli, Leonardo, and the Science of Power* [Notre Dame: University of Notre Dame Press, 1996] , 240–47).

56. Cf. Frontinus III 8.2.   58. See Frontinus III 3.5.

57. Cf. Frontinus III 3.2.

59. In 212 B.C., outside of Tarentum; see Frontinus III 3.6; cf. Livy XXV 8–9; Polybius VIII 24–29; the traitor or traitors are variously named in these texts.

60. See Frontinus III 10.1–4; the Hannibal mentioned at III 10.3 is not the famous Hannibal of the Second Punic War, but his relative who fought in the First Punic War; cf. Diodorus Siculus XIII 59–62, where the withdrawal of this Hannibal's troops from their camp near Himera in 409 B.C. is in earnest, not a stratagem.

Phormio.[61] [115] The besieged ought to beware of men among them of whom they have suspicions. But sometimes it is customary to secure oneself against them as much with reward as with punishment. [116] Marcellus, knowing how Lucius Banzio Nolano had turned to favor Hannibal, used so much humanity and liberality toward him that from an enemy he was made very much a friend.[62] [117] The besieged must use more diligence on guard when the enemy is far away than when he is near by. And they must guard those places better by which they think they can be hurt less. For many towns have been lost when the enemy assaults them on the side on which they do not believe they can be assaulted. [118] This deception arises from two causes: either through the place being strong and the belief that it is inaccessible, or through art being used by the enemy to assault them on one side with mock noises and on the other quietly and with true assaults. [119] Therefore, the besieged must take this great precaution, and above all at every time, and especially at night, have good guards on the walls, and post not only men but dogs, and have ferocious and ready ones who by smelling have presentiment of the enemy and with their barking uncover him. [120] And not only dogs, but geese, it was found, have saved a city, as happened to the Romans when the French besieged the capitol.[63] [121] While Athens was being besieged by Sparta, Alcibiades, so as to see if the guards were being vigilant, ordered that when he raised his lamp at night all the guards should raise theirs, instituting a punishment for anyone who did not obey it.[64] [122] Iphicrates the Athenian killed a guard who was sleeping, saying he left him as he had found him.[65] [123] Those who are besieged have various modes of sending messages to their friends. So as not to send messages by mouth, they write letters in cipher and hide them in various modes. The ciphers are according to the will of whoever orders them; the mode of hiding them is varied. [124] Someone has written on the inside of a sheath of a sword; others have put letters in unbaked bread, and then baked it and given it as [if it were] his own food to him who carries them. [125] Some have put them in the most secret places of the body. [126] Others have put them in the collar of a dog that is familiar with him who carries them. [127] Some have written ordinary things in a letter and then, between one line and another, written with waters that, when washed and warmed, later re-

61. In 432 B.C.; see Frontinus III 11.1.

62. See Frontinus III 16.1; cf. Livy XXIII 15–16.

63. See Livy V 47; cf. Vegetius IV 26: "Marvelous was the watchfulness or good fortune, whereby one bird saved the men destined to send the whole world under the yoke." Cf. also Ovid, *Metamorphoses* XI 599: "solicitous dogs, or even more sagacious, a goose."

64. See Frontinus III 12.1.   65. At Corinth; see Frontinus III 12.2.

veal the letters.[66] [128] This mode has been very astutely observed in our times when someone, wanting to signify to friends of his who lived inside a town things to keep secret, and not wanting to trust anyone, sent communications written according to custom and interlined as I said before, and had them suspended from the doors[67] of the temples. Recognized by those who recognized them by passwords, they were detached and read.[68] [129] This mode is very cautious because whoever carries them can be deceived in this and not run any risk. [130] There are infinite[69] other modes that each one can read for himself and find. [131] But one can write to the besieged with more ease than the besieged [can write] to their friends outside. For they cannot send such letters to them except through one who under the shadow of a fugitive goes out of the town, which is a thing doubtful and dangerous when the enemy is at all cautious. [132] But [as to] those who send [messages] inside, he who is sent can go to the camp that besieges under many colors and from there take a convenient opportunity to jump into the town.[70] [133] But let's speak of the present stormings. I say that if it happens that you are attacked in your city, which is not ordered with ditches in the inside part, as we showed a little while ago,[71] and you want the enemy not to enter through the breaches in the walls that the artillery makes (for there is no remedy to keep it from making a breach), it is necessary for you while the artillery is battering to put a ditch at least 30-braccia wide inside the wall that is struck, and to throw all that is dug toward the town; this makes an embankment and makes the ditch deeper. And you must hasten this work so that when the wall falls the ditch is dug at least five- or six-braccia [deep]. [134] It is necessary, while it is being dug, to close up this ditch on every side with casemates. And when the wall is so hardy that it gives you time to make the ditch and the casemates, the battered part ends up being stronger than the rest of the city. For such a redoubt ends up having the form that we prescribed for inside ditches. [135] But when the wall is weak and does not give you time, then there is need to show your virtue, and to resist with armed men and with all of your forces. [136] This mode of making repairs was obeyed by the Pisans when you went to encamp there. And they were able to do so because they had very hardy walls that gave them time and sticky soil very fit for raising embankments and making redoubts. [137] If

---

66. Cf. Frontinus III 13.   67. *Porta*, usually translated "gates."

68. Perhaps an allusion to papal briefs censuring the Dominican friar Savonarola (1452–98). The briefs were circulated by his enemies. Savonarola was excommunicated in 1497; less than a year later his political opponents in Florence had him tried, tortured, hanged, and burned.

69. Lit.: very or most infinite.   71. See *AW* VII 6–17.

70. Cf. Frontinus III 13.

they had lacked this convenience, they would have lost.[72] [138] Therefore, one always acts prudently by providing beforehand by making ditches all the way around the inside of one's city, as we explained[73] a little while ago.[74] For in this case one awaits the enemy in idleness and security, since the redoubts are made. [139] Many times the ancients occupied towns with underground mines in two modes: either they secretly made an underground passage that led into the town and through which they entered (in this mode the Romans took the city of the Veientes); or the mines undermined a wall and made it fall in ruin.[75] [140] This last mode is hardier today and makes cities placed high weaker because they can be mined better. Then, putting the powder that lights in an instant in the mines not only ruins a wall, but mountains are opened up and whole fortresses are broken into many pieces. [141] The remedy for this is to build on a plain and to make the ditch that surrounds your city so deep that the enemy cannot dig deeper than it without finding water, which is[76] the only enemy of these mines. [142] If, however, you find yourself in a town that you defend on a hill, you cannot remedy this otherwise than to make many deep shafts within your own walls, which are like vents for those mines that the enemy is able to order against you. [143] Another remedy is to make a mine against him once you notice where he is digging. This mode impedes him easily, but is foreseen with difficulty if one is besieged by a cautious enemy. [144] He that is besieged ought above all to take care not to be oppressed in times of rest, as after a battle has been waged, after the guards are changed[77] (in the morning at daybreak and in the evening between day and night),[78] and, above all, when eating. At that time many towns have been stormed and many armies have been ruined by those inside [cities]. [145] Therefore, with diligence in every respect[79] one should be always on guard and in good part armed.[80] [146] I do not want to fail to tell you that what makes defending a city or an encampment difficult is having to keep disunited all the forces you have in them. For since the enemy can assail you from any side all together, you must keep every side guarded. He thus assaults you with all of his forces and you defend yourself with part of yours. [147] Also, the besieged can be beaten entirely; he who is outside can only be repelled. Hence, many who have been besieged either in their encampment or in a town have (although inferior in strength) at a stroke gone outside with all of their troops and have overcome

---

72. A reference to Florence's ten-year war to retake Pisa; Machiavelli played a significant role in its recovery and entered the city with the victorious army.

73. Lit.: divided.   77. Lit.: made.

74. Cf. *AW* VII 6–17.   78. Parentheses in the original.

75. See Vegetius IV 24; cf. Livy V 7–22.   79. Lit.: part.

76. Lit.: waters, which is.   80. See Vegetius IV 27.

the enemy. [148] Marcellus did this at Nola.[81] Caesar did it in France when his encampments were being assaulted by a very great number of Frenchmen. Seeing that he could not defend due to having to divide his own forces into several parts and that he could not charge the enemy with force[82] by remaining inside his palisades, [Caesar] opened one side of the encampment; and, turning all of his forces to that side, he made such a thrust against them and with so much virtue that he overcame them and won.[83] [149] The constancy of the besieged also makes the besiegers despair and be afraid. [150] When Pompey was before Caesar and the Caesarian army was suffering much from hunger, some of its bread was brought to Pompey. Seeing that it was made of grass, he commanded that it not be shown to his army so as not to frighten it, seeing what enemies it had against it.[84] [151] In the war against Hannibal, nothing did the Romans so much honor as their constancy. For in any of the most hostile and adverse fortune, they never asked for peace and never made any sign of fear. Indeed, when Hannibal was near to Rome, the fields where they had placed their own encampments were sold at a higher price than they would ordinarily have been sold at other times.[85] And they stuck so obstinately to their enterprises that when the Romans were besieging Capua at the same time that Rome was being besieged, they did not want to leave off their attacks [on Capua] so as to defend Rome.[86] [152] I know that I have told you many things that you must have understood and considered by yourselves. Nonetheless, as I already said today,[87] I have done so so as to be able better to show you, by means of these things, the quality of this army, as well as to satisfy those, if there are any of them, who have not had the advantage that you [have had] for understanding them. [153] It seems to me that nothing is left other than to tell you some general rules with which you will be very familiar, which are these:[88]

[154] That which helps the enemy hurts you, and that which helps you hurts the enemy.

[155] In war, he who is more vigilant in discerning[89] the plans of the enemy

---

81. Claudius Marcellus against Hannibal at Nola in 216 B.C.; see Livy XXIII 16.

82. Lit.: impetus.

83. See Caesar, *Gallic War* III 5, where it is Galba rather than Caesar in "France" in 57 B.C.

84. See Suetonius, *Julius Caesar* 68, where Pompey comments, "I am fighting wild beasts."

85. In 211 B.C.; see Frontinus III 18.2; cf. Livy XXVI 11.

86. In 211 B.C.; see Frontinus III 18.3; cf. Livy XXVI 7–8.

87. Presumably *AW* III 10, VI 20, 102.

88. For the following rules, cf. Vegetius III 26.

89. Lit.: observing.

and endures more trouble in training his army will incur fewer dangers and will be more able to hope for victory.

[156] Never lead your soldiers to battle if you have not first confirmed their spirit and known them [to be] without fear and ordered; and never test them except when you see that they hope to win.

[157] It is better to beat the enemy with hunger than with iron; in victory by [means of] the latter, fortune can [do] much more than virtue.

[158] No policy is better than that which remains hidden from the enemy until you have executed it.

[159] To know in war how to recognize an opportunity and seize it is better than anything else.

[160] Nature produces few hardy men; industry and training makes many.

[161] In war, discipline can [do] more than fury.

[162] When some leave the side of the enemy and come into your service, if they are faithful they will always be great acquisitions for you. For the forces of adversaries are more diminished by the loss of those who flee than of those who are killed, even though the name of deserter is suspect to new friends and hateful to old ones.

[163] In ordering for battle, it is better to place many reserves behind the first front than to disperse your soldiers so as to make a greater front.

[164] He who knows how to gauge[90] his own forces and those of his enemy is beaten with difficulty.

[165] The virtue of soldiers is more valuable than their number; sometimes the site helps more than virtue.

[166] New and sudden things frighten armies; accustomed and slow things are little esteemed by them. Therefore, you will have your army practice and recognize a new enemy in small fights before you come to battle with him.

[167] He who pursues an enemy in disorder after he is beaten wants nothing other than to change from being victorious to losing.

[168] The one who does not prepare the food supplies necessary for living is beaten without iron.

[169] Whoever trusts more in horse than in infantrymen, or more in infantrymen than in horse, [should] accommodate himself to the site.

[170] In the daytime when you want to see if any spies have come into camp, have each [soldier] go into his own encampment.

[171] Change policy when you become aware that the enemy has foreseen it.

90. *Conoscere.*

[172] Take counsel from many on the things that you must do; what you later want to do, tell few.

[173] When they remain in garrison, soldiers are maintained with fear and punishment; when they are then led to war, with hope and reward.

[174] Good captains never come to battle if necessity does not constrain them or opportunity does not call them.

[175] Make it that your enemies do not know how you want to order your army for the fight; and in whatever mode you order it, make the first squadrons able to be received by the second and by the third.

[176] In the fight, if you do not want to disorder [things], never use^{91} a battalion for anything other than that for which you had assigned it.

[177] Sudden accidents are remedied with difficulty, known ones with ease.

[178] Men, iron, money, and bread are the sinew of war; but of these four, the first two are more necessary; for men and iron find money and bread, but bread and money do not find men and iron.

[179] The unarmed rich man is the reward of the poor soldier.

[180] Accustom your own soldiers to disdain delicate living and luxurious clothes.

[181] This is as much as occurs to me to remind you of generally, and I know that many other things could have been said in all of this reasoning of mine. For instance, how and in how many modes the ancients used to order their lines, how they used to dress, and how in many other things they used to train themselves. And many particulars could have been added that I did not judge necessary to narrate, both because you can see them for yourselves, and also because my intention has not been to show you exactly how the ancient military was made, but how in these times one might order a military that would have more virtue than the one that is used [today]. [182] Hence, concerning ancient things it has not seemed [well] to me to reason beyond^{92} that which I have judged necessary for such an introduction. [183] I also know that I would have had to enlarge more on the military on horse back and then to reason about naval war,^{93} because whoever differentiates the military says how there is an army for the sea and for the land, on foot and on horse. [184] Of that for the sea I would not presume to speak, through not having any knowledge of it; rather, I will leave it to be spoken of by the Genoese and Venetians, who with similar studies have in the past done great things. [185] Of horse I also want to say nothing but what I have said before, since, as I said, this part is less corrupt.^{94} [186] Besides this, having ordered good infantries, which are the sinew of the army, of necessity one ends

91. *Adoperare.*   93. Cf. Vegetius IV 31–46 on naval warfare.
92. Lit.: other than.   94. See *AW* II 319

up making good cavalrymen. [187] I would only remind whoever may order a
military in his own country to make two provisions for filling it with horses. One
[is] to distribute mares of good breeding throughout his countryside and to accustom his own men to buy up[95] colts as you do in this country with calves and
mules. The other, so that the dealers might find buyers: I would prohibit anyone
who does not keep a horse from being able to keep a mule, such that whoever
wants to keep one mount only would be constrained to keep a horse; what is
more, whoever does not keep a horse would not be able to dress in fine clothes.[96]
[188] I understand this order to have been made by a certain prince in our times,
and in a very brief time to have brought back to his country a first-rate cavalry.
[189] About the other things concerning horses, I submit myself to as much as I
said to you today and to what is customary. [190] Would you perhaps also desire
to understand what parts a captain ought to have? [191] On that I will satisfy you
very briefly, because I would not know how to select another man than him who
knows how to do all those things that have been reasoned about by us today.
Even these would not be enough, if he did not know how to find them by himself. For without invention no one was ever a great man in his own trade; and
if invention brings honor in other things, in this above all it honors you. [192]
And one sees every invention, even though weak, celebrated by the writers, as one
sees that they praise Alexander the Great, who, so as to decamp more secretly,
did not give the sign with a trumpet, but with a hat upon a lance.[97] [193] He[98] was
also praised for having ordered it that his own soldiers, on joining with the enemy, kneel with the left foot, so as to be better able to withstand their thrust
hardily. By having given him victory, this also gave him so much praise that all
the statues built in his honor stood in this guise.[99] [194] But because it is time to
finish this reasoning, I want to return to the purpose, and I will meanwhile flee
that punishment to which it is customary to condemn those in this land[100] who
do not return to it. [195] If you remember well, Cosimo, you said[101] to me that
you were unable to find out the cause for this: that, on the one hand, I am the exalter of antiquity and blamer of those who in grave things do not imitate it, and,
on the other, I have not imitated it in the things of war, where I have exerted my-

95. *Fare incette* can mean "corner the market on" or simply "deal in."

96. *Droppo*, especially in and around Florence, refers to cloth woven of silk and used as work
clothes, but also for religious vestments.

97. Source unknown; perhaps an invention of Machiavelli.

98. The manuscripts leave a blank space in which some name other than Alexander's was
perhaps to be added; the first printing ignores the blank space, leaving the impression that Alexander was the subject of this sentence as well as the previous sentence.

99. See notes 97 and 98.   101. See *AW* I 36.

100. Or: town.

self. To this I responded[102] that men who want to do something, must first prepare themselves to know how to do it, so as then to be better able to do[103] it when
the opportunity permits. [196] Whether I would know how to return the military to ancient modes or not, I want for judges you who have heard me dispute
at length on this matter. From this you have been able to recognize how much
time I have consumed in these thoughts, and also I believe you can imagine how
much desire there is in me to manage them with effect. [197] If I had been able
to do this, or if I had ever been given the opportunity, you can conjecture it. [198]
Yet so as to make you more certain of this, and for my greater justification, I also
want to adduce the causes. And in part I will observe the promises[104] to you by
demonstrating to you the difficulties and the ease[105] that there are at present in
such imitations. [199] I say, therefore, that no action that may be done today
among men is more easy to return to ancient modes than the military, but only
by those who are princes of so large a state that they can put together from their
subjects at least 15 to 20 thousand youths. [200] On the other hand, nothing is
more difficult than this to those who do not have such a convenience. [201] And
so that[106] you may better understand this part, you have to know that there are
two kinds[107] of captains praised. [202] One is those who have done great things
with an army ordered by its own natural discipline, as were the greater part of
Roman citizens and others who have guided armies. These have had no other
trouble than to keep them good and see to guiding them securely. [203] The
other is those who not only have had to overcome the enemy, but, before they
arrive at that, have been necessitated to make their army good and well ordered.
These without doubt merit much more praise than those have merited who have
operated virtuously with ancient and good armies. [204] Of these such were
Pelopidas and Epaminondas, Tullius[108] Hostilius, Philip of Macedon, father of
Alexander, Cyrus, king of Persia, and Gracchus the Roman. [205] All of these
first had to make the army good, and then fight with it. [206] All of these were
able to do this both through their prudence and through having subjects whom
they could direct in similar training. [207] Nor would it ever have been possible
that any one of them, even though a man full of every excellence, would have
been able to do any praiseworthy work in an alien province full of corrupt men
not used to any honest obedience. [208] Knowing how to govern an army [al-
ready] made is, then, not enough in Italy; rather, it is first necessary to know how
to make it and then know how to command it. [209] And of these, it must be

102. See *AW* I 39.

103. *Operare.*

104. See *AW* I 44.

105. Plural in Italian.

106. Lit: because.

107. Lit: reasons.

108. Following the reading of Marchand et al., Tullus is misspelled as Tullius.

those princes who have the convenience to do it through having a large state and many subjects. [210] I, who never commanded nor can command any but foreign armies and men obligated to others and not to me, cannot be among them. [211] Whether or not it is possible for them to introduce any of those things reasoned about by me today, I want to leave to your judgment. [212] When could I make one of the soldiers who practice today carry more arms than they are accustomed to, and, besides the arms, food for two or three days, and a hoe? [213] When could I make him dig and keep him every day for many hours under arms in fake drills, so as later to be able to avail myself of him in true ones? [214] When would they abstain from games, from acts of lasciviousness, from curses, from acts of insolence that they do everyday? [215] When would they be reduced to so much discipline and to so much obedience and reverence that one tree full of apples in the middle of their encampments may be found there and left intact as one reads happened many times in the ancient armies?[109] [216] What thing can I promise them, by means of which they might hold me in reverence with love or fear, when, the war having finished, they no longer have anything to connect them to me? [217] With what would I make ashamed those who have been born and raised without shame? [218] Why would those who do not know me have to observe[110] me? [219] By what God, or by what saints would I make them swear? [220] By those that they adore, or by those that they curse? [221] I do not know any that they adore, but I know well that they curse them all. [222] How would I believe that they would observe their promises to those whom every hour they disparage? [223] How can they who disparage God revere men? [224] What good form, then, could there be that one could impress on this matter? [225] And if you allege to me that the Swiss and Spaniards are good, I would confess to you that they are by great lengths better than the Italians. But if you would note my reasoning and the mode of proceeding of both, you would see how many things are lacking for them to reach the perfection of the ancients. [226] And the Swiss have been made good by one usage natural to them caused by that which I said[111] to you today, these other by a necessity. For being in the military in a foreign province and it seeming to them that they are constrained to die or to win, they have become good through it not seeming to them that they have a place to flee to. [227] But it is a goodness in many parts defective. For in it nothing else is good except that they are accustomed to await the enemy at the point of the pike and the sword. [228] Nor would anyone be fit to teach them that which they lack, and so much less whoever is not of their language. [229] But let us return to the Italians. Through not having had wise princes, they have not taken any good order;

109. Frontinus IV 3.13.   111. Cf. AW I 98, II 29.
110. Or: obey.

and through not having had that necessity that the Spaniards have had, they have not taken any by themselves, such that they remain the scorn of the world. [230] The people are not to blame for it; but their princes are indeed so. They have been punished for it, and for their ignorance they have borne just penalties by ignominiously losing their states, and without any virtuous example. [231] Do you want to see if what I say is true? [232] Consider how many wars there have been in Italy from the passing of King Charles to today. And while wars usually make men bellicose and reputed, these, as much as they have been more grand and fierce, have so much more made the members and their heads lose reputation. [233] This must arise because the accustomed orders were not and are not good; and as to new orders, there is not anyone who has known how to seize them. [234] Never believe that reputation may be rendered by Italian arms, except by the way that I have shown and by means of those who have big states in Italy. For this form can be impressed on simple, coarse men of one's own, not on malicious, badly cared for foreigners. [235] One will never find any good sculptor who believes [he can] make a beautiful statue from a piece of marble badly blocked out; but from one in the rough [he may] very well [think so]. [236] Before they tasted the blows of the ultramontane wars, our Italian princes used to believe that it was enough for a prince to know how to think of a sharp response in his studies, to write a beautiful letter, to show wit and quickness in his deeds and words, to know how to weave[112] a fraud, to be ornamented by gems and gold,[113] to sleep and eat with greater splendor than others, to keep many lascivious ones around, to govern subjects avariciously and proudly, to rot in idleness, to give promotions in the military by favor, to despise anyone who may have shown them any praiseworthy way, to want their speeches to be responses of oracles. Nor did these wretches perceive that they were preparing themselves to be the prey of whoever assaulted them. [237] From here then arose in 1494 great terrors, sudden flights, and miraculous losses; and thus three very powerful states[114] that were in Italy have been sacked and wasted. [238] But what is worse, those who are left persist in the same error and the same disorder. And they do not consider that those who anciently wanted to keep their states used to do and used to have done all those things that have been reasoned about by me, and that their studies used to prepare their bodies for hardships and their spirits not to fear dangers. [239] From this it arose that Caesar, Alexander, and all those men and excellent princes were the first among combatants, went

---

112. Cf. *P* 2.   113. Cf. pr. 4.

114. The five most powerful Italian states were Florence, Milan, Venice, the "papal states," and Naples. But it is a matter of speculation as to which, if any, of these Fabrizio refers to here.

armed on foot and, if somehow they lost their states, they wanted to lose their
lives. Thus did they live and die virtuously. And if in them, or in part of them,
one could blame too much ambition to rule, never will one find that one may
blame in them any softness or anything that makes men delicate and unwarlike.
[240] If these things were read and believed by these princes, it would be impossible that they not change their form of living and their provinces not change
their fortune. [241] And because you, at the beginning of this reasoning of ours,
complained[115] of your militia here, I say to you that, if you had ordered it as I
have reasoned above and it had not given a good proof[116] of itself, you could
complain of it reasonably. But if it is not ordered and trained just as I have said,
it can complain of you that you have made an abortion, not a perfect figure.
[242] The Venetians also, and the duke of Ferrara,[117] began one and did not continue it, which has been through their defect, not that of their men. [243] And I
assert to you that whichever of those who today keep states in Italy first enters by
this way, he will be lord of this province before anyone else. And it will happen
to his state as to the kingdom of the Macedonians. Coming under Philip, who
had learned the mode of ordering armies from the Theban Epaminondas—and
since the rest of Greece[118] was in idleness and attended to the performance of
comedies—it became so powerful with this order and these armies that he[119]
could in a few years occupy all of [Greece], and leave to his son[120] such a foundation that he was able to make himself prince of all the world. [244] Hence, he
who disparages these thoughts, if he is a prince, disparages his own principality;
if he is a citizen, his own city. [245] And I complain against nature, which either
should not have made me a knower of this, or should have given me the ability[121]
to be able to execute it. [246] Nor do I think that now, since I am old, I can have
any opportunity for it. And because of this I have been liberal toward you. If[122]
the things said by me please you, in due time you, being young and qualified,
could help and counsel your princes to their benefit. [247] I do not want you to
be afraid or distrustful of this, for this province seems born to resuscitate dead
things, as has been seen in poetry, painting, and sculpture. [248] But I am distrustful of how much may be expected from me, as [I am] getting on in years.

115. See *AW* I 148–56.   116. Lit.: experience.

117. Ercole (Hercules) I of Este (1433–1505) in 1479.

118. Lit.: the other Greece.

119. Or: it, referring back to the kingdom of the Macedonians.

120. Or: to the son.   122. Lit.: when.

121. Lit.: faculty.

[249] And truly, if in the past fortune had conceded to me enough for a like enterprise, I believe in a very short time I would have shown to the world how much ancient orders are worth, and without doubt I would have either increased it with glory or lost it without shame.

THE END OF THE SEVENTH AND LAST BOOK OF THE ART OF WAR

BY NICCOLÒ MACHIAVEGLI,

FLORENTINE CITIZEN AND SECRETARY

FIGURES

———— ❧ ————

Niccolò Machiavegli,
Florentine Citizen and Secretary,
to the Reader[1]

[1] I believe it to be necessary, in wanting you readers to understand without difficulty the order of the battalions and armies and encampments as arranged in the narration, to show you the figures of each of them. [2] So it must be explained to you under what signs or characters infantrymen, cavalrymen, and every other individual member are shown.

[3] Know then that this letter

o	signifies	Infantrymen with shield
♂		Infantrymen with pike
✗		Decurions
⭲		Ordinary velites
t		Extraordinary velites
c		Centurions
?		Constables of battalions
φ		Head of brigades
ω		Captain-General
ʃ		Music
z		Flag
⅄		Men-at-arms
⅄		Light cavalrymen
θ		Artilleries

[4] In the first figure is drawn the form of an ordinary battalion[2] and in what mode it is doubled along the flank,[3] as its ordering was described.

---

1. Lit.: to him who reads or to whoever reads.

2. See *AW* II 193–96.

3. See *AW* II 185–88, 191–92.

[5] In the same figure is shown how with the same order of 80 files (just by changing to the rear the five files of pikes that are in the front) all the pikes are made by doubling to turn to the back; this is done when one marches ahead and fears the enemy to the rear.[4]

[6] In the second figure is shown how a battalion is ordered that marches ahead and has to fight along the flank, as contained in the treatise.[5]

[7] In the third figure is shown how a battalion is ordered with two horns, and then with a piazza in the middle, as arranged in the treatise.[6]

[8] In the fourth figure is shown the form of an army ordered to do battle with the enemy, as arranged in the treatise.[7]

[9] In the fifth figure is shown the form of a squared army, as contained in the treatise.[8]

[10] In the sixth figure is shown the form of an army turned from a squared army back into the ordinary form for doing battle, as contained in the text.[9]

[11] In the seventh figure is shown the form of the encampment, as is discussed[10] above.[11]

---

4. Cf. *AW* II 226.

5. See *AW* II 221–22.

6. The top of figure 3 shows the marching order described at *AW* II 232–36; the bottom left of figure 3 shows the battalion with two horns described at *AW* II 242–46; the bottom right of figure 3 shows the battalion with a piazza in the middle described at *AW* II 248–49.

7. See *AW* III 50–63.

8. See *AW* V 14–36.

9. See *AW* V 44–50.

10. Lit.: is reasoned.

11. See *AW* VI 23–88.

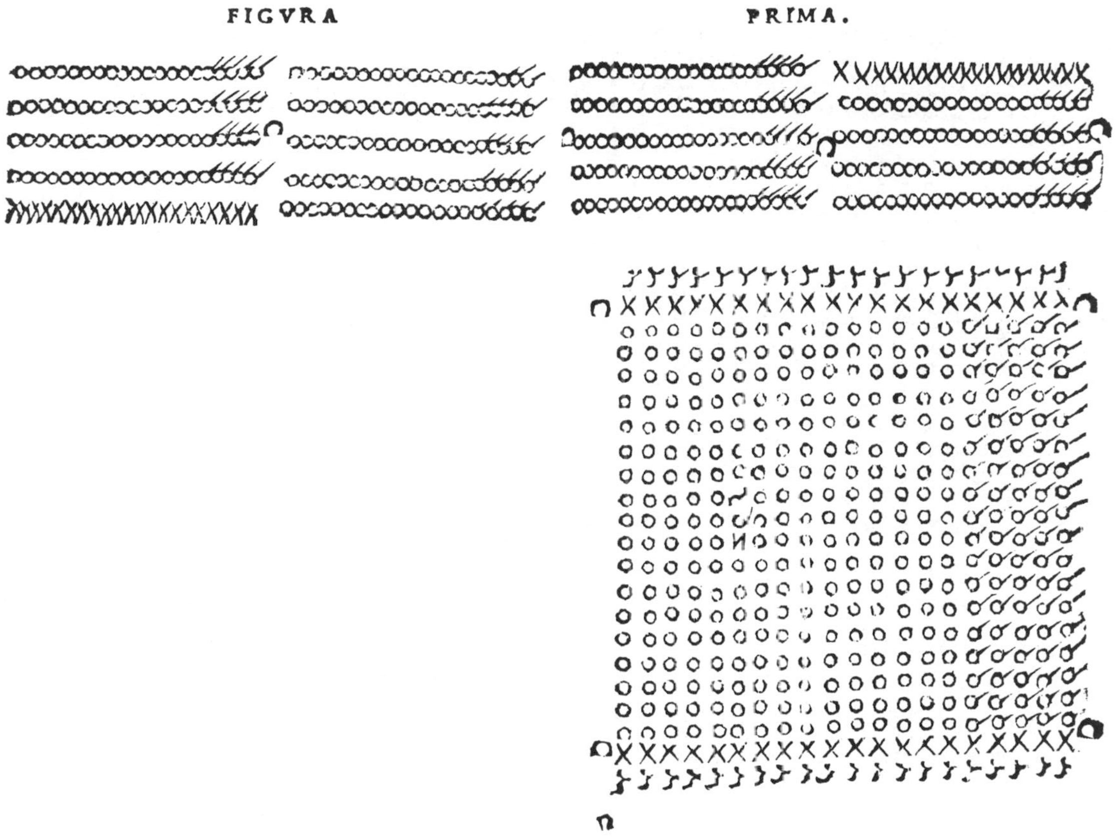

Figure 1

FIGVRA SECVNDA.

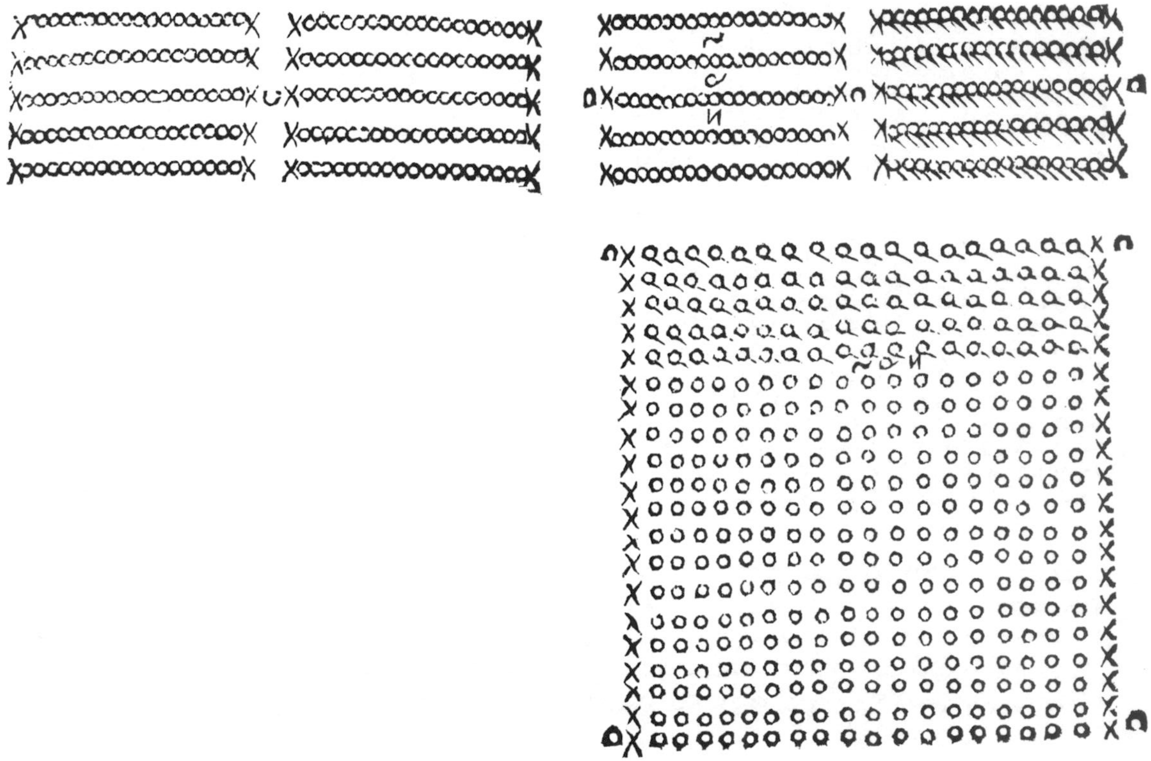

Figure 2

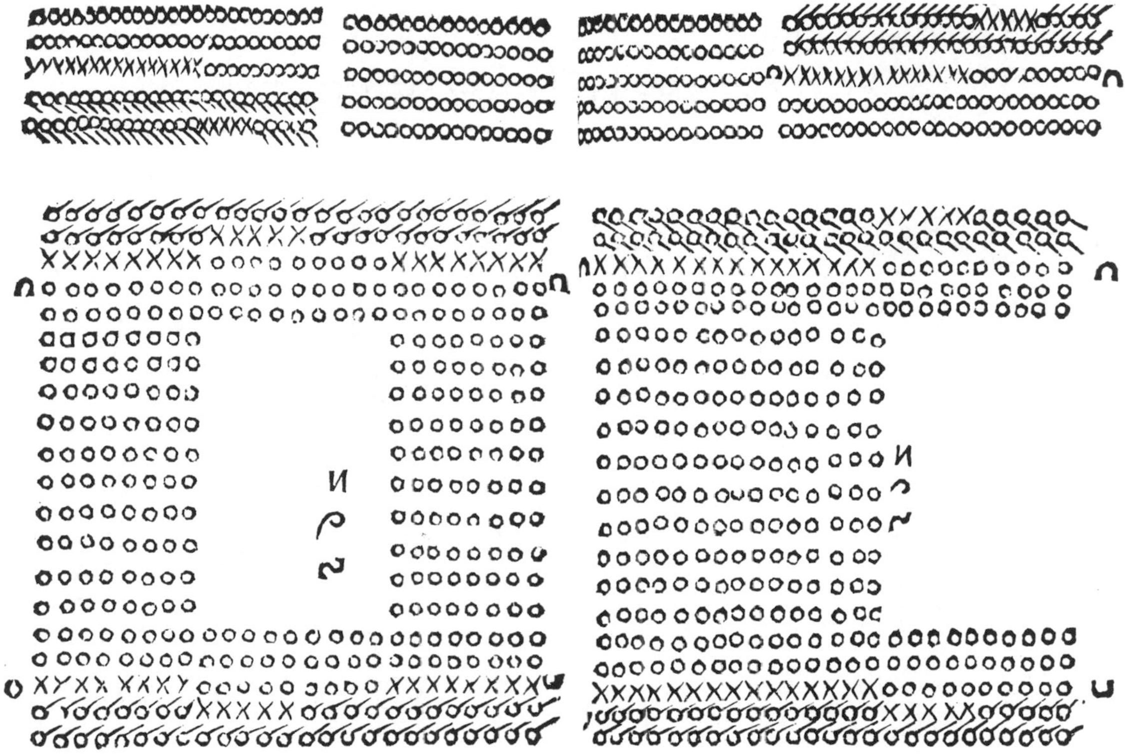

Figure 3

FIGVRA QVARTA.

CARRIAGGI·ET· DISARMATI·

Figure 4

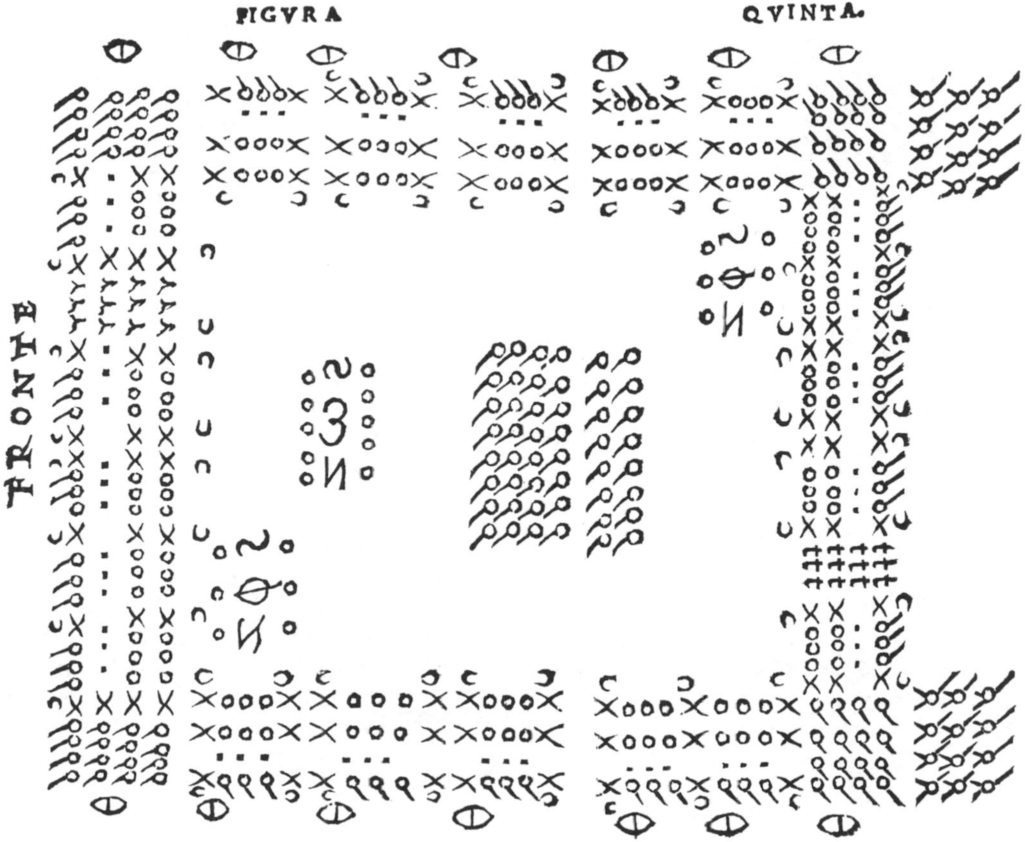

Figure 5

FIGVRA SEXTA

Figure 6

SETTIMA. FIGVRA

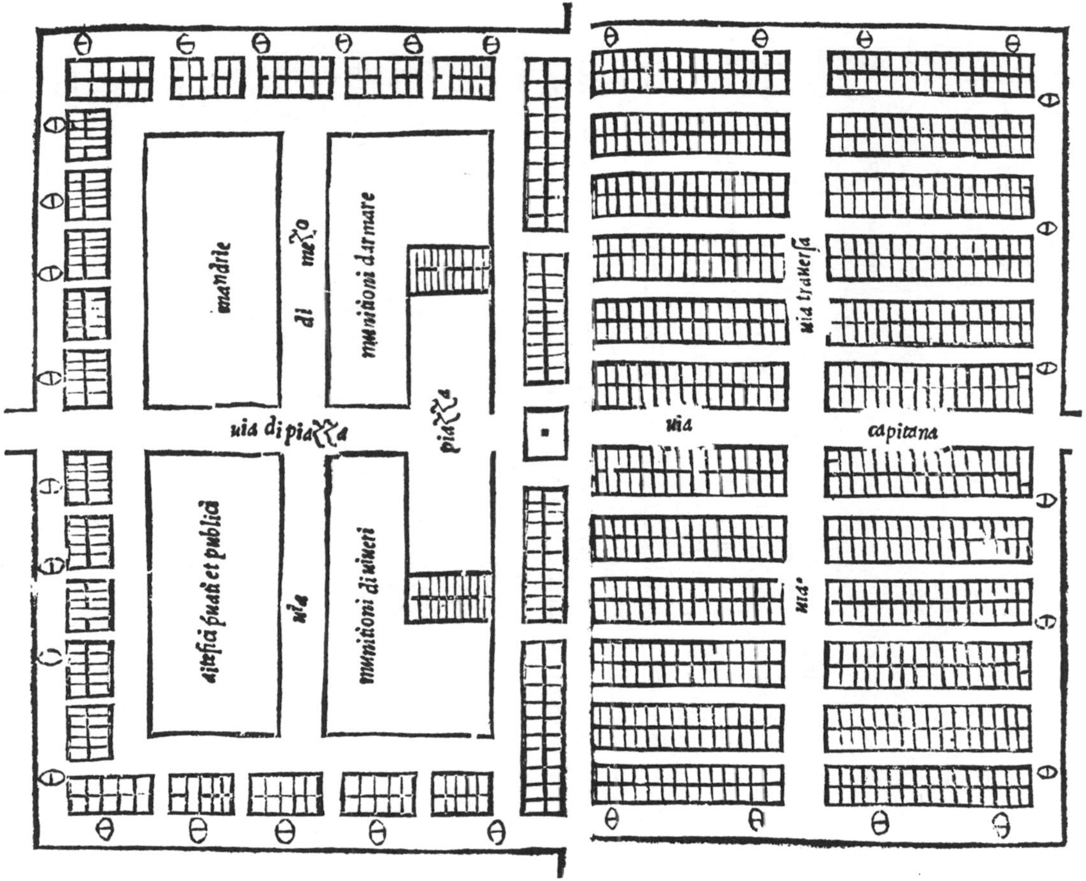

Figure 7

Notes on Figures

In the original Italian explanation of figures, the symbol signifying a constable of a battalion ("Connestaboli delle battaglie") seems to be a reversed Greek sigma (ꙅ), though in the figures themselves (and in the translation of the explanation of figures on page 167) it resembles the Arabic numeral 9. In the figures this symbol and others (especially those signifying the flag and the music) are often reversed or upside down or both.

Figure 1   *Top* (when figure is held such that "Figura Prima" reads from left to right): The constable, music, and flag do not appear in the figure. The text (*AW* II 194) says they should be in the midst of the second century, after the last rank of pikes and in the first rank of shield-men, occupying the spaces of three shield-men.

                 Bottom: The constable, music, and flag seem to be out of place. The text (*AW* II 191) says they should be between the last rank of pikes and the first rank of shields.

Figure 2   *Bottom:* The constable, music, and flag seem to be out of place. The text (*AW* II 224) says the constable should be "in the middle," presumably between the tenth and eleventh ranks rather than the fifth and sixth files.

Figure 3   *Top:* The constable, music, and flag do not appear in the figure. The text (*AW* II 234) says they come between the second and third centuries.

                 Top and bottom right: The text leaves unspecified where the pike decurions should be; that is, whether they should be on the extreme flanks or one file in from the extremes. If the diagram on the bottom left of figure 3 is the standard, then the first and fourth centuries should be changed such that the pike decurions are one file in from the extremes; they should also be so placed on the left horn of the diagram on the bottom right of figure 3.

                 Bottom left: If the text (*AW* II 248–49) is followed, then there should be seven ranks left at the rear (though the figure gives eight) and ten ranks along the sides of the piazza (though the figure gives nine).

Figure 4   The symbol for centurions ("**C**") is often missing from or backward in most of the ten battalions in the brigade on the left; the symbol for ordinary velites ("**ꞇ**") is missing from the sides of many of the same battalions.

                 Bottom: "CARRIAGGI ET DISARMATI" means "wagons [or baggage] and [those who are] unarmed."

Figure 5   According to the text (*AW* V 14), the five battalions along each flank should be placed front to back rather than side by side, such that these battalions face in the same direction as those along the front and rear.

                 According to the text (*AW* V 15–16), the ordinary velites ("**ꞇ**") that are on the front between the fourth and fifth battalions should be moved to the left, between the first and second battalions. Similarly, the extraordinary velites ("**t**") that are on the rear between the first and second battalions should be moved to the right, between the fourth and fifth battalions.

The symbol for centurions ("**C**") is often missing or backward.

Figure 6   As with the correction of figure 5, the five battalions along each flank should apparently be placed front to back rather than side by side.

Several symbols for centurions ("**C**") are missing.

Figure 7   *Right:* There are two columns of twenty-four large rectangles, each made up of thirty-two smaller rectangles. In eight of the twenty-four large rectangles, one of the smaller rectangles is slightly larger than the others. According to the text (*AW* VI 34, 37), instead of eight such slightly larger rectangles, there should be twenty-four, one at the outer end of each large rectangle.

Other irregularities (such as missing or added lines or dots) appear to be the result of the imperfections of the original woodcuts or of the copies.

The microfilm of the original eliminated the words "via di croce," which belong on the street running vertically down the center of the figure. The phrase means cross street (or way of the cross). Translations of the labels of the other streets are as follows: "Via capitana" means captain street; "via traversa" means transverse street; "via di piazza" means piazza street.

Left: Translations of the labels for the enclosed areas are as follows: "artefici p[ri] vati and publici" means private and public artisans; "mandrie" means herds; "munitioni di viveri" means provisions for living; "munitioni d'armare" means privisions for arming; "piazza," left untranslated in the text, means marketplace or square.

INTERPRETIVE ESSAY

Like *The Prince* and *Discourses on Livy,* Machiavelli's *Art of War* is a carefully ordered whole. Separation of the intellectual world into discrete academic disciplines, however, has led to partial treatments of this whole. Each discipline has tended to focus on some aspect of the *Art of War,* underestimating the importance of the rest or even mistaking that part for the whole. An interdisciplinary approach would not dispose of the difficulty, since it would incorrectly assume that some combination of our contemporary disciplines correspond to and exhaust the many aspects of Machiavelli's works. Under the spell of such partial approaches, the reader is in danger of failing to appreciate the many unexpected gifts that Machiavelli places before him. At the very least, one must resist the temptation to let one's own field answer in advance the question Machiavelli has left as a riddle: What kind of work is the *Art of War*? For anyone who seeks to understand this useful and beautiful book, an unwavering determination to answer this question must be matched by an equally steadfast patience not to rush to judgment.

These potential pitfalls notwithstanding, I have reaped much from many fields and offer the following in return. The first part of this essay, on Machiavelli's solutions to the military problems of his day, will be of most use to those interested in military and Renaissance history, and the last section of this part to students of strategic thought. Especially on my mind as I wrote the bulk of the first part were the trenchant and detailed criticisms of Machiavelli's military writings put forth so thoughtfully by Piero Pieri in *Guerra e politica negli scrittori italiani.*[1] Point-by-point responses to Pieri would have been out of place here, but I implicitly defend Machiavelli against Pieri (as well as others mentioned in this book's introduction), not by challenging Pieri's excellent military history, but by challenging him and other critics to pay even closer attention to exactly what Machiavelli said and to take even greater pains to discern what he

---

1. Piero Pieri, *Guerra e politica negli scrittori italiani* (Milan: Riccardo Riccardi, 1955).

might have meant. Political scientists and those interested in civil–military relations will likely find the second part of this essay, on the relationship between war and politics, to be the more useful. Those whose interests are literary or philosophical would do well to begin with the last part, which concerns Machiavelli's overall intention in the *Art of War*.

Machiavelli's Solutions to the Military Problems of the Early Sixteenth Century

Carl von Clausewitz asserted that Machiavelli was a "very sound judge of military matters," and treated him as a writer whose insights into the conduct and nature of war possessed permanent value.[2] Military writers since Clausewitz's time have been less generous and—as the following seeks to suggest—less correct than Clausewitz regarding Machiavelli's military judgment. I first consider his solutions to the relatively ephemeral problems surrounding recent innovations in battlefield tactics, developments in the areas of manpower and organization, and technological changes related to fortifications and sieges. Then I turn to Machiavelli's treatment of more permanent problems of strategic thought.

The Field of Battle

Controversy abounds as to what caused the dizzying military changes during Machiavelli's day. Also debated is whether these changes constituted a full-blown military revolution or instead represented a particular moment in a long-term evolution. In considering these questions, it is important to remember that the sense at the time was that tumultuous change was indeed afoot, but not rapid change in a single direction driven by gunpowder technology. On the tactical level especially, each of the battles that occurred on the Italian peninsula, from the battle of Fornovo in 1495 to that of Pavia in 1525, seemed to offer a new lesson to be learned, a new innovation that transformed the ways armies ought to be armed, ordered, led, and used.

In late medieval warfare, heavy cavalry had come to dominate the battlefield. The primary function of these well-armored men on powerful, armored chargers was to overwhelm their enemies by means of shock, crashing into them with the maximum force needed to drive them from the field. To be effective, this par-

---

2. Carl von Clausewitz, *Historical and Political Writings,* ed. and trans. Peter Paret and Daniel Moran (Princeton: Princeton University Press, 1992), 281; Peter Paret, *Clausewitz and the State* (New York: Oxford University Press, 1976), 161.

ticular weapon system—and any weapon system at anytime, for that matter—
had to be intelligently combined with the other available weaponry. Heavy cavalry had to be coordinated with heavy infantry and with light cavalry and light
infantry and their many ballistic weapons (especially the crossbow), in addition
to a variety of small, stationary artillery pieces whose projectiles were for the
most part not propelled by gunpowder. As the Middle Ages waned, many factors
no doubt contributed to the eventual decline of the dominance of the heavy cavalryman. But from the tactician's point of view, the most critical development
was the advent of heavy infantry that could defend against the onslaught of
heavy cavalry and even, in many cases, take the offensive against it. Medieval
warfare had seen significant but isolated instances of heavy infantry able to put
up considerable resistance to attacking heavy cavalry; but not until the Swiss
"came down from the mountains" could heavy infantry consistently challenge
heavy cavalry.

The secret of the Swiss success consisted in the deployment of tightly packed,
massive squares of around twenty-five hundred highly trained and disciplined
men. The vast majority of these men carried pikes eighteen feet in length that
they had trained with since their youth; a much smaller number placed at the
center of the squares still carried the shorter halberds that had once been carried
by all. Because of the pikes' great length, four to six rows of pike points extended
in front of the first line of men in whichever direction they chose to face. Like the
heavy cavalry they came to displace, their chief function was offensive. They too
strove to crush or drive from the field anyone who got in their way. As soon as
men in the front ranks fell, those directly behind would step up to take their
places, while the halberdiers in the center would fend off any infantry or cavalry
that managed to penetrate the square. Although offense was their preferred mode,
when assaulted on their flanks by heavy cavalry they were forced to assume a
defensive position. Each man would stop and plant the butt of his pike against
the inside of one foot with the point facing in the direction of the oncoming
enemy, thereby presenting an almost impenetrable wall of pike points. This defensive posture was very effective, but being forced to assume it kept the pikemen
from performing their aggressive, offensive function. Because heavy cavalry
could, in principle, force pike squares onto the defensive, it retained an important battlefield role, if not the regnant role it enjoyed in the past.

A close descendent of the medieval heavy cavalryman was the fifteenth- and
sixteenth-century condottiere, so named for the *condotta* or contract stipulating
the terms of his employment by the political authority that hired him. The word
had a less pejorative tone than our "mercenary," but still clearly resonated with
the cold cash exchange at the basis of the condottiere's military service. These
soldiers were less willing than their medieval predecessors to charge either Swiss

pikes or the many (often less effective) imitators of the Swiss that had cropped up by the early 1500s. Thus the Swiss square and its offshoots presented two major problems to Italian military theorists and practitioners: how to counter or effectively imitate the Swiss pikes, and how to make effective use of the recently dethroned heavy cavalry arm. The tacticians of Europe, and especially of Italy, were still grappling with these two problems when the other major battlefield innovation of the era, the development of gunpowder technology, began to make itself felt.

Early in the sixteenth century—most notably at the battles of Cerignuola in 1503 and Bicocca in 1522—it was discovered that sufficiently protected arquebusiers could do considerable damage to the enormous, and therefore easy to hit, pike formations. The arquebus (pronounced AR-ka-bus) was a handheld, matchlock firearm that was less reliable, less accurate, and of less range than the crossbow, but it had an equal rate of fire and at least as powerful an impact; it also required less training, and, most important, was cheaper to produce than the crossbow. Yet for successful employment of arquebusiers, protection was essential since they could easily be driven from the field by pike squares or cavalry. Thus their effectiveness at Cerignuola was, as it would still be almost twenty years later at Bicocca, completely dependent on the willingness of their targets to charge them while they remained secure behind heavy entrenchments. It was not immediately obvious in what other way such protection could be provided. The early sixteenth century also saw the first decisively effective use of field artillery (as opposed to siege artillery, the effectiveness of which had been shown much earlier). For at the battle of Ravenna in 1512, the Spanish–papal forces (and in particular the heavy cavalry commanded by the *Art of War*'s chief interlocutor, Fabrizio Colonna) were subjected to such blistering artillery fire that they were driven out of their entrenchments and forced to give battle in a weakened and shaken condition rather than receive battle from behind the security of their embankments. The result was a Spanish–papal loss, displaying field artillery's ability to play a crucial battlefield role for the first time in its centuries-long existence. Both handheld firearms and field artillery had begun to show their power.

It is very easy to mistakenly assume that the moment these gunpowder weapons appeared on the battlefield everything immediately changed. In fact, the effectiveness of arquebuses took centuries to establish, and another century to be systematically incorporated into battlefield tactics. Arquebuses (and muskets, their heavier and more powerful successors) did not begin to play a significant, independent battlefield role until the second decade of the 1500s. Furthermore, no widespread tactical transformation can accurately be said to have taken place in direct connection to firearms until the middle of that century. Not even by then can it be said that these many elements were put together into anything like a systematic whole. For this feat Europe would have to wait for Maurice of Nassau and, especially, Gustavus Adolphus to come on the scene at the turn of the next century. It was the latter who also found a place on the battlefield for artillery, but only by decreasing its size in order to increase its mobility and by loading it with grape shot (multiple balls the size of musketballs) to make up for its slow rate of fire. Even then its tactical utility was quite limited, and it was useless once the battle had been joined because then it produced as many casualties among friends as among enemies.

Throughout this process of change, good tacticians strove to achieve the optimal combination of the various weapon systems. Shortly after Machiavelli's day, solutions to the three problems discussed above slowly emerged. The dominance of the pike could only be countered by the combination of cavalry and some type of shot. Since this combination of cavalry and shot could only be countered by its own kind, pike squares needed cavalry and shot on their own side; yet given that shot and cavalry without their own pikemen were vulnerable to enemy pike, they needed their own pikemen. In a word, each element needed the others to carry out its own function successfully. The tactical way of the future was to be found in this effective combination of heavy and light infantry, cavalry, and—when circumstances required or permitted it—artillery. But during Machiavelli's time, no one had alighted on this exact combination, though all the best theorists and practitioners, including Machiavelli, were groping in that direction. A brief look at Machiavelli's own analysis of the battle of Ravenna illustrates his firm grasp of the contemporary tactical problems and of the need for a well-balanced coordination of arms in order to solve them. And a summary of the basic characteristics of the army advocated in the *Art of War*, with reference to the imaginary battle staged in book III, specifies the content of Machiavelli's solutions.

It is remarkable that Machiavelli should pause to give technical military advice in the midst of his poetic and apparently impassioned conclusion to *The Prince*, in which Machiavelli echos Julius II's exhortation to expel the barbarian invaders from the land. The battle he uses to illustrate his advice is that of Ravenna. It will be recalled that without the effective use of field artillery before the battle, the French would have been forced either to storm an extremely difficult Spanish position or to skulk off the field. Instead, the already outmatched Spanish cavalry was seriously weakened by the enemy's artillery fire and then forced out of its position. The consequent rout of the Spanish cavalry freed the French cavalry to relieve their own heavy infantry, armed like the Swiss, just then losing to the Spanish infantry. Thus the key factors in this battle in their order of occurrence are (1) the devastating and unprecedented use of field artillery at the beginning of the battle as a means of softening up and dislodging a partially fortified enemy whose best chances for victory depended on receiving rather than giving battle; (2) the effectiveness of the Spanish infantry against pikes *alla svizzera;* and (3) the vulnerability of the Spanish infantry to unmolested heavy cavalry. I focus on the latter two points first.

In the oddly technical digression in the midst of *The Prince*'s hortatory conclusion, Machiavelli notes that although both Swiss and Spanish infantry are considered terrifying, each has a specific defect: Spanish infantry is vulnerable to French cavalry, while Swiss infantry is vulnerable to Spanish infantry. He continues:

> And although a complete experiment of this last has not been seen, yet an indication of it was seen in the battle of Ravenna, when the Spanish infantry confronted the German [infantry] battalions [fighting for the French], who use the same order as the Swiss. There the Spanish, with their agile bodies and aided by their shields, came between and under the Germans' pikes and attacked them safely without their having any remedy for it; and if it had not been for the cavalry that charged them, they would have worn out all the Germans. (*P* 26.105)

Thus Machiavelli's solution to the problem of pikes *alla svizzera* is heavy infantry like that of the Spanish, armed with swords and shields so as to be able to close with relatively unprotected pikemen whose long pikes were of no use at close quarters. But armaments were not all that was at stake. Machiavelli's reference to agile bodies is not just an observation about Spanish physiques. A passage from the *Art of War* indicates that the reference is to the relatively small bodies of approximately four hundred men into which the Spanish were grouped to allow for greater articulation of their formations and therefore greater flexibility than could ever be achieved with massive pike squares: "[I]t is necessary that there be many bodies in an army, and that each body have its own flag and its own guide. For having this, it must have many souls and, as a consequence, many lives" (*AW* II 275). But because of their vulnerability to cavalry, infantry like the Spanish could live so many lives only with the aid of pikes to repel cavalry. Machiavelli therefore suggested a "third order" that "might not only oppose but also be confident of overcoming" infantries like the Spanish and the Swiss (*P* 26.104).

Thus was first suggested the scheme fully put forth for the first time in the *Art of War*. Machiavelli proposed the systematic combination of pikes with shieldmen similar to the ad hoc arrangement developed earlier in the century by "the Great Captain," Gonzalo de Córdoba. In Machiavelli's version, a front of twenty pikes a mere five ranks deep is followed by fifteen ranks of shieldmen. Ten such battalions of four hundred each are placed side by side to make the front of

the whole army arrayed in battle order. This long, articulated front is then followed by a second line, this time composed of six identically ordered battalions
with large spaces in between from side to side. Machiavelli allowed his humanist readers to believe that he was simply copying a battle order of the ancient
Romans. In that scheme the front line, with similar large spaces from side to side,
would withdraw into the second line when pressed by the enemy, and they together would, if need be, withdraw into a third line of four similarly ordered battalions. But Machiavelli considerably alters this Roman model (which seems actually to have been a parade ground drill rather than an actual battle order) to
make it less impracticable. Two innovations are worth noting: first, rather than
follow the Roman practice of leaving gaps in the front line—thereby making at-
tractive targets of the battalions' flanks—Machiavelli places the battalions relatively close together; second, in recognition of the considerable difficulties in-
herent in any involuntary retreat, Machiavelli replaces the overly precise Roman
procedure of having the front line back up so as to incorporate itself into the second with the more general principle that the second line must be able to relieve
the first. Machiavelli thus increases the practicality of the Roman order by sim-
plifying it.

For all his attention to detailed orders, Machiavelli shows himself to be
strongly attached to precious few, if any. For instance, before offering the very
general and flexible principle of always providing a tactical reserve, his Fabrizio
emphatically asserts that one should not hold exclusively to the formation described above. Luigi asks, "Would you always use this form of order when you
want to do battle?" Fabrizio answers, "Not in any mode. For you have to vary the
form of the army according to the quality of the site and the quality and quantity of the enemy" (AW III 172–73). Indeed, greater flexibility than that of any
potential enemies was what Machiavelli strove for above all else. Thus his battle
lines, while less flexible than the ancient Roman, were more flexible than the
pike squares over which he sought the relative advantage. To buy this greater
flexibility, Machiavelli was even willing to pay the same price that Maurice and
Gustavus Adolphus, men in no small part inspired by Machiavelli, were willing
to pay one hundred years later. That price was a certain vulnerability on the
flanks. The thin line of pikes and the light infantry deployed along the side of
Machiavelli's army could approximate, but not replicate, the impenetrable wall
of pike points presented by a solid square of pikes. Such vulnerability, however,
is the necessary consequence of gaining more flexibility by means of linear as
opposed to block formations. The Romans' linear formations had been more
vulnerable on their flanks than their Macedonian opponents just as Gustavus
Adolphus's linear formations would prove more vulnerable to pikes ordered like
the Swiss. But they and Machiavelli knew that the price was worth the paying,

and that it could be lessened by the proper use of light infantry and, especially, cavalry.

The other lesson that Machiavelli gleaned from the battle of Ravenna was the vulnerability of Spanish infantry, the model for his own shieldmen, to heavy cavalry. The thin line of pikemen in front of his shieldmen was part of his solution to this problem, but for a full solution heavy cavalry of its own was indispensable. It is often thought that Machiavelli assigned to cavalry no significant battlefield role. This misunderstanding has arisen from incorrect interpretations of the *Art of War* and *Discourses on Livy*. Fabrizio's claims about the *relative* importance and esteem that ought to be accorded to infantry and cavalry have been mistaken for a prohibition against using cavalry in battle. But Fabrizio merely asserts that cavalry is to be esteemed *less* than infantry because the latter is *more* useful in battle, not that cavalry is useless in battle. Similarly, claims about the relative value of cavalry's various functions are mistaken for a derogation of its utility in battle. But Fabrizio says only that cavalry is *more* useful in reconnaissance, harassment of the enemy, and cutting lines of communication and supply than it is in battle (*AW* II 72–100; cf. *D* II 18).

It is wrong to take these statements to mean that Fabrizio wishes to exclude cavalry from having a significant role in battle or even to reduce it as much as possible. Moreover, the action of the imaginary battle of book III highlights the importance of heavy cavalry. There we witness the light cavalry charge the enemy's arquebusiers and neutralize their dangerous fire to the flank, and the heavy cavalry—after having been compelled to take cover amidst their pikemen—repulse and kill many of the enemy's heavy cavalrymen that are so threatening to their own shieldmen (*AW* III 81–91). Finally, it should be emphasized that Fabrizio's statements about infantry and cavalry pertain to the *esteem* in which each is to be held, not to the specific use to which each should be put. The point is as much political as military, and is made to offset to the excessive dependence on mercenaries on horseback. In *The Prince*, Machiavelli says that the first thing mercenary captains did in order to establish their dominance was take reputation away from infantry and give it to cavalry, that is, to themselves (*P* 12.53). In an effort to replace these condottieri, Machiavelli's Fabrizio seeks to institutionalize a restoration of the infantry's reputation.

It should be noted that in order to attain this accurate understanding of Machiavelli's position regarding infantry and cavalry, careful attention must be paid to his exact wording. Machiavelli aimed not just for the kind of technical precision reached in those passages. He also chose his words and general rhetoric carefully so as to avoid running afoul of the numerous political obstacles through which he was compelled to navigate in order to gain a hearing in the Florence and Europe of his day. The subject of Machiavelli's rhetoric is treated at length in the last part of this essay, where I consider Machiavelli's aim in writing the *Art of War*. It must also be briefly addressed in this context, however. Throughout almost all of the *Art of War,* the arguments are presented in the form of a dialogue—that is, in a form resembling, for example, a Shakespearean play. To assume that Fabrizio, the most vocal participant of the dialogue, simply speaks for Machiavelli is similar to assuming that Hamlet's words reveal Shakespeare's full understanding. It is true that, unlike *Hamlet,* the *Art of War* is a treatise on warfare that seeks to convey technical information. But if it were nothing more than a technical treatise, Machiavelli would not have undertaken the cumbersome business of providing a setting, discussing the attributes of the various characters, and so forth. It so happens that no attribute of the characters is stressed more emphatically than their ages. Indeed, many of Fabrizio's carefully worded statements are made in response to probing, sometimes pointed questions put to him by the much younger participants in the discussion, all friends of Machiavelli who attended regular intellectual gatherings in the gardens that provide the setting for the *Art of War.* The case discussed above regarding cavalry illustrates well the primary difference between Fabrizio and the young participants. It is only after persistent questioning by the young men that Fabrizio admits not only that modern cavalry is superior to ancient, but that the ancients whom Fabrizio at first pretends to worship were themselves fatally vulnerable to ancient cavalry, to say nothing of the modern cavalry that owed its superiority to technical innovations such as stirrups and horned saddles. Machiavelli uses the old Fabrizio to appeal to the work's primary audience, "lovers of ancient actions" (*AW* pr. 11), while appealing to a wider and younger audience by means of the young men who, Machiavelli emphasizes, are "on fire for" all great things, regardless of whether they are ancient or modern.

Such rhetorical considerations must be kept in mind at every step, but especially when questions arise regarding innovations, including technological innovations. Thus by the end of the dialogue even Fabrizio himself is willing to pay tribute to the spirit of invention: He ends the military part of the work with the assertion that "if invention brings honor in other things, in [war] above all it honors you. And one sees every invention, even though weak, celebrated by the writers" (*AW* VII 191–92). He then goes on to offer two examples of inventions used by Alexander the Great. But because the examples cannot be corroborated by any ancient source or ruin, it would seem that they are the inventions of Machiavelli's Fabrizio. We thus see that Fabrizio, like Machiavelli, knows how to make good use of the supposition, planted in his readers by him, of his love of antiquity.

Attention to rhetoric is also important for a proper understanding of Machiavelli's treatment of another technological innovation, the most significant of his age and perhaps the most significant in the history of warfare: firearms. Much as Cosimo extracted from Fabrizio the admission that modern cavalry was much superior to ancient cavalry and that modern armies must be armed and ordered differently as a result, so the youngest participant in the discussion, Luigi, extracts the concession that the newest technology, the arquebus and small artillery, can indeed inflict such great harm in battle that tactics must be altered in order to neutralize it (*AW* III 134). Thus Machiavelli again satisfies the lovers of antiquity with the authority of the more restrained and older Fabrizio at the same time that he satisfies the youthful fascination with modern innovation by means of the insistent, if usually polite, questioning of the young men. But Fabrizio goes even further than the above concessions. Without pressure from any of the younger interlocutors, he asserts that the use of the arquebus has become a necessity and insists not just that a portion of already enlisted soldiers be trained in its use, but that *all* young men, soldiers or not, be so trained. "I would add the arquebus, a new instrument, as you know, and a necessary one. And I would accustom all the youths of my state to these drills" (*AW* II 125). By making what must be one of the earliest—if not *the* earliest—prescriptions for universal arquebus training, Fabrizio shows himself to be more than receptive to the innovations of his day.

But Machiavelli is also aware of the limits of his audience's patience for concessions to modern innovations. This is reflected in Fabrizio's refusal (*AW* III 150) to enlarge on the uses of field artillery and his enjoinder to look up Machiavelli's more thorough treatment of the subject in the *Discourses on Livy*. There Machiavelli reveals that he knew full well when field artillery is and is not useful. The only circumstance in which it is useless is when both armies are willing to do battle on the open field without delay. For there, as noted earlier, once the armies meet, friend cannot be adequately distinguished from foe. But under other circumstances it can be of decisive importance. When artillery is deeply dug in behind well-prepared field fortifications on high ground, it gives an advantage to a defender who wishes to hold that position without giving battle. If one wishes to draw such an enemy into battle, one must have recourse to a variety of stratagems to cajole the enemy from his position or (in a beautiful illustration of what we could call Machiavelli's philosophical stance toward the power of necessity) one must open gaps in one's ranks in the areas at which the artillery is firing, "[f]or this is a general rule: that one has to give way to those things which cannot be withstood" (*AW* III 160). Far from obstructing the development and use of modern innovations, Machiavelli "gave way to" them and sought to put them to as much use as possible.

The other circumstance in which artillery is very useful brings us back to the battle of Ravenna and to another instance of Machiavelli's improvements on the ancients. Machiavelli notes that field artillery tends to give the advantage to whoever is on the offensive, moving aggressively from one battle to the next and from one part of any given battlefield to another before the enemy has time to prepare his defenses. Such a modern defender who wishes to maintain an underfortified position is "on account of artillery at a greater disadvantage" than was an ancient defender. For with artillery, the attacker "dislodges you at once and without your having any remedy, and you are forced to go out from your fortresses and come to fight. . . . This happened to the Spanish at the battle of Ravenna." Machiavelli concludes that the Romans, who even without the advantages of artillery preferred the offensive, "would have had more advantage, and would have made their acquisitions more quickly if there had been [artillery] in those times" (D II 17.3). As he recommends the offensive to his contemporaries, he also indicates that they have a distinct advantage over their predecessors.

It is hard to imagine that a theorist who revealed himself to be open to, and even eager for, military innovations in general, and to training in the arquebus in particular, would not have embraced a particular development that took root while the *Art of War* was being written, one that was to flower in the following decades. The development was the increased use of arquebusiers to accomplish the task that Fabrizio set for his shieldmen, namely, to combine with pike squares to offer them mutual protection. The very Spaniards whose shieldmen Machiavelli's Fabrizio imitated were the most successful at incorporating this innovation into the kind of effective combined arms synthesis Machiavelli sought. And there is one passage in particular in the *Art of War* that suggests that Machiavelli favored this practice in instances in which an individual battalion engaged in an action on its own. He mentions, as though in passing, that the Swiss had a formation "in the mode of a cross" between the arms of which arquebusiers found protection from the enemy (*AW* II 253–54). If this mode were to prove useful *en masse*, there is every reason to think that Machiavelli would have been more than willing to replace his shieldmen with arquebusiers, thus achieving the optimal coordination of weapons systems for which he was clearly striving.

Manpower, Organization, and Training

Closely related to the developments in battlefield tactics discussed above were changes in the areas of manpower, organization, and training. The footloose and often predatory mercenary bands of the fifteenth century were being replaced in Machiavelli's day by a more stable arrangement wherein mercenary captains, with varying numbers of their own men, would hire themselves out to the same state for longer periods of time. And they increasingly began to lead or fight alongside individuals and groups, whether militias or semifeudal lords and vassals, that were part of the state that had hired them. Not until well into the next century did this arrangement begin to be replaced by professional standing armies that drew their soldiers almost entirely from among their own citizens or subjects. Throughout these centuries of transition, most of the leading military commanders in Europe, such as Maurice of Nassau and Gustavus Adolphus, strove with but limited success to replace mercenaries with native professionals.

During this general period of transformation the peculiarities of each of the major European powers, especially those of Florence, should be noted. The tactical success of the Swiss and the related search for a new combination of weapon systems presented challenges that were met in various ways by the French, Germans, Spanish, and Italians. Among the French, the fear of an armed populace slowed considerably the formation of a substantial heavy infantry, leading them to rely on their heavy cavalry supported by light infantry and light cavalry armed with arquebuses and crossbows and supplemented by pikes in the hands of Swiss or German mercenaries. The Germans and Spanish were moving more rapidly in the direction of state-supported, professional heavy infantry, but were slowed down for financial rather than political reasons. Among the Germans and Spanish, infantry *alla svizzera* existed in large numbers but were paid by and loyal to quasi-feudal lords; cavalry, drawn as they were from the lesser nobility, were often paid by government ministries. In Italy, all the states but Florence were moving slowly but perhaps more quickly than the non-Italian states in the direction of professional standing armies, with some combination of feudal and hired arms in service to governments of various kinds. The difference between the Italian states and the other major European powers was the implacable antagonisms that existed among them, as well as the relative lack of central power. Among these many Italian powers, Florence alone had no new or old aristocracy with a strong military bent that could serve as heavy cavalry or call on dependents as infantry. Civil strife and the rise to dominance of the trade and banking classes served to extirpate any landed aristocracy bound by long tradition (cf. *FH* III 1, 10, 12, 13, 18; cf. also *FH* II 11–13, IV 2, 27, V 4; *D* I 55). Florence was utterly reliant on and prey to mercenaries, primarily from the papal states (*FH* I 39). Although many of these soldiers, especially in the upper ranks, were highly skilled, the overall organization and training among the rank and file was very uneven.

The road along which other European powers were creeping in the direction of well-disciplined, professional standing armies was simply closed to Florence. It was completely dependent on mercenaries for lack of any native group or class with any substantial military expertise or tradition. The middle way of attaching mercenaries and militias to feudal or aristocratic natives was not a possibility for Florence. Likewise, it is easy for us to forget that our alternative of a professional army in the service of an impersonal "state" was even less possible: the very notion—let alone the actual existence—of an impersonal state in whose name a professional armed force could serve would not be born till the time of Thomas Hobbes.

Thus the practical danger confronting Florence was that it would prolong a dependency on mercenary and foreign forces that had become militarily and financially crippling. To form an army from scratch, the only place to turn was to the citizens of Florence and her subjects and allies in the towns and countryside throughout Tuscany, much as Machiavelli himself had done while serving republican Florence. Given the enormity and necessity of this task and the inertia of the mercenary system, which all deplored but few knew how to escape, it made sense to push the deprecation of mercenaries to its rhetorical limit, while at the same time praising the only available alternative of a citizen soldiery in the only available terms, namely, those provided by the old and faltering—but still hallowed—tradition of Florentine "civic humanism." The dream nurtured by the civic humanists of resurrecting the even older golden days of the Florentine citizen soldiery had been at or near the core of this intellectual movement for over a hundred years. Machiavelli was thus faced with a very difficult but potentially fruitful rhetorical situation. The best allies Machiavelli had in his efforts to convince Florence to arm herself were part of a humanist tradition that looked to the ancients with the devotion that Machiavelli is (incorrectly) assumed to have shared. An obvious way to convince Florence was to adopt the language and conventions of the group most likely to give him an initial hearing, and then ease at least some of them into the realization that when it came down to practice they would have to part with some of their more cherished beliefs—or better yet, first ease them into the advantages of the practice, and let the limitations of their old beliefs come to light on their own.

But if the Florentines were persuaded to accept a new militia, could it ever possess the complex but cohesive hierarchy needed to support a modern army? Part of the answer lay in who would serve—in our terminology—as officers and NCOs. Regarding officers we can only speculate, since Machiavelli left few clues. Fabrizio states that captains are to be rotated from region to region on an annual basis and cannot serve in their home region. It therefore seems to be implied that these captains would constitute a *de facto* officer corps. On the move from year to year, they could have no occupation separate from their military responsibilities. Based on the actual militia Machiavelli formed while Florentine secretary, we might speculate that this corps would at first be made up of mercenaries. But it seems likely that the hope was to replace mercenaries with Tuscan natives paid by Florence. More specifically, it is clear from the *Purpose of the Militia* of 1506 that if Florentines themselves were to take part, they would insist on positions of authority. Therefore, the officer corps would most likely be made up of politically powerful Florentines. To say so openly would have been to play with political dynamite, for it is precisely the thought of arms in the hands of their fellow citizens that incensed most Florentines. But such an arrangement would seem to follow from the premise of a group of rotating officers. Contrary to Fabrizio's insistence in book I that no well-ordered state would allow its citizens or subjects to be employed as full-time soldiers, a professional officer corps of some kind seems to be embedded in Fabrizio's army. And it is not as though members of such a corps would have no model elsewhere in the dialogue. For Fabrizio himself constitutes such an ambiguous case. He is his king's advisor in peacetime, and his captain in time of war. At the end of the dialogue we learn that what he regards as his most important peacetime advice concerns how to prepare for war. Thus it may well be that these rotating captains would have an equally murky status in times of peace so as to be able to maintain their positions as rotating captains.

Regarding NCOs, matters are much clearer. Fabrizio places great emphasis on the importance of what he calls decurions and constables. Their primary functions are to keep small groups of men in their battle orders and to act as examples (*AW* II 266–82). Fabrizio takes steps to ensure that the best men will end up in positions of authority, such as instituting a system of rivalry for promotion at all levels and establishing criteria on the basis of which men suited to lead could be chosen during training. It would seem that all the elements are in place for the well-articulated hierarchical structure necessary to support a large, well-trained army.

And well trained it is. Large parts of the second, third, and fifth books are devoted, respectively, to training men individually and at the battalion level, training them for battle at the brigade and army levels, and training them for being on the march in enemy territory at the brigade and army levels. Although in the earlier, more political parts of the work, Fabrizio minimizes the frequency of the training required, he later says that one must train the whole army "as many times as one can" (*AW* III 199), again suggesting that rhetorical considerations keep him from admitting how very much preparations for war could end up dominating peacetime life. Be that as it may, one of the keys to the army's success is the order that comes only from disciplined training. Fabrizio asserts that it is not enough to have toughened up and trained one's men individually:

[T]here is also the need for them to learn to be in their orders, to obey the signals by sound and at the words of the captain. . . . For without this discipline,
observed and practiced with utmost care [and] diligence, never was an army
good. And without doubt, ferocious and disordered men are much weaker
than timid and ordered ones. For order chases fear from men and disorder
lessens ferocity. (*AW* II 140–41)

It is clear that Machiavelli takes himself to be conveying a timeless truth regarding military excellence. But he also asserts that in a period of comparatively lax
military discipline and training, good discipline would nearly guarantee success:
"[A] disciplined army is nothing other than an army that is well practiced in
these orders; and it would not be possible that whoever used similar discipline
would ever, in these times, be beaten." Recruited, well organized, and well
trained, Machiavelli's army would seem to be up to the task.

Fortifications and Sieges

In 1494, the bold invasion of Italy by King Charles VIII of France demonstrated
conclusively that the fortification systems that had dominated European strategy
for nearly a millennium were no match for modern artillery and the new massive
siege trains that made its deployment possible. The rising tide of large offensive
operations that engulfed Italy over the next decade was at last stemmed by 1527
and had all but receded by midcentury. The counterforce that slowed and finally
put a stop to this decided shift toward the strategic and operational offensive was
the development of fortifications capable of resisting both powerful artillery fire
and, perhaps more important, attempts to take fortresses by storm. The keys to
resisting the power of modern artillery fire lay in the modification of fortress
walls. It was found that by decreasing their height, increasing their thickness,
and changing their composition, walls could hold at bay a well-armed and well-
supplied attacker for many months and in some cases for years. The key to resisting attempts to storm fortresses lay in two design modifications that denied attackers any area near the walls that was free from the defenders' fire and in which
the attackers might securely amass themselves for an attempt on the walls.

The first modification involved what came to be called angled bastions, or
trace italienne. These bastions replaced the high, circular or square towers projecting above the already high medieval walls. The walls of the new bastions were
slightly sloped toward the bottom and were no higher than the fortress walls,
thereby allowing the defenders to fire directly down on attackers at the base of
the walls without having to expose themselves by hanging far over the edge of

the walls. But more important was the replacement of the square or circular shape with one that, when viewed from above, resembles an arrowhead laying flat on the ground. The neck of the bastion (like the very beginning of the shaft coming from the arrowhead) connects it to the fortress wall. Imagine a fortress in the shape of a pentagon that has one such bastion projecting outward from each of its five angles. If the sides of the bastions are built at just the right angle, an artillery piece placed in the neck of one bastion can direct its line of fire right along the straight side of the neighboring bastion. At the same time, the other side of that bastion can be completely covered by the fire coming from an artillery piece placed in the neck of a bastion on the opposite side; and so on all the way around the pentagon. If instead of these straight-sided, arrow-shaped bastions there were old-fashioned circular bastions, the line of fire coming from another bastion could cover only one point along the whole curve of the bastion, leaving all the other spots along the curve free for attackers to gather themselves in safety.

The second modification involved improving internal and external ditches. In addition to increasing, in effect, the height of walls without also making them less stable, an external ditch provided protection for defenders to await the attacking enemy. If beyond the ditch the ground was made to slop gently away from the ditch until completely flat, then the well-protected defender had an open field of fire that provided the attacker no place to hide. Internal ditches presented yet another obstacle to an attacker that has opened a breach in the wall. On the opposite side of the ditch from the place where the breach is expected, defenders could erect a new fortified line so that when the attackers stepped into the breach they found themselves forced to descend into a ditch into which the defenders could rain down all types of fire.

As one finds in book VII of the *Art of War,* Fabrizio lays out all of the principles, and many of the specific features, of modern fortress design just then being developed but not yet fully put into practice. Not until Machiavelli's report on his above-mentioned visit to the walls of Florence in 1526 does he add all of the details of the angled bastions that would continue to protect fortresses until well into the Napoleonic era. But even by 1521, Machiavelli had laid all of the foundations. For Fabrizio asserts that fortress walls should be much lower and thicker than their predecessors in order to increase their resistance to artillery, should be filled with recesses and turns to create fields of fire into which to draw the attacking infantry, should have towers approximately every four hundred feet apart to provide artillery fire, and should, if possible, have ditches on the inside and the outside, but certainly on the inside so as to provide the advantages of the "double pisan rampart." In addition to these and other engineering innovations, Machiavelli supplies details regarding logistics for a long siege, and regales us with a feast of tricks for deceiving the enemy, destroying his morale while maintaining one's own, and sending messages from and delivering them to the besieged.

Strategy, "Culture," and the Commander's Character

The *Art of War* seems to contain flatly contradictory statements on strategy. For example, Fabrizio says that the entire purpose of an army is to present battle to the enemy on the open field, but later asserts that a captain must never present battle unless he is forced to do so. On the question of whether one ought to seek victory with military force or by means of starving the enemy into submission, Fabrizio offers the "general rule" that "men and iron" (the use of force) are more necessary than "money and bread" (food and the means to get it) because "men and iron find money and bread, but bread and money do not find men and iron." Elsewhere, however, he assures his listeners that to seek victory by starvation "is more secure and more certain" than doing so by force. To explain these and many similar contradictory statements, interpreters have advanced the usual explanations, including varied dates of composition and outright confusion on Machiavelli's part. But in this case, and not only in this case, an adequate explanation is contained within the work itself.

In the first item in each pair of contradictory statements cited above, students of strategic thought will recognize essential elements of Clausewitzean doctrine. Without denying the significance of other aspects of war, Clausewitz, the great nineteenth-century Prussian theorist of war, stresses the need to destroy the enemy's military forces (the principle of destruction), the importance of concentrating one's forces, the unreliability of intelligence reports, the difficulty of attaining surprise, and the ideal of victory by means of the decisive battle. The list of Fabrizio's Clausewitzean sayings is long, but perhaps the most telling concerns what Clausewitz called the principle of continuity, the need to pursue the enemy with the utmost vigor without slackening the pace for even a moment. In accordance with this principle Fabrizio says:

> [O]ne must follow up the victory with utmost speed and in this case imitate Caesar and not Hannibal, who, by staying put after he had beaten the Romans at Cannae, lost the empire of Rome. The former never paused after a victory, but followed the beaten enemy with greater impetus and fury than [when] he had assaulted it in its entirety. (*AW* IV 74–75)

The principle of continuity and the Clausewitzean approach to war suffuse the *Art of War.*

In each pair of contradictory statements above, the second item is an instance of an altogether different strategic doctrine, one often associated with Sun Tzu. The Chinese sage emphasizes the importance of avoiding harm, the utility of evasive maneuvers, the necessity of obtaining accurate intelligence, deception as an excellent means for attaining surprise, and the ideal of a bloodless victory. Fabrizio's Sun Tzuian sayings are as numerous as his Clausewitzean ones. Two stand out: "it is more important for one to guard against being hit than it is important to hit the enemy" and whoever "pursues an enemy in disorder after he is beaten wants nothing other than to change from being victorious to losing" (AW III 111, VII 167). Securing the absolute minimum risk of harm to oneself far outweighs striving to inflict the greatest harm possible on the enemy. But it is in the area of deception that Fabrizio is most like Sun Tzu and least like Clausewitz. Clausewitz deeply distrusted intelligence reports. He thought they further thickened the fog of war and tended to divert the general from the most pressing task of destroying the enemy by the most direct and simple route. Fabrizio, by contrast, coaches his listeners on every trick: how to handle double agents, pass secret messages, lull opponents with repetitive habits to be broken at just the right moment, goad the enemy into dispersing his forces, manage passwords, and so forth. And he is just as intent on not being deceived by the enemy as he is on deceiving him. The importance of deception and military intelligence is best revealed in his desire to "provide perfect knowledge (scienza)" of how to avoid ambushes. The cornerstone of this science is that you must "never believe that the enemy does not know how to conduct his own affairs. Indeed, if you want to be deceived less and want to bear less danger, the more the enemy is weak [or] the less the enemy is cautious, so much more must you esteem him" (AW V 108, 116; cf. D III 18, 48). Fabrizio might well have agreed with Sun Tzu when the latter went so far as to define war itself as the art of deception.

The presence of these two opposed understandings raises a question that is just as relevant to current divides within contemporary strategic thought as it is to the heart of Machiavelli's own thinking. It is whether there exist "strategic cultures" that provide the vocabularies and conceptual frameworks that both make possible and limit the content of any strategic theory. The most common version of the question asks whether there are specifically "Eastern" and "Western" ways of war. A negative answer to this question would seem to be provided by virtue of the fact that Machiavelli shares ideas essential to these two putatively opposed strategic cultures. Machiavelli seems to agree with the cultural relativists in that he thinks there are indeed two fundamentally opposed ways of war. But he departs from them in indicating that some combination of the two is possible and necessary.

Machiavelli casts the entire question in terms of Europe versus Asia. After patiently listening to Fabrizio extol the ability of the ancient Roman infantry to withstand and even beat cavalry, Cosimo finally suggests to Fabrizio that perhaps cavalry is now superior to infantry due to the saddles, stirrups, and armor of modern heavy cavalry. Even after Fabrizio explains the position considered above regarding the relative esteem in which cavalry and infantry ought to be held in light of the perniciousness of mercenaries, Cosimo persists. This time he is less polite in that he pointedly contradicts Fabrizio's previous claim that Rome had conquered the whole world. Cosimo raises two "doubts," one of which is that "the Parthians used nothing other than cavalrymen in war, and yet they divided the world with the Romans" (*AW* II 80). Fabrizio, reticent to "give reasons for what is customary in Asia," nonetheless responds with the following sweeping admission:

> [T]he Parthians' military was entirely contrary to that of the Romans, because the Parthians all soldiered on horseback, and in fighting they proceeded confused and dispersed. It was an unstable mode of fighting and was full of uncertainty. The Romans were, it can be said, almost all on foot and fought together, tight and solid. One or the other alternately won according to whether the site was wide or tight. For in the latter the Romans were superior; in the former, the Parthians, [who] were able to make a great showing with that military thanks to the region they had to defend. (*AW* II 83–84)

The Asian and European ways of war are "altogether contrary," and each prevails on a particular type of terrain. In itself, this is no assertion of two diametrically opposed "cultures." But it begins to resemble one given Fabrizio's refusal to give reasons for things Asian, his apparent derogation of their "altogether contrary" way of war as confused, dispersed, unstable, and uncertain, and his apparent praise of the Romans' way of war as firmly planted on the ground, tight, solid, and ordered—in a word, a way of war for which one *can* give straightforward reasons.

This whole speech might be taken as a fit of Eurocentrism if not for three facts. First, the whole interchange is elaborately staged by Machiavelli. Readers are meant to observe and reflect on this confrontation between what one might be tempted to call incipient modern Western rationalism and an "exoticized" East against which the modern West defines itself. Second, Fabrizio admits that under the right circumstances, the West is not the best. The apparent derogation of the Eastern way of war as unstable and uncertain yields to the fuller understanding that its very instability leads to certain victory under the right circumstances. Indeed, the Parthians would seem to be the more careful rational calculators by virtue of the fact that their hit-and-run approach affords maximum gains at minimum cost. The kind of warfare for which Fabrizio is more willing to give reasons is not necessarily but only circumstantially superior. Finally, Fabrizio's willingness to accord cavalry the status of "the second foundation" after infantry can now be seen as a significant incorporation of Asia within the West. Indeed, the primary role he assigns to cavalry (harassment and cutting lines of supply) and his subsequent use of it for surprise and maneuver all accord well with what contemporary theorists call the Eastern way of war. If this passage is an expression of Eurocentrism, it is self-conscious, deliberate, and "revisionist." Specifically, it would seem that Machiavelli judges the ancient version of Western warfare to have been especially vulnerable to the Eastern way of war; he seeks to guard against this vulnerability by combining East and West.

The difficulty as well as the necessity of this combination becomes apparent when one recognizes that the opposition between these two approaches devolves on the opposition between two different dispositions to the sway of chance in war and in human life more generally: boldness versus caution. The Parthians seek the maximum gain at the minimum cost by always keeping a safe distance from their powerful adversary while raining down destruction on him. Similarly, Fabrizio prizes military intelligence, the attempt to reduce one's risk to a minimum by means of deception and superior knowledge. The common denominator is caution, the disposition to act only when the risk of failure is low and the chance of success is high. The contrary disposition to take major risks is exemplified by the Romans. Their armies sought to close with the enemy as rapidly as possible and bring to bear the maximum amount of force in shortest amount of time. In the worst case, as against the Parthians, the Romans followed the principle of continuity all the way to their own destruction, such that the maximum risk resulted in the maximum loss. In the best case, the Romans followed the same principle from one victory to another, keeping the enemy always on his heels and reeling from loss to loss.

Would Fabrizio, the professed advocate of all things Roman, always choose the commander with a bold rather than a cautious disposition? The way to Machiavelli's political answer to this question is provided by a mundane observation charged with more than mundane implications: sometimes it is better to be bold, at others it is better to be cautious. The cautious commander who carefully feels his way along, preferring to find his enemy's weak spots and avoid his strengths, who seeks by maneuver and deception to catch his enemy with his forces dispersed rather than attack him straight on, is better in certain circumstances. In other circumstances, the bold commander who goes for the jugular is required. A political expedient for handling this situation is provided by the

republican form of government itself. Since a republic (as opposed to a principality with a single prince) can produce "infinite most virtuous princes" or captains (*D* I 20), it can choose whichever type of commander the particular circumstances call for. When Hannibal threatens to destroy the Roman army on
Italian soil, the cautious Fabius Maximus Cunctator is required; when it is time
boldly to bring the war home to Hannibal's Carthage, Fabius must be pushed to
the side and Scipio Africanus brought to the fore. Rome's constitution allows it
to choose at will among such diverse types. Although prudent individuals (who
have their own natural dispositions with which to contend) are required to pick
a captain who most accords with the times, considerable military flexibility is
gained by what can be called constitutional means.

The trouble is that it is difficult to gauge which type "the times" call for. If
the Romans' failures in Asia highlight the defects of the bold, Western approach,
Machiavelli's own times highlight the defects of the cautious, Eastern approach.
The proper imitation of Fabius is the perfect test for whether one has a proper
orientation to fortune. For the moderns (that is, Christian Europeans, Italians
in particular, and Florentines especially) believe they imitate Fabius by sending
their captains into the field and forbidding them to do battle. In effect, however,
they thereby entrust their arms and their captains to another, which is to say to
fortune, because the enemy can then do battle when he sees fit rather than when
it is best for their army. But Fabius can also be imitated well. For, as Fabrizio
claims, "you can very well do with art what happened to Fabius Maximus by
chance" (*AW* IV 129). The wider context of this passage indicates that what is at
stake is how to balance prudently the demands of necessity and the scope of
chance. Do not seek to evade the pinch of necessity, but submit to it willingly so
that you might make use of your submission; and when necessity demands that
you either trust fortune or try her, always do the latter, for you might come out
ahead, while to do the former is to entrust yourself to your enemy.

Fabrizio sums up the way that boldness and caution are combined in the
very structure of his army:

> [Y]ou must never believe that the enemy does not know how to conduct his
> own affairs. Indeed, if you want to be deceived less and want to bear less dan-
> ger, the more the enemy is weak [or] the less the enemy is cautious, so much
> more must you esteem him. And in this you have to use two diverse means, for
> you have to fear him in thought and in order, but with words and with other
> extrinsic demonstrations, show that you despise him. For this last mode makes
> your soldiers hope more to have victory; the other one makes you more cau-
> tious and less apt to be deceived. (*AW* V 116–17)

Bold in word, deed, and reputation; cautious in thought and order. A bewildering mixture is demanded. Knowledge of how and when to mix them is the key.

War and Politics

In the chapter of *The Prince* in which Machiavelli goes "more deeply" into the character of mercenary arms and discusses their "origin and progress," he argues that they gained such prominence in Italy as a result of the popes' efforts to make the Church a temporal power (*P* 12.52). When Italy rebelled against the Holy Roman Empire, the Church gained a toehold in cities by siding with the people. But since the priests did not have knowledge of arms, the Church was compelled to hire foreigners. Nor could the priests acquire military knowledge and at the same time retain their authority with the people (*P* 12.52–53). For just as "arms did not fit [the pope] as a man of religion" (*FH* I 39.50), neither could his vicars take them up.

These condottieri were not brought forth and honored from among a populace that feared for its life and property; instead, they were hired by a power whose state was essentially spiritual and only incidentally temporal. They faced other such captains, for virtually all on the other side were brought forth in the same manner or in reaction to the same power:

> Since they depended on war, they had made a sort of bond and understanding together and had reduced war to an art in which they would temporize so that most of the times both one side and the other of those who were waging war would lose; and in the end, they reduced it to such vileness that any mediocre captain in whom only a shadow of ancient virtue had been reborn would have despised them, to the astonishment of all Italy, which, because of its lack of prudence, honored them. (*FH* I 39.50)

Once the practice of warfare falls entirely into the hands of such mercenaries, there is no pressing motive for any prince to make his own subjects or fellow citizens into soldiers. For those condottieri that might come against him are repelled well enough by others of their kind. This arrangement might be tolerable for all concerned were it not for the "ultramontane" troops that prey with impunity on an Italy so armed. For the same popes who hire condottieri bring these outside forces into Italy for the same reasons they hire the condottieri. Finally, even if one city or region decided to arm itself and seek to "dominate the others" (*FH* V 1.186), the popes would still have tremendous power, especially among the people whom they tend to favor, to foster internal divisions within such a city. If a prince of a region large enough to challenge the pope wished to turn his subjects or fellow citizens into soldiers, he would have to contend with a pope who can threaten the "ultimate ruin" and "last misery" and promise infinite rewards with which such a prince could never compete by means of his own merely temporal punishments and rewards.

It is often supposed that Machiavelli agreed with the civic humanists of his day who sought to transform the men of Tuscany into citizens-soldiers selflessly dedicated to the "common good," by which they meant the good of a particular, temporal city. The claim that soldiers must be or become so dedicated to the common good might seem to be bolstered by some of Machiavelli's more famous remarks, especially his resounding condemnation of mercenaries. After listing the many qualities that make mercenaries useless, Machiavelli writes, "The cause of this is that they have no love nor cause to keep them in the field other than a small stipend, which is not sufficient to make them want to die for you" (P 13.48–49). From this it might be inferred that the object of a prince is to get his soldiers to "want to die for" him, and that the object for a republican captain is to get the soldiers under his command to want to die for the city or for the sake of the common good. Moreover, since deaths occur on the winning as well as on the losing side, we tend to assume that men willingly give their lives, and we praise them for so doing. In our own popular understanding a good soldier is willing "to lay down his life" for his country. But to state an obvious point, it is killing, being able to kill, and seeming to be able to kill rather than dying that bring victory to the army and glory to the captain. The question raised by the above quoted passage from *The Prince* is not how to get men to want to die for their prince, city, or country, but how to "keep them in the field" so that they can and will "fight well" for their captain (D III 12).

The political question of what constitutes good citizens thus becomes the military question of how to keep men in the field and make them fight well. In the language of the *Art of War,* the question is about how a captain can make his soldiers obstinate in battle. We will discover that the captain's goal is to prevent his soldiers from ever being in a situation in which each must choose between saving his own life or property, and serving the common good (or his country or prince), and that Machiavelli's Fabrizio is not averse *in principle* to a standing professional army. One begins to suspect that Fabrizio is quietly sending anyone who might be persuaded of his prescriptions down a path that has less, and perhaps nothing at all, in common with a civic humanist dedication to the common good, and more in common with a coercive and centralized (if not impersonal) state, regardless of whether that state is a principality or republic.

Professionalism

The first subject Fabrizio treats as he sets out to form his army is what we would call recruiting or conscription, called by Fabrizio "selection." This part of the dialogue has three main sections, which are rather short and are divided by two explicitly identified long digressions, on the desirability of a militia "similar" to the one Machiavelli himself had established while he was Florentine secretary (*AW* I 148–90, 220–61). In the first two of these main sections Fabrizio establishes that the will of the political authority, not the will of the men themselves, must be the determinative factor in the selection. The "prince," as this authority is later called by him with indifference as to whether it be a republican captain or an actual monarch, will chose the men; they will not choose to serve him. Thus even with the very first step, a top-down relationship is established.

Although Fabrizio usually keeps up the front that he is opposed to a professional army, he tips his hand by making a reference that would have been jarring to the contemporary readers of the dialogue and that should leap out at readers of the *Discourses on Livy* and *The Prince*—one that demonstrates his freedom from moralism or any ultimate adherence to civic humanism. Toward the end of his second digression, Fabrizio stops to give *ex post facto* advice to a number of Roman emperors, including the notorious Septimius Severus. He says that if an emperor such as Severus had rotated captains from region to region, keeping them from gaining the exclusive loyalty of their soldiers, he could have both protected himself from tumultuous captains while he lived and have accorded the Senate sufficient authority after he died to choose his successor, thus allowing the Senate to manage the volatile passions and politics endemic to a state with a professional army (*AW* I 89). In the *Discourses on Livy*, similar to but not as extreme as the *Art of War* in its deference to humanistic sensibilities, Severus is openly called a criminal (*D* I 10.4). But in the sole reference to him in the *Art of War*, there is not even a hint of blame. From *The Prince*, we can see why he would be considered a criminal by any civic humanist: he came to rule the empire by "persuading his army, of which he was captain" to march on Rome so as to have the current emperor put to death and to terrify the Senate into electing him as the new emperor. What is more, in *The Prince* Severus is *the* representative of the most extreme possibility offered in that work: a prince who must, that is, can, ignore the desires and even incur the hatred not just of the great but of the people by satisfying the deeply entrenched professional military (*P* 19.78–20.83). To give opened-handed advice to such a man, and to do so in the midst of a discussion of how to keep captains from overthrowing their rulers is most jarring indeed.

Machiavelli's Fabrizio is not at all squeamish about recognizing the possibility of the military and political effectiveness of a permanent and professional military establishment. Indeed, the real point of this whole discussion of recruitment is about establishing a framework within which control and obedience can be secured by means of first giving in to, and then managing, soldiers' and captains' passions, rather than trying to overcome them in the name of the common good or the fatherland. Just before he gives advice to Severus, Fabrizio makes the case that well-ordered men, whether armed or unarmed, will obey the laws. It might reasonably be thought that Fabrizio is presuming moral goodness on the part of these armed men. But just as being poorly ordered denotes having armed men who have "heads" over them that incite them to rebellion, so being well ordered denotes having heads who keep them under strict control. Orders are bad or absent when these heads derive their "reputation" or authority from the men they lead; whereas when they have their own reputation or authority from the political authority, they have less motive to drum up partisan support by means of encouraging factious disputes. And when they are rotated regularly they have no opportunity to do so. As the example of Severus and the other emperors to which Fabrizio then turns makes clear, this entire line of reasoning applies just as well to permanent professional soldiers as to part-time citizen soldiers. Thus the problem is not professionalism as such, but captains who are and are perceived to be independent of the political authority of whatever type.

Discipline

Perhaps the single most important aspect of Fabrizio's army is its discipline. Lest "discipline" be mistaken for a mere corollary of patriotism or selfless dedication to the common good, it is important to recognize the psychological ambivalence of the new recruit before going on to consider the subtle and often coercive management of the soldiers' passions. Early in book I Fabrizio describes the psychological state of a new recruit. At the basis of the soldier's military service is an ambivalence of will brought about by, on the one hand, his aversion to present pain and, on the other hand, his fear of the prince's disdain. While discussing the problem of the intransigence of soldiers who are forced against their will into military service and the intractability of those, on the other hand, who are eager to go to war because they are good for nothing else, Fabrizio says:

> [Y]ou have to understand that the men who are inducted into the military by
> commandment of the prince have to come to it neither altogether forced nor
> altogether willingly. . . . [O]ne should take a middle way where there is neither
> complete force nor complete willingness; rather, they must be drawn through
> the respect that they have for the prince, where they fear his disdain more than

present pain. And it will always happen that it is force mixed with willingness, so that such a discontent as to have bad effects will not be able to arise from it. (*AW* I 166–67)

Their spirits being thus "suspended" and not of any determinate character (cf. *P* 21.88), they are more fit to be molded by the captain's form, since they are neither bent on nor repulsed by any particular course of action.

Fabrizio places next to no reliance on the natural or patriotic spirit of the soldiers. Rather, the industry and art of the captain produce a fighting spirit by means of imposing orders on the soldiers. Fabrizio says, "And without doubt, ferocious and disordered men are much weaker than timid and ordered ones. For order chases fear from men and disorder lessens ferocity." Later he says "a spirited army is not made so by having spirited men in it but by having well-ordered orders" (*AW* II 141, 167). Those in the front line of attack should know from where their help will come, while those behind know where and when to help—and, in a spirit of rivalry, the latter hope to do so. Furthermore, Fabrizio warns that an army organized into one rigid body is rendered susceptible to one devastating blow, and is therefore subject to one fortune. "It is necessary that there be many bodies in an army, and that each body have its own flag and its own guide. For having this, it must have many souls and, as a consequence, many lives." Fabrizio then observes how important music is in maintaining this many-souled unity, and launches into a stirring discussion of how the ancients used music to inflame or firm up their soldiers' spirits. "It would be necessary to find all of these modes again," he says in summation, but immediately adds, "and if this were difficult, one would at least not want to leave behind those that teach the soldier to obey" (*AW* II 275, 281). In the end, the captain's concern is not with those modes that inspire or firm up patriotic or other kinds of spiritedness, but instead with those that make soldiers more receptive and obedient to his command.

Up to this point it can seem that all there is to soldiering well comes from the order imposed on the soldiery. But the most pressing necessities of the captain's soldiers, the fear of death and the desire for individual profit, emanate from the soldiers themselves with great force and can be manipulated to great effect by the captain.

Obstinate Defense of One's Own Body and One's Own Property

To unite the soldiers' passion for self-preservation with the captain's aim of victory is the most pressing need, hence the first goal, of the captain. Fabrizio says that some captains have constrained their soldiers

to fight by necessity, taking away from them every hope of saving themselves,
outside of winning. That is the most hardy and the best provision that one,
wanting to make his own soldiery obstinate, can make. That obstinacy is increased by confidence and by the love of the captain or of the country. (*AW*
IV 148)

After briefly explaining these latter means, Fabrizio returns to the primary necessity: "Necessities can be many, but the one that is strongest is that which constrains you to win or to die" (*AW* IV 152). This principle is later confirmed by
examples from both the attacker's and the defender's perspectives (*AW* VI 223,
VII 27–28).

Given Machiavelli's apparent hatred of mercenaries, it perhaps comes as a
surprise to discover that property or individual profit turns out to be "no less a
ground" for rendering soldiers obstinate than their desire for self preservation.
Nor is this property to be associated with the idyllic farm, plow, and ox that any
decent man would defend, or with wealth earned by means of one's civilian occupation. The spoils of war are what motivates Fabrizio's soldiers:

> [Y]ou must, above everything, take this precaution in wanting to make your
> soldiery obstinate in the fight: do not permit them to send any of their prop-
> erty home or to put it in some place until the war has ended, so that they
> understand that if in fleeing they save their lives, they do not save their posses-
> sions, the love of which is no less a ground for rendering men obstinate in de-
> fense. (*AW* IV 134)

Not only are the individual soldiers kept from desertion by this management of
property, but the whole army itself is so motivated. Fabrizio says that whereas in
the present times even the victor loses money and belongings, "anciently . . . the
winner of wars got rich" because the ancients did not leave the spoils to "the discretion of [individual] soldiers" but "order[ed] it that all the spoils belong[ed]
to the public, and that the public then dispens[ed] it as seemed [best]" (*AW* V
95–98).

These last passages could be mistaken for evidence of a civic humanist's priz-
ing of the common good over the good of the individual. But it is the efficacy of
the procedure for dispensing spoils that Fabrizio prizes so highly. It is this dispensation, based on the love of individual property, that is shown to be responsible for the maintenance of the very orders discussed above. Spoils were used

> to give the ordinary pay to the soldiers, to help the wounded and the sick, and
> for the other needs of the army. The consul was very able, and often did, use

it to yield spoils to the soldiers. But this concession did not make disorder. For having beaten the army, all the spoils were put in the middle and distributed by head, according to the qualities of each. This mode made the soldiers attend to winning and not to robbing. And the Roman legions used to conquer the enemy and not follow him, because they never departed from their orders. (*AW* V 99–100)

Therefore, both regular pay and rewards for extraordinary performance comes from the spoils of victory, thereby uniting the soldier's love of property with his desire for victory. Furthermore, the love of property not only motivates the army as a whole, keeps men in the army and well ordered in the field, but, if managed well, can even be used to make men fight well in the midst of battle.

The ancients considered another thing well: they wanted each soldier to deposit a third of the money that they gave him next to the one who carried the flag of his battalion, who never reconsigned it to him unless the war was finished . . . because they knew that their belongings were next to the flag, they were forced to take more care of it and defend it with more obstinacy (*AW* V 104–5)

Finally, Fabrizio notes how individuals who received rewards for their success in battle display them to their friends and relatives with solemnity and pomp, thereby emphasizing that the outward esteem of public wealth and deprecation of private wealth lead in practice to considerable private wealth. Men bring their spoils home.

Punishment and Reward

Even properly managed orders are not enough. The laws for their observance must be fortified, and the "fortification must be harsh and hard, and the executor very hard." Fabrizio supplies a list of rules governing both camp life and combat. He states that individuals who broke those rules should be punished, adding that among the Romans when a whole cohort was to blame the terrifying mode of decimation was used so that "if each did not feel it, each nonetheless feared it." But because one wishes "that men fear and hope at one stroke," Fabrizio also lists those deeds that are rewarded. In addition to the "glory and the fame" received from the others, soldiers who performed such deeds received the gifts mentioned before, which they paraded among their friends and relatives (*AW* VI 114–15). Just as in fighting, so also in general discipline, the fear of death and punishment and the hope of reward are nearly all in all.

The harsh discipline and other means of motivating the soldiers of Fabrizio's army would indicate that he was not counting on patriotic dedication. He would seem instead to be prescribing means for the almost perfect control of the soldiers, a control that would be at times be brutal, at other times subtle, and occasionally both. For even or especially the harshest measures have their subtle side, as in the Roman practice of "decimation" recommended by Fabrizio. The means for superiors to exert this kind of control and manipulation would require far more authority than any Florentine captain or commissioner had ever been able to exert. One must thus inquire who would ultimately command the obedience of these soldiers. A consideration of this question shows that the *Art of War* reaches beyond offering prescriptions for Florence to touch the very nerve of civil–military relations.

What Makes an Excellent Captain Obey?

If it is primarily the captain who makes the common soldiers obey, who or what makes *him* obey? If his control of his soldiers brings him success in battle, he can become an enormous problem to the political authorities. For as his success gains him reputation with his soldiers, the political magistrates of his republic or his prince come to fear him more than he fears them. Here the captain faces a grave danger—or a great opportunity. Machiavelli treats this problem thoroughly in the *Discourses on Livy* and *The Prince*, but in the *Art of War* he, or his Fabrizio, all but covers it up. Thus one might well conclude that Machiavelli thinks that all we need is a few good men in order to solve the thorny problem of the relationship between civil and military orders and authorities. That is, it seems that nothing stands between the successful captain and his seizure of political authority but the moral goodness of the captain. Good and able men, such as Scipio and Marcellus, are celebrated while men who are merely able, such as Caesar and Pompey, seem to be disparaged. More than in Machiavelli's other works, glory and honor are presented as being free from every taint of the low necessities of fear and profit as well as ambition (cf. *AW* I 58, II 29, VII 239 for the three instances of "ambition" in the work). One might be led to think, and to a large degree it seems we are meant to think, that in the *Art of War* honor and glory are the highest goods, the crown atop the head of moral goodness. But even here, Machiavelli plays his game of bait and switch.

To see this game clearly, it helps to look from the vantage point provided by the *Discourses on Livy* and *The Prince*. Although there are numerous indications in the *Discourses* that captains obey because they are morally good, another view is developed early on. Toward the end of his discussion of ingratitude (which in fact is about the problem posed by the captain's success), Machiavelli says one ought to

> follow the same modes the Roman republic followed so as to be less ungrateful than the others. This arose from the modes of its government. For since the whole city—both the nobles and the ignobles—was put to work in war, so many virtuous men emerged in every age, decorated from various victories, that the people did not have cause to fear any one of them, since *they were very many and guarded one another.* (*D* I 30.2, emphasis added)

Rome kept its captains good through "the modes of its government" founded on the fear a captain had of the many once-and-future captains who guarded him. Machiavelli does not so much as imply that moral goodness or a sense of obligation to the common good keeps the captain in check. Because the others know he is afraid, they do not suspect him of seeking to rob them of their security or wealth; because they do not suspect him, he does not suffer or fear ingratitude at the hands of his fellow citizens.

But what exactly happens when the magistrates come to fear the successful captain more than he fears them? Of necessity the authorities are ungrateful in that they have to punish rather than reward the successful captain by taking away his reputation and authority for fear that he will seize the state.[3] When he foresees this necessity, what should the captain do? Should he patiently suffer the ingratitude of the city? Machiavelli is ruthless in his advice to the successful captain in a principality: he must seize the necessarily ungrateful prince's state. There are, in fact, two options in addition to this one. One option is not to win such reputation in the first place by being less successful. Not surprisingly, this option is never suggested.[4] The other is to be so cautious as not to inspire suspicion or envy after having gained great reputation. In the case of a captain in a principality, Machiavelli openly reveals that this option is impossible. When it comes to a successful captain in a republic, he brings one to the very brink of recognizing that the captain must do what he must in order to protect himself from the ingratitude suffered by Scipio and Camillus (see *D* I 29; cf. *D* III 22, 23) and preemptively avenged by Caesar. Caesar is not Scipio's moral inferior because he did what he had to do given the corruption in Rome in his day; indeed, he is his

---

3. Cf. Machiavelli, *Dell'Ingratitudine*, in *Tutte le opere*, ed. Mario Martelli (Firenze: Sansoni, 1992), 980–83, esp. lines 116–24, 146–54; on the vital importance of gratitude or morality for politics, see Aristotle, *Nicomachean Ethics* V 6–7; Xenophon, *Education of Cyrus* I ii 6.

4. Contrast Shakespeare, *Antony and Cleopatra* III i.

superior in prudence because he did what he had to in order to keep from suffering Rome's ingratitude (*D* I 29–30; cf. *D* I 10, 17, 29, 37 II 6 III 22–25).

Similarly, in *The Prince*, Machiavelli educates the careful reader's expectation that a captain who seizes a state by overthrowing a republican government and who commits other immoral acts deserves blame. In his treatment of Agathocles, he first establishes an opposition between an excellent captain and an excellent man, allowing the reader to infer that the former is inferior to the latter. He then blurs and finally erases the very principles on which the distinction rests. In brief, first it is said that Agathocles, a man of uncommon "virtue of body and spirit," is undeniably a "most excellent captain" but nonetheless cannot be "celebrated among the most excellent men" because of his crimes and his "savage cruelty and inhumanity" (*P* 8.35). For Agathocles had, among other things, seized the principate from a republican government by using his military command to butcher the leading citizens. Agathocles's conspicuous lack of moral virtue seems to preclude the possibility that he could gain glory as an excellent man. But Machiavelli then proceeds to excuse Agathocles's cruelty, well-used cruelty in general, inhumanity, and, finally, criminality. For in the same chapter, Agathocles is offered as an example of cruelty "well used" and Machiavelli expatiates on the benefits of all forms of well-used cruelty (*P* 8.37–38). Still later in *The Prince*, Hannibal, a most excellent man, is likewise characterized as having practiced inhuman cruelty (*P* 17.67–68; cf. *D* III 19–21). Finally, as to Agathocles's crimes preventing him from being considered an excellent man, the example of Severus the criminal tyrant shows that one can acquire glory despite and by means of one's crimes (*P* 19.78–79). The distinction between the excellent captain and the excellent man does not hold up.

Tutored by these examples from *The Prince* and the *Discourses on Livy*, we are able to see that there are many indications within the *Art of War* that obedience to political authorities is merely a contingent good and that the possibility of the captain's seizing a state is on Fabrizio's mind. The opposition in *The Prince* between an excellent captain and an excellent man corresponds to the distinction in the *Art of War* between an able man who acquires only fame and an able and good man who acquires glory. To see this, consider again what Fabrizio says in book I:

> I say that Pompey and Caesar, and almost all those captains who were in Rome after the last Carthaginian war, acquired fame as able, not as good, men; those who had lived before them acquired glory as able and good. This arose because these men did not take the practice of war as their art, and those that I named first used it as their art. And while that republic lived immaculately, never did

> any great citizen presume by means of such a practice to take advantage of the
> peace by breaking the laws, despoiling the provinces, usurping and tyrannizing
> the fatherland and taking advantage in every mode. (*AW* I 65–67)

Fabrizio does not indicate any agreement with the one or the other kind of
praise. He merely points to the limits that one would need to observe—or alter—to seek one or the other type of praise. What is more, we are left to wonder
how all the able men before one particular point in time were also good while all
such men after that time were not good. But as we have already seen, it was fear
under the watchful gaze of their peers (*D* I 30), rather than moral goodness, that
kept the captains of the republic "good." Fabrizio is careful not to preclude this
possibility. Likewise, when he mentions Caesar toward the end of the dialogue
he speaks with a care reminiscent of the Agathocles passage from *The Prince*. He
says of Caesar and Alexander:

> [I]f in them, or in *part* of them, one *could* blame too much ambition to rule,
> never will one find that one may blame in them any softness or anything that
> makes men delicate and unwarlike. If these things were read and believed by
> these princes, it would be impossible that they not change their form of living
> and their provinces not change their fortune. (*AW* VII 239–40, emphasis added)

Not only does he make the three italicized hedges of his previous apparent blame
of Caesar, but he offers Caesar along with Alexander the Great as prime examples for contemporary imitation. Finally, the distinction between fame and
glory (on the basis of which the praise of Caesar and Pompey was distinguished
from that of Scipio and Marcellus) is ignored in the crucial context of rewards
for success in battle (*AW* VI 115; cf. *D* II pr. 1). Taken together, especially in the
light of the *Discourses* and *The Prince*, these points complicate Fabrizio's assessment of the "bad" captains and the basis on which it was made.

   As to modern examples, Fabrizio refers three times to Machiavelli's favorite
mercenary captain, Francesco Sforza, who seized the state of his prince. Sforza
is said to have entered into "an honorable wickedness" (*AW* I 62). The patina of
opprobrium fails to cover the admiration implicit in Fabrizio's favorable comparison of Sforza to other mercenary captains who failed to seize a state. But a
more—if not the most—important modern example is Fabrizio himself. While
openly admitting that the only way to put his counsel into practice is to be a
prince, Fabrizio's excuse for not becoming one is not, as one would expect, that
a morally good man would never think of such a thing. Instead, he points to the
logistical obstacles to gaining the loyalty of the troops under his command, cit-

ing the facts that the troops are foreign and obligated to another and that he does not even speak their language. In other words, he might be willing to take the step of seizing his king's state if he could take the first step of retaining his troop's obedience. Second, he says that because of his age he doubts he will have the occasion to do what he so dearly desires. Again he leaves open the possibility that if the obstacle of old age could be overcome, the steps necessary for seizing a state might be taken. Later, while still in the flush of his victory in an imaginary battle staged for his interlocutors, he reveals how much he is pining for the chance to do in fact what he now, as a mere captain, can do only in speech. And last, while speaking of himself at the head of a tired army in need of refreshment, he refers to its leader as "prince" (*AW* VII 210, VII 246, III 98, V 83). These points lead one to question his excuse for not having put into practice the military transformation he has outlined.

Fabrizio seeks to defend himself against the accusation that he both blames the moderns for not imitating the ancients and fails to do so himself. In his defense (or his excuse, as he calls it), he asserts one must prepare for such enterprises with the utmost industriousness so that when the opportune moment arises, one can spring into action; at the same time, he indicates that such preparations should be made with the utmost caution so as to go undetected (*AW* I 39–40). Thus in his eagerness to acquit himself of the charge of negligence or hypocrisy, Fabrizio all but admits that he has been lying in wait for his "opportunity." When pressed a bit by Cosimo, who has not yet figured out, or is acting as though he has not yet figured out, that "the opportunity" here refers to is becoming a prince, Fabrizio says,

> [B]ecause I know that you can doubt whether or not this opportunity has
> come, I want to discourse at length, if you want to listen to me with patience,
> on what preparations are necessary to make before, what opportunity must
> arise, what difficulty impedes so that preparations do not help and so that the
> opportunity does not come, and how this thing is, though the terms seem con-
> trary, at once very difficult and very easy to do. (*AW* I 44)

As stated earlier, Fabrizio openly admits that the only way to put his counsel into practice is to be a prince. Not being a prince is the primary "difficulty" that impedes him. The need for a prince's authority also comes to the surface in the discussion of the mode of selecting the troops, considered above. Finally, at the conclusion of the dialogue Fabrizio makes plain what he has been getting at all along: that the "preparations" referred to in the passage just quoted are his reflections revealed in the foregoing military prescriptions, the "opportunity" he sought or awaited was to be a prince, and the primary "difficulty" that prevented his introduction of his military reforms was the lack of a principality (*AW* VII 240–41).

For a prince, the only way to forestall this incursion of war into politics is to preempt it by being, rather than seeking to control, the successful captain. The expanding republic, too, can forestall it by channeling it outward, but cannot prevent it altogether, for the great military successes of an expanding republic will of necessity lead to the rise of Caesars (*D* III 24). The *Art of War* points in the direction of a path more fully charted in the *Discourses*.

Machiavelli's Aim

The preface and the beginning of the first book of the *Art of War* are the only parts of the work in which Machiavelli speaks in his own voice. They reveal the particular aim of the work and indicate how that aim fits into his entire enterprise as carried out in *The Prince* and *Discourses on Livy*.

In the preface, Machiavelli states a problem, the dissimilarity or disharmony of the civilian and military lives, and offers a solution, the reformation of the present military in accordance with ancient modes and past virtue. One might infer that all is well among those leading civilian lives, and that greater unity will be brought about by making the military life more like civilian lives. This inference is correct insofar as the most basic practical reform suggested in the work is to replace mercenary soldiers with soldiers that are citizens or subjects. But in the preface itself Machiavelli does not state this practical side of the problem or its solution; he even leaves unclear the reason why the disunity of the two lives is a problem at all.

A closer look indicates that a fundamental intellectual or spiritual reformation must take place before or in conjunction with the military's reformation more obviously called for in the preface and in the work as a whole. To understand his preface, it is essential to recognize that Machiavelli treats the *opinions about* the military and civilian lives more than the character of those lives themselves. More specifically, the coherence of his argument in the preface ultimately depends on a strangely unexplained assertion that nonmilitary men hold "sinister opinions" that cause them to flee from and to hate military men.

Machiavelli begins by stating an opinion that "many have held and hold"— namely, how very little the military and civilian lives fit together and how dissimilar they are. The flight of military men from the ways of civilians is an instance of this opinion in action. Young men who aspire to successful careers as soldiers do not believe they can be violent, manly, and frightening if they live as civilians do. They therefore change from the civilian to the military way of life, altering everything from the way they dress to the words they speak. Machiavelli concludes this long sentence with the perplexing assertion that this situation makes "very true" the opinion about the dissimilarity of the two lives. But what aspect of "this" situation makes the opinion true? What causes the dissimilarity between the two lives? It could be inferred that it is the aspiring soldiers' action that causes the dissimilarity. But it must be recalled that they take their action in the first place because of their belief or opinion that the two lives are dissimilar. The questions therefore arise: Is the aspiring soldier correct about the disharmony of the two ways of life? If so, what is its cause?

Machiavelli goes on to assert that the two lives—military and civilian—were united in ancient times, without saying exactly in what the unity consisted or what is desirable about it. Such unity was called for by the recognition of the "necessity" for defense. He says that if in some "other order" the ancients used every diligence "to keep men faithful, peaceful, and full of the fear of God, in the military it was redoubled" (*AW* pr. 5). No other order received more care than the military. At the moment that Machiavelli raises the question of some "other order" than the military, he asks—not only rhetorically—what man ought to be more faithful, more a lover of peace, and more fearful of God than a soldier. Machiavelli leaves the reader to answer the question. In Machiavelli's time, what man and what order were expected to be more full of faith, more lovers of peace, and more God-fearing than any other man or order, including the military man and his order? The answer is the priest and the priesthood. The moderns, we are led to infer, separate the military order from the religious order and, I conjecture, subordinate the former to the latter. The ancients did neither. It may be that the unity of the civilian and military lives in antiquity was dependent on the subordination of the religious life to the military. However this may be, Machiavelli quietly but clearly holds up the priesthood and the military as parallel objects of inquiry.[5] But where does such an inquiry fit into Machiavelli's more general analysis of politics?

Much of Machiavelli's analysis of politics revolves around his understanding of the "two humors," that of the people, who wish only to enjoy their security and comfort, and that of the great, who seek to dominate the people (*P* 9.39; *D* I 5.2). But the question as to which humor priests belong, and as to which soldiers belong, does not arise until one of these two orders has more strength or authority than the people or the great. What happens then is explained by Machiavelli in *The Prince*, where he discusses the case of the soldiers in a principality. When the soldiers constitute a deeply entrenched and sufficiently strong "humor"

---

5. Cf. Leo Strauss, *Thoughts on Machiavelli* (Chicago: University of Chicago Press, 1958), 184.

or "third difficulty" or "extraordinary force," as Machiavelli variously calls them there, they immediately become the force to watch (*P* 19.76, 77). For the prince can and must satisfy them at the expense of the people and the great. The phrase "extraordinary force" is also used in the *Florentine Histories;* but here it is applied to the Church and its ministers, who are said to keep Italy in vileness. Thus the priest and the warrior, the unarmed and the armed, are left to vie with one another for this position of the third force.[6] In "these times," given the reigning belief, the priests would appear to have secured this position for themselves and to have reduced soldiers to the status of hirelings who, by a pact made among them, fight nonwars (*FH* V 1; I 39).

In the preface to the *Art of War,* Machiavelli asserts that recognition of the necessity for defense leads, in a way he does not spell out, to the recognition of the necessity for the unity of the civilian and military lives. He asserts that this unity was brought about in ancient times by lawgivers and military trainers. But given that these two types merely represent a particular instance of civilian and military orders—albeit at a high level—the origin of their accord in antiquity remains obscure. Perhaps one of these orders was clearly subordinate to the other. Or perhaps there was a still higher or more comprehensive order, such as that provided by poetry (mentioned by Machiavelli at the beginning of book I), that ensured the unity of lawgivers and military trainers by imparting shared opinions about the most important things. In any case, the combined activity of lawgivers and military trainers instilled in civilian men an esteem for soldiers sorely lacking in "these times." Through the corruption of military orders and their separation from ancient modes, "these sinister opinions regarding them have arisen that make [men] hate the military and flee association with those who practice it." Whereas at the beginning of the preface Machiavelli draws the reader's attention to the opinions of aspiring soldiers that lead to their antipathy to civilian life, now he draws attention to the civilians' opinions that lead to their antipathy to the military and its soldiers. To whose "sinister opinions" does Machiavelli refer? They are distinct from the civilians' hatred for the military, for this hatred is itself the result of the sinister opinions. Nor can he mean the already-mentioned opinions of the aspiring soldiers, for their opinions are about civilian life and its inadequacy for getting them what they desire. Nor, yet again,

---

6. For pertinent instances of this rivalry, see *Decennale primo,* in *Tutte le opere,* 943; also Francesco Guicciardini, *History of Italy,* trans. Sidney Alexander (Princeton: Princeton University Press, 1969), 139; cf. Machiavelli, *The Life of Castruccio Castracani of Lucca,* in Machiavelli, *The Chief Works and Others,* vol. 2, trans. Allan Gilbert (Durham: Duke University Press, 1989), 535; cf. also "Fabrizio Colonna," in *Dizionario biografico degli italiani,* vol. 27 (Rome: Instituto della Enciclopedia Italiana, 1982), 288–89.

can it be that he is implicitly criticizing the aspiring soldiers' desires, for they are explicitly endorsed or implicitly accepted later in the work—not to mention in his other works.

Of course there were many influential opinions current in Florence, Italy, and Europe during Machiavelli's time to which he might have been referring. But the only other use in the *Art of War* of the suggestive phrase "sinister opinion," along with its sole use in the *Discourses on Livy,* pinpoint Christianity as the source of the sinister opinions and limn the nature and scope of Machiavelli's aim in writing the *Art of War.*[7] The second of the two uses of "sinister opinion" in the *Art of War* occurs in book IV. In response to a question concerning the manner in which deserting soldiers can be induced by means of speech to fight, Fabrizio asserts:

> To persuade or dissuade a few of a thing is very easy. For if words are not enough, you can then use authority or force. But the difficulty is in removing from the multitude a sinister opinion that is also contrary either to the common good or to your opinion. There one can use only words that are heard by all, wishing to persuade all of them together. (*AW* IV 137)

The context suggests that the same issue is at stake as in its first use in the preface: how to make deserting soldiers fight. It is remarkable that Fabrizio—and perhaps even Machiavelli—seems to think that it is possible to do so with mere words (cf. *D* II 15.1; *FH* III 27).[8] The task Machiavelli sets for himself begins to come into focus: to replace the current sinister opinion of "the multitude" with an entirely new opinion that accords with the common good.

Words that can be spoken to the multitude are explicitly distinguished from the authority and force that can be used with a few, and implicitly distinguished from the words that can be spoken to a few. What about the multitude makes it unwilling or unable to hear certain words, and which words does it hear? It may seem that Fabrizio is merely echoing the claim of ancient political philosophers that the multitude can never be philosophic,[9] but here the emphasis is on how words can effect a change in the multitude's opinion to bring it into accord with some other opinion, not on how to make the multitude philosophic or lead it to seek to replace its opinions with knowledge. While suggesting that his innovation would be for the common good, Machiavelli's Fabrizio would seem to

---

7. Cf. *AW* VI 207; Marsilius of Padua's use of "opinio perversa," *Defender of the Peace* I 1.3.

8. Cf. Xenophon, *Education of Cyrus* III 49–55.

9. See Plato, *Republic* 493a.

occupy neither the position of Machiavelli's predecessors, who held that the many could never be philosophic, nor that of his successors, who would maintain that Enlightenment of the multitude is a reasonable goal.

A parallel passage in the *Discourses* clarifies why Machiavelli thought it so difficult to change the multitude's opinion:

> I do not know if I shall take upon myself a hard task full of so much difficulty that it may suit me either to abandon it with shame or continue it with disapproval, since I wish to defend a thing that, as I said, has been accused by all the writers. But however it may be, I do not judge nor shall I ever judge it to be a defect to defend any opinion with reasons, without wishing to use either authority or force for it. (*D* I 58)

The opinion he is preparing himself to defend regards the constancy of the multitude. The distinguishing characteristic of a people or a multitude is that it "is seen to begin to hold a thing in horror and to stay with that opinion for many centuries" (*D* I 58.3). This tendency to hold things in horror for long periods of time makes the people the keeper of morality, but it also makes them very difficult to persuade. If one seeks to change something that conflicts with that morality, one must walk softly. If one seeks to change that morality itself, one does well to depute others to do the walking (*D* II pr. 3.). Once the multitude has an opinion, it holds on to it regardless of whether that opinion is for its own good, for the common good, or in accord with the opinion of the wisest men.

But what specific aspect of public opinion does Machiavelli seek to change? A look at the only use of "sinister opinion" in the *Discourses* points us in the direction of an answer. That use is closely connected to the passage in book IV of the *Art of War* just summarized. The clue to the connection between these two passages lies in the prominent status accorded Manlius Capitolinus in the *Discourses*.

In *Discourses on Livy*, Manlius is said to sow "various sinister opinions within" the plebs (*D* I 8 1). Machiavelli discusses only one of these opinions, in which Manlius falsely claims that there is a treasure belonging to the plebs that has been usurped by private citizens. "These words were able to do very much among the plebs." But the Senate crushed Manlius's influence with the plebs by the prudent use of its well-established order of accusations in which Manlius was forced to verify publicly his claim to private knowledge of the alleged treasure. Later in the *Discourses* we find that once the people had condemned Manlius to death, they greatly desired his return to life (*D* III 8). It is at a signal moment that Machiavelli recounts this instance of the people's fervent desire for the resurrection of a man who promised great but unverifiable rewards to his faithful followers. That moment is at the beginning of the very passage discussed above in which Machiavelli makes the case that the people tend to hold to opinions for centuries at a time. Who else sowed the unverifiable opinion, held "for many centuries" by the people yearning for his return, that there was wealth laid up in an inaccessible place to be enjoyed by those among the humble people who sided with him and his ministers against the great? Belief in the story and promise of the Gospels is the "sinister opinion" that Machiavelli seeks to eliminate and replace. Its elimination would be required to stop the headlong flight of soldiers, who are both too afraid and not afraid enough because of the promises and threats of prelates. Only once it is removed can the priests, the well dug in "third force," be dislodged from their entrenchments.

The Corruption of the West

Toward the end of book II of the *Art of War* is an account of the "clash of civilizations" as well as one of the most outspoken criticisms of Christianity in Machiavelli's corpus—albeit from the mouth of his captain, Fabrizio. Cosimo says to Fabrizio, "I would like to understand from you . . . from where so much vileness and so much disorder and so much neglect of" proper military training come from (*AW* II 283). Fabrizio responds at length, stating that excellent captains arise when there are many rulers or empires striking fear of servitude and death into one another with the result that each state is forced to honor those who excel in war. But Christianity undermines that honor by taking from men that fear. Fabrizio says that "today's mode of living, on account of the Christian religion, does not impose that necessity to defend oneself that there was in antiquity." In antiquity the conquered were killed or subjected to miserable slavery, and the towns, whose goods where taken and inhabitants dispersed, were razed "so those overcome in war suffered every last misery." Fabrizio indicates that Christian mercy is near the root of the problem because none of these horrors is visited upon the conquered, "so that the greatest evil that is feared is a ransom." Because they do not "fear an ultimate ruin," men "do not want to submit themselves to military orders and to struggle along beneath them so as to flee those dangers they little fear" (*AW* II 305–9). And by speaking once more in the same passage of men "buying themselves back with ransoms," Fabrizio brings to mind the belief that Christ performs the greatest act of mercy by offering himself as the ransom that frees the many who believe in him from death.[10] Earthly death is no longer the "last misery" or "the ultimate ruin." Christianity keeps the world in weakness by robbing men of a salutary, earthly fear.

10. Cf. Mark 10:45.

Yet Christianity is only the proximate cause of Rome's corruption and its eventual inability to produce excellent captains. Roman corruption came about as an inevitable result of its military success. The extinction of the fear of strong neighbors resulting from Rome's success in war is therefore the ultimate cause behind the proximate cause that has "rendered the world weak" (D II 2.2).

Machiavelli thus suggests that, to end its corruption, the West must return to (or approximate) a situation in which a multitude of republics and principalities vie with one another, such that each is motivated by an essentially secular fear to reward virtue and the captains who best display it. How very much this dispensation would differ from that in which quasi wars are fought by mercenaries and brokered by priests. How similar in appearance but opposed in effect to the "renaissance" sought by those humanists who longed for many republics filled with selfless love of the "common" good. For an incorrupt West would be founded on a self-love fueled from below by bodily fear and from above by the desire for martial glory. But how could such an incorrupt West be brought into being? The only alternative would seem to be the spiritual or intellectual elimination of Christianity itself. But what evidence is there that Machiavelli aimed this high? To answer this question, we must first appreciate how for Machiavelli Catholic Christianity resembles Asia, for it is against the East that Fabrizio leads his army.

"Asia" functions as *the* standard of corruption: "from which it arose that virtuous men came to be as few in Europe as in Asia." So few virtuous men arose in Asia because "that province was altogether under one kingdom in which, through its greatness, since it was idle most of the time, it could not give birth to excellent men," whereas Europe, before its corruption, was made up of "several kingdoms and infinite republics." Thus "many valiant men [sprang] up" there (AW II 283 ff). But this does not mean that Asian princes or tyrants did not have soldiers. On the contrary, each Asian king was surrounded by soldiers while his people remained unarmed. Indeed, when Fabrizio gives advice to the criminal tyrant Severus as to how to make his tyranny more enduring, it is the Assyrian king whom he offers as a model. The Assyrian king not only had a disarmed people (as did Severus, thanks to the work begun by Octavius and Tiberius [AW I 87]), but always rotated his captains from region to region so that they would be more attached to him than the soldiers would be to them. If Severus were to be more Asiatic in this respect, he would thereby give more authority to the Senate when the time came to elect his successor. The people would be no less despised and the soldiers no less satisfied if Severus would have made the proper adjustments. But in doing so, he would have created an elective, almost constitutional framework for tyranny.

In contrast to the aggressive coexistence he sought to foster, Machiavelli saw a sick and corrupt Italy whose illness was the product of a multiplicity of temporal states infected by a single pervasive spiritual state. It was therefore the presence of Asiatic unity in the midst of Western multiplicity that had kept the West in vileness for so long. But that combination may also have provided the pattern by which Machiavelli formed both temporal and spiritual armies of his own.

In the early pages of book I of the *Art of War*, Machiavelli announces a project of civilizational reform to be carried out (or "executed," he would say) posthumously in his *Discourses* and *The Prince*. First, in the *Art of War* Machiavelli draws attention to how writing helps one overcome the obstacles fortune places in one's way. Next, the broadest subjects of the work are shown to be how to introduce reforms in an age of corruption and what the character of those reforms should be. Finally, Machiavelli indicates that he himself is engaged in such a project of reform and sketches the nature of that project. Machiavelli performs these tasks by establishing parallels between his own activity and situation and those of the only other characters developed in these early pages: Cosimo, Bernardo (Cosimo's grandfather), and Fabrizio.

Machiavelli and Cosimo: Writing

The parallel between Machiavelli and Cosimo shows that Machiavelli sought to overcome or elude fortune by means of writing. In the preface, Machiavelli presents himself as one who decided to write about war despite his inexperience as a warrior. In his eulogy to Cosimo immediately after the preface, Machiavelli presents Cosimo as one who decided to write about love despite his inexperience as a lover. In the preface he presents himself as one who writes so as not to pass his idle times in vain. In the eulogy, he presents Cosimo as a writer in exactly the same way and in similar words. Finally, in the preface Machiavelli opposes the deeds of others to the words he wrote, which he then submitted to the judgment of Lorenzo di Filippo Strozzi. In the eulogy, Machiavelli contrasts the deeds that Cosimo never performed to the words that Cosimo wrote, and says that by means of the latter we can judge Cosimo's worth.[11] Just as one can do deliberately or by art what happened by chance to Fabius Maximus (*AW* IV 129), so can one do by design what happened to Cosimo by chance. By leaving writings behind to be interpreted after his death, Machiavelli can elude intentionally the fortune that Cosimo eluded by the same means but by chance. The striking parallel between Cosimo and Machiavelli suggests that Machiavelli intended to give fortune the slip by means of his posthumous writings, just as Cosimo did by means of his. But how? And to what end?

11. Cf. letter to Francesco Vettori, April 16, 1527.

Bernardo and Fabrizio: Ancient Models for Reform

The parallel between Bernardo and Fabrizio indicates how one ought to introduce reforms as well as the nature of the reforms needed in their corrupt times. Both Bernardo and Fabrizio are accused of having failed to institute reforms that their respective defenders claim they each dearly desired. Each had wished to do so in accordance with ancient models. Thus they are both ardent but failed reformers who looked to antiquity for guidance.

Fabrizio himself is the accuser of Bernardo. After being seated by Bernardo's grandson Cosimo in the "most secret and shady part" of his garden, Fabrizio seems puzzled by his surroundings, and especially by the trees that cast the shade in which at least some of those present sit. Cosimo satisfies Fabrizio's evident perplexity by telling him that some of the trees were "more celebrated by the ancients than by the common usage today." Machiavelli then informs us that Cosimo tells Fabrizio the names of the ancient trees and of how his grandfather had "exerted himself in so much cultivation of them." Fabrizio responds, "I was thinking that what you say might be so; and this place and this study were making me remember some princes of the Kingdom who delight in these ancient growths *(culture)* and shades" (*AW* I 15). The "kingdom" is the customary way of referring to the kingdom of Naples, where Fabrizio is the lord of several towns and cities, most notably Tagliacozzo. The court of the kingdom of Naples (especially under Alfonso I [1442–58] but also under his successors) had been well known for its attention to humanist studies. Thus the conversation that is about to take place would occur under the cool cover of antiquity as cultivated by contemporary humanists.

But after pausing to reflect a moment, and then expressing his belief that he will not offend anyone with what will soon be characterized as his accusation of Cosimo's grandfather, Fabrizio continues:

> How much better they would have done, may it be said with everyone's leave, to seek to be like the ancients in the strong and harsh things, not in the delicate and soft ones, and in those that they did under the sun, not in the shade, and to take up the modes of the true and perfect antiquity, not the false and corrupt one. (*AW* I 17)

Before he makes the last distinction between the true and perfect and the false and corrupt antiquities, it seems that Fabrizio is suggesting that Bernardo should have looked to "the ancients" in general as his model, separating their choiceworthy elements and leaving behind the rest, for example, separating their strong things from their delicate things and choosing the former. But once the last distinction is made it is clear that there are two different antiquities, and that a reformer might therefore safely take all the things of the true and perfect one, leaving behind those of the false and corrupt one. Bernardo, it seems, chose the wrong antiquity.

But which antiquity is the right one? Fabrizio adds, "[F]or after these studies pleased my Romans, my fatherland went to ruin" (*AW* I 17). Thus the Romans, at least for a time, were the true and perfect antiquity. Seeking to be like them would therefore be the proper course. Or would it? For Fabrizio introduces his chosen Romans hand in hand with their corruption and ruin. A passage in the *Florentine Histories* elucidates the ruin of Rome. At the very center of that work (*FH* V 1.185), Machiavelli discusses the natural cycle of the order and disorder of worldly things. Order leads naturally to disorder, and disorder in turn to order. The means by which provinces come, and by which the Romans especially came, "to ruin" were "letters" and the "leisure" so necessary to "philosophers" whom youths, and "the Roman youth" in particular, seem so willing to "follow" with "admiration." Ordinarily, once a province comes to ruin by these means, order again arises because men have "become wise from their afflictions." Just as philosophers and their letters are the means to corruption, disorder, and ruin, so captains and their arms lead back to order. Thus "letters come after arms" and "captains arise before philosophers" (*FH* V 1.185). But in the case of Italy, something extraordinary happened to prevent captains who would restore order from arising. It was Christianity that kept Italy in weakness after Roman arms defeated all opponents and with them their own fear. Here in the *Florentine Histories*, Christianity is obliquely referred to with the phrase "an extraordinary force."

For Machiavelli, Catholic Christianity is like philosophy, and a branch of Athenian philosophy in particular, in that it arose on the heels of the order imposed in part by military might. In this respect it seems to be philosophy writ large, because it arises out of the same source as philosophy and it leads to the prolongation and expansion of the political–military results of philosophy. But it is also unlike philosophy; for instead of eventually giving rise to harsh wars and the excellent captains who in turn restore order and "dominate the others," it gave rise to neither peace nor war.

> For one cannot affirm it to be peace where principalities frequently attack one another with arms; yet they cannot be called wars in which men are not killed, cities are not sacked, principalities are not destroyed, for these wars came to such weakness that they were begun without fear, carried on without danger,

> and ended without loss. So that virtue which in other provinces *used to be* eliminated in a long peace was eliminated by the vileness in the provinces of Italy. (*FH* V 1.186)

The ordinary way that virtue "used to be" eliminated has itself been eliminated, and not just in Italy, by the extraordinary force of Christianity. The very breaking or stopping of the cycle is itself a remarkable occurrence, and in itself not something entirely bad. Perhaps the most remarkable thing is that it *has* been broken by a belief or opinion that is universal in its claims and potentially in its dissemination. Now that there is a sphere of universal opinion, perhaps that universal opinion can be replaced by another that encourages at the same time that it manages the passions at the root of the particularity of the many republics and principalities. This takes us beyond the *Art of War*. But Fabrizio's words in this instance, as in others, prepare the way for Machiavelli's own later words. In this case, Fabrizio hints at the need for improving on Rome even as he introduces Rome as his model.

The actual Rome of the past contains within itself certain corruption. An element of the Greek past represents the chief deceit by means of which that corruption is accomplished. This Roman–Greek cycle is played out in the parallel between Bernardo and Fabrizio as they trade accusations and excuses through Cosimo. Bernardo's preference for an overly harsh antiquity plays into the hands of the current corruption by aiming too high. Cosimo claims that although Bernardo loved the ancient "harshness of life" praised by Fabrizio, he recognized that its imitation by him or his children would result in their being "defamed and vilified." To deny the body for the sake of wisdom as the Greek philosopher did, to brutalize children into simulating courage by making them love life less as the Spartans did, or to restrain one's desire for wealth like the most morally austere of Romans (*AW* I 25–27)—to enjoin men to imitate any or all of these practices is to aim too high even to get a hearing in such corrupt times, and perhaps too high at any time if one would avoid the Greek and Roman cycle as suggested above. That Cosimo allows wisdom, courage, and moderation into the picture only as maniacal wisdom, bestial courage, and coerced restraint indicates Machiavelli's critique of Greek philosophy, as does the absence of justice in this vignette of the classical virtues. They have had their chance, and we have seen what that chance has brought the world to; if yet another version of them were given another chance, we can reason that it would do so again. Besides, virtue for its own sake does not sell well in times such as those in which Bernardo and Fabrizio find themselves.

Instead of Bernardo's harsh modes, Fabrizio offers "more human modes." He would like to introduce modes "similar" to those of the Roman republic:

>To honor and reward the virtues, not to despise poverty, to esteem the modes
>and orders of military discipline, to constrain the citizens to love one another,
>to live without sects, to esteem the private less than the public, and other simi-
>lar things that could easily accompany our times. (*AW* I 33)

As stated, they sound like little more (or less) than "civic humanist" ideals. But
Fabrizio does not claim that these are the best modes, only that they are better
than the rarefied studies that the humanists fall back on in lieu of Bernardo's
harsher modes. He says too that these modes, like Bernardo's, are useful not so
much in themselves as for the shadow they cast: "Whoever orders that thing
plants trees under the shade of which one resides more happy and more glad
than under this" shadow cast by the effete humanists beneath which they sit. He
suggests, then, that his humanistic modes serve the purpose of providing cover
for something else.

The shadow cast by these modes conceals the full character of Fabrizio's
army. "To esteem the modes and orders of military discipline" could be and was
suggested by the "civic" humanist Bruni as well as by Machiavelli in both the
Discourses on Livy and *The Prince*. But the type of the military discipline in Fabrizio's army in no way resembles that which Bruni advised, in that it consists of
a kind of coercive or subtle manipulation of the passions that is antithetical to
the spirit of dedication to the common good advanced by the civic humanists.[12]
Likewise, in Fabrizio's army the private is indeed esteemed less than the public,
but only in an instrumental sense: all the soldiers stay in their common orders
so that they can more securely seize the spoils that later each enjoys individually.
The way in which these modes are more human or humane than Bernardo's can
be seen by the work's only statement on "humanity." Much later in the dialogue
Batista says to Fabrizio, "Your humanity is so much that it has us follow our desires without being afraid of being held presumptuous, since you freely offer us
what we would be ashamed to ask of you" (*AW* VI 233). Human beings want
things for which they are ashamed to ask. It would be inhuman to deny them
what they want, what they *must* want. Fabrizio's proposals allow and even encourage us to "follow our desires."

Fabrizio claims that it is not difficult to persuade men of common talent of
these modes. It is at this moment that Cosimo narrows the focus of the discussion to more strictly military matters, saying that he will leave to some unspeci-
fied "these" the judgment as to whether such persuasion is as easy as Fabrizio

---

12. Leonardo Bruni, *De militia*, in *The Humanism of Leonardo Bruni: Selected Texts*, ed. and
trans. Gordon Griffiths, James Hankins, and David Thompson (Binghamton, N.Y.: Medieval and
Renaissance Texts and Studies, 1987), 130, 144.

claims (*AW* I 35). We are left to wonder for the remainder of the dialogue whether such persuasion is easy, difficult, or impossible. If Fabrizio represents Machiavelli himself, then we can conclude that Machiavelli intended that we judge the ease, difficulty, and possibility of his enterprise as well.

Fabrizio and Machiavelli: Mercenary Captains as Teachers of the Young

The parallel between Fabrizio and Machiavelli leads us to see that the principal feature of Machiavelli's reform is the education of the young. This parallel is first hinted at near the beginning of the *Art of War:* just as Fabrizio would reject the ancient modes that few or none would praise, follow, or imitate (in that order) and seeks other ancient models, so Machiavelli approvingly notes how in antiquity soldiers were "*praised* by other men and *followed* and *imitated* with utmost attention" (*AW* pr. 8, emphasis added). More tellingly, Fabrizio's words about himself and his activity at the end of the work clearly allude to Machiavelli and his own activity as described at the end of the preface to that book of the *Discourses on Livy* devoted to foreign affairs and war. The dialogue ends with Fabrizio giving advice to his interlocutors whose youth has been emphasized from the beginning of the dialogue (*AW* I 4, I 6, I 11, I 47, III 5, IV 2, VII 246–49; cf. I 86, I 225). Here he rails against nature and fortune for giving him the knowledge but not the ability to reform his corrupt age. Likewise, in the *Discourses on Livy,* Machiavelli observes:

> Human appetites are insatiable, for since from nature they have the ability and the wish to desire all things and from fortune the ability to achieve few of them, there continually results from this a discontent in human minds and disgust with the things they possess. This makes them blame the present times, praise the past, and desire the future, even if they are not moved to do this by any reasonable cause. (*D* II pr. 3)

Machiavelli goes on to wonder whether he is being unreasonable in praising the times of ancient Rome while blaming his own times. He concludes that it is not unreasonable to do so because the virtue of the ancient and the vice of the present times are obvious to everyone. In reaching this conclusion, however, Machiavelli presents himself, just as Fabrizio did, as one moved by nature to be a reformer of his day but lacking the capability to do so because of fortune:

> I will be spirited in saying manifestly that which I may understand of the former and of the latter times so that the spirits of youths who may read these writings of mine can flee the latter and prepare themselves to imitate the former at whatever time fortune may give them opportunity. For it is the duty of a

good man to teach others the good that you could not work because of the malignity of the time and of fortune, so that when many are capable of it, someone of them more loved of heaven may be able to work it. (*D* II pr. 3)

The chapter in the *Discourses on Livy* that immediately precedes the preface just quoted, the last one of the first book, ends with words about the "very young" (*D* I 60). In it Machiavelli discusses the connection between virtue and the hope for the reward of glory, and the necessity of feeding this hope in the young if one chooses, as did Rome (*D* I 6), to arm the plebs. It is a necessity that "the prudence of the old," that is, Aristotelian prudence,[13] be foregone in favor of the multitude's election of an outstanding youth to be their captain (*D* I 60). Machiavelli places his hope in the youthful hope for glory that is achieved by winning the multitude to opinions and orders that accord with those taught by Machiavelli in the *Discourses on Livy* and *The Prince*. The youthful desire for glory is as much a necessity for the success of Machiavelli's enterprise as it is for the young themselves. But just as Fabrizio obscures this necessary and therefore unexalted character of glory, so Machiavelli gives countless examples of great actions by great men to inspire youths to action even while he teaches some of them that necessity rules. Like the excellent captain whose spirit *(spirito)* is present even and especially in his absence (*D* III 31.4), Machiavelli seeks to control the youth of the coming ages.

Machiavelli announces the advent of a spiritual army that is both the necessary condition for the flourishing of his temporal armies and the means by which the breaking of the natural cycle of order and disorder discussed above can be turned to the common benefit of each.

In the passage on this natural cycle in the *Florentine Histories* in which letters (that is, philosophy or its variant, Christianity) are said to be the means by which ordered cities come to ruin, Machiavelli also says, "The strength of well-armed spirits cannot be corrupted by a more honorable leisure than that of letters, nor can leisure enter into well-instituted cities with a greater and more dangerous deceit *(inganno)* than this one" (*FH* V 1.185). In the *Art of War*, Fabrizio says that "one bears more and greater dangers than in doing battle" when one marches against the unseen but always feared enemy because of the many ways one can be ambushed by some "deceit *(inganno)*" (*AW* V 118, 114–15). Fabrizio wishes to provide "perfect knowledge of this exercise" of guarding against such deceits (*AW* V 108). Here, in a key passage for understanding Machiavelli's art of writing, he advises that in the presence of such an army "you have to fear him in thought and in order, but with words and with other extrinsic demonstrations,

13. Cf. Aristotle, *Nicomachean Ethics* VI viii 5–8.

show that you despise him. For this last mode makes your soldiers hope more to have victory; the other one makes you more cautious and less apt to be deceived"(*AW* V 117). The bold words for which Machiavelli is famous and with which he shows that he despised Christianity are but "extrinsic demonstrations" to give his soldiers hope of victory over this unseen enemy. In his own thoughts, however, he had high esteem for this greatest deceit and danger. But to know his thought, one must make one's way from his bold pronouncements to consider his cautious manner of proceeding and especially his "order."

Only the organizing principle of this order can be mentioned here. Near the point in book II at which Cosimo confronts Fabrizio with the manifest superiority (in certain circumstances) of the Asian way of war, Fabrizio alters the proposed order of topics to be discussed with the result that the entire remainder of the work is reordered in light of the distinction between two kinds of warfare: that against an enemy one sees before one and that against an unseen but always feared enemy (*AW* II 165, V 1; cf. I 114–17, II 160–73, and pages xliii–xliv above). The *Art of War,* then, was meant by Machiavelli not only as a treatise on fighting physical armies but also as a guide for battling the unseen but always feared God whose religion and Church have kept the West in ruin. Should He be revered and feared as a believer reveres and fears Him, or esteemed and feared as Machiavelli esteems and fears Him, that is, as the deceit always ready to turn military–political order into disordered weakness. Whatever may be the correct answer to this most pressing question, Machiavelli was well prepared indeed to wage a war of indefinite duration against His orders.

GLOSSARY

English terms appearing in the translation are in boldface, followed by the Italian terms they translate in italics and the listing of their occurrences by book and sentence number. The abbreviation "pr." refers to the preface; "figs." refers to the explanation of the illustrations (pages 176–77). A parenthetical number followed by "X" indicates multiple occurrences. Negatives and other words with prefixes are listed with their root words. Indicators of parts of speech (n. for noun, v. for verb, adj. for adjective, part. for participle) are given only where the English terms are identical. *See also* refers to another English term used to translate that Italian term; *Cf.* refers to an etymologically or conceptually related term. An asterisk next to an English or an Italian term indicates that not all instances of that term are listed in the glossary. The glossary does not include words inserted in the translation in brackets for clarification.

absolute: *assoluto,* I 80

accident: *accidente,* I 252, I 254, II 205, IV 8, IV 63, V 1, V 107, V 127, VI 186, VI 208, VI 231, VII 69, VII 177. *Cf.* chance

accuse: *accusare,* I 20 (2X), I 40, I 157, VI 121; **accuser:** *accusatore,* I 35; **accusation:** *accusa,* I 42. *Cf.* excuse

accustom: *assuefare,* I 210, II 111, II 125, II 212, II 281, III 207, III 211, IV 140, V 66, VII 226; **accustom:** *avvezzare,* II 179, VII 180, VII 187; **accustom:** *solere,* I 48; **accustomed:** *consueto,* I 141, I 184, I 209, II 41, II 212, IV 37, IV 40, IV 43, VI 135, VII 72, VII 166, VII 214, VII 233

acquire: *acquistare,* I 65 (2X), I 70, I 251, I 252, II 111, VI 117, VI 118; **acquisition:** *acquisto,* II 47, VI 230, VII 162

action: *atto,* II 171; *see also* apt; fit; **action:** *azione, fazione,* I 35, I 36, I 120, II 104, II 121, II 200, II 228, II 258, II 270, II 271, III 42, III 44 (2X), V 120, VI 19, VI 46, VI 172, VI 183, VI 187, VII 199

administer: *sumministrare,* II 326

adore: *adorare,* VII 220, VII 221

advantage: *commodità,* II 126, VII 152; *see also* comfort; convenience; easy, make it; opportunity

advantage: *vantaggio,* II 44, II 46, II 49, II 57, II 117, IV 14, IV 87, IV 95, IV 96, IV 100, IV 119, VI 240; **to take advantage of:** *valersi, prevalendosi,* I 67 (2X)

advise: *avvisare,* VI 170. *Cf.* counsel

to be afraid: *temere,* I 176, III 146, III 188, IV 115; **to be afraid:** *avere paura,* II 42, II 67, VI 217, VI 233; **to be afraid:** *dubitare,* II 66; **to be afraid:** *sbigottirsi,* II 168, IV 52, VI 180, VII 150, VII 248; **to make afraid:** *fare paura,* II 313, II 322. *See also* fear; frighten

age: *età,* I 6, I 86, I 143, I 147, I 192. *See also* old; *Cf.* young

agreement: *convenienza,* pr. 1; *see also* convene; fit; inconvenience; **agreeable:** *grato,* I 157 (2X); *see also* grateful; favor

alive: *vivo,* II 130, II 294, II 306, IV 77, VI 119. *See also* lively; to live

allow: *permettere,* I 64, I 89, II 265. *See also* permit

ambassador: *ambasciatore,* VI 175, VII 164; **ambassadors:** *oratori,* VI 191, VI 192; *see also* orators

ambition: *ambizione,* I 58, II 29, VII 240

ancient, anciently, ancients, antiquity, in antiquity: *antico, anticamente, antichità* pr. 3, pr. 9, pr. 10 (2X), I 14, I 15, I 17 (2X), I 23, I 28 (2X), I 32, I 35, I 36 (3X), I 41, I 50, I 104, I 112 (2X), I 120, I 124, I 133, I 136, I 164, I 262, II 1, II 9, II 20, II 28, II 29, II 30, II 34, II 72, II 73, II 74, II 75, II 93, II 101, II 105, II 117, II 118, II 121, II 137 (2X), II 144, II 146, II 148, II 191, II 205, II 210, II 273, II 277, II 290, II 305, II 310, II 319, III 10, III 13, III 30, III 56, III 108, III 122, III 137, III 139, III 140 (2X), III 145, III 149 (2X), III 160, III 213, III 226, IV 26, IV 49, IV 141, IV 142, V 13, V 14, V 78, V 85, V 88, V 91, V 93, V 95, V 96, V 104, VI 70, VI 99, VI 125, VI 147, VI 153, VI 155, VI 207, VI 208, VI 211, VI 220, VI 225, VI 235, VI 237, VII 40, VII 43, VII 75, VII 102, VII 108, VII 139, VII 181 (2X), VII 182, VII 195, VII 196, VII 199, VII 203, VII 215, VII 225, VII 238, VII 250

animal: *animale,* II 91, IV 54; **animal:** *bestiame,* V 87, VII 68; *see also* beast

appetite: *appetito,* IV 6

apt: *atto,* II 96, III 162, III 214, V 117. *See also* action; fit

arbiter: *arbitro,* VI 122

arm, armed: *armare, armato,* I 117, I 150, I 165, I 172, I 179, I 180, I 225, I 246, I 247, I 267, I 270, I 272, II 1, II 15, II 22, II 23, II 25, II 27, II 29, II 34, II 36, II 42, II 43, II 46, II 47 (2X), II 48, II 59, II 60, II 68, II 69, II 72, II 75, II 76, II 101, II 102, II 129, II 147, II 148, II 150, II 174, II 190, II 318, II 321 (2X), II 322, III 63, III 95 (2X), III 139, III 145, III 161, III 217, IV 111, V 11, V 154, VI 27, VI 28, VI 29, VI 70 (2X),VI 104, VI 125, VI 133, VII 70, VII 91, VII 135, VII 145, VII 238; **heavily armed:** *gravemente armato, grave armadura,* II 2, II 5, IV 51; **light armed, lightly armed:** *leggermente armato,* II 2, III 15, III 16, IV 35, IV 37, V 101. *See also* armor

armor (v.): *armare, armato,* II 27, II 56 (2X), III 141, III 144. *See also* arm

army: *esercito, passim*

arquebus, arquebusier: *scoppietto, scoppiettiere,* II 28, II 70, II 125, II 132 (2X), II 148, II 253, II 322 (2X), III 28, III 89, III 134, IV 60

art: *arte,* title, pr. title, pr. 3, pr. 10, I title, I 36, I 50, I 51 (4X), I 52 (2X), I 57, I 60, I 63, I 64 (2X), I 66 (2X), I 67, I 68 (2X), I 70, I 71 (2X), I 74, I 75, I 77, I 82, I 83 (2X), I 85, I 89, I 92, I 93, I 98, I 100, I 104, I 106, I 108 (2X), I 193, I 194, I 195, I 196, I 197, I 202, I 264, IV 50, IV 64, IV 129, V 109, VI 12, VI 14, VI 17, VI 70, VI 162, VI 187, VI 199, VI 248, VII 118. *See also* artifice; artisan; *see* page 33 note 1 for six additional instances of **art:** *arte* in book titles omitted from the translation; the coda to book VII on page 165.

artifice: *arteficio,* I 78. *See also* art; artisan

artisan: *arteficio,* VI 71. *See also* art; artifice

artillery: *artiglierie,* figs. 3, II 246, II 249, III 63, III 64 (2X), III 80, III 81, III 84, III 103, III 105, III 107, III 108, III 110, III 112, III 118 (2X), III 119, III 121, III 126, III 128, III 129, III 131 (2X), III 133, III 134 (2X), III 137, III 139, III 140, III 141, III 143, III 146, III 148 (2X), III 149, III 151, III 154, III 156 (3X), III 157 (3X), III 159, III 160, III 211, III 220, IV 18 (2X), IV 30, V 11, V 26, V 33, V 44, V 54, V 61, VI 69, VI 75, VI 79, VI 88 (2X), VII 2, VII 5, VII 8, VII 11, VII 12, VII 14 (2X), VII 25, VII 29, VII 37, VII 46, VII 50, VII 64, VII 76, VII 133 (2X)

assail: *assailire,* III 70, V 12, VI 164, VI 179, VII 146

assault (v.): *assaltare,* II 32, II 39, II 50, II 165, III 70 (2X), III 71, III 81, III 121, III 124, IV 56, IV 57, IV 75, IV 77, IV 97, IV 101, IV 106, IV 123, V 1, V 8, V 9, V 14, V 65, V 115, V 121, V 126, V 156, V 157, VI 161, VI 179, VI 186, VI 193, VI 196, VI 197, VI 214 (2X), VI 217, VI 222, VI 244, VI 246, VII 73, VII 74, VII 75, VII 86, VII 98, VII 103, VII 112, VII 117 (2X), VII 118, VII 146, VII 148, VII 236; **assault (n.):** *assalto,* II 166, III 134, III 215, III 230, IV 56, V 38, V 39, V 43, V 51, VII 78, VII 86, VII 118. *See also* assail; attack; charge

astuteness: *astuzia,* I 141, IV 83; **astutely:** *astutissimamente,* VII 128

attack (v.): *affrontare,* III 77, III 87, III 90, V 54; **attack (v.):** *assaltare,* III 224, VII 92, VII 93; **attack:** *assalto* (n.), III 211; **attack (v.):** *combattere,* VI 87, VII 133; **attack (v.):** *offendere,* VII 76; **attack (n.):** *offesa,* VI 246, VII 72, VII 77, VII 151; **attack (v.):** *urtare,* III 177. *See also* assail; assault; charge; fight

attention: *studio,* pr. 8, II 102, II 205; *see also* study; **attention:** *osservanza,* VI 118; *see also* observance

augurs: *auguri,* VI 207

authority: *autorita,* I 135, I 251, I 252, I 254, I 257, II 268, III 2, IV 137, VI 125, VI 204, VII 109

avariciously: *avaramente,* VII 236

bad, badly: *male,* I 119, I 129, I 167, II 35, III 71, IV 16, V 63, V 72, V 154 (3X), VI 107, VI 141, VI 244, VII 31, VII 234, VII 235; **bad:** *cattivo,* II 49; **bad:** *malvage,* VI 142;. *See also* evil; malicious; wicked

barbarian: *barbaro,* II 305

battalion: *battaglia, battaglione,* figs. 1, figs. 3, figs. 4, II 10, II 18, II 57, II 70, II 145, II

147 (2X), II 149, II 152, II 156, II 157, II 159 (2X), II 160 (2X), II 162, II 163 (2X), II 171, II 172, II 174, II 176, II 180, II 187, II 188 (2X), II 189, II 191, II 192, II 193, II 197 (2X), II 202, II 206, II 208, II 216, II 219, II 221 (3X), II 224, II 225, II 226 (2X), II 227, II 230, II 231 (2X), II 237, II 242, II 246, II 248, II 250, II 251, II 253, II 254 (2X), II 255 (2X), II 258 (2X), II 260 (2X), II 263, II 265, II 266, II 318, II 323, II 328, III 32, III 34 (2X), III 49 (2X), III 50, III 51, III 52, III 54, III 55, III 56 (2X), III 60 (2X), III 61 (2X), III 67, III 74, III 76, III 89, III 92, III 135, III 140, III 145, III 153 (2X), III 156, III 162, III 163, III 171, III 177, III 178, III 183, III 185, III 186, III 187, III 189, III 192 (2X), III 193, III 195 (2X), III 199, III 200 (2X), III 201 (2X), III 203, III 204 (2X), III 205 (2X), III 206, III 211, IV 26, IV 35, IV 36, V 14 (2X), V 15, V 16 (3X), V 18 (3X), V 19, V 20 (2X), V 21, V 22, V 23, V 24, V 25, V 28, V 33, V 35 (2X), V 36, V 47 (2X), V 48 (2X), V 50 (3X), V 71, V 78, V 104, V 125, V 159, VI 21, VI 40 (2X), VI 41, VI 42, VI 43, VI 44, VI 47, VI 48, VI 49, VI 62, VI 78, VI 79, VI 97, VII 176. *See also* battle; brigade

battle: *zuffa,* II 7, II 77, II 162, II 166, III 37, III 189, IV 8, IV 26, IV 32, IV 35, IV 56, IV 66, VI 224; **battle:** *battaglia,* II 37, II 166, VI 224, VII 144; *see also* battalion; brigade; **battle:** *giornata,* figs. 8, figs. 10, I 115, I 119 (2X), I 272, II 13, II 17, II 66, II 70, II 79, II 99, II 101, II 104, II 164, II 165, II 170, II 172, II 230, II 329, III 9, III 11, III 12, III 27, III 38, III 45, III 46, III 47, III 48, III 64, III 78, III 97, III 101, III 114, III 123, III 124, III 130 (2X), III 134, III 153, III 161, III 163, III 164, III 172, III 189, III 198 (2X), III 211, IV 1, IV 19, IV 28, IV 38, IV 42, IV 65, IV 73, IV 95, IV 103, IV 112, IV 116, IV 117, IV 118, IV 119 (2X), IV 120, IV 121, IV 122, IV 123, IV 124, IV 125, IV 127, V 1, V 43, V 118, V 128, VI 93, VI 94, VI 166, VI 192, VI 207, VI 225, VI 239 (2X), VII 156, VII 163, VII 166, VII 174

beast: *fiera,* I 26

beat*: *rompere,* I 168, II 76, II 79, II 107, III 127, IV 33, IV 35, IV 60, IV 74, IV 75, IV 77 (2X), IV 92, IV 101, IV 120, IV 123, IV 131, V 68, V 100, VI 243, VI 246 (2X), VII 167; *see also* break; **beat:** *vincere,* II 43, III 20, III 34, IV 61, IV 108, VI 215, VI 217 (2X), VI 219, VII 147, VII 157, VII 164, VII 168; *see also* conquer; defeat

beautiful: *bello, begli* I 227, II 19, II 272, VI 229, VII 52, VII 235, VII 236; **beauty:** *bellezza,* VII 52

begin: *cominciare,* I 50, I 87, I 89, I 112, I 114, I 209, II 94, II 207, II 304, III 107, IV 34, IV 108, VI 2, VI 31, VI 39, VI 180, VII 24, VII 243; **beginning:** *principio,* I 114, I 205, I 206, III 25, VI 37, VI 156, VII 25, VII 242

believe: *credere,* pr. 2, pr. 11, I 1, I 16 (2X), I 24, I 29, I 42, I 47 (2X), I 48, I 77 (2X), I 96 (2X), I 169, I 183, I 205, I 206, I 219, I 225, I 229, I 259, II 1 (2X), II 71, II 73, II 74, II 190, II 266, II 325, III 49, III 101, III 106, III 123, III 128, III 138, III 141, III 145, III 154, III 161, III 165, III 177, III 199, III 228, IV 5, IV 72, IV 78, IV 83, IV 84, IV 115, IV 116, IV 118, IV 128, V 70, V 95, V 107, V 114 (2X), V 116, V 130, V 136, V 143 (2X), V 152, V 158, VI 1, VI 4, VI 27, VI 76, VI 168 (2X), VI 169, VI 170, VI 174, VI 202, VI 215, VI 221, VI 224, VII 7, VII 52 (2X), VII 92, VII 96, VII 98, VII 104, VII 117, VII 118, VII 196, VII 222, VII 234, VII 236, VII 241, VII 250; **believable:** *credibile,* II 23; **believability:** *fede,* VI 222; *see also* confidence; faith; trust; vouch

belongings: *mobile,* V 95, V 105

besiege: *assediare,* II 62, V 130, V 133, VI 139, VI 142 (2X), VI 183, VI 184, VII 74, VII 80 (2X), VII 81 (2X), VII 96 (2X), VII 97, VII 99, VII 101, VII 107, VII 113, VII 115, VII 117, VII 119, VII 120, VII 121, VII 123, VII 131 (2X), VII 132, VII 143, VII 144, VII 147 (2X), VII 149 (2X); VII 151 (2X); besiege: *espugnare,* VI 232; *see also* storm

blame (v.): *biasimo, biasimare,* pr. 12, I 57, I 153, I 154, I 170, I 179, I 220, I 260, III 1, VI 116; blame (v.): *dannare,* VII 240 (2X); blame (v.): *inculpare,* I 41; not to blame: *non avere culpa,* VII 230; blamer: *biasimatore,* VII 195. *See also* condemn; culpable; fault

blind (v): *accecare,* III 128, III 129, III 130; blind (adj.): *cieco,* III 128

blood: *sangue,* I 256, VI 204

body: *corpo,* I 203 (2X), I 209, II 40, II 65, II 103, II 110, II 163, II 219, II 275 (2X), III 19, III 21, III 24, III 26 (X), III 29 (X), V 50, VI 229, VII 125, VII 238; body: *persona,* II 77, III 134

break*: *rompere,* I 67, II 67, II 71, II 108, II 117, II 141, II 155, II 205, III 24, III 116, III 177, IV 24, V 31, VI 222 (2X). *See also* beat

brigade: *battaglione,* figs. 1, figs. 3, figs. 4, figs. 6, figs. 7, II 144, II 147, II 150, II 154, II 156 (2X), II 158, II 164, II 255, II 328, III 27 (3X), III 28, III 31, III 32, III 48, III 49, III 50, III 61, III 62, III 63 (2X), III 75, III 76, III 165, III 166, III 182 (2X), III 183, III 186, III 202, III 203, III 204, III 219, V 10, V 11, V 13, V 34 (2X), V 35 (2X), V 36, VI 21 (2X), VI 23 (2X), VI 25, VI 31, VI 32, VI 33, VI 38, VI 39, VI 40, VI 49, VI 50 (2X), VI 51, VI 57, VI 61, VI 62 (2X), VI 66, VI 67, VI 134, VI 135, VI 136, VI 156; brigade: *battaglia,* II 18; *see also* battalion

bucklers: *brocchieri,* II 65; bucklers: *rotelle,* II 148

build (v.): *edificare,* VII 3, VII 8, VII 22, VII 31, VII 34, VII 44, VII 45, VII 141; build (v.): *rizzare,* VII 193

bury: *sotterrare,* IV 83. *Cf.* land; town

calm: *ozio,* III 92. *See also* idle; holiday

calumniate: *calunniare,* I 16

campaign: *impresa,* III 42; *see also* enterprise; undertaking; campaign: *campagna,* VI 247

captain: *capitano,* figs. 3, I 53, I 63, I 65, I 68, I 69, I 137, I 150, I 181, I 183 (2X), I 255, I 256 (3X), I 257 (2X), II 50, II 76, II 97, II 104, II 129, II 140, II 156, II 165, II 171, II 243, II 249, II 290, III 63 (2X), III 74, III 85, III 88, III 114, III 134, III 189, III 200, III 201, III 206, III 209, III 212, III 218, III 220, III 222, III 226, III 227, III 230, IV 8, IV 26, IV 32, IV 33, IV 58, IV 68 (2X), IV 76, IV 79, IV 85, IV 94, IV 95, IV 99, IV 106, IV 111, IV 113, IV 121, IV 138, IV 139, IV 140 (2X), IV 142, IV 149, IV 150, IV 151, V 13, V 19, V 38, V 68, V 72, V 92, V 107, V 109, V 113, V 119, V 151, V 156, VI 1, VI 12, VI 26 (2X), VI 29, VI 30 (5X), VI 31 (2X), VI 32, VI 38, VI 39, VI 49, VI 52, VI 54, VI 55, VI 56 (2X), VI 57 (2X), VI 58 (2X), VI 59 (2X), VI 60, VI 61, VI 82, VI 93, VI 113, VI 132, VI 143, VI 146, VI 153, VI 179, VI 183, VI 187, VI 199, VI 204, VI 205, VI 207 (2X), VI 208, VI 215, VI 221, VI 229, VI 238, VI 239, VII 34, VII 82, VII 99, VII 102, VII 108, VII 174, VII 190, VII 201; captain (v.): *capitanare,* II 318 capital: *capitale,* III 134, V 105, VI 113; **capitally:** *capitalmente,* VI 101

care, take care: *custodire,* I 69, I 70, VII 234; **care:** *curare,* III 205, VI 19; **give care, take care:** *avere cura, tenere cura,* II 78, II 210, IV 21, V 105, VII 78, VII 144; **take care:** *riguardare,** VI 188; **not cared for:** *straccurare,* II 262

career: *esercizio,* I 2, I 52, I 60, I 62, I 64. *See also* exercise; drill; practice; train

castle: *castello,* VI 241, VII 37, VII 80, VII 85, VII 101, VII 103, VII 111; **castle:** *rocca,* I 88, VII 1, VII 23, VII 26 (2X), VII 27, VII 28 (2X), VII 29, VII 30, VII 34 (2X), VII 58. *See also* stronghold; *Cf.* citadel; fortress

cause (n.): *cagione,* I 1, I 10, I 100, I 107, I 169, I 187, I 196, I 237, I 247, I 249, I 256, I 257, II 66, II 137, II 139, II 173, II 302, II 309, II 315, III 111, III 120, III 126, III 139, III 140 (2X), III 198, III 224, III 225, IV 43, IV 57, IV 80, IV 91, IV 93, IV 105, IV 126, IV 146, IV 147, V 50, V 123, VI 186, VI 187, VI 201, VI 208 (2X), VI 210, VI 220, VI 243, VII 25, VII 118, VII 195, VII 198; **cause** (n.): *causa,* IV 150, VI 121; **cause** (v.): *causare,* I 246, IV 150, IV 151, VII 226

cavalry: *cavalleria, cavallo, cavagli,* I 104, I 261, I 262, I 263, II 78, II 80, II 84, II 86, II 129, II 326, III 81, III 89, III 118, III 164, III 222, IV 37, IV 59 (2X), IV 60, V 6, V 29, V 101, VI 43, VI 44, VI 214 (2X), VII 188; **cavalryman, cavalrymen:** *cavagli, cavalli, cavallo,* figs. 2, figs. 3, II 31, II 32, II 34, II 38, II 42 (2X), II 43, II 44 (2X), II 46, II 51, II 52 (2X), II 66, II 67, II 70, II 72, II 74, II 76 (2X), II 79, II 80, II 87, II 88, II 89, II 91, II 93, II 100 (2X), II 318, II 321, II 322, II 323, II 326, II 328, III 15, III 19 (2X), III 34, III 35, III 37, III 40, III 41 (2X), III 42, III 59, III 72 (2X), III 82, III 86, III 89 (2X), III 130, III 133, III 142, III 164, III 165, III 170, III 171, III 224, IV 24, IV 25, IV 36 (2X), IV 37, IV 51 (2X), IV 59, IV 70, IV 111, V 3, V 10, V 27, V 30, V 33, V 38, V 41, V 44, V 45, V 54, V 56, V 61, V 119, V 126, V 136, V 138, V 148, VI 19 (2X), VI 21, VI 25, VI 37 (2X), VI 38, VI 39, VI 40 (2X), VI 45, VI 46 (2X), VI 49, VI 50, VI 61, VI 224, VII 186. *See also* horse; mare

centurion: *centurione,* II 152, II 153 (2X), II 156, II 191, II 193 (2X), II 194, II 195 (2X), VII 197 (6X), II 209, II 212, II 221, II 222, II 224, II 225 (2X), II 232, II 235, II 236, II 237, II 238, II 240 (2X), II 241, II 243, II 244, II 264, II 265, III 56, III 204

century: *centuria,* II 221, II 222 (3X), II 223 (2X), II 226

ceremony: *cerimonia,* IV 5, VI 125

chance: *sorte,* IV 105; **chance:** *caso,* IV 129, VI 146, VII 52. *Cf.* accident

chastity: *castità,* VI 229

charge (v.): *urtare,* II 38, II 94, III 65, III 67, III 88, III 89, III 142, III 177, IV 17, IV 61, V 30, V 65, VI 224, VII 148; **charge** (n.): *urto,* II 38, II 253, III 29; **charge** (n.): *foga,* II 98 (2X)

chariot: *carro,* III 160, IV 49, IV 50 (2X). *See also* wagon

check, keep in check (v.): *frenare, raffrenare, tenere in freno,* I 88, II 94, VI 126. *See also* restraint

children: *fanciugli,* VII 70; **children:** *figliuoli,* I 24, I 26, VI 188; **childhood:** *fanciugli,* II 169. *See also* son

church: *chiesa,* VI 227

citadel: *cittadella,* VII 28. *Cf.* castle; fortress; stronghold citizen: *cittadino*, pr. title, I title, I 1, I 33, I 51, I 64, I 67, I 69, I 73, I 76, I 85, I 106, I 137, I 159, I 171, I 173, I 175, I 176, I 181, I 184, I 185 (2X), I 186, II 121, III 40, VI 116, VII 202, VII 245; *see* page 33 note 1 for six additional instances of citizen: *cittadino*, in book titles omitted from the translation; the coda to book VII on page 165.

civilian: *civile*, pr. 1, pr. 2 (3X)

civilization: *civiltà, civilità*, pr. 3, I 31

clarify: *dichiarare*, III 224, III 225. *See also* declare; describe; explain

close: *addosso*, I 88; *see also* near; close: *presso*, II 56; *see also* near; close: *serrato*, III 144; close: *stretto*, III 146; close quarters: *presse*, II 38; close, to be: *accostare*, V 15; *see also* approach; near, side with; stop

combatant: *combattitori*, II 167, II 168, III 24, VI 224, VII 244

comfort: *commodità*, II 265. *See also* advantage; convenience; easy, make it; opportunity

command: *comandare*, I 87, I 137, I 159, I 220, II 162, II 215, II 276, III 73, III 76, III 88, III 201, IV 26, IV 35, IV 41, IV 54, IV 92, V 68, V 71, V 72, V 73, V 122, V 142, V 159, VI 168, VI 221, VI 224, VII 149, VII 208, VII 210 (2X)

commission: *commissione*, III 61, V 38

community: *comunità*, I 94, I 98

company : *compagnia*, I 54, I 100, II 231, II 289, IV 133

compared to: *rispetto* a*, II 309, VI 195, VII 42. *See also* respect; thanks

conceal, concealed: *celare, nascosto*, IV 57, VI 113. *See also* hide

condemn: *condannare, dannare*, I 36, I 152, III 139, VI 120, VI 123, VII 194. *See also* blame; culpable; fault

confederate (n.): *confederato*, III 41; confederate (v.): *collegare*, VI 178

confess: *confessare*, I 3, I 225, VI 76, VII 225

confidence, to have: *confidare, avere confidenza*, III 44, III 83, IV 38, IV 111, VI 187; confidence: *confidenza*, IV 149, IV 150, VI 180; confidence, to lack; to not be confident: *diffidare, essere male confidente*, I 183, IV 115, IV 127; confidence, lack of: *diffidenza*, I 183. *See also* trust; vouch

conform, to be in conformity: *conformare, avere conformità*, pr. 3, I 29, IV 72, V 54

conjecture (n.): *coniettura*, I 69, I 200, I 202, I 206, I 217, I 218, I 220, I 224, VI 142; conjecture (v.): *conietturare*, I 195, I 203, II 18, II 48, VII 197

conquer: *vincere, vinto*, I 69, I 168 (3X), II 31, II 38, II 299, II 305 (2X), II 307, II 328, IV 3 (2X), IV 25, IV 26, IV 29, IV 39, IV 52, IV 58, IV 60, IV 119 (2X), V 93, V 101, V 138, V 141, VI 150 (2X), VI 151, VI 163, VI 180, VI 197, VI 223, VI 225; *see also* defeat; win; conquest: *vittoria*, VII 91; *see also* victory

conscript: *descrivere*, II 256, II 328. *See also* describe; enroll

contemplate: *speculare*, V 119

contend: *disputare*, I 104; *see also* dispute; contend (with): *contendere*, V 131

convene: *convenire,** I 8, I 213, I 227. *Cf.* agreement; convenience

convenience, convenient, conveniently: *accomodato, commodi, commodità*, IV 18, IV

46, IV 62, IV 77, V 92, VI 68, VI 81, VI 169, VI 186, VI 201, VII 12, VII 67, VII 137, VII 200, VII 209; **convenient:** *conveniente,* VII 132. *See also* advantage; agree; convene; comfort; easy, make it; opportunity

corrupt: *corrompere, corrotto,* pr. 9, I 17, I 86, I 99, I 102, I 105, I 106, I 173, II 304 (2X), II 319, IV 133, VI 100, VII 108, VII 185, VII 207; **corruption:** *corruttela, corruzione,* I 24, I 78, I 205, II 325. *See also* poison

counsel, take counsel: *consigliare,* I 81, I 109, V 109, V 144, VII 172 VII 247; **counsel** (n.): *consiglio,* I 81, IV 25, VI 109, VI 189, VII 24, VII 26; **counselor:** *consigliere,* VI 188. *Cf.* advise

country: *patria,* IV 149, IV 151; *see also* fatherland; **country:** *paese,* I 54, I 121, I 124, I 224, I 227 (2X), I 236, I 240, I 242, I 246, I 247, I 248, II 79, II 97, II 158, II 261, III 65, IV 57, IV 62, V 2, V 10, V 12, V 14, V 27, V 93, V 110 (2X), V 118 (2X), V 119, V 156, VI 179, VI 182, VI 193, VI 196, VI 215, VII 67, VII 105, VII 114, VII 187 (2X), VII 188

crazy: *pazzia, pazzo,* I 25, III 108

create: *creare,* I 89, I 104, I 192, I 212

crossbows: *balestriere,* VII 45; **crossbowmen:** *balestieri,* II 28, II 321, III 15

culpable: *essere in colpa,* VI 202. *See also* fault

cultivation, cultivating: *coltura, cultivare, culto, cultura,* I 15, I 93, I 97 (2X), VII 63

curse (v.): *bestemmiare,* VII 220, VII 221; **curse** (n.): *bestemmia,* pr. 2, VII 214. *See also* swear

danger: *pericolo,* pr. 7, I 73, I 83, I 84, II 10, II 91, II 111, II 308, III 140, III 156, IV 131, IV 139, V 72, V 102, V 116, V 118, V 129, VI 92, VI 94, VI 203, VI 223, VI 238, VII 155, VII 238. *See also* risk; peril

day: *dì,* I 12, I 100, IV 21, V 158, VI 145, VI 147, VI 221, VII 144; **day:** *giornata,* II 84, V 141; *see also* battle; **day:** *giorno,* I 9, I 10, I 11, I 70, I 227, II 111, II 164, III 207, V 42, V 88, V 158, VI 105, VI 150, VI 168, VI 173, VI 183, VI 192 (2X), VI 214, VI 220, VII 95, VII 111, VII 212, VII 213; **daybreak:** *fare del dì,* V 157; **daybreak:** *fare del giorno,* VII 144; **daytime:** *giorno,* VII 170

deceive: *ingannare,* I 56, IV 52, IV 62, V 116, V 117, VI 100, VI 168, VI 170, VI 221, VII 37, VII 112, VII 114, VII 129; **deception:** *inganno,* I 53, IV 139, V 114, V 115, VI 184, VII 96 (2X), VII 118

decide: *diliberare, divisare,* pr.10, I 9, VII 138; **decision:** *diliberazione,* I 80

deed*: *opera,* I 200

defamed: *infame,* I 24

defeat: *vincere,* I 17, I 45 (2X), VII 90. *See also* conquer; win

defend, defender, defense: *defendere, difendere, difendersi, difeso, difesa,* pr. 3, pr. 5, I 107 (2X), I 177, I 181, I 231, II 14, II 15, II 26, II 29 (2X), II 55, II 56, II 60 (2X), II 84 (2X), II 301, II 305, II 309, III 13, III 64, III 72, III 82, III 108, III 115, III 121, III 141 (2X), III 143, III 148, III 161, III 188, IV 134, IV 108, V 105, V 130, V 154, V 159, VI 13, VI 121, VI 123, VI 169, VI 179, VI 193, VI 198, VI 223, VI 224, VI 232, VI 249, VII 8, VII 12 (2X), VII 13, VII 19, VII 23, VII 24, VII 25 (2X), VII 27, VII 31, VII 36 (2X),

VII 37, VII 45, VII 46, VII 49, VII 69, VII 71, VII 73, VII 75, VII 76, VII 142, VII 146 (2X), VII 148, VII 151

degree: *mezzo,* I 34. *See also* half; means; midday; route

delight: *dilettarsi, diletto,* I 15, I 227; **delightful:** *dilettevole,* I 13, I 227

demonstrate, demonstration: *dimostrare, dimostrazione, mostrare,* I 114, I 189, I 211, II 178, II 197, II 221, II 254, II 262, III 9, III 30, III 49, III 158, V 117, VI 24, VI 117, VI 131, VI 133, VI 167, VII 198. *See also* show

describe*: *descrivere,* figs. 4; I 6; II 125; V 119; *see also* conscript; enroll; **describe:** *disegnare,* VI 26; *see also* design; draw; plan

deservedly: *meritamente,* VI 151. *See also* merit

design (v.): *disegnare,* IV 87, IV 140; **design** (n.): *disegno,* IV 93, V 120. *See also* describe; draw; plan

desire (v.): *disiderare,* I 1, I 21, I 37, I 49, I 71, I 81, I 113, I 241, II 45, II 72, II 86, II 166, II 168, II 318, III 94, III 225, IV 2, IV 8, IV 126, IV 130, V 71, VI 8, VI 9, VI 175, VII 42, VII 103, VII 190; **desire** (n.): *desiderio,* I 12, I 68, I 113, III 38, III 77, IV 126, IV 130, VI 121, VI 169, VI 233, VII 196

despise: *dispregiare, disprezzare, spregiare,* I 27, I 33, III 126, IV 133, V 117, VII 236. *See also* disdain; disparage

devices: *industrie,* I 59

dictatorship: *dittatura,* III 2, IV 2

die, dead: *morire, morto, per morte cadere,* pr. 5, I 5 (2X), I 89, II 66, III 24, III 94, III 95, III 134 (2X), IV 58, IV 70, IV 83, IV 107, IV 152, VI 114, VI 119, VII 226, VII 239, VII 248; **deadly:** *mortale,* II 116; **death:** *morte,* I 1, I 4, I 26, II 65, IV 65, VI 123. *See also* kill

dignity: *dignità,* VI 206

disadvantage: *disavvantaggio,* II 43, II 53, II 57, IV 18, IV 83, IV 87, IV 98, IV 126, VI 244; **disadvantage:** *disfavore,* VII 107; **disadvantage:** *incommodo,* VI 119

discharge: *licenziare,* I 72

discipline, disciplined : *disciplina, disciplinato,* I 33, I 119, I 188, I 189, II 24, II 140, II 161, III 45, III 83, III 90, III 91, IV 14, IV 16, V 67, V 68 (3X), VI 14, VI 125, VI 163, VI 163, VI 239, VI 240, VI 241 (2X), VI 242 (2X), VI 247, VII 161, VII 202, VII 215

discontent: *mala contentezza,* I 165, I 167

discord: *discordia,* VI 199, VI 203, VI 206, VI 222

discourse: *avere discorso, discorrere,* I 44, II 283. *See also* discuss; reason

discuss: *ragionare, avere discorso,* figs. 11, I 10, I 113, II 314, III 151, III 196, IV 7, VII 34; **discussion:** *ragionamento,* I 8, I 20, I 38, I 46, I 104, I 111, I 112, I 156, II 81, II 85, III 1. *See also* discourse; reason

disdain (v.): *spregiare,* VII 180; **disdain** (v.): *sdegno,* I 167. *See also* despise; disparage

dismay: *sbigottire,* VII 24

disparage: *dispregiare, spregiare,* III 108, VII 222, VII 223, VII 245 (2X). *See also* despise; disdain

dispute: *disputare,* I 7, I 8 (2X), I 16, I 64, I 164, VI 231, VI 201. *See also* contend

ditch: *fossa,* II 108, IV 13, IV 62, V 129, V 131 (2X), V 132 (2X), V 136, V 151, V 152, VI 53,
    VI 56, VI 61, VI 62, VI 63, VI 65, VI 66, VI 67, VI 68, VI 69, VI 75, VI 79 (2X), VI
    80, VI 85 (2X), VI 88 (3X), VI 99, VI 101, VII 6, VII 7, VII 8, VII 10 (4X), VII 11,
    VII 12, VII 14 (4X), VII 15, VII 16 (2X), VII 17, VII 18, VII 19 (2X), VII 20, VII 22,
    VII 28 (2X), VII 34 (2X), VII 35, VII 37, VII 38, VII 64, VII 133 (4X), VII 134 (3X),
    VII 138, VII 141; *see also* hole; ditch: *grotta,* VI 13
do*: *operare,* pr.10, I 39, II 79, II 126, II 163, III 189, IV 138, VI 118, VII 195
dominion: *dominio,* I 180
double: *raddoppiare,** figs. 4, figs. 5, II 184, II 185, II 198 (2X), II 199, II 200, II 223 (2X),
    III 196 (2X), III 197 (2X), VI 22 (2X); *see also* redouble; double: *doppio,* I 197, II
    113, II 171, V 110, VI 47, VI 48, VI 50, VI 52, VI 61, VI 63, VI 65 (2X), VI 66 (2X), VI
    104; double: *duplicare,* V 61, VI 192
doubt (v.): *dubitare,* I 44, II 173, II 266, III 79, III 155, III 178, V 81, VI 9, VI 225, VI 226;
    doubt (n.): *dubitazione,* I 49, II 80, II 316, III 100, III 152. *See also* to be afraid; fear;
    hesitate
drill (n.): *esercizio,* I 210, I 211, I 227, II 103, II 105, II 106, II 121, II 124, II 125, II 127, II
    130, II 137, II 138, II 139, II 140, II 213, II 259 (2X), II 261, III 211 (2X), III 212, III 221,
    V 67, VI 89, VII 213; drill (v.): *esercitare,* II 114, II 164, VI 89. *See also* career; exer-
    cise; practice; training

earth: *terra,* IV 62, VII 10 (2X). *See also* country; town; ground
ease: *facilità, facultà,* II 212, II 307, III 29, IV 80, IV 133, V 137, VI 215, VI 217, VII 131,
    VII 177, VII 198; easily (adv.): *facilmente,* I 33, I 35 (2X), I 87, I 158, I 159, I 183, I
    210, I 222, I 245, I 254, II 48, II 123, II 161, II 163, II 218, II 260, II 276, II 326, III 34,
    III 73, III 142, III 159, III 160 (2X), III 162, III 171, III 201, IV 17, IV 39, IV 52, IV 59,
    IV 60, IV 85, IV 106 (2X), V 32, V 65, V 69, V 88, V 114, V 122, VI 98, VI 166 (2X),
    VI 167, VI 180, VI 207, VI 216, VI 219, VII 4, VII 5, VII 13, VII 45 (2X), VII 55, VII
    59, VII 63, VII 65, VII 105, VII 145; easy (a.): *facile,* I 38, I 44, I 99, I 173 (2X), II 130,
    II 199, II 212, II 215, III 76, IV 137, IV 142, VI 106 (2X), VI 221, VII 5, VII 91, VII 92,
    VII 105, VII 107, VII 110, VII 199; make easy: *dare faciltà, facilare, fare facile,* II 201,
    VI 230, VII 8, VII 20; easily (adv.): *commodamente,* IV 18, IV 112; make it easy:
    dare commodità, III 156; *see also* advantage; convenience; comfort; opportunity
education: *educazione,* I 205
effect: *effetto,* I 166, I 167, III 16, III 209, IV 7, IV 13, V 152, VI 72, VI 177, VII 201
effeminate: *effeminato,* pr. 2, I 249
effort: *fatica,* pr. 12, II 171; *see also* exert; exhaust; fatigue; tiresome; toil; trouble;
    effort: *sforzo,* VII 32; *see also* force
elephants: *liofanti,* III 160, IV 25, IV 38, IV 41 (2X), IV 50, IV 59, IV 91
eliminate: *spegnere, spenso,* I 211, VI 191. *See also* extinguish
embankment: *argine,* II 98, II 108, III 112, III 114, VI 69, VI 79, VI 85, VI 87, VI 104, VII
    63, VII 64, VII 133, VII 136
empire: *imperio,* pr. 8, pr. 12, I 87, I 89, I 90, I 129, I 255, I 256, I 257 (2X), I 303, I 304, I
    305, I 306, IV 1, IV 74, VI 118. *See also* rule

employ: *adoperare,** I 97. *See also* work

encamp: *alloggiare,* II 103, II 104, III 44, IV 119, V 42, V 136 (2X), VI 8, VI 9, VI 14 (2X), VI 16, VI 18, VI 20 (3X), VI 23, VI 24, VI 25, VI 26, VI 28, VI 31, VI 33, VI 37 (2X), VI 39, VI 40, VI 41, VI 42, VI 43, VI 46, VI 47, VI 48, VI 49, VI 50 (2X), VI 52, VI 57, VI 61, VI 62 (3X), VI 64, VI 65, VI 66 (2X),VI 67, VI 69, VI 81, VI 94, VI 107, VI 108, VI 138, VI 144, VI 156, VI 157, VI 166, VI 238; **encamp:** *accampare,* IV 116, VII 65; **encamp:** *andare a campo,* VII 136; **encamp:** *essere a campo,* VII 84; **encampment:** *alloggiamento,* figs. 1, figs. 11, II 265, II 326, III 64, III 123, III 163, IV 103, IV 120, IV 131, V 145, VI 11, VI 15, VI 16, VI 24, VI 26, VI 28, VI 29, VI 30 (4X), VI 31 (3X), VI 32, VI 33 (3X), VI 34, VI 37 (2X), VI 38 (2X), VI 39, VI 40 (2X), VI 41 (3X), VI 42 (2X), VI 43, VI 44, VI 45, VI 47 (2X), VI 48, VI 49, VI 50 (2X), VI 51, VI 52, VI 53, VI 54, VI 55, VI 56 (4X), VI 57 (2X), VI 58 (4X), VI 59, VI 60, VI 61 (4X), VI 63 (2X), VI 64 (2X), VI 65 (3X), VI 66 (3X), VI 67, VI 68, VI 71, VI 73, VI 77, VI 79, VI 80, VI 82 (2X), VI 83, VI 88, VI 89, VI 92, VI 94, VI 95, VI 97,VI 104, VI 108, VI 110, VI 113, VI 116, VI 137, VI 145, VI 148, VI 156, VI 158,VI 159, VI 166, VI 171, VI 172, VI 183, VI 212, VI 214 (3X), VI 217, VI 222, VII 113, VII 146, VII 147, VII 148 (2X), VII 151, VII 170, VII 215. *See also* lodge

end (v.): *capitare,* V 63; **end** (v.): *terminare,* IV 134; **end** (n.): *fine,* I 76, II 79, II 104, II 328, VI 166, VI 236, VII 32; **end** (n.): *punta,* VI 63, VII 60; **end** (n.): *termine,* III 181, IV 34; *see also* limits; means; terms; purpose, ultimate; **end** (n.): *testa,* VI 47; *see also* beginning; front; head

engage*: *affrontare,* III 11. *See also* attack

enroll: *descrivere, descritto,* I 147, I 236, I 253, II 133. *See also* conscript; describe; design

enterprise: *impresa,* I 231, IV 57, IV 142, V 83, V 92, VI 169, VI 170, VII 31, VII 151, VII 250. *See also* campaign; undertaking

equal: *pari,** pr. 13, I 216, II 319, III 205; *see also* peers; **equal:** *equale,* III 181, IV 32; **equal:** *uguale,* V 48; **equally:** *equalmente,* III 70, V 11; **equally:** *parimente,* VII 54; **equally:** *ugualmente,* VII 54

era: *secolo,* I 24

error: *errore,* I 11 (2X), I 119, I 188, I 225, II 128, III 175, IV 141, VI 114, VI 122, VI 197, VI 237, VII 238; **err:** *errare,* I 110, II 277, II 327, III 178, VII 52

evil: *male,* I 26, II 308, IV 141, VI 118, VI 220; **evil:** *malvagio,* I 186, I 258. *See also* bad; malicious; wicked

exalt: *esaltare,* II 301; **exalter:** *esaltatore,* VII 195

example: *esemplo, esempio,* I 30, I 124, I 164, I 188, I 255, I 258, II 33, II 45, II 61, II 268, II 310, II 312, II 313, II 314, III 30, III 31, III 76, III 122, III 130, III 173, III 178, III 179, IV 26, IV 132, V 141, VI 123, VI 225, VI 229, VII 27, VII 43, VII 59, VII 95, VII 230; **example, use as an:** *esemplificare sopra,* I 108; **for example:** *verbigrazie,* I 223, I 229. *See also* for instance

excellent: *eccellente,* I 36, I 63, II 171, II 285, II 287, II 290, II 291, II 293, II 299, II 306, IV 26, IV 138, VI 82, VII 82, VII 239; **very excellent:** *eccellentissimi,* II 295; **excellence:** *eccellenza,* VII 207; **Excellency:** *eccelenza,* I 9 excuse, excused (v.): *scusare, escusati,* I 20 (2X), I 23 (2X), I 29, I 259, I 260, VI 6; excuse (n.): *scusa,* I 38, I 42

execute: *esequire,* I 112, III 5, III 61, III 63, V 68, VI 168, VII 158, VII 246; executor: *esecutore,* VI 112; executioner: *esecutore,* VI 121; execution: *esecutione,* I 118

exercise: *esercitare, esercizio,* I 6, I 64 (2X), II 159 (2X), II 169, II 175, II 258, II 320, VI 147. *See also* career; drill; practice; training

exert oneself: *affaticarsi,* V 68, VII 195; exertion: *fatica,* II 261. *See also* effort; exhaust; fatigue; force; tiresome; toil; trouble

exhaust (v.): *affaticare,* II 127, II 171, V 83. *See also* effort; exert; fatigue; force; tiresome; toil; trouble

expand: *ampliare,* I 182

experience (n.): *esperienza,* I 165, I 200, I 202, I 206, I 217, I 224 (3X), II 32, II 93, II 130, IV 16, VII 72; experienced (v.): *esperimentato,* I 217; *see also* test; inexperience: *inesperienza,* I 165 (2X); inexperienced: *inesperto,* I 161

experiment: *esperienza,* II 95

extrinsic: *estrinseche,* V 117

extinguish: *spegnere, spento,* II 293, II 302, II 303, II 304, IV 139, VII 43. *See also* eliminate; spend

extraordinary: *estraordinario,* II 150 (2X), II 153 (2X), II 156 (2X), II 255 (2X), III 49, III 56, III 57 (2X), III 60, III 61, III 62, III 69, III 81, III 91, III 153, III 164, III 171, III 186, III 192, III 205 (2X), III 211, III 220, III 224, V 17, V 19, V 46, V 56, VI 62 (4X), VI 66, VI 67, VI 73, VII 80

extreme: *estremo,* III 52, III 54, VI 30; extremity: *estremità,* VI 30

faith: *fede,* pr. 5, VI 169, VI 178 (2X), VI 225, VI 227; *see also* believability; faith: *fedele,* IV 64; faithful: *fedele,* pr. 5, IV 111, VII 162; most faithful: *fidatissimi,* IV 70; *see also* confidence; trust; vouch

fame: *fama,* I 63, I 65, II 111, VI 117

fancy: *fantasia,* VI 7

father: *padre,* I 56, I 58, I 101, I 129, IV 120, IV 146, VI 229, VII 204

fatherland: *patria,* pr. 5, I 1, I 2, I 17, I 67, I 180, VI 117. *See also* country

fatigue (n.): *fatica,* II 40, II 254, IV 112. *See also* effort; exert; exhaust; tiresome; toil; trouble

fault: *colpa,* V 64. *See also* blame; culpable

favor (v.): *favorire,* II 290, IV 98, VI 121, VI 122, VII 116; *see also* protect; favor (n.): *favore,* VII 247; favor (n.): *grazia,* VI 57, VII 236; favorable: *favorevole,* pr. 2; to be unfavorable: *disfavorire,* IV 20. *See also* disadvantage

fear (n.): *paura,* II 307, III 134, IV 3, IV 65, VI 203, VI 207, VII 72, VII 103, VII 111, VII 156; fear (n.): *sbigotto,* III 134; fear (n.): *timore,* pr. 3, pr. 5, pr. 7, I 175, I 185, II 118, II 141, II 294, II 306, III 134, IV 139, V 120, VI 111, VI 123, VII 153, VII 175; fear (v.): *dubitare,* I 171, II 98, IV 34, IV 78, VI 170 (3X), VI 197; *see also* doubt; fear (v.): *avere paura,* V 39; fear (v.): *temere,* I 26, I 67, I 81, I 82, I 98, I 160, I 167, I 174, I 175,

I 176, I 186, I 246, I 257, II 10, II 70, II 100, II 120, II 293, II 308, II 309 (2X), II 314 (2X) III 134, III 143, III 147, III 148, III 188, IV 70, IV 81, IV 108, IV 141, IV 142, IV 147, V 1, V 12, V 66, V 115, V 117, V 151, VI 85, VI 115, VI 116, VI 125, VI 227, VII 216, VII 238; *see also* frighten; afraid

felicity: *felicità,* I 6. *See also* happy

ferocious: *feroce,* I 246, II 141, VII 119; **ferocity:** *ferocia,* I 249, II 141

fierce: *fiere,* VII 232

fight (v.): *azzuffare,* III 30, IV 115, VI 10; **fight** (v.): *combattere,* I 115, I 181, I 183 (2X), I 184, II 5, II 10, II 29, II 42, II 43, II 49, II 52, II 56, II 57, II 83, II 84, II 96 (2X), II 104, II 120, II 123, II 140, II 165, II 166, II 167, II 170, II 171 (2X), II 221, II 226, II 254 (2X), II 259, II 299, III 19, III 23, III 24, III 44, III 67, III 68, III 83, III 93, III 158, III 175, III 182 (2X), III 183, III 189, III 195 (2X), III 216, IV 29 (2X), IV 33, IV 37, IV 38, IV 55, IV 63, IV 68, IV 70, IV 71, IV 83, IV 86, IV 97, IV 98, IV 103, IV 109, IV 118, IV 126, IV 127, IV 128, IV 130, IV 131, IV 133 (2X), IV 135, IV 148, V 13, V 20 (2X), V 25, V 66, V 128, V 136, VI 9, VI 22, VI 96, VI 113 (2X), VI 116 (2X), VI 146, VI 157, VI 195, VI 212, VI 216, VI 223, VII 49, VII 48, VII 66, VII 74, VII 89, VII 205; **fight** (n.): *combattere,* II 83, II 103, II 268, III 66, III 68, III 75, III 156, IV 35, IV 36, IV 39, IV 42, IV 62, IV 99, IV 133, IV 145; **fight** (n.): *assalto,* II 327; **fighting:** *zuffa,* V 13; **fight** (n.): *zuffa,* II 37, II 79, III 11, III 13, III 16, III 17, III 18, III 33, III 35, III 37, III 92, III 136, IV 51, IV 52, IV 56, IV 58, IV 62, IV 63, IV 72, IV 94, IV 108, IV 109, IV 130, IV 133, IV 134, V 13, VI 1, VI 10, VI 148, VI 166, VI 186, VI 212, VII 166, VII 175, VII 176. *Cf.* combatants

fit (adj.): *atto,* I 147, II 103, II 107, II 108, II 110, II 115, II 134, III 5, III 63, III 98, III 218 (2X), IV 57, IV 111, V 78, V 110, V 144, V 148, VII 136, VII 228; *see also* action; apt; **fit** (adj.): *idoneo,* I 213; **fit** (v.): *convenire,* pr. 2, III 210; **fit** (adj.): *sufficiente,* I 198; **fitting:** *conveniente,* pr. 2, III 210; *see also* convenient; agreement

flee: *fuggire,* pr. 9, I 12, I 78, I 86, I 141, II 96, II 111, II 308, III 36, III 95, III 96 (2X), III 139, III 156, III 160, III 230, IV 15, IV 39, IV 61, IV 66, IV 68, IV 69 (2X), IV 70 (2X), IV 81, IV 83, IV 116, IV 117, IV 118, IV 119 (2X), IV 123, IV 124, IV 125, IV 134, IV 139, V 73 (2X), V 74, V 122, V 159, VI 119, VI 140 (2X), VI 144, VI 152, VI 195, VI 212, VI 223 (2X), VI 244, VI 248, VII 90, VII 112, VII 162, VII 194; *see also* take refuge; **flee to, to:** *alla fuga,* VII 226; **flee:** *volgere,* IV 135

follow: *seguire,* pr. 8, I 27, II 79, II 107, II 140, II 170, II 232, II 298, II 302, III 5, III 144, III 206, III 220, IV 2, IV 33 (2X), IV 62, IV 74, IV 75, IV 80, IV 102, V 4, V 6, V 87, V 101 (2X), V 122, V 143, VI 6, VI 8, VI 33, VI 37, VI 42, VI 206, VI 214 (2X), VI 223, VI 224, VII 8; **follow:** *conseguire,* VI 233; **follow:** *succedere,* II 166, II 167, III 13, III 37, **followers:** *sussidi,* II 165. *See also* succeed

for instance*: *verbigrazie,* II 207, II 220, III 204. *See also* example

force (v.): *forzare, sforzare, fare forza,* I 62 (2X), I 83, I 131, I 166, III 18, III 195 (2X), IV 87, V 105, V 151, V 156, VII 74, VII 78, VII 88; **force** (n.): *forza, sforzo,* I 161 (2X), I 165 (2X), I 166 (2X), I 167 (2X), I 231, II 18, II 92, III 43, III 70, III 154, IV 71, IV 87, IV 105, IV 137, V 63, V 151, VI 101, VI 160, VI 163, VI 184, VI 185, VI 186, VI 187, VI

194, VI 195 (2X), VI 196 (2X), VI 220, VI 247, VII 72, VII 135, VII 146 (2X), VII 148, VII 162, VII 164. *See also* effort

foreign: *forestiero,* I 173, I 175, II 47, VI 19, VI 25, VII 210, VII 226; **foreigner:** *forestiero,* I 173, I 175, I 246, II 78, VI 57, VII 234

form: *forma,* pr. 10, I 136, I 189, II 160, II 164, II 181, II 182, II 183, II 191, II 193, II 225, II 253, II 328, III 66, III 75 (2X), III 172, III 173, III 174, III 181, III 199, IV 8, IV 11 (2X), IV 59, IV 85, IV 86 (2X), V 12, V 13, V 43 (2X), V 49, V 66 (2X), V 69, V 90, VI 10, VI 15, VI 16 (2X), VI 24, VI 82, VI 84, VI 138, VII 41, VII 134, VII 224, VII 234, VII 241; **form** (v.): *formare,* II 188

fortress: *fortezza,* I 95, I 97, VII 28, VII 31, VII 140. *See also* strength; *Cf.* castle; citadel; stronghold

fortune: *fortuna,* I 6 (2X), I 7, I 67, II 298, II 313 (2X), III 12, III 20, III 163, IV 1, IV 34, IV 98, VII 151, VII 157, VII 241, VII 250; **fortune:** *ventura,* I 53, V 65. *Cf.* perhaps

found (v.): *fondare,* I 15, I 32, II 146, III 174, VI 221, VII 37; **foundation:** *fondamento,* I 189, II 79, VII 244

fraud: *fraude,* VII 236; **fraudulent:** *fraudolento,* I 52

free (adj.): *libero,* I 172 (2X), I 210, II 10, III 84, III 135, III 159, III 166, V 8, V 155, VI 207, VII 70; **free** (v.): *liberare,* II 98, II 307, V 152, VI 184, VI 185; **freely:** *liberamente, libero,* I 3, I 89, II 29, VI 233. *Cf.* liberty

frighten: *fare paura,* pr. 2; **frighten:** *sbigottire,* I 2, I 28, III 148, IV 52 (2X), IV 63 (2X), IV 64, IV 65, IV 127, VII 149, VII 162. *See also* afraid; fear

front: *testa,* II 197 (2X), II 199, II 200, II 221, III 91, V 8, V 9, V 15 (3X), V 18 (2X), V 19, V 25, V 32, V 48, V 54 (2X), V 55, V 56, V 59, V 60, V 66 (2X), V 71, V 75, VI 28, VI 30, VI 33, VI 58, VI 59, VI 60, VI 63, VI 72; *see also* head; **front:** *fronte,* II 10, II 70, II 164, II 182, II 186, II 187, II 191 (2X), II 197, II 214 (2X), II 215, II 221, II 242, II 249, III 12, III 14, III 34 (2X), III 51, III 65, III 66, III 99, III 129, III 130, III 162, III 171, III 177, III 180, III 189, III 203, IV 12, IV 14, IV 19, IV 22, IV 32 (2X), IV 35, IV 38, IV 41, IV 61, IV 85, IV 91, IV 92, V 8, V 16, V 18, V 21 (2X), V 35 (2X), V 49, V 50, V 53, V 75, VII 4, VII 163 (2X); **front:** *dinanzi,* II 21, II 187, III 189; **front:** *davanti,* II 187, II 226, III 24, III 189, V 16, V 17, V 18, V 30, VII 12; **front:** *innanzi,* II 197, IV 39, IV 68 (2X), IV 82, V 114, VI 85, VII 6

future: *avvenire,* VI 5

gain (v.): *guadagnare,* I 165, V 102, VII 224 (2X), VII 225; *see also* profit; **regain:** *riguadagnare,* IV 71

general (n.): *generale,* II 154, III 61, III 63, III 200, III 204, III 209, III 218, V 19, V 35, VI 57; **general** (adj.): *generale,* III 134, III 160, IV 87, V 73, VII 153; **general** (adj.): *universale,* II 164; **generally:** *generalmente,* III 220, VI 129, VII 67, VII 181; **generality:** *generalità,* III 174, IV 14, V 29

generate: *generare,* I 121, I 254, II 280, VI 207. *Cf.* kind

gentlemen: *gentili,* I 9, I 93, I 94

girl: *fanciulla,* IV 146, VI 229. *Cf.* children; son; young

glory, glorious: *gloria, glorioso,* I 9, I 63, I 65, I 71 (2X), I 75, I 187, VI 117, VI 167, VII 250

God: *Iddio,* pr. 3, pr. 5, pr. 7, IV 143, IV 145, IV 146, VI 125 (2X), VII 210, VII 223; **God:** *Dio,* IV 141; **gods:** *dii,* I 63

gold: *oro,* pr. 4, I 27, II 118, VII 236

goodness: *bontà,* I 195, I 200, I 229

govern: *governare,* I 76, I 93, I 108, I 110, I 158, I 250, II 165, II 312, II 313, V 10, V 91, V 93, VI 5, VI 46 (2X), VII 208, VII 236; **governance:** *governo,* II 326; **government:** *governo,* I 186 (2X), I 254 (2X), I 256

grace: *grazia,* I 203. *See also* favor

grandfather: *avolo,* I 15, I 23

grateful: *grato,* pr. 13, I 22. *See also* agree

grate (n.): *graticco,* V 149

grating: *graticola,* VII 41, VII 48, VII 49, VII 60; **with grating:** *ingraticolata,* VII 61

gratifying, very: *gratissimo,* III 3, VI 7. *Cf.* grateful; favor; agree

grave: *gravo,* I 35, I 100, I 240, II 51, IV 99, VII 195; **gravity:** *gravità,* III 214. *See also* heavy

greed: *cupidità,* V 97; **greedy:** *cupido,* V 97

ground: *terra,* II 5, II 52, II 57, II 114, III 130, IV 50, IV 92; **ground:** *terreno,* III 51, VII 64. *See also* country; earth; land; soil; town

guard: *guardare, guardia,* I 95, I 97 (2X), I 98 (2X), II 100, II 322, III 56, III 111, III 152, IV 115, V 20, V 21, V 22, V 23, V 41, V 109, V 110, V 120, V 130, V 154 (2X), VI 91 (2X), VI 92, VI 98, VI 99 (2X), VI 101, VI 104, VI 106, VI 113, VI 171, VI 193, VII 19, VII 21, VII 86, VII 96, VII 98, VII 102, VII 103, VII 104, VII 105 (2X), VII 109, VII 111, VII 117 (2X), VII 119, VII 121 (2X), VII 122, VII 144, VII 145, VII 146; **rearguard:** *retroguardo,* III 163; **vanguard:** *antiguardo,* I 163

habit: *abito,** III 83; **habit:** *consueto,* IV 37; *see also* accustomed; **habit:** *consuetudine,* VI 221

habituate: *avvezzare,* II 40. *See also* used to

half: *metà,* II 69 (2X), III 62, VII 59 (2X); *see also* middle; **half:** *mezzo,* II 6, II 151 (2X), III 166 (2X), III 167, III 168 (2X), IV 101, VI 45 (2X), VI 50 (2X), VII 45, VII 57; *see also* means; midday; route; degree

happy: *felice,* I 34; **happier:** *felice,* II 118; **very happily:** *felicissimamente,* III 97; **happiness:** *felicità,* I 187, III 98. *See also* felicity

harm (v.): *offendere, fare offensione,* I 6, II 11, I 77, III 81 (2X), III 112, III 115, III 116, III 148, V 111, V 113, VI 169, VII 11, VII 64; **harm** (v.): *nuocere,* I 250, III 134; **harm** (n.): *danno,* pr.11, I 86, I 100, I 171, I 227, I 240, II 51, II 84, III 24, III 131, III 134, V 83, V 40, V 64, VI 167, VI 217, VI 242, VI 243, VII 95, VII 96; **harmful:** *dannoso,* I 89, I 255, IV 79

hate (v.): *odiare,* pr. 9; **hateful:** *odiozo,* VII 162

head: *capo,* I 26, I 48, I 53, I 55, I 106 (2X), I 171, I 245, I 246 (2X), I 247 (2X), I 248 (2X),

I 249, I 250, I 251, I 253, I 254, I 266, II 4, II 20, II 27, II 39, II 60, II 152, II 154, II 156, II 163, II 190, II 225, II 241, II 262, II 266, II 269, II 309, II 311, II 323, III 21, III 49, III 61, III 69, III 73, III 109, III 199, III 200, III 204 (4X), III 205, III 206, III 219, IV 65, IV 81, IV 136, V 35 (2X), V 36, V 52 (2X), V 120, V 124, V 159, VI 33, VI 34, VI 37 (2X), VI 39, VI 41, VI 44, VI 47, VI 57, VI 68, VI 109, VI 200, VI 228, VII 232; **head:** *testa,* II 114, II 186, II 187, II 193, II 209, II 221 (2X), II 222, II 224 (2X), II 225, II 226, II 239, II 240, III 15, III 21, III 23, III 56, III 57, III 61, III 63, III 81, III 131 (2X), III 165, V 100, VI 33; *see also* front; **head-to-head:** *attestati,* IV 35; **capitol:** *capo,* VII 105

healthy: *sano,* VI 139, VI 144, VI 147, VI 148

heart: *cuore,* II 268; **heart:** *animo,* III 102; *see also* spirit

heaven: *cielo,* I 182, VI 26

hesitate: *dubitare,* pr. 1; **hesitation:** *rispetto,* I 171. *See also* to be afraid; doubt; fear

hide: *nascondere,* III 92, IV 57, IV 83, V 114, V 142, VI 170, VII 14, VII 123 (2X), VII 158. *See also* conceal

hire: *soldare,* I 131**history:** *istoria,* I 164, II 13, II 24, II 46, II 70, III 230. *Cf.* soldier

hit*: *ferire,* IV 19; **hit:** *offendere,* VII 11

hole: *fossa,* I 141. *See also* ditch

holiday: *giorno ozioso,* I 227, II 125, II 134. *See also* calm; idle

honest: *onesto, onestà,* I 205, VII 207; **honestly:** *onestamente,* I 51; **dishonest:** *disonesto,* I 205

honor (v): *onorare,* pr. 13, I 6, I 12, I 33, I 118, I 120, II 293, II 294, II 298, II 306, II 314, III 204, VII 191; **honor** (n.): *onore,* I 12, I 119, II 104, III 204, IV 3, VII 32, VII 151, VII 191, VII 193; **honorable, honorably:** *onorevole, onorevolmente,* I 12, I 56, I 62, I 63, IV 1, VI 155; **unhonored:** *inonorato,* I 4

hope (v.): *sperare,* I 10, I 68, I 112, II 328, V 117, VI 118, VI 240, VII 155, VII 156; **hope:** *speranza,* IV 139, IV 148, V 120, VII 26, VII 72, VII 173; **unhoped for:** *insperato,* I 106

horse: *cavallo,* I 268, I 269, II 52, II 78, II 90, II 91, II 94, II 95, II 99, II 325, IV 114, IV 204, VII 62 (2X), VII 187 (3X). **horses:** *cavagli,* II 29 (2X), II 75, II 96, II 97 (2X), II 98, II 129, II 325, II 326, IV 130, IV 132, V 87, V 154, V 155, VI 46, VII 169 (2X), VII 185, VII 187, VII 189. *See also* cavalry; mare

human: *umano,* II 290, IV 139, VI 212; **humanity:** *umanità,* VI 233, VII 116. *See also* humane

humane: *umano,* I 29. *See also* human

hunger: *fame,* IV 97, VI 144, VI 149, VI 151, VI 152, VI 212, VII 78, VII 79, VII 81, VII 150, VII 157

hurt: *nuocere,* VII 154 (2X); **hurt:** *offendere,* III 115, III 116, III 160, IV 16, IV 18, IV 78, VI 244, VII 117; **hurt:** *urtare,* II 109

husband: *marito,* VI 229

idle, in idleness: *ozio, ozioso,* pr. 10, I 129, I 227, II 291, VI 124, VII 148, VII 236, VII 244. *See also* calm; holiday

ignominy, ignominious, ignominiously: *ignominia, ignomioso, ignominiosamante,* IV 119, VI 119, VII 230

ignorance: *ignoranza,* I 258, IV 99, VII 230

image: *immagine,* IV 144; **imagine:** *immaginare,* III 77, VII 196

imitate, imitation, imitator: *imitare, imitatore, imitazione,* pr. 8, I 28, I 35, I 266, II 33, II 323, II 326, III 10, III 76, III 134, III 140 (2X), IV 74, V 10, V 141, VI 1, VI 18, VI 95, VI 164, VI 211, VII 195 (2X), VII 198

impetus: *foga,* II 94, II 95, II 99; **impetus:** *impeto,* IV 41, IV 50, IV 75, VI 224

impregnable: *inespugnabile,* VII 15. *Cf.* besiege; storm

inconvenience: *incommodità,* II 40, VI 244; **inconvenience, inconvenient:** *inconveniente,* I 100, I 102, I 166, II 10, III 36, V 100, VII 7, VII 70

indignant, make: *fare sdegnare,* IV 133; *see also* disdain; despise; disparage; **indignant:** *indegnato,* IV 133

individual, one: *uno,* II 207, II 267, II 280, VI 121, VI 122, VI 173, VI 174, VI 176; **individual, an:** *uno,* I 25, I 26, I 124, I 171; **individual, each:** *ciascuno,* II 96

indulgence: *perdonanza,* VI 227. *Cf.* pardon

industry: *industria,* I 118, I 124, II 125, II 171, IV 79, V 91, V 107, VI 12, VI 17, VI 126, VI 197, VI 239, VI 248, VII 1, VII 3, VII 4, VII 160; **industriousness:** *industria,* I 39

inequality: *inequalità,* III 132

infantries, infantry: *fanteria, fanterie,* I 82, I 83, I 91, I 96, I 230, II 2, II 19, II 27, II 30, II 42 (2X), II 43, II 46, II 49, II 55, II 59, II 62, II 65, II 66 (2X), II 67, II 71 (2X), II 72, II 75, II 78, II 101 (2X), II 137, II 151, II 319, III 88, III 131 (2X), VI 38, VI 78, VII 186; **infantryman, infantrymen:** *fante, fanti, fanterie,* figs. 2, figs. 3 (2X), I 83, I 93, I 95, I 131, I 229, I 272, II 22, II 26, II 36, II 42, II 44, II 51, II 62, II 63, II 66 (2X), II 67, II 70 (2X), II 75, II 76, II 80, II 86, II 87, II 88 (2X), II 89, II 91, II 93, II 97, II 137, II 148, II 149, II 150, II 156, II 176, II 193 (2X), II 200, II 206, II 212, II 228, II 242, II 276, II 319, II 324, III 15, III 19, III 35, III 37, III 40, III 41 (3X), III 42, III 45 (2X), III 49, III 66, III 81, III 90, III 131 (2X), III 132, III 140, III 142, III 152, III 178, IV 30, IV 37, IV 111, IV 141, V 126, V 138, VI 19 (2X), VI 21 (2X), VI 25, VI 42, VI 43, VI 45, VI 46, VI 47, VI 50, VI 62, VI 64 (2X), VI 65, VI 66, VI 158, VII 172 (2X)

infinite: *infinito,* pr. 7, I 237, II 286, IV 139, VII 130

inhabit: *abitare,* I 177, VI 178; **inhabitants:** *abitatori,* II 84, II 305, VI 141; **inhabitants:** *abitanti,* II 131, II 133. *See also* live

injury: *ingiuria,* III 86

insolence: *insolenza,* I 89 (2X), I 98; **insolence, acts of:** *insolenze,* VII 214; **insolent:** *insolente,* I 104, VI 206

inspirit: *inanimare,* III 85. *See also* spirited

institute (v.): *costituire,* VII 123

intent: *intento,* VI 186; **intention:** *intenzione,* I 35, I 208, II 254, VI 81, VII 181. *See also* think interpret: *interpretare,* V 72, V 73, VI 207 (2X), VI 208

judge (v.): *giudicare,* pr. 2, pr. 10, I 12, I 35, I 36, I 52, I 88, I 140, I 188, I 224, II 75, II 212, II 229, III 26, III 126, III 137, III 189, III 214, IV 85, V 128, VI 100, VI 122, VII 181, VII 182; judge (n.): *giudice,* VI 123, VII 196; judgment: *giudicio,* pr. 12, I 12, I 22, I 35, III 141, VII 7, VII 211

just: *giusto,* * VII 230; justice: *giustizia,* I 62, VI 122, VI 149, VI 229; justice: *giusto,* * VI 230; justify: *giustificare,* I 157; justification: *giustificazione,* VII 198

kill: *ammazzare,* II 52, II 305, II 307, III 92, IV 49, IV 65, IV 70, VI 119, VI 120, VII 14, VII 111, VII 122, VII 162; killed, to be: *morire,* I 59, II 57, III 91, IV 64, IV 69, IV 77, VI 114, VI 116, VI 217, VII 81, VII 88, VII 101. *See also* death; die

kind: *generazione,* II 24, II 131, III 30, IV 38, VII 49; kind: *genere,* VI 71; kind: *ragioni,* I 142, VII 201; kind: *sorte,* II 183

king: *re,* I 9, I 58, I 77 (2X), I 78, I 80, I 82, I 83, I 91, I 104, I 107, I 109, I 110, I 159 (2X), I 188, I 190, II 17, II 33, II 76, II 158, II 287, II 309, III 216, IV 120, IV 122, IV 146, VI 162, VI 163, VII 25, VII 27, VII 31, VII 44, VII 204, VII 232; kingdom: *regno,* pr. 5, I 15, I 51, I 58, I 59, I 64, I 78, I 89 (2X), I 80, I 82, I 83, I 122, I 177, I 188, I 255 (2X), II 62, II 139, II 286, II 291, II 293 (2X), II 295, II 310, VII 244

knowledge: *notizia,* I 14, VII 109, VII 184; knowledge: *scienza,* V 108; knowledge: *sapere,* VII 72; knowledgeable: *sapiente,* I 8; knowledgeable: *consapevole,* VI 107; known, let it be: *dire voce,* VI 195; *see also* voice

lance: *lancia,* II 26, III 23 (2X), VII 49, VII 192

land: *terra,* I 180, I 181 (2X), I 183 (3X), I 184 (2X), I 185, I 194, I 196, II 127, V 63, VII 183, VII 194. *See also* country; earth; ground; town; *Cf.* bury

language: *lingua,* II 144, VII 229

lasciviousness, acts of: *lascivie,* VII 214; lascivious ones: *lascivie,* VII 236

laudable: *lodevole,* I 205. *See also* praiseworthy

lauded: *lodato,* IV 38. *See also* praise

laugh: *ridere,* III 126

law: *legge,* pr. 3, pr. 8, I 67, I 98, I 171, I 246, II 105, II 261, VI 112, VI 125 (2X)

lawgiver: *datore di legge,* I 179

legion: *legione,* I 86, I 206, I 212 (2X), I 213, I 214 (3X), I 215, I 216, I 262, II 143, II 147, III 14, III 25, III 26, III 29, III 30, III 31, III 32, III 40, III 41, III 44, III 46, III 47, III 48, III 66, III 75, III 178, IV 28 (2X), IV 41, IV 68, V 6 (2X), V 101, V 102, V 142, V 143, VI 19 (3X), VI 21, VI 114, VI 133, VI 195 (2X); legionary (a.): *legionario,* III 45; legionary (n.): *legionario,* V 101

levy (n.), *deletto,* I 120 (2X), I 125 (2X), I 126, I 127, I 128 (2X), I 130, I 131, I 140, I 147, I 166, I 191, I 206 (2X), I 207, I 208, I 209, I 212, I 214, I 217 (2X), I 218, I 220, I 223, I 225, I 259, I 260, I 261

liberal: *liberale,* VII 247; liberality: *liberalità,* pr. 13 (2X), I 10, VII 116

liberty: *libertà,* I 56, I 159, II 301. *Cf.* free

limits: *termini*, II 81, II 212, V 106, VI 81. *See also* end; means

life: *vita*, pr. 1, pr. 8, I 8, I 24, I 26, I 29, I 31, I 57, I 68, I 209, I 225, II 268, II 275, II 305, III 26, IV 134, IV 139, VI 116, VII 239. *See also* live

live: *abitare*, VII 34, VII 129; live: *vivere*, pr. 3, I 33, I 48, I 51, I 56, I 62, I 65, I 67 (2X), I 71, I 82, I 83, I 91, I 92, I 104, I 105, II 29, II 139, II 262, II 310, V 88, VI 70, VI 205, VII 66, VII 239; living: *il vivere*, I 53, VI 70, VII 168, VII 180; living, form/ mode of: *forma/modo del/di vivere*, I 28, I 29 (2X), II 305, V 83, V 90, VII 241. *See also* life

lively: *vivo*, I 204. *See also* alive

lodge: *alloggiare*, II 268, II 324, IV 133, VI 134, VI 141. *See also* encampment

Lord: *signore*, I 8, III 77, IV 5, VI 6; lord: *signore*, I 8, I 94, I 137, II 314, III 4, III 209, V 95, VI 1, VII 29, VII 30, VII 35, VII 244; lord, to be: *signoreggiare*, II 313 (2X)

lot, by: *a sorte,** I 214

Love: *Venere*, VI 129; love (n.): *amore*, pr. 6, I 91, IV 134, IV 149, IV 151; love (v.): *amare*, pr. 3, I 11, I 26, I 33, I 108, VII 216; love (a.): *amoroso*, I 6; to be in love: *innamorarsi*, I 6; lover: *amatore*, pr. 10, I 24, I 110 (2X)

magistracy: *magistrato*, I 206, I 212

magnanimous: *magnanimo*, VII 31

magnificent: *magnifico*, pr. 3

maintain: *mantenere*, pr. 2, pr. 3, I 171, I 249, II 30, II 123, II 140, II 171 (2X), II 270, II 304, II 314, III 210, V 69, V 86, V 124, VI 144, VI 147, VI 171, VI 206 (2X), VII 89, VII 173

malicious: *maligne*, VII 234; malignity: *malignita*, I 57, II 290, II 298; malice: *malizia*, I 86, I 141. *See also* bad; evil; wicked

man*: *uomo*, pr. 2, pr. 3, pr. 5 (2X), pr. 8, I 1, I 3 (2X), I 8, I 10, I 12, I 24, I 26, I 39, I 48, I 51 (2X), I 52, I 53, I 60, I 64, I 65, I 66, I 67, I 71, I 72, I 86 (2X), I 89, I 91, I 92, I 98, I 100, I 107, I 112, I 117, I 120, I 121, I 122, I 130, I 133, I 141, I 147, I 153, I 162, I 166, I 169, I 173, I 183 (2X), I 195, I 201, I 204, I 213, I 217, I 220 (2X), I 224, I 225, I 227 (3X), I 230, I 237, I 240, I 246 (2X), I 253, I 254, I 258, I 261, I 262, II 1, II 20, II 41, II 46, II 49, II 52, II 90, II 97, II 117, II 118, II 120, II 121, II 140, II 141 (2X), II 142 (3X), II 147 (3X), II 160 (3X), II 161, II 167, II 185, II 186, II 190, II 191 (2X), II 212, II 215, II 242, II 255, II 260, II 261, II 268, II 270, II 278, II 285, II 287, II 288, II 290, II 291 (2X), II 293 (2X), II 295, II 299, II 301, II 302 (2X), II 304, II 305, II 306, II 308 (2X), III 22, III 23, III 61, III 63, III 75, III 116, III 147, III 178, III 180 (2X), III 184, III 192, III 205, III 227, IV 78, IV 106, IV 111, IV 134, IV 141, V 19, V 32, VI 19, VI 27, VI 50, VI 82, VI 108 (2X), VI 116, VI 125 (3X), VI 162, VI 165, VI 168, VI 175, VI 187, VI 210, VI 226, VI 228, VII 10, VII 26, VII 39, VII 62 (2X), VII 74, VII 85, VII 111, VII 114, VII 115, VII 119, VII 160, VII 178 (3X), VII 187, VII 191 (2X), VII 195, VII 199, VII 207 (2X), VII 210, VII 223, VII 232, VII 234, VII 239, VII 240, VII 243; men: *gente, genti*, II 52, III 17, III 48, III 129, IV 13, IV 16, IV 28, IV 29, IV 121, VI 14, VI 153, VI 224, VII 135; *see also* people; man-at-arms, man-of-arms: *gente d'arme, uomo d'arme*, figs. 3, I 95, I 99 (2X), I 102, II 52, II 56, II 59, II 60, II 63, II 74, II 76, III 59, III 83, II 321, II

323, II 324, II 325 (2X), III 58, III 88, III 91 (2X), III 133, V 28, VI 33 (4X), VI 36, VI 37 (2X), VI 41. *See also* troops

manage: *maneggiare*, I 173, II 9, II 12, II 230, III 37, III 90, III 211 (2X), VI 79, VI 166, VII 201; **management:** *maneggio*, II 322

mares: *cavalle*, VII 187. *See also* cavalry; horse

marvel (v.): *maravigliare*, I 14, II 91, II 117, II 319, VI 186, VI 242; **marvelous:** *maraviglia*, VI 118

master: *maestro*, IV 130, IV 132; **master:** *padrone*, II 168, VI 46; **quartermaster:** *maestro di campi*, VI 57

matter: *materia*, I 10, I 130, II 140, II 318, VI 191, VI 235, VII 196, VII 224; **materials:** *materia*, Pr 11, I 114, I 173, III 8, IV 7, V 135, V 146, VI 8, VI 11, VI 231, VII 15

means: *termini*, I 36, I 50, I 211, V 117, VI 216, VII 82, VII 102; *see also* end; limit; **means:** *mezzo*, III 196; *see also* half; midday; route; degree

member: *membro*, I 68, I 203, II 262, II 311, IV 147, V 25, VII 29, VII 232

memory: *memoria*, I 7, I 8 (2X), I 54, III 49

mercy: *piatà*, I 53

merit: *meritare*, pr. 12, I 37, I 57, I 179, I 224, I 259, VI 118, VI 236, VII 32, VII 203 (2X). *See also* deservedly

midday: *mezzo dì*, V 126; **midday:** *mezzogiorno*, V 157. *See also* half; means; route; degree

middle: *mezzo*, I 58, I 167, II 12, II 182, II 222, II 224, II 232, III 44, III 52, III 56, III 61, III 159, III 177, III 182, III 203, IV 28 (2X), IV 29 (2X), IV 30, IV 56, IV 92, V 19, V 46, V 56, V 100, V 129, VI 3, VI 19, VI 54, VI 55, VI 56, VI 57, VI 61, VI 72 (2X), VI 133, VII 34, VII 35, VII 80, VII 215; *see also* degree; means; midday; route; **middle:** *metà*, VII 46; *see also* half

military (n.): *milizia*, pr. 5, pr. 9, I 41, I 57, I 89, I 129, I 144, I 147 (2X), I 163 (2X), I 166, I 208, I 210, I 217, I 218, I 229, I 236, II 78, II 83, II 84, II 85, II 142, II 144, II 314, II 319, II 323, II 329, III 10, IV 140, V 78, V 106, VII 181 (2X), VII 183 (2X), VII 187, VII 196, VII 199, VII 236; **military, to be in the:** *militare*, I 72 (3X), I 125, I 129 (2X), I 161, I 198, IV 141, VI 57, VI 167, VII 226; *see also* soldier; **military** (adj.): *militare*, pr. 1, pr. 4, pr. 8, pr. 9, I 8, I 33, I 47, I 147, I 189, I 209, I 210, I 212, II 125, II 272, II 294, II 306, II 308, V 68, VI 123, VI 239

militia: *ordinanza*, I 104, I 148, I 151, I 154, I 170, I 189, I 190, I 199 (2X), I 201, I 220, I 222, I 227, I 228, I 234, I 238, I 240 (2X), I 260, I 263, II 171, VII 242. *See also* order; *cf.* military

mind (n.): *mente*, I 12, I 49; **mind** (v.): *curare*, IV 88; *see also* care; **mind** (v.): *rincrescere*, VI 232

minister (n.): *ministro*, I 78, III 60, VI 88

misfortune: *sventura*, V 64

mix: *mescolare*, I 167, I 209, II 65, II 123, II 188, III 34, IV 142, VII 39; **mixture:** *mescolare*, I 206

mobile: *mobile*, VI 84

modern (a.): *moderno,* II 61, II 93, II 101, II 146, III 161, V 89, VI 154; **modern** (n.): *moderno,* III 137

monarchy: *monarchia,* I 178

money: *danari,* II 135, IV 97, V 95, VII 178 (3X); **money:** *soldo,* II 271, V 104, V 105

multitude: *moltitudine,* * I 242, III 29, IV 137, V 156, VI 13, VI 161, VII 85

music: *suono,* figs. 3, II 155, II 156, II 162, II 163, II 191, II 194, II 222, II 234, II 276 (2X), II 277, II 278, II 279, II 280 (2X), II 282, II 323, III 61, III 63, V 71, V 73, V 77, V 124; **music:** *musica,* II 277; **musician:** *suono,* II 156, II 269; **musical instrument:** *suono,* II 277, III 212, III 213 (2X), III 217, III 218 (2X), III 219, III 220

mutiny, in: *tumultuariamente,* I 55. *See also* tumult

name (v.): *nominare,* I 66, II 131, II 134, II 279, II 285, II 290 (2X), II 298, III 163; **name** (v.): *chiamare,* V 35; **name** (n.): *nome,* I 1, I 15, I 19, I 120 (2X), II 4, II 142, II 146, II 148, VI 21, VI 70, VI 230, VII 109, VII 162

narrate: *narrare,* VI 20, VI 38, VI 166, VII 181; **narration:** *narrazione,* VI 18. *See also* tell; relate

nation: *nazione,* II 33, II 142, III 34, III 217, VI 161

nature: *natura,* I 124 (2X), I 252, I 253, II 10, III 156, IV 151, VI 142, VII 1, VII 2, VII 14, VII 160, VII 246; **natural, naturally:** *naturale, naturalmente,* I 253, II 86, II 97, II 262, IV 3, VI 13, VI 161, VI 162 (3X), VI 208, VI 212, VI 217, VII 202, VII 226

necessary, necessity: *necessario, necessità, passim;* **necessitate:** *necessitare,* I 52, I 211, II 29, III 67, IV 39, IV 95, V 12, VI 244, VII 203

new: *nuovo,* I 144, I 178, I 192, I 199, I 206 (2X), I 209 (3X), II 125, II 169, II 171, II 203, II 213, IV 51, IV 52, IV 97, IV 140, VI 79 (2X), VI 105, VI 172, VI 186, VII 37 (2X), VII 107, VII 162, VII 166 (2X), VII 233; **anew:** *di nuovo,* I 192, I 201 (2X), I 218, III 67, III 201, VI 138, VI 234, VII 43. *Cf.* renew

nobility: *nobiltà,* pr. 13 (2X); **nobles:** *nobili,* VI 190

noise: *romore, rumore,* II 282, III 218, III 224, III 226, III 228, III 229, III 230, IV 59, IV 60 (2X), V 39, V 60, VII 118; **to make noise:** *romoreggiare,* III 230

number*: *numero,* I 96, I 97, I 98, I 130, I 131, I 220 (2X), I 221 (2X), I 222, I 223, I 228, I 230, I 237 (3X), I 239, I 240, I 270, II 32, II 142, II 149, II 160, II 176, II 190, II 199 (2X), II 210, II 211 (2X), II 290, II 323, III 41 (2X), III 116, III 180, III 181 (2X), III 201 (2X), III 202, III 203 (2X), III 204, III 208, IV 14 (2X), IV 16, IV 111, IV 126, V 11, V 35, V 78, V 119, V 143, VI 19, VI 51, VI 106, VI 156, VI 161, VI 164, VII 148; **number** (v.): *numerare, mettere nel numero,* I 29, III 202, VI 70

oath: *sacramento,* I 67; **oath:** *giuramento,* V 138. *Cf.* swear

obey: *obediscere, ubbidire,* I 159, II 88, II 140, II 166, II 199, II 277, II 281, II 309, III 73, III 200, IV 132, VI 15, VI 16, VI 168, VI 241; **obey:** *osservare,* IV 110, VII 121, VII 136; *see also* observe; **obedience:** *ubbidienza,* VI 162, VII 207, VII 215; **obedient:** *ubbidiente,* I 229

oblige, obligated: *obligare, obligato,* I 227, I 230, II 82, II 134, II 138, II 162, II 326, III 12, III 163, VI 46, VII 71, VII 210

observe: *osservare,* I 206, I 208 (2X), I 255, II 103, II 140, II 160, II 161, II 207, II 226, II 230, III 13, IV 23, IV 142, V 37, V 60, V 106, VI 16, VI 18, VI 20, VI 46, VI 84 (2X) VI 105, VI 107 (2X), VI 110, VI 111, VI 118, VI 119, VI 120, VI 124, VI 138, VI 150, VI 152, VI 154, VI 164, VI 242, VII 128, VII 155, VII 198, VII 218, VII 222; *see also* obey; **observe:** *notare,* III 35; **observance, observant:** *observante, osservanza,* V 99, VI 111, VI 125; *see also* attention

obstinate: *ostinato,* II 49, IV 134 (2X), IV 148; **obstinacy:** *ostinazione,* II 301, IV 139, IV 148, V 105, VI 163; **so obstinately:** *in tanto ostinato,* VII 151

offend, offence: *offendere, offesa,* I 16, I 248, II 6, II 14, II 15, II 26, II 55, III 125, III 152, III 154, IV 18, IV 21, IV 49, V 12, V 62, V 121, VI 80, VII 48, VII 90

office: *ufficio, uffizio,* I 212, II 28, II 191, II 259, II 260, II 269, III 35 (2X), III 56, III 82, III 156, IV 2, V 36, V 78, VI 1, VI 57

old: *vecchio,* I 192, I 199, I 206, I 209, II 169, II 202, II 213, VII 70, VII 162, VII 247; **old age:** *vecchiezza,* II 134. *Cf.* age; youth

operate: *operare,* I 139, VII 203. *See also* do; work

opinion: *opinione,* pr. 1, pr. 2, pr. 9, I 16, I 142, I 155, I 221, I 237, I 243, II 312, II 315, III 145, III 149, III 226, IV 57, IV 121, IV 137 (2X), VI 210, VII 19, VII 74. *See also* reputation

opportunity: *occasione,* I 10, I 12, I 39, I 40, I 41, I 43, I 44 (3X), I 112, I 257, II 126, IV 71, IV 77, IV 99, IV 102, IV 123, IV 127, VI 175 (2X), VI 183, VI 195, VII 113, VII 132, VII 159, VII 174, VII 195, VII 197, VII 247

oppress: *opprimere,* I 173, IV 77 (2X), VI 98, VI 168, VI 170, VI 200, VII 104, VII 114, VII 144

oracle: *oraculo,* VII 236

orators: *oratori,* IV 138. *See also* ambassador

order (n.): *ordine, passim;* **order** (v.): *ordinare, ordinato, passim;* **order:** *ordinanza,* V 125, VI 78. *See also* militia

ordinary: *ordinario,* pr. 2, I 36, II 27, II 125, II 148 (2X), II 149 (2X), II 152, II 156 (3X), II 188, II 216, II 258, III 40, III 49, III 60, III 92, III 204, IV 41, V 17, V 99, VI 40, VI 49, VI 50, VI 50, VI 94, VI 160, VII 37, VII 52, VII 127; **ordinarily:** *ordinariamente, per l'ordinario,* II 193, II 226, III 44, V 3, V 7, V 21, V 42, V 87, VI 85, VI 104, VII 57, VII 151

overcome*: *superare,* II 40, II 44, II 71, II 167, II 305, III 17, III 20, III 99, III 161, III 230, IV 25, IV 39, VI 151, VI 175, VII 74, VII 87, VII 147, VII 148, VII 203

palisade: *steccato,* VI 85, VI 86, VI 230, VII 148

pardon (v.): *perdonare,* VII 90. *Cf.* indulgence

partisan: *partigiano,* II 148

party: *parte,** I 248

passage*: *via,** III 159 (libera), V 32, VII 139. *See also* path; road; way

passion: *passione,* I 188, II 290, IV 139, VI 212

path: *via,** I 35. *See also* passage; road; way

peace: *pace*, pr. 6, I 17, I 52 (3X), I 53 (2X), I 56, I 61, I 67, I 75, I 81, I 83, I 91, I 93 (3X), I 94, I 95, I 96 (2X), I 97 (2X), I 98, I 99, I 104, I 105, I 106, I 107, I 108, I 109, I 110, I 236, I 248, II 164, VII 151; **peaceful:** *pacifico*, pr. 5

peers: *pari*, I 94. *See also* equal; even

penalty: *pena*, II 119, V 120, VII 230. *See also* punishment

people: *popolo, populare*, I 73, I 87, I 88, I 93, I 159, I 188, I 223, II 29 (2X), II 78, III 300, III 302, III 305, III 315, IV 78, VI 118, VI 122 (2X), VI 123, VI 168, VI 169, VI 178, VI 227 (2X), VI 229, VII 230; **people:** *gente*, V 78; *see also* men

perfect: *perfetto*, I 17, I 222, V 110, VI 8, VI 24 (2X), VII 225, VII 241; **perfection:** *perfezione*, I 170, III 110, VII 225; **perfectly:** *perfettamente*, I 278; **imperfect:** *imperfetto*, III 181

perhaps*: *per avventura*, I 14. *Cf.* fortune

peril: *pericolo*, II 84. *See also* danger; risk

permit: *permettere*, I 85, III 41, IV 134, VI 127, VII 195; **permission:** *licenza*, I 46, I 69, I 70. *See also* allow

pernicious: *pernizioso*, IV 30; **pernicious:** *pernicioso*, III 229

perpetual: *perpetuo*, II 305

pike: *picca*, figs. 3, figs. 5, II 18, II 26, II 27, II 31, II 38, II 55, II 56, II 57 (2X), II 60, II 65, II 70 (3X), II 92, II 94 (2X), II 132, II 148 (2X), II 149, II 150 (2X), II 151, II 153, II 156, II 191 (2X), II 193, II 194, II 196 (2X), II 221 (2X), II 223, II 224, II 225, II 226 (2X), II 229, II 232 (4X), II 235 (2X), II 245, II 247, II 255, II 258, III 31, III 34 (2X), III 35, III 36 (2X), III 37, III 49, III 56, III 57, III 60, III 61, III 62, III 66, III 69, III 72, III 90 (3X), III 91, III 92, III 95, III 141, III 145, III 153, III 164, III 165 (2X), III 166 (2X), III 167, III 170, III 171, III 186, III 189, III 196, III 208, IV 36 (2X), V 19 (2X), V 21, V 22, V 24, V 39, V 46, V 50, V 56, VI 62 (3X), VI 66, VI 67, VI 73, VII 227; **pike:** *palo*, IV 50; **piker:** *picchiero*, II 132. *See also* stake

plan (v.): *disegnare*, pr. 2, I 130, IV 87, V 14, VI 171; *see also* design; draw; **plan** (n.): *disegno*, IV 87, VI 169 (2X), VI 170 (2X), VI 172, VI 173, VI 216, VII 155; **plan** (v.): *pensare*, I 52; *see also* think

please, pleasing, pleasure: *compiacere, piacere*, I 12, I 17, I 49, I 77, I 114, I 227, III 7, IV 3, IV 4, IV 6, VI 77, VI 127, VII 247; **pleasant:** *grato*, VI 234

plebs: *plebe*, VI 190

plunder*: predare, II 259, V 155. *See also* prey; spoils

poetry: *poesia, poetica*, I 6, VII 247

poison (v.): *avvelenare*, VI 219; **poison** (v.): *corrompere*,* VII 106; *see also* corrupt

policy: *partito*, I 182, I 187, II 136, V 129, V 157, VII 38, VII 158, VII 171, VII 180

poor: *povero*, II 29, VII 179; **poverty:** *povertà*, I 33, II 29; **impoverish:** *impoverire*, V 95

Pope: *papa*, I 98, VII 20, VII 27

power: *podestà, potestà*, I 80, I 125, II 288, II 313; **power:** *potenza, potere*,* I 87, II 18, II 52, VI 212; **powerful:** *possente, potente*, I 173, I 184, II 33, III 195, IV 33, V 126, VI 237, VII 244

practice, practiced: *praticare, practico*, II 140, II 166, II 202, II 213, V 67, V 68, VI 82,

VII 166, VII 212; **practice** (n.): *pratica,* * II 130, II 164, II 201, II 205, II 217, II 219, II 220, II 227, II 281, III 45, III 211, VI 6; *see also* proceed; **practically:** *praticamente,* * VI 82; **practice** (v.): *esercitare,* pr. 9, I 6, I 51, II 104; **practice** (n.): *esercizio,* I 66, I 67, I 72, I 74, I 76, I 77, I 85, I 86, I 105; *see also* career; drill; exercise, train

Praetorian: *Pretoriano,* I 88

praise (v.): *laudare, lodare,* pr. 8, I 1 (2X), I 11, I 13, I 24, I 27, I 151, II 34, IV 139, VI 117, VII 192, VII 193, VII 201; *see also* lauded; **praise** (n.): *lode,* I 12, VI 118, VII 33, VII 193, VII 203; **praiseworthy:** *lodevole,* I 5, VII 207, VII 236; *see also* laudable. *Cf.* blame

pray: *priegare,* III 224

prevail: *prevalere,* II 52, II 84, II 294. *See also* succeed

prey (n.): *preda,* I 70, IV 82, IV 128, IV 139, VII 6, VII 100, VII 236; **prey** (v.): *predare,* II 305, VII 114. *See also* plunder; spoils

prince: *principe,* I 15, I 29, I 56, I 93, I 94, I 122, I 132, I 135, I 137, I 166, I 167, I 208, I 254, II 29, II 130, II 261, II 287, II 297, II 313, III 209, IV 140, V 68, V 83, V 98, VI 228, VII 188, VII 199, VII 209, VII 229, VII 230, VII 236 (2X), VII 239, VII 241, VII 244, VII 245, VII 247

private: *privato,* I 33, I 67, I 68

proceed: *procedere,* I 90, I 206, I 255, II 67, II 83, II 179, II 277, III 214, IV 11, IV 28, VII 225; *see also* progress; **proceed:** *toccare,* * IV 2; **proceedings:** *pratica,* VII 84; *see also* practice

profit: *guadagno,* II 170. *See also* gain

progress (v.): *procedere,* I 165. *See also* proceed

promotion: *grado,* VII 236. *See also* rank

proof: *esperienza,* VII 242

property: *facultà,* * V 131

proportion: *proporzione,* I 95, II 216, II 221

proud: *superbo,* pr. 4; **proudly:** *superbamente,* VII 236

proverb: *proverbio,* I 61

province: *provincia,* I 53, I 67, I 70, I 125, I 129, I 249, II 213, II 291, II 309, VI 197, VI 228, VI 230, VII 207, VII 226, VII 241, VII 244, VII 248

prudence, prudent, prudently: *prudente, prudentemente, prudenza,* I 8, I 110, I 121 (3X), II 30, II 52, II 136, III 61, III 102, III 128, III 145, III 155, IV 63, IV 100, IV 106, IV 111, V 10, V 62, V 119, VI 2 (2X), VI 27, VI 236, VI 237, VI 246, VII 31, VII 138, VII 206; **lacking prudence:** *poco prudente,* V 63; **imprudent:** *imprudente,* I 187, VI 238

public: *publico,* I 33, I 75, I 87, I 173, I 249 (2X), II 135, V 11 (2X), V 98 (2X), V 103, VI 70 (2X), VI 71, VI 134, VI 136; **publicly:** *publicamente,* IV 139, VI 115

punish: *punire, fare punitore,* I 74, III 134, VI 101, VI 108, VI 113, VI 121, VI 124, VI 201, VI 202, VI 205, VI 206; **punishment:** *punizione,* VI 116, VI 121, VI 201, VI 205; **punish:** *gastigare,* VI 200, VI 205, VII 230; **punishment:** *pena,* III 134, VI 113, VI 115, VII 117, VI 118, VI 119, VII 123, VII 173, VII 194; *see also* penalty purge: *purgare,* I 94

purpose,* ultimate: *fine,* I 6, I 115. *See also* end

Queen: *reina,* I 58

rank: *grado,* pr. 11, III 204 (3X), III 205 (2X), VI 206; *see also* promotion; rank: *stiera,* II 15; to close rank: *premere,* V 76

read: *leggere,* pr. 10, I 8, I 55, I 190, II 13, III 10, IV 139, VI 20, VII 128, VII 215, VII 241

reason (v): *ragionare,* I 203, I 234 (2X) I 260, I 261, II 24, II 25, II 172, III 5, III 107, IV 111, IV 118, V 25, V 82, V 83, V 95, VI 98, VII 94 (2X), VII 182, VII 183, VII 191, VII 211, VII 238, VII 242; *see also* discuss; reasoning: *ragionamento, ragionare,* I 94, I 165, I 220, I 259, I 260, I 271, II 172, II 316, III 44, III 173, IV 4, IV 48, IV 72 (2X), V 150, VI 1, VI 2, VI 6, VI 234, VII 17, VII 77, VII 181, VII 194, VII 225, VII 242; reason (n.): *ragione,* I 61, I 96, I 161, I 162, I 177, I 185, I 222, II 16, II 82, III 122, III 168, III 179, III 215, V 105, VI 239, VII 15, VII 53; reasonableness: *ragionevole,* V 114; reasonable, reasonably: *ragionevole, ragione vuole, ragionevolmente,* II 299, III 195, III 230, V 93, V 102, VI 150, VII 242; unreasonable: *non ragionevole,* V 115; reason (n.): *cagione,* I 243, II 319

reborn: *rinato,* II 305

redouble: *raddoppiare,** Pr 5, I 113, III 116, III 148, V 119, VII 14. *See also* double

redoubt: *ridotto,* VII 23, VII 26, VII 30 (2X), VII 35; redoubt : *riparo,* VII 134, VII 136, VII 138

relate: *narrare,* V 107. *See also* narrate; tell

relatives: *parenti,* VI 117

religion: *religione,* I 129, II 305, V 138, V 139, VI 126, VI 210; religious: *religioso,* V 139

remedy (n.): *rimedio,* I 7, I 54, II 52, II 57, III 18, III 106, III 125, III 134, III 151, III 155, IV 8, IV 13, IV 18, IV 67, IV 87, IV 118, V 148, V 151, V 155, VI 121, VI 122, VI 146, VI 168 (2X), VII 15, VII 24, VII 88, VII 89, VII 133, VII 141, VII 143; remedy (v.): *rimediare,* I 169, II 218, II 267, II 313, III 159, VII 70, VII 142, VII 177

renew: *rinnovare,* I 85, III 17, VI 106. *Cf.* new

republic: *republica,* I 31, I 51, I 64, I 67, I 77, I 106, I 122, I 137, I 177, II 105, II 118, II 130, II 137, II 139, II 158, II 261, II 286 (2X), II 287, II 290, II 292, II 293, II 294, II 295, II 297, II 303, II 314, IV 140

reputation: *reputazione, riputazione,* I 239 (2X), I 248, I 257, II 33, III 129, IV 140, VI 201, VII 24, VII 74, VII 232, VII 234, VII 237 (2X), VII 246; reputation: *opinione,* IV 150; *see also* opinion

respect*: *rispetto,* I 21 (2X), I 49, I 167, II 290, III 228, IV 8, IV 94, V 8, VI 121, VI 137, VI 138. *See also* thanks to, hesitate

restore: *instaurare,* I 144, I 192, III 24 (2X), III 169; restore: *ristorare,* III 66, V 83; restoration: *instaurazione,* I 199

restraint: *freno,* I 129. *See also* check

reverence: *reverenza,* VI 163, VII 215, VII 216; **revere:** *riverire,* VII 223

reward (v.): *premiare,* I 33, I 109, VI 117; **reward** (n.): *premio,* I 107, I 220, IV 71, IV 139, V 120, VI 116 (2X), VII 173, VII 179; **reward** (n.): *merito,* VII 115

rich: *ricco,* I 262, I 266, II 29, IV 139, VII 179; **get rich:** *arrichire,* V 95, V 103. *Cf.* wealth

risk: *pericolo,* VII 129. *See also* danger; peril

road*: *via,** V 41, V 119, V 125, V 154 (2X). *See also* passage; path; way

route: *mezzo,* VII 109. *See also* degree; half; means; midday

rule (n.): *imperio,* I 80, IV 1; *see also* empire; **rule** (v.): *empierare,* VI 123; **rule** (v.): *regnare,* VII 240; **rule** (n.): *regola,* I 121, I 122 (2X), I 225, II 212, II 230, III 160, III 174, IV 87, V 13, V 144, VI 38, VII 153

satisfy: *sodisfare,* I 10, I 12, I 35, I 39, I 77, I 111, I 228, II 231, III 7, IV 4, IV 9, IV 84, V 86, V 94, VI 169, VII 152, VII 191; **satisfactio:** *sodisfazione,* pr. 10, I 38; **dissatisfied:** *non sodisfatto,* I 63

scandal: *scandolo,* I 205, I 242, I 245, I 247, I 248, I 249; **scandalous:** *scandoloso,* I 129, I 249

science: *scienza,* III 174

secret (a.): *segreto,* I 12; **secret** (a.): *secreto,* VII 125; **secret** (n.): *secreto,* VI 175; **secret** (n.): *segreto,* VI 177; **secretly:** *secretamente,* VII 93; **secretly:** *segretamente,* VII 139, VII 192; **keep secret:** *tenere secreto,* VI 172, VII 128. *Cf.* the titles of the preface, book I, and page 33 note 1 for eight instances of **secretary:** *secretario;* see also the coda to book VII on page 165.

sect: *setta,* I 33

sedition: *sedizione,* VI 199

senate: *senato,* I 67, I 69, I 88, I 89, I 257, VI 123

shade, shadow, shady: *ombra, ombroso,* I 12, I 13, I 15, I 17, I 34, I 141, II 144, VI 144, VII 131

shame, shamefilled, shameful: *vergogna,* I 205, II 75 (2X), V 64, VI 76, VII 217, VII 250; **to bring shame:** *vergognare,* VII 31; **to be ashamed:** *vergognare,* IV 68, IV 133, VI 233; **to make ashamed:** *fare vergognare,* VII 217

shield: *scudo,* figs. 3, II 5, II 9 (2X), II 11, II 12, II 14, II 16, II 17, II 20, II 21, II 38 (2X), II 39, II 60, II 70 (2X), II 114, II 148, II 151, II 191 (2X), II 193, II 194, II 196, II 211, II 221, II 222, II 232 (2X), II 233, II 234, II 235 (2X), II 239, III 31, III 34 (2X), III 37 (2X), III 62, III 90, III 92, III 162, V 50, V 130, V 159; **shield:** *rotella,* II 4; **shield-men:** *scudati,* II 148, II 149, II 156, II 194, II 238, II 240, II 241, III 92, III 189

show*: *dimostrare, mostrare,* figs. 1, figs. 2, figs. 5, figs. 6, figs. 7, figs. 8, figs. 9, figs. 10, figs. 11, pr. 13, I 6, I 41, I 98, I 162, I 208, II 57, II 70, II 77, II 157, II 165, II 166, II 171, II 231, III 197 (2X), IV 52, V 49. *See also* demonstrate

sin: *peccato,* II 78, IV 99

site: *sito,* II 84, II 98, II 205, II 260, III 173, IV 11 (2X), IV 96, IV 126, V 8, VI 12, VI 13, VI 14, VI 15 (2X), VI 16 (2X), VI 17, VI 26, VI 59, VI 84 (2X), VI 141, VI 143, VI 241 (2X), VI 249, VII 165, VII 169 slavery: *schiavi*, II 305

slingers: *fundatori*, II 28, III 15

soil: *terreno*, VII 137. See also ground; terrain; *cf.* bury

soldier, soldiery (n.): *soldo, soldato*, pr. 2, pr. 8, I 53, I 54, I 55, I 56, I 58, I 60, I 63, I 72, I 74, I 97, I 122, I 123, I 142, I 197, I 200, I 203, I 204, I 209 (2X), II 78, II 102, II 107, II 111, II 116, II 166, II 179, II 202 (3X), II 203, II 211, II 225, II 261, II 281 (2X), III 75 (2X), III 76, III 139, III 141, III 143, III 200, III 201, III 216, III 230, IV 25, IV 63, IV 64, IV 70, IV 112, IV 114, IV 126, IV 127, IV 134, IV 135, IV 140, IV 141, IV 147, IV 148, V 11, V 66, V 71, V 78, V 81, V 86, V 96, V 97, V 99, V 100, V 101 (2X), V 104, V 105, V 107, V 118, V 121, V 154, VI 1, VI 19, VI 70, VI 89 (2X), VI 117, VI 119, VI 120, VI 125, VI 129 (2X), VI 144, VI 154, VI 156, VI 160, VI 164, VI 180, VI 199, VI 205 (2X), VI 207, VII 99, VII 101, VII 156, VII 163, VII 165, VII 174, VII 179, VII 180, VII 193, VII 212; *see also* hire; **soldier** (v.): *militare*, I 9, I 72 (3X), I 73, I 132, I 220, II 83, II 123, II 128; *see also* military, to be in the; **soldierly:** *soldati*, II 122

son: *figliuolo*, VI 28, VII 244. *See also* children

soul: *anima*, I 2, II 275, III 26

sound (n.): *suono*, II 140, II 166, III 206, VI 133; **sound** (n.): *voce*, III 222; **sound** (v.): *sonare*, VI 132, VI 224

spare: *avanzare*, IV 5. *See also* exceed; leave; remain; stick; surplus

spear: *asta*, II 9 (2X), II 10 (2X), II 11, II 12, II 13 (2X), II 14, II 15 (2X), II 21 (2X), II 22, II 27, II 56, VI 82; **spear:** *dardo*, II 7

speech: *parole*, III 230, VII 236. *See also* word

spirit: *animo*, I 3, I 4, I 8, I 10, I 13, I 94, I 121, I 165 (2X), I 203, I 205, II 90, II 122, II 167, II 268, II 278, II 280, III 101, III 216, III 227, IV 63, IV 116, IV 139, VI 169, VI 170, VII 31, VII 74, VII 156, VII 238; *see also* heart; **spirit:** *spirito*, I 225. *See also* inspirit

spirited: *animoso*, pr. 11, I 121 (2X), II 90 (2X), II 167 (2X), IV 3

spoils: *preda*, I 68, V 93, V 96, V 97, V 98, V 99, V 100 (2X), V 102, V 103, V 114, VI 79, VI 180, VI 215; **spoils:** *predare*, V 97. *See also* plunder; prey

stake: *palo*, II 265, II 324. *See also* pike

state*: *stato*, I 84, I 98, I 100, I 158, I 171, I 230, II 125, II 290, II 309, II 311, II 313, II 314, V 95, VII 95 (2X), VII 199, VII 209, VII 230, VII 234, VII 237, VII 238, VII 239, VII 244 (2X)

storm, storming: *espugnare, espugnazione*, III 64, IV 116, VI 166, VI 232, VII 20, VII 22, VII 85 (2X), VII 92, VII 98, VII 104, VII 105, VII 133, VII 144; *see also* besiege; **stormed, could not be:** *essere inespugnabile*, VII 30; *see also* impregnable

strength: *forze*, I 86, VII 146; **strength:** *fortezza*, II 109, III 61, III 69, III 145, V 49, VI 17, VI 175, VII 52; **strength:** *gagliardo*, V 86. *See also* strong

strike* (v.): *ferire*, II 115, II 116 (2X). *See also* hit; wound

stroke: *tratto*, I 44, I 175, II 129, III 201, V 8, VI 116, VII 86, VII 147

strong: *forte*, I 17, I 204, II 106, II 121, II 267, II 319, III 69, III 113, III 144, IV 26 (2X), IV 28, IV 116 (2X), IV 152, V 61, V 76, V 152, VI 11, VI 12, VI 13, VI 84, VI 85, VI 150, VI

182, VI 202, VI 222, VII 1, VII 2, VII 3, VII 8, VII 16, VII 37, VII 51, VII 56, VII 74, VII 118, VII 134; **strong:** *gagliardo,* II 114, IV 26, IV 27. *Cf.* strength

stronghold: *rocca,* VII 22. *See also* castle; *cf.* citadel; fortress

study: *studio,* I 15, I 75, II 329, VI 243. *See also* attention

succeed: *prevalersi,* pr. 2, I 52; *see also* prevail; **succeed:** *riuscire,* I 59, VI 216, VII 106; **succeed:** *succedere,* III 3, VII 93; *see also* follow; **likely to succeed:** *riuscibile,* IV 78

sun: *sole,* I 17, I 25, I 70, I 141, III 127, IV 19, IV 21, V 42, VI 207

suspect, suspected: *sospetto,* II 250, V 2, V 12, VI 166, VI 169, VI 187, VII 162; **suspicion:** *sospetto,* I 1

swear: *giurare,* VI 125; *cf.* oath; **the Sworn:** *i Giurati,* II 134, II 135; **swear:** *bestemmiare,* VII 219; *see also* curse; **swearer:** *bestemmiatore,* I 129

sword: *spada,* II 6, II 13, II 14, II 15, II 21, II 26, II 38 (2X), II 55, II 56 (3X), II 65, II 66, II 70, II 92, II 113, II 148, III 31, III 37, III 93, III 95, III 141, IV 68, V 39, VII 124, VII 227

tax (v.): *tassare,* VI 150

teach: *insegnare,* II 116, II 121, II 171, II 213, II 214, II 281, II 310, III 138, VI 225, VII 228; **teacher:** *maestro,* I 209, II 122; *see also* master

tell: *narrare,* III 9, V 1. *See also* relate; narrate

temerarious: *temerario,* IV 113

temple: *tempio,* IV 144, VII 100; **temple:** *templo,* VII 128

term: *vocabolo,* II 3; **terms:** *termini,* I 44. *See also* limit, means

terrain: *terreno,* III 132. *See also* ground; soil

terror: *spavento,* VII 237; **terrible:** *terribile,* II 19, VII 73

thank: *ringraziare,* I 113; **thanks to:** *rispetto a,* I 206, II 84. *See also* compared to; respect

think: *pensare,* I 15, I 34, I 35, I 40, I 67, I 70, I 87, I 94, I 177, II 59, II 60, II 117, II 284, III 145, III 177, III 216, IV 1, IV 39, IV 49, V 85, VI 98, VI 126, VI 163, VI 168, VI 169 (2X), VI 186, VI 222, VII 29, VII 117, VII 236, VII 247; *see also* plan; **think:** *intendere,* III 102; **thought:** *pensiero,* I 6, I 12, I 53, V 117, VI 169, VII 196, VII 245; **thought, to give:** *fare pensiero,* III 78; **thoughtlessly:** *inconsideratamente,* IV 102

thrust: *impeto,* II 89 (2X), II 91, II 109, III 12, III 61, III 72, III 88, III 163, III 180, IV 49, IV 50, IV 106 (2X), V 155, VI 245, VII 86, VII 87, VII 148, VII 193. *See also* impetus

tiresome: *fatica,* II 260. *See also* effort; exert; exhaust; fatigue; toil; trouble

toil (n.) : *fatica,* I 71, I 141, III 108; **toil** (v.): *affaticarsi,* II 125. *See also* effort; exert; exhaust; fatigue; force; tiresome; trouble

town: *terra,* I 54, II 37, II 39, II 84, II 305, II 310, II 311, III 64, III 148, IV 116, IV 117, V 93, V 133, VI 116, VI 166, VI 193, VI 225, VI 226, VI 227, VI 232, VI 249, VII 1, VII 25, VII 37, VII 38, VII 59, VII 64, VII 65, VII 69, VII 70, VII 72, VII 75, VII 86, VII 88, VII 97, VII 99, VII 100 (2X), VII 101, VII 102, VII 106, VII 108, VII 109, VII 112, VII 113, VII 117, VII 128, VII 131, VII 132, VII 133, VII 139 (2X), VII 142, VII 144, VII

147; **townspeople:** *terrazzani,* VII 88, VII 89, VII 90, VII 98, VII 100. *See also* country; earth; ground land; *cf.* bury

train: *esercitare,* I 117, I 150, I 165, I 207, I 209, I 210, I 217, I 225, I 227, I 240 (2X), I 263, I 266, II 102, II 112, II 118, II 121, II 125, II 127 (2X), II 128, II 134, II 137, II 138, II 165, II 172, II 202, II 255, II 256, II 259 (2X), II 260, III 11, III 198, III 210, III 221, IV 111, VII 155, VII 181, VII 242

treasure: *tesoro,* V 103

tribune: *tribuno,* I 212, I 213, I 214 (3X), I 215, VI 119

tribute, make to pay: *taglieggiare,* V 93; **tribute, levy:** *taglieggiare,* I 54, I 58

triumph (n.): *trionfo,* I 68, V 103

troops: *genti, gente,* III 191, IV 14, IV 22, IV 39, IV 57 (2X), IV 63, IV 68, IV 77, IV 92 (2X), IV 96, IV 97, IV 111, IV 116, IV 123, V 8, V 39 (2X), V 62 (2X), V 63, V 65, V 71, V 113, V 141, V 142 (2X), V 154, V 159, VI 19, VI 22 (2X), VI 23, VI 25, VI 172, VI 186, VI 187, VI 188, VI 193, VI 195, VI 215 (2X), VI 241, VI 244, VI 245 (2X), VII 29, VII 59, VII 95, VII 97, VII 105, VII 147; *see also* men; people; **troops:** *aiuti,* VII 107

trouble (n.): *fatica,* II 111, III 93, III 117, IV 3, V 91, VI 91, VI 166, VI 223, VI 241, VII 46, VII 95, VII 155, VII 202. *See also* effort; exert; exhaust; fatigue; tiresome; toil

true: *vero,* pr. 2, pr. 6, I 17, I 21, I 72, I 77, I 98, I 129, I 150, I 165, I 217, I 219, II 13, II 145, II 216, II 302, II 314, II 326, III 11, III 110, III 134, III 182, III 197, IV 85, V 56, V 71, V 147, VI 66, VII 104, VII 118, VII 231; **true one:** *vero,* I 210, II 113, II 115, II 121, II 166, IV 56, VII 213; **truly:** *veramente, in vero,* I 94, I 114, II 173, III 77, III 174, VII 250; **truth:** *verità, il vero,* I 20, I 29, I 34, I 127, II 173

trust, entrust oneself (v.): *confidare, confidarsi, fidare, fidarsi,* I 11, I 158, II 100, III 102, IV 114, VI 100, VI 227, VII 96, VII 128, VII 168; **trust** (v.): *prestare fede a,* VI 189; **trust** (n.): *fede,* VII 109; **distrustful, to be:** *diffidare,* VII 248, VII 249. *See also* believability; confidence; faith

tumult (n.): *tumulto,* I 255, VI 124, VI 168, VI 206, VI 222, VII 71; **tumult** (v.): *tumultuare,* I 257, V 37; **tumultuous:** *tumultuario,* V 38, V 39; **tumultuous:** *tumulto,* V 40; **tumultuous:** *tumultuariamente,* VII 69. *See also* mutiny

type: *ragione,* V 11. *See also* reason

tyrant: *tiranno,* I 185, I 186; **tyranny:** *tirannide,* I 78; **tyranny:** *tiranno,* I 185; **tyrannical:** *tirannico,* I 67; **tyrannize:** *tiranneggiare,* I 66, I 186

undertaking: *impresa,* I 2. *See also* campaign; enterprise

unfavorable, to be: *disfavorisce,* IV 20

union: *unione,* I 249 (2X), I 254

unite: *unire,* pr. 3, I 209, I 246, I 247, I 249 (2X), II 254, III 44, III 67, IV 41, VI 203, VI 204, VI 241, VI 242, VI 245; **disunited:** *disunito,* I 246, I 247, I 249, VI 241, VII 152

unstable: *instabile,* II 83, IV 1

unwarlike: *imbelle,* VII 23

unwilling: *male volentieri,* II 91, VII 94

usage: *usanza, uso,* pr. 2 (3X), I 14, I 24, I 102, II 101, VII 50. VII 226; *see also* manner;

usage; **used to:** *uso, usato,* I 183, I 196, I 220, IV 62, IV 139, VI 172; **used to*:** *avvezzo,* I 141; **get used to:** *avvezzare,* II 110; *see also* habituate. *Cf.* accustom

useful: *utile,* I 8, I 163, I 171, I 196, I 197, I 248, I 255, II 31, II 79 (2X), II 126, II 170, II 182, II 322 (2X), II 323, III 35, III 42, III 45, III 130, III 137, III 145, III 167, IV 30, V 66, V 120, V 122, VI 21, VI 25, VI 46, VI 147, VI 168, VI 172, VI 183; **useless:** *inutile,* I 158, I 234, I 240, I 247, II 10, II 11, II 30, II 37, II 38, II 56, III 35, III 37, III 95, III 108, III 121, III 136, III 137, III 139, III 169, III 175, III 189, IV 54, VI 126; **uselessly:** *inutilmente,* VI 149; **uselessness:** *inutilità,* I 160, I 161, I 163, I 169; **uselessness:** *inutile,* II 77. *See also* utility

usurp: *usurpare,* I 67

utility: *utile,* I 57, I 87; **utility:** *utilità,* I 52, I 195, I 233, I 249, IV 76, VI 215. *See also* useful

vehemence: *impeto,* I 27

vent (v.): *sfogare,* I 58; **vent** (n.): *sfogatoi,* VII 142

victor: *vincitore,* I 23, II 299, VI 177; **victory:** *vittoria,* II 57, II 65, II 111, II 168, III 16, III 85, III 96, IV 27, IV 51, IV 54, IV 57, IV 58, IV 74, IV 75, IV 77, IV 91, IV 93, IV 115, IV 143, IV 146, IV 150, V 119, VI 151, VI 221, VII 93, VII 107, VII 155, VII 157, VII 193; **victory:** *vinta,* III 130, IV 63; **victorious:** *vittorioso,* IV 25 (2X), IV 107, V 97, VI 148, VII 167. *See also* conquer

vile: *vile,* II 90 (2X), V 71, VI 228; **vileness:** *viltà,* I 249, II 283, II 315, IV 99, IV 106

violate: *violare,* I 67

violence, violent: *violenza, violento,* pr. 2, I 52, I 53

virtue: *virtù,* pr. 10, I 8, I 33, I 62, I 201, I 205, II 24, II 32, II 33, II 79, II 80, II 86, II 267, II 287, II 290, II 293, II 301, II 302, II 303, II 304 (3X), II 305, II 313 (2X), II 314, III 20, III 35, III 44, III 83, III 88, III 92, III 123, III 149, III 175, III 212, III 216, IV 25, IV 45 (2X), IV 108, IV 151, V 107, VI 204 (2X), VI 247, VI 248, VII 32, VII 74, VII 135, VII 148, VII 157, VII 165 (2X), VII 181; **virtuous, virtuously:** *virtuoso, virtuosamente,* I 158, I 180, II 262, II 290, II 293, II 302, II 304, IV 39, VI 117, VII 203, VII 230, VII 239

voice: *voce,* pr. 2, III 212, III 230, V 71, V 77. *See also* known, let it be

volume: *suono,* III 222

vouch: *fare fede,* I 5, II 24. *See also* believability; confidence; faith; trust

wagon: *carrette, carriagi, carro,* II 246, II 249, II 263, II 265 (2X), II 324, II 325, III 56, III 157 (3X), IV 6, V 5, V 6 (3X), V 8, V 9, V 10, V 11 (2X), V 32, V 47, V 57, V 80, V 122, VI 70, VI 71, VII 50, VII 53, VII 54, VII 56 (2X), VII 57, VII 110. *See also* chariot

war (n.): *guerra,* title, pr. title, I title, I 6, I 10, I 8, I 36, I 48, I 50, I 52, I 53, I 54, I 55 (2X), I 62, I 65, I 66, I 67, I 70, I 71, I 75 (2X), I 81, I 82, I 83 (2X) , I 84, I 85, I 91, I 93 (2X), I 95, I 96, I 97, I 98, I 106, I 107, I 108 (2X), I 109, I 110, I 112, I 115, I 119 (2X), I 121, I 180, I 181, I 183, I 184, I 188, I 206, I 210, I 212, I 224, I 235, I 247, I 248, I 255, I 256, II 79, II, 80, II 81, II 119, II 122, II 131, II 134, II 142, II 202, II 213, II 285, II 305 (2X), II 312, II 322, III 216, III 54, IV 111, IV 112, IV 120, IV 135, IV 146, V 95 (2X), V

104, V 120, VI 150, VI 161, VI 162, VI 166, VI 175, VI 178, VI 188, VI 193, VI 235, VI
237, VI 238, VI 239, VI 244, VI 247, VII 43, VII 105, VII 151, VII 155, VII 159, VII 161,
VII 173, VII 178, VII 183, VII 195, VII 216, VII 232 (2X), VII 236; **warfare:** *guerra,* I
118; **war** (n.): *bellum* (L), I 246; **war** (v.): *guerreggiare,* VI 242; **warlike:** *bellica,* II
121. *See* page 33 note 1 for six additional instances of "war" in book titles omitted
from the translation; the coda to book VII on page 165.

way*: *via,** I 20, I 133, I 134, I 139, I 167, II 303, III 159, III 160, IV 36, IV 41, IV 51, IV 85,
IV 139, V 71, V 156, VI 139, VI 223, VII 90. *See also* passage; path; road

weak, weakness: *debile, debole, debolezza,* I 188, II 52, II 78, II 80, II 98, II 140, II 141, II
309, III 69, III 177, III 180, III 182 (2X), IV 20, IV 26 (3X), IV 28, IV 29, IV 31, V 116,
V 156, VI 172, VI 187, VI 196, VII 2, VII 34, VII 44, VII 56, VII 64, VII 70, VII 135,
VII 140, VII 192; **weaken:** *indebolire,* III 71

wealth: *ricchezze,* pr. 13 (2X). *See also* rich

wicked: *reo,* VI 117 (2X), VI 119; **wicked:** *cattivo,* I 48, I 74, I 129, I 130, I 155, I 166, I 258;
wicked: *malvagio,* VI 167; **wickedness:** *cattività,* I 62. *See also* bad; evil; malicious

win: *vincere,* I 115, I 119, I 169, I 184, II 57, II 58, II 70, II 84, II 309, III 16, III 97, III 98,
III 101, III 161, III 175, IV 1, IV 70, IV 73, IV 74, IV 99, IV 109, IV 115, IV 148, IV 152,
V 1, V 95, V 101, VI 166, VI 196, VI 239, VI 240, VII 148, VII 156, VII 226; *see also*
conquer; defeat; **winner:** *vincitore,* V 95; *see also* victor

wine: *vino,* V 84, V 85 (2X), V 89, V 91, VI 217, VI 219

wise, wisely: *savio, saviamente,* I 7, I 8, I 22, I 23, I 85, I 106, I 107, I 110, I 112, I 153, I 154
(2X), I 169, I 178, IV 132, V 62, VII 38, VII 229; **unwise:** *non savio,* I 183

women: *femmine,* VI 127; **women:** *donne,* VII 70

word: *voce,* II 140, II 166, IV 58, V 72, V 73 (2X), V 74, V 76; **word:** *parola,* pr. 2, pr. 11, I
50, II 178, II 268, IV 133, IV 137 (2X), V 117, VII 236. *See also* speech

work (n.): *operazione,* pr. 2; **work** (n.): *opera,* pr. 11, pr. 13, I 5, VI 94, VII 133, VII 207;
work (v.): *operare,* pr. 11, I 40, I 119, VI 144, VI 191; **work** (v.): *adoperare,* I 141, I
249; **work** (v.): lavorare, I 196; **worker:** *lavoratore,* I 69, I 194. *See also* do; employ,
operate

world: *mondo,* I 122, I 178, II 8, II 23, II 80, II 286, II 290, II 304, II 305, III 78, VI 165,
VII 43, VII 229, VII 244, VII 250

worthy, to be; to be worth: *valere,* I 119, VI 148

wound (v.): *ferire,* II 21, II 114, III 24, III 89, III 95, III 169, III 195, V 101, VI 116, VII 4,
VII 21, VII 112. *See also* hit; strike

write: *scrivere,* pr. 10, pr. 11, I 141, I 204, II 77, II 210, II 211, VI 20, VI 178, VI 191, VII 123,
VII 124, VII 127 (2X), VII 128, VII 131, VII 236; **write:** *descrivere,* III 201; **write
above:** *soprascrivere,* II 230; **writings:** *scritti,* I 6; **writer:** *scrittore,* I 194, II 9, II 16,
II 117, II 298, II 301, III 10, VII 192. *See also* conscript; enroll

you (singular, informal only): *tu, ti, te, tuo,* and verbs in the second person singular
with no subject pronoun, I 84 (2X), I 120 (3X), I 126 (5X), I 129, I 130 (4X), I 131, I
171, I 197, I 200, I 231 (2X), I 232 (2X), I 233 (2X), I 237, I 238 (2X), I 239 (2X), I 240
(2X), I 268 (2X), II 96 (2X), II 97 (2X), II 116, II 125 (2X), II 164, 170 (2X), II 196, II

198 (6X), II 199, II 211 (2X), II 231, III 20, III 70 (3X), III 71 (3X), III 72(4X), III 121, III 128, III 131, III 159, IV 12 (3X), IV 13 (5X), IV 14 (6X), IV 16 (2X), IV 17, IV 18 (3X), IV 21 (2X), IV 24 (3X), IV 63 (2X), IV 77, IV 80, IV 88 (4X), IV 89, IV 90 (2X), IV 97 (4X), IV 98 (4X), IV 100 (2X), IV 102 (4X), IV 103 (4X), IV 105, IV 112, IV 114, IV 115, IV 116 (5X), IV 126 (3X), IV 127 (3X), IV 128, IV 129, IV 130, IV 134, IV 137, IV 147 (2X), IV 152, V 1, V 12 (3X), V 30, V 39, V 41, V 43 (2X), V 44, V 51, V 62 (4X), V 63 (4X), V 64 (2X), V 65 (5X), V 73 (2X), V 109 (2X), V 111 (2X), V 112 (2X), V 114 (3X), V 115 (3X), V 116 (2X), V 117 (4X), V 118, V 121 (3X), V 126 (4X), V 129 (5X), V 140, VI 109 (2X), VI 143 (2X), VI 149 (3X), VI 150 (4X), VI 151 (2X), VI 166 (2X), VI 168 (4X), VI 169 (7X), VI 170 (11X), VI 171 (2X), VI 172 (4X), VI 175 (2X), VI 183, VI 198 (3X), VI 200, VI 201, VI 205 (2X), VI 206 (2X), VI 209, VI 212 (4X), VI 221, VI 225 (3X), VI 239 (2X), VI 241 (7X), VII 6, VII 8, VII 13 (2X), VII 14 (4X), VII 15, VII 19, VII 24 (4X), VII 25 (4X), VII 64 (2X), VII 67, VII 68, VII 71, VII 80, VII 87, VII 92 (3X), VII 93 (2X), VII 112, VII 133 (4X), VII 134, VII 135 (2X), VII 141, VII 142 (5X), VII 146 (6X), VII 154 (2X), VII 156 (4X), VII 158, VII 162, VII 166 (3X), VII 170 (2X), VII 171 (2X), VII 172 (4X), VII 175 (3X), VII 180, VII 191

young (adj.): *giovane*, I 4, I 227, II 114, II 127, III 5 (2X), IV 2, V 105, VII 70, VII 247; **young:** *gioventù*, III 5; **young** (n.): *giovanetti*, I 210; **youth:** *giovane*, I 11, I 47, I 225, I 227, II 113, VII 199; **youth:** *gioventù*, II 106, II 125; **youth** (abstract noun): *gioventù*, I 47, II 130; **youthful:** *giovenile*, I 6

INDEX OF PROPER NAMES

⎯⎯ ❧ ⎯⎯

Names in italics are referred to but not used by Machiavelli; portions of names, monikers, and titles in italics are omitted by Machiavelli. A reference in italics (e.g., *III 13*) indicates an implicit reference to the person, place, or thing named in the entry. Multiple references within Italian sentences are not indicated. Writers' names are given only when explicitly mentioned in the text. The abbreviation "pr." refers to the preface.